LOST PROPERTY

Lost

JENNIFER SUMMIT

Property

THE WOMAN WRITER AND ENGLISH LITERARY HISTORY, 1380–1589

THE UNIVERSITY OF CHICAGO PRESS
CHICAGO AND LONDON

JENNIFER SUMMIT is assistant professor of English at Stanford University.

The University of Chicago Press, Chicago 60637
The University of Chicago Press, Ltd., London
© 2000 by The University of Chicago
All rights reserved. Published 2000
Printed in the United States of America
09 08 07 06 05 04 03 02 01 00   1 2 3 4 5
ISBN: 0-226-78012-0 (cloth)
ISBN: 0-226-78013-9 (paper)

The details of illustrations on pages ii, 22, 60, 108, and 162 are reproduced here with permission. The illustrations are presented in their entirety and attributed in the text as, respectively, figures 3, 1, 2, 7, and 9.

An earlier version of chapter 4 appeared as "'The Arte of a Ladies Penne': Elizabeth I and the Poetics of Queenship" in *English Literary Renaissance*, 26 (1996): 395–422. Reprinted by permission of the editors.

Library of Congress Cataloging-in-Publication Data

Summit, Jennifer.
    Lost property : the woman writer and English literary history, 1380–1589 / Jennifer Summit.
        p. cm.
    Includes bibliographical references and index.
    ISBN 0-226-78012-0 (cloth : alk. paper)—ISBN 0-226-78013-9 (pbk : alk. paper)
    1. English literature—Middle English, 1100–1500—History and criticism.
    2. English literature—Early modern, 1500–1700—History and criticism.
    3. English literature—Women authors—History and criticism.   4. Women
    and literature—England—History—16th century.   5. Women and literature—
    England—History—To 1500.   I. Title.

PR275.W6S86   2000
820.9'9287'0902—dc21   99-087252

♾ The paper used in this publication meets the minimum requirements of the American National Standard for Information Sciences—Permanence of Paper for Printed Library Materials, ANSI Z39.48-1992.

Contents

Illustrations

Acknowledgments

A number of individuals supported this project from its inception. It is a pleasure to single out some of them for particular thanks: Jonathan Goldberg inspired and helped shape my work on women writers and early books from the start. I am grateful to him and to Elaine Tuttle Hansen for their generous and acute readings of my first written versions of this work, as well as to Gabrielle Spiegel and Stephen G. Nichols, who also offered valuable help. Many of the ideas behind this book were initially fostered in graduate seminars: to Robert Calkins, R. James Goldstein, John Guillory, Mary Poovey, Winthrop Wetherbee, and, for a remarkable seminar on women writers at the Folger, Ann Rosalind Jones, I remain especially indebted.

At Stanford I have found a supportive intellectual community; among the colleagues who helped me with this project at various levels, I would like to extend special thanks to Brad Gregory, Terry Castle, Paula Findlen, Seth Lerer, Stephen Orgel, Patricia Parker, and David Riggs. Sara S. Poor offered moral as well as intellectual support and was a generous reader and interlocutor. The wonderful students in my "Materials and Methods for Studying Early Women Writers" seminar will, I hope, recognize the marks of their inspiration here, as should Jenn Kao. In the late stages of this project, I benefited from the acumen and energy of my two research assistants, Karen Gross and Amy Tigner.

For the opportunity to present parts of this book, I am grateful to Susan Groag Bell, Julia Boffey, Marilynn Desmond, Linda Gregerson,

Seth Lerer, Sharon Marcus, Catherine M. Mooney, Janel Mueller, Stephen Orgel, and Sara S. Poor. David Baker, Constance Jordan, Ethan Knapp, Lisa Lampert, David Wallace, and Nicholas Watson offered comments on written portions or drafts of chapters that helped shape the project in important ways.

In the last stages of pulling together the book, I enjoyed a luxurious year at the Stanford Humanities Center; I am grateful to Keith Baker, Bliss Carnochan, Susan Dunn, the staff, and the fellows, whose collective intellectual energy and generosity kept this project and its author going.

I thank in addition Alan Thomas, Randolph Petilos, and the editorial staff at the University of Chicago Press, as well as the two readers who read this book in manuscript.

For debts of a more personal nature, I acknowledge with pleasure and gratitude the ongoing support of my family. Simon Firth saw this book develop from the very first stages, read every word, and contributed in many other ways, large and small; to him, my heartfelt thanks. This book is dedicated to my parents, Roger and Virginia Summit.

I am grateful to the librarians of the British Library and the Bodleian Library for permission to reprint material from manuscript sources. I would also like to acknowledge the support of the librarians and staff of Cambridge University Library, the Folger Shakespeare Library, University of London's Senate House and Institute for Historical Research, and Stanford University's Green Library. A fellowship from the American Association of University Women supported my research and early stages of writing.

An earlier version of Chapter 4 originally appeared as "'The Arte of a Ladies Penne': Elizabeth I and the Poetics of Queenship," *English Literary Renaissance* 26 (1996): 395–422; I thank Arthur Kinney for permission to reprint it here.

Introduction

English literary history has been haunted by the figure of the lost woman writer. Today the figure calls to mind the female-authored texts that have gone unremarked and unpreserved by literary tradition, many of which have recently been restored to view. But even when the very notion of an English literary tradition was still in its formative stages, the lost woman writer exerted a powerful presence in the early literary-cultural imagination. Writing in 1641, Richard Brathwait invokes the figure when he considers why the works of women writers have gone missing from the ledgers of literary history. He concludes that this absence could only have been voluntary:

> These [women writers] desired to doe well, and not to be applauded; to advance vertues, and not to have their names recorded: nor their amiable features with glorious *Frontispices* impaled. To improve goodnesse by humility, was their highest pitch of glory. This their sundry excellent fancies confirmed; their elegant labours discovered; whereof though many have suffered Oblivion through the injury of time, and want of that incomparable helpe of the *Presse*, the benefit whereof wee enjoy: yet shall wee find by the testimony of

our approvedst Authors, that many of these women, which for brev-
ity sake wee have onely shadowed, have become *assistants* to the
highest and most enlivened Composures that ever derived birth or
breath from *Helicon*.[1]

By Brathwait's reckoning, women write themselves into thin air. Representing the inverse of male literary fame, women writers seek obscurity out of feminine modesty, a model that starkly differentiates
writing by social categories of gender. In Brathwait's vision, gender
difference rules even the technologies of writing: where the "glorious
frontispiece" immortalizes male authors by fixing their portraits at
their books' openings, it holds the opposite effect for female authors,
not preserving their features but threatening to "impale" them—that
is, to deface by piercing or dividing them.[2] And while the printing
press brings men's works to public attention, it denies the same service to women, consigning them instead to the textual obscurity and
fragility of the manuscript. In the end, the lost women writers of
Brathwait's account are recovered as male authors' anonymous "assistants," a position that makes their disappearance strangely necessary
to the maintenance of literary tradition. Brathwait's other writings
include well-known conduct books for men and women as well as
some of the earliest English critical commentaries on Chaucer; here,
his interests in gender and literary history come together to make the
woman writer synonymous with loss.[3]

Brathwait's discussion shows that the idea of the lost woman writer
has a past, which has been bound up with changing ideas about writing, gender, and the nature of literary tradition. That past bears relevance to our own, more recent attempts to locate women writers
within the histories of English literature that have traditionally excluded them. Recent scholarly undertakings have established not
only that women wrote literary texts far earlier than had been previously believed but also that many of these texts were familiar to and
even celebrated by contemporaries.[4] But if we now know more about
women's historical literary activities than did preceding generations
of literary historians, we still know little about what "the woman
writer" meant to those earlier periods; nor do we know what relation
this figure bore to the broader idea of English literature as it was then
conceived.[5]

This book asks how contemporary definitions of "the woman
writer" participated in and helped to shape ideas about the nature and
identity of "English literature" from the late fourteenth through the

late sixteenth centuries. It thus traces a prehistory of Brathwait's insistence that "the woman writer" is by definition excluded from ruling concepts of authorship and literary tradition. To turn to the late medieval and early modern periods is to show that those concepts, especially applied to vernacular writing, are not absolute; rather, as many recent studies have confirmed, they were under construction in ways that reflected changing legal practices in the book market and a growing presence of state control in vernacular literary culture.[6] If the categories of authorship and English literature can be shown to have a history, and one that is linked to the history of literate institutions, this book seeks to trace a parallel history of the woman writer—and in the process to demonstrate how the categories "woman writer," "English literature," and "literary tradition" came to define one another during a key stage in their development.[7]

This approach both contributes to and modifies several of the major focuses of feminist literary history as they have been defined up to now. Instead of surveying women writers to consider what unites them as women—a question that has both tantalized and vexed feminist literary historians in the past—I examine the history of representations of women writers to consider how and to what specific ends and effects printers, readers, and other agents of literary culture variously conceived the category of "woman writer" to be a coherent and culturally significant term.[8] Furthermore, those representations differed according to time and circumstance, thus revealing that "the woman writer" was not a unified, absolute category during this period but one that took its relative meanings from a range of historical contexts. This history of "the woman writer" offers an important corollary to the history of authorship and the book, by showing how the signs of female authorship were variously imported to explain, taxonomize, or assign value to texts by allowing them to be gathered together under the rubric of gender. Thus, rather than seeking to integrate women writers into an existing canon of medieval and Renaissance English literature, this book seeks to understand how the history of representations of women writers participates in a broader history of ideas about English literature and canonicity. At a time when these ideas were under negotiation, the figure of the woman writer formed a subject of heightened interest. Examining the specific shapes that contemporary representations of women writers take reveals that the concept of "the woman writer" became a major cultural cornerstone around which fundamental notions of authorship, writing, and literary tradition were first constructed.

Ideas about "the woman writer" as they emerge over this period bear a contiguous, but not coterminous, relation to the historical activities of women who wrote. While medieval and early modern representations of women writers reflect cultural awareness that women could and did write, the meanings that attached to those representations exceeded the historical writing activities of women, in the same way that the meanings that have accrued to the figure "woman" have always exceeded the historical activities and positions of women.[9] Representations of "the woman writer" in the medieval and early modern periods mark the convergence of contemporary understandings of gender with ideas about writing and literary culture and, in turn, pose a new set of questions for the history of authorship in this period: At what historical moments, and in what particular forms, did it become possible to conceive "the woman writer" as a coherent figure? How did understandings of this figure reflect changing expectations about literary genre, history, and the history of the book? And finally, how did "the woman writer" become "lost"?

Until recently, women writers of the Middle Ages and Renaissance were considered to be literally lost. Famously, Virginia Woolf concluded that any woman who dared to write in the age of Shakespeare could only have ended her life and career in despair.[10] Yet in the same British Library where Woolf pondered the absence of women writers, early female-authored texts already existed in numerous volumes, both in print and in manuscript; had she known where and how to look, Woolf might have faced the different challenge of accounting not for women writers' absence but for the specific mechanisms of textual evaluation that kept their work from entering the English canon.[11] Similarly, in the seventeenth century, Richard Brathwait need not have looked far in English literary history to uncover women writers who were not the victims of obscurity, voluntary or otherwise: only twenty years before Brathwait wrote, Lady Mary Wroth published her scandalous *Urania*, proving through her boldness anything but the desire "to doe well, and not to be applauded; to advance vertues, and not to have [her name] recorded."[12] Moreover, the very year in which Brathwait recorded his reflections on the lost woman writer, 1641, witnessed a fresh burst of writing by women on the eve of the Civil War: in 1641 Katherine Chidley published her *Justification of the Independent Churches of Christ*, the same year that printed petitions were presented to Parliament by "the gentlewomen, and tradesmens-wives, in and about the City of London."[13] The fact that these and similar texts subsequently dropped from view while others like Milton's *Areopagitica* have remained, Hilary Hinds has argued, demands new understandings of the historical and gender-differentiated construction of terms such as canonicity, authorship, and literature itself.[14] In light of such contemporary or recent texts by women that were clearly in the public eye, Brathwait's comment on the universal "oblivion" of women writers needs to be understood not as an accurate description of women writers' "loss" from literary history but as an active construction of it, which obscures the specific, historical processes through which women's writing was culturally defined, circulated, and assigned value, by turning women writers themselves into history's shadowy ghosts. But Brathwait's portrayal of women writers' loss, by mystifying these material processes, represents a significant gesture within the broader history of English canon formation that begs further analysis as such. Instead of seeing women writers as literally lost from literary history, I want to consider how the idea of loss has served as a powerful fiction that shaped the cultural place of the woman writer as well as the abstract model of a literary history that excluded her.

If it is now commonplace to conceive "the woman writer" in opposition to literary tradition, *Lost Property* historicizes this opposition by considering how it dialectically fashioned both "the woman writer" and "English literature" in the medieval and early modern periods. Rather than assuming that English literary tradition and authority preceded the woman writer's emergence—and thus that her marginalization was meant to protect an institution that was already fully in place and fully masculinized—it is my argument that producing the woman writer as "lost" from literary history was part of the process of conceiving what literary history was in a fundamental way. The idea of the "lost" woman writer can be traced to the medieval and early modern periods, in which "the woman writer" emerged as a unified cultural category through her perceived opposition to literary tradition. This is not to argue that women writers were thereby removed from literary history—to the contrary, they are present to a surprising degree at the key sites at which "English literature" is first invented. But they enter these sites as emblems of loss and figures of a literature that tradition fails to enshrine. In so doing, they give shape to the question of what it meant to write outside tradition in ways, I argue, that became instrumental for the conception of English literature.

English literature was not always conceived as a unified entity with a tradition of its own. The idea of literary tradition as it was inherited by the medieval and early modern periods was based on classical or patristic models, which identified the literary past as an ancient source of authority to be endlessly cited and deferred to.

However, such a model was not directly applicable to vernacular writers and writing, as A. J. Minnis and, more recently, Ralph Hanna III have made clear.[15] Before Chaucer, writing in Middle English existed as what Hanna calls "a prenational literature" whose polyvocality and multiple literary communities belied any sense of a unified literary tradition.[16] Inventing that tradition would become a corollary to the project of consolidating national identity, and across the fifteenth and sixteenth centuries this project was abetted by a number of historical developments: official acts to circumscribe the vernacular, the secularization of literary production, the centralization of the English court as a site of literary production, and the development of print culture chief among them.[17]

But these developments were by no means in alignment; nor did the process of inventing literary tradition conform to a single direction or aim. As the contested process of canonizing Chaucer in these periods made clear, the task of defining the literary past was overlaid with competing efforts to determine England's linguistic, religious, and cultural identities.[18] If the models of literary tradition that we have inherited from later periods stress the timelessness of what has been passed down (a promise that lies at the root of *traditio*), they do so by suppressing the material practices of selection and competition that went into the production of that tradition.[19] Those practices are visible in medieval and early modern discussions of "English literature." To literary historians in later periods, the Middle Ages and Renaissance became the bulwark of English literary tradition, providing the celebrated names—Chaucer, Spenser, Shakespeare, Milton— that guaranteed its timelessness and unity. In contrast, to medieval and early modern writers the relationship between "English literature" and "tradition" was far from certain; rather than appealing to ideals of timelessness and unity, those who theorized the status of "English literature" in the medieval and early modern periods continually called attention to the category's instability, stressing the cultural chasm that separated English writing from classical and patristic authority and lamenting its perceived secondariness, belatedness, and alienation from the literary past.[20]

"Tradition" as derived from classical or clerical institutions by definition excluded women. The universities and clergy, grounded in patristic tradition, comprised a literate community so exclusively masculine that when Chaucer came to define the figure "woman writer," he made her the natural opponent of "clerks."[21] Similarly, the classical tradition and its authors entered medieval and early modern culture as instruments of boys' education, in ways that made antifeminism as fundamental a tool for the fashioning of masculine selves as Latin grammar.[22] As English writers and other agents of literary culture contemplated the distance between vernacular writing and the classical and patristic canons, the woman writer emerged as a powerful cultural symbol for the obverse of such authoritative models, representing an unauthorized form of writing that could become alternately an object of desirous identification or one of fearful disavowal. Defined through her alienation from tradition, the figure of the woman writer became a focal point for many of the questions that were pivotal to the conceptual development of "English literature." Thus for those concerned about the status of English letters, "the woman writer" gave shape to the question of what it meant to write from a position of estrangement from tradition, and in a linguistic form that appeared to have neither past nor future—indeed, from a position that was culturally analogous to that of English literature itself.

Lost Property examines representations of women writers by late medieval and early modern English writers, readers, editors, and printers as they overlap with a series of defining moments in the production of "English literature" as a unified cultural category. A number of the women writers who are the objects of these representations are now familiar names: Margery Kempe, Christine de Pizan, Anne Askew, Elizabeth I, and Mary Stuart, Queen of Scots. Others are more iconic than they are historical, such as St. Bridget, to whom a set of popular prayers were apocryphally ascribed, and Corinne, a "lost" classical woman writer who is named in Chaucer's *Anelida and Arcite.* Representations of these and other writing women became unexpectedly central to medieval and early modern discussions of the cultural and historical place of English writing. Many of these discussions have been long recognized as major sites for the development of English literary history: Chaucer's meditations on the shape of vernacular writing, John Bale's Reformation attempts to formulate schematic models of English literary history, or George Puttenham's seminal assertion of a native poetic practice that would shape ideas about English poetry for his own and subsequent generations. However, the roles that women writers play in these works have not yet been recognized. I find that in these and other works, the woman writer forms a nodal point around which ideas about the nature of vernacular writing and canonicity are formulated. These works' parallel representations of English letters and women writers share important features with the work of editors, publishers, and translators who materially shape the work of women writers for the consumption of a literary public. Together, these responses to women writers and their work not only construct "the woman writer" as a significant and recognizable cultural figure during this time; in the process, they produce a new vocabulary for discussing the problems of writing, tradition, and literary value that attended the formation of a vernacular canon.

My focus on early representations of women writers and women's writing, then, stresses their embeddedness within a broader history of writing and the book. This emphasis departs from the now-common practice of metaphorizing women's writing through terms such as "voice," "speech," or "silence"—terms that, despite their theoretical and polemical utility, obscure the material ways in which writing differs from speech.[23] Whatever the restrictions that were placed on women's speech in this period—and they were clearly manifold, as much recent work has established—women's writing was produced under a very different set of institutional conditions. Not the least of these conditions concern the layers of textual mediation that intervene between the moment of composition and that of reception, which raise important questions in turn about the very processes through which writing comes to be assigned gender at all. While speech clearly issues from a gendered body, writing yields fewer internal markers of gendered authorship, and even those must be viewed critically, as editors of women's writing remind us.[24] It is difficult to link material writing in archival sources with any certainty to writers of either gender, Julia Boffey has observed, given the pervasiveness of anonymous composition in the earlier periods and "the general impossibility of deducing the gender of a scribe from the appearance of a hand."[25] Considering women's writing as writing, rather than as voice, requires a different program of analysis, which illuminates the material conventions through which texts are established to be the products of women writers, the specific meanings that attach to the genders of authors in particular circumstances, and the uses to which the category of "women's writing" is put in the production and circulation of books. Such a bibliographical approach promises to historicize "the woman writer" in ways that demonstrate the mutual relevance of textual criticism and feminist literary history.[26]

In books, a key site for differentiating authors as male or female is what Gérard Genette calls the paratext—the formal textual conventions by which editors, translators, scribes, or other figures mediate texts to readers.[27] Such paratextual mechanisms as the title, printer's or translator's preface, illuminations or woodcuts, and marginal annotation have already proven to be important sources for the history of authorship. The practice of assigning names to texts first takes shape in manuscript collections as a way of fixing those texts within particular contexts, and studies have shown that legal contests over intellectual property gave rise to the formal marks of literary authorship in books.[28] Paradoxically, these practices in turn helped to shape a notion of singular authorship that invested the individual writer with creative control. *Lost Property* extends a similar scrutiny to the material contexts that helped to fashion "the woman writer" within specific literary-cultural milieux. Much of its focus, then, falls on materials that have in the past seemed literally marginal to the study of women writers: editors' apparently self-interested prefaces to patrons or readers; the paratextual details that shaped the circulation of a female-authored text, sometimes by distorting it beyond recognition; works of translation or collation that occasionally mistranscribe or inaccurately reflect the original. Such materials shape female-authored texts in ways that can seem very far from their authors' intended aim, and many of them offer representations of the woman writer that appear to willfully misread their subjects. They have thus more often been seen as signs of corruption from which women's writing needs to be recovered than as objects of analysis that are valuable in their own right for the study of women writers. But such paratextual evidence reveals the specific ways in which women's writing was presented, circulated, and evaluated as such, a question that is always an implicit subject of feminist literary history but has been less frequently considered as a historical, material process.[29] As this evidence shows, early editors do not act as "gatekeepers" in any simple sense: their project is not to keep women's writing from public eye or to enact censorship upon it. Rather, in their efforts to mediate texts by women to readers, they reveal the historical and often contested processes through which "the woman writer" emerged to form a significant category within a broader history of ideas about the book, the author, and English literature itself.

For many of the late medieval and early modern readers, writers, and editors whose work I present here, "women's writing," by virtue of its alienation from tradition, is almost by definition writing that is shrouded in literary-historical obscurity. In their representations of women writers, Chaucer, Bale, and Puttenham show how "loss" became a constitutive characteristic of the woman writer, making the work of editing, translating, or publishing it an act of recovery. But, as the work of the early editors reveals, that act can also be so permeated with desire and identification as to blur the distinction between recovery and creation. In Bale's editions of Anne Askew and Elizabeth Tudor, for example, the editor becomes as visible an agent as the

woman writer, and his frequent interventions betray his desire to produce both Askew and Tudor as icons of a nascent Protestant identity.[30] But calling attention to the interventions and desires of the editors, writers, and translators who represent them does not mean that
women writers themselves were without agency in the historical construction either of English literature or of "the woman writer." To the
contrary, the editorial and representational acts that I examine here
are dialectical, showing how female-authored texts both shaped and
were shaped by the conventions of literary culture in which they were
received. The encounter between editor and woman writer is never a
unidirectional assertion of editorial will onto a wholly passive text;
indeed, editorial paratexts often yield signs of interpretive struggle
that indicate points of the texts' resistance to the editors' intended
framing of them.[31] Other editors reveal themselves to be canny readers of the texts they present, as does George Puttenham in his treatment of the poetry of Elizabeth I; as editor, he adopts the rhetorical
tropes and postures of his subject, indicating the extent to which the
text controls him, rather than the reverse.

Women writers, in turn, frequently reveal their awareness of the
literary-cultural meanings that defined "women's writing." As Margaret Ferguson notes, the figure of the woman writer occupies a consistently "eccentric" position to the side of literary authority and
tradition, a position of which women who wrote in the late medieval
and early modern periods were strikingly conscious.[32] Indeed, the literary mode in which early women writers most consistently frame
their work is the apology. In the Middle Ages, Julian of Norwich excuses her writing by noting that "I am a woman, leued, fabille and
freylle."[33] In similar terms, the early modern writer Elizabeth Jocelin
describes her own reluctance to write: "I thought of writing, but then
mine own weakness appeared so manifestly that I was ashamed and
durst not undertake it"; both thus employ an apologetic topos that
Elizabeth Hageman finds characteristic of the early woman writer
who acknowledges in various ways through her writing that she is
"only a woman."[34] These women writers' repeatedly apologetic self-
positionings not only reflect their cultures' attitudes about women,
they also help to fashion the literary-cultural category of "women's
writing," while demonstrating the different ends and effects to which
it could be manipulated.[35] Identification with this category did not
keep women from writing; indeed, several scholars have suggested
that the apology as a literary mode enabled women writers to emphasize their outsider status and thereby to present their work as a new
form of writing, beyond the boundaries of traditional authority. Thus

Nicholas Watson finds that Julian of Norwich's apologetic mode transforms medieval patristic culture's de-authorization of women into the basis of a new form of literary authorship, while Wendy Wall points to the ways in which an early modern woman writer such as Elizabeth Jocelin, credited by her seventeenth-century editor with "a prophetical sense of her dissolution," turns abnegation into an enunciatory position.[36] The apology topos does not remove women's writing from circulation—nor, these examples suggest, should it be seen as a transparent attempt to do so. Rather, it serves as a convention of circulation that shapes the conditions in which that writing will be received. The production of women's writing as marginal or lost, therefore, also produces the possibility of viewing literary tradition and authority from the outside.

The alienation that defined "women's writing" in the medieval and early modern periods made it a focal point for the historical alienation that was perceived to afflict English letters more generally. John Skelton's "Phyllyp Sparowe" (c. 1500), a poem that confronts the problem of English literary history at a self-consciously formative moment, offers one example of how English letters' perceived alienation from the authoritative literary past is concentrated in the figure of the woman writer.[37] Skelton's poem follows its female narrator, Jane Scrope, in her travails of composition as she attempts to write an elegy for her pet sparrow. But her attempt falters when she finds herself at a loss for the classical influence she desires—"these poetes of auncyente / They ar to diffuse for me" (767–68)—because, she laments, as a "maid," she is excluded from the Latinate tradition of the classical authors:

> But for I am a maid,
> Tymerous, halfe afrayde,
> That never yet asayed
> Of Helicon's well
> Where the Muses dwell. (607–11)

If Jane's femininity restricts her access to classical traditions, it also identifies her with the vernacular, which is, like Jane, alienated from the past and limited in its vocabulary and rhetorical expressiveness. While her own language is, by her own admission, awkward and unformed, so too is English itself: "our natural tongue is rude / And hard to be ennewed" (774–75). Lamenting her alienation from the classical traditions because she "can but little skill / Of Ovid or Virgil" (755–56), Jane declares a natural affinity with the authors of the vernacular texts she does read, among which she names Chaucer's

Canterbury Tales and *Troilus and Criseyde*, together with the poems of Gower and Lydgate. In this, she becomes a focal point for Skelton's larger reflection on the state of English letters. Skelton is one of the first English writers to conceive English literature as a body of texts linked by a common national and linguistic identity, and the major figures he identifies—Chaucer, Gower, and Lydgate—remain the touchstones of the medieval literary canon. However, Skelton unites this early survey of Middle English literature by defining its spokesperson as a young woman writer, a gesture in which is concentrated his own sense of that literature's inadequacy. Thus Jane's alienation from the classical canon gives form to the parallel alienation of English literature itself.

The perception that English literature was estranged from or bore only the most tenuous connection to tradition and the literary past recurs throughout the works that I examine—indeed, it would continue to be expressed through the seventeenth century.[38] But what counted as tradition, and whether alienation from it was therefore positive or negative, was subject to change across the medieval and early modern periods, as the imaginary relationship between English literature and the literary past was redefined. If Skelton presents English literature as a debased cultural form that could never hope to attain the cultural authority of the classical canon, in the later sixteenth century its perceived distance from ancient literary authority made vernacular literature a source of England's national identity. This shift is apparent in the contrast between two figures who frame this book's historical focus: Geoffrey Chaucer and George Puttenham. Both are fundamentally concerned with the possibility of a vernacular literary tradition, as exemplified by Chaucer's *Troilus and Criseyde* and Puttenham's *Arte of English Poesie*, two works that have been taken to be that tradition's founding texts.[39] Both personify this tradition through lists of male authors, such as when Chaucer invokes the names of "Virgile, Ovide, Omer, Lucan, and Stace" at the end of *Troilus and Criseyde* as models for the English poet, or when Puttenham offers an inventory of English poets of note that begins with Chaucer himself and progresses through Skelton, Wyatt, Surrey, Sidney, and Ralegh.[40] Yet both Chaucer and Puttenham concentrate their discussions of writing and literary history in figures of women writers. For Chaucer, the spectacle of masculine poetic authority is drawn up against the figure of the woman writer, epitomized by Criseyde, shown in the act of writing "of hire hond," while for Puttenham, the central figure of English poetry is Elizabeth I, who represents the most exalted of what he terms "gentlewoman makers." In my reading it is these figures, rather than the better-known successions of famous male poets, in whom Chaucer and Puttenham focus their most historically responsive meditations on the complex state of English letters. Chaucer and Puttenham are united in stressing the woman writer's exteriority to classical models of writing, yet the implications of that exteriority differ fundamentally: where for Chaucer, it implies a position of abjection, expressed by Criseyde as a phobia about writing, for Puttenham it promises new forms of English literature, exemplified in the brutal but ornamental poetry of Elizabeth I. Indeed, the representations of women writers that form my focus throughout the following chapters show that the meanings of "the woman writer" are supremely contingent across the late medieval and early modern periods; but in their contingency, they reflect and participate in changing conceptual models of English literary history.

My first chapter sets up the major terms of the book's broader argument by reading a series of Chaucerian texts in which the "lost woman writer" embodies the disjunction between vernacular writing and the classical canon. Where literary history has installed Chaucer as the "father of English poetry" and thus the origin of a patrilineal model of literary influence and inheritance, my first chapter revisits this paradigm by considering the unexpectedly instrumental roles that his works assign to women writers. In the pivotal middle years of his career, Chaucer turned to classical forms and settings in *The House of Fame, Anelida and Arcite, Troilus and Criseyde,* and *The Legend of Good Women,* all of which stage a deliberate encounter between English writing and the classical canon. If the classical authors exemplify a level of cultural permanence and authority that would always be unattainable for the vernacular poet, their foils are the women writers who appear throughout Chaucer's classical works and embody opposing threats of textual loss and cultural instability. In the figure of the woman writer Chaucer explores the problem of writing outside authoritative models of literary tradition, a problem that attends the project of vernacular canon formation. The woman writer's marginalization from the classical canon makes her a potent symbol in Chaucer's work for the cultural instability of the literary vernacular, with its vulnerability to language change and the vagaries of manuscript transmission. If subsequent generations credited Chaucer with elevating English letters to the level of the classical canon, Chaucer's representations of women writers manifest the limits of this project.

While the woman writer's perceived distance from tradition is to Chaucer an occasion of pathos and loss, to later readers that same position offers new models of authorship and literary activity. As secular literary production moved to the fifteenth-century aristocratic household and the newly consolidated English court, a new class of courtly literati articulated its growing sense of distance from earlier medieval institutions of literacy by finding models for its own literary work in the figure of the medieval woman writer.[41] My second chapter traces this movement in the English translation and circulation of the work of the French medieval writer Christine de Pizan (c. 1364–c. 1431). Christine's works have attracted recent scholarly attention for their representations of the learned woman and critique of the medieval institutions that excluded her, notably the misogynist traditions of clerical writing and the literary conventions of chivalry and courtly love. These elements won Christine an appreciative readership in England over the century following her death, when her works entered the nascent canon of fifteenth- and early sixteenth-century court literature. However, in this new milieu the principal readers, translators, and editors of Christine's works were not women but gentlemen. As the paratextual evidence of Christine's circulation in England puzzlingly shows, the books that carried Christine's works in late fifteenth- and early sixteenth-century England were explicitly addressed to gentlemen readers and in the process were frequently represented as the work of men. At the same time, Christine's self-representations as a female author, which recur throughout her always-autobiographical works, were not excised or ignored but were rather carefully appropriated by those works' translators and editors for the new literary communities that emerged within England's aristocratic households and royal courts. This chapter therefore demonstrates that Christine's revisions of medieval institutions of literacy established the terms by which early modern male courtiers understood the nature of their own literary work in the changing institution of the household and court. But in turn, the editors, translators, and printers of Christine's work also registered in their paratexts the degree of their resistance to Christine's definition of "the woman writer."

Where Christine de Pizan, like Chaucer, defines the woman writer in opposition to the figures of traditional literary authority such as the medieval "clerc," that same symbolic opposition to clerical institutions of pre-Reformation literacy made the woman writer a foundational figure for English readers and writers during the English Reformation. My third chapter focuses on the work of early sixteenth-century English antiquarians and editors who, following the destruction of the monastic libraries, worked to salvage and catalogue the textual remains of the English literary past. The bibliographical and editorial work of John Bale, whose voluminous catalogues construct a nascent English literary history, presents the woman writer as a potent figure of opposition to the Catholic medieval church, and thus the unexpected representative of a native, proto-Protestant English literature. But doing so required him to refigure the literary history of religious women writers from England's recent past, whose work had not long before been pressed into the service of orthodoxy. In his attempt to write a literary history of women writers that is also a prehistory of English Protestantism, Bale recovers the religious woman writer as a figure for the conflict-ridden relationship between English writing and the literary past. As a dedicated editor of women's writing as well as arguably England's first literary historian, Bale presents the work of contemporaries Anne Askew and the future Elizabeth I as the inheritrixes and contemporary exponents of a native tradition of women's writing. He thereby inspires a new interest in writing by women among sixteenth-century Protestant bibliophiles, including the Elizabethan Thomas Bentley, whose *Monument of Matrones* (1582) presents an extensive anthology of writing by ancient and contemporary women that is centered on the religious writing of Elizabeth I.

Where Bale and Bentley present the writing of Elizabeth Tudor as the cornerstone of a new, Protestant English literature, my fourth chapter further argues that Elizabeth's literary works and their reception were crucial to the establishment of the vernacular, national literature associated with her reign. Lauded by her contemporaries as a female poet on the model of Sappho, Elizabeth promised a vernacular poetry that could rival the classical canon. This promise takes shape in George Puttenham's *Arte of English Poesie* (1589). While Puttenham's treatise has been widely recognized as a formative text for a new, English courtly poetry, my reading reveals and explores the central role that Puttenham assigned to Elizabeth herself as an exemplary poet for this new art. By making a female poet into a representative English author, Puttenham revises the humanistic opposition between oratory, the classical site of masculine political authority, and poetry, an ornamental and contrastingly feminine mode of communication. In Puttenham's work, poetry replaces oratory as the medium of politics. Furthermore, in its privacy, ornamentality, and linguistic doubleness, it forms a vernacular model of textual production ideally suited to what he calls "gentlewomen makers," women like the queen whose production and circulation of poetry at once maintain humanist models of feminine privacy and silence and uphold poetry as a locus of political interest of the highest order.

Across the fourteenth through the sixteenth centuries, then, "the woman writer" becomes an index for changing ideas about the nature of English literature. What made women writers figures of loss for Chaucer at the end of the fourteenth century—their alienation from ecclesiastical literacy and the traditions embodied in the classical canon—also made them figures of new literary and national identity in the sixteenth century. For Bale the woman writer's alienation from clerks prefigured a native literary history of English Protestantism; similarly, for Puttenham, the woman writer's exclusion from classical oratory formed the condition for a new English poetry that was explicitly opposed to the orator's art. The survey I offer is representative rather than exhaustive; but by investigating the meanings of women writers in the key sites for the formation of "English literature," I argue that the woman writer is therefore not "lost" or "absent" from English literary history during this formative period. Rather, defined within those sites as a figure outside tradition, she becomes central to English literature's very invention.

Medieval and early modern representations of the woman writer's exteriority to tradition made her a charged emblem of literary modernity. Whether "tradition" takes the form of an inherited body of texts and *auctores* or the metaphorical inheritance conferred by humanist classicism, by promising a literary model outside tradition's borders, the woman writer embodies a species of literary newness that, as Paul de Man observes of literary modernity, "exists in the form of a desire to wipe out whatever came earlier, in the hope of reaching at last a point that could be called a true present, a point of origin that marks a new departure." [42] The "modernity" of the woman writer designates less a particular chronological moment than a position that is perceived to depart from the past, a position that has been identified with women throughout literary history and theory. For Brian Stock, the medieval woman defines a position from which it becomes possible to critique tradition: as he puts it, "women in general, whom the traditions of the church had so completely isolated," became in the late Middle Ages figures who were "modern in a new sense," promising a dissident alternative to the "blind adherence to tradition." [43] Recent work in later periods has advanced related arguments linking women and modernity: Alice A. Jardine finds the figure of woman representative of what she calls "the crisis-in-narrative that is modernity" which is "intrinsic to new and necessary modes of thinking, writing, speaking."[44] Similarly, David Simpson has recently argued that "the very notion of the modern subjectivity came into being as a feminized entity."[45] Likewise, the representations of women writers that I examine in this book concentrate contemporary responses to modernity, understood as a split from tradition. But they also offer an opportunity to historicize and qualify the linkage of "woman" with "modernity" as it has obtained in current theoretical models. Women's writing in itself is not necessarily dissident or resistant; indeed, it can be enlisted on behalf of orthodoxy as easily as on behalf of dissent, as my third chapter on Reformation editions of women writers shows.[46] What makes the texts I examine here emblems of literary modernity is not the fact that they were written by women per se, but that they were circulated and interpreted within a broader category of "women's writing," which was shaped in opposition to "tradition." In this model, "women's writing" and "literary tradition" come to define one another dialectically, in ways that recall Stock's point that "tradition and modernity are not mutually exclusive; they are mutually interdependent."[47] By this argument, the modernity of the woman writer enabled early literary culture to define literary tradition by imagining forms of writing that stood outside it. But by giving form to that which lies outside tradition, "the woman writer" also absorbed the cultural uncertainties and dangers associated with this position of exteriority and thus also became the focal point for resistance to modernity in its various forms across this period.[48]

As focal points for the encounter between tradition and modernity, the authorized past and the unknown future, representations of women writers from the fourteenth through the sixteenth centuries reflect their makers' perceptions of their own periodicity. They thus offer a vantage from which to rethink the models of periodization that have organized women's writings in the more recent past. Teaching anthologies of early women writers commonly attempt to place their subjects into established periods such as "medieval" and "Renaissance," sometimes by distorting their chronological specificity.[49] In contrast, some important collections of scholarly essays on women writers have defined their focus with greater diachronic breadth as "late medieval and early modern," allowing the study of writing by women to define new schemes of periodization in literary history.[50] Such a gesture follows the lead of Joan Kelly's landmark essay "Did Women Have a Renaissance?" which asserts: "One of the tasks of women's history is to call into question accepted schemes of periodization."[51] Where recent critiques of the categories "medieval" and "Renaissance" have questioned the assumptions that such schemes

uphold, particularly as informed by Jacob Burckhardt's model of epochal change from a period of corporate identity to one of liberal in-
dividualism, feminist scholars such as Kelly have long pointed out
that Burckhardtian schemes of "medieval" and "Renaissance" were
never relevant to the history of women.[52] Women writers such as Margery Kempe and Christine de Pizan encourage a rethinking of periodization because they wrote in the fifteenth century, a period that falls
between traditional divisions of "medieval" and "Renaissance" and
has until recently been neglected in English literary history. Defining
its focus across the fourteenth and sixteenth centuries, *Lost Property*
does not operate within the period boundaries of a traditionally defined Middle Ages or Renaissance; instead, it investigates the models
by which writers, readers, and editors understood their own place in
literary history and, furthermore, defined that literary history through
models of gender. The woman writer's perceived alienation from tradition and the authorized past makes "women's writing" a category
that can appear to float free of sequential narratives of literary history.
But that alienation also made "the woman writer" a figure in which
local responses to questions of historical change were most urgently
concentrated. The shifting representations of the woman writer
across this period reflect the numerous levels of negotiation that attended these moments of change, as well as the layers of appropriation
that went into making a new literary culture in the sixteenth century:
for example, the woman writer becomes a point of struggle for definition during the Reformation between those who would claim her on
behalf of Catholic orthodoxy and those like John Bale who would advance her as an emblem of native dissidence along the lines that Stock
describes. Tracing the representation of women writers across this period, along with the responses to cultural change that they embody,
reveals that English literary history is not a stable grid into which
women writers can simply be imported, but a contingent narrative
that ideas about women writers helped to create.

   The history of "the woman writer" that *Lost Property* proposes
both contributes to and modifies the history of authorship as it has
recently been written. Medievalists such as David Hult and A. J.
Minnis and Renaissance scholars such as Jeffrey Masten and Joseph
Loewenstein indicate that from the fourteenth through the sixteenth
centuries, ideas about authorship underwent a series of shifts that
dislocated literary authority from communal structures of writing
to the individual writer.[53] These and related studies show, following Foucault, that "the author" has a history that is linked to the
broader histories of reading, writing, and textual culture, emerging as

a "principle of a certain unity of writing," as Foucault puts it, that enables texts to be classified in reference to a model of individual identity.[54] The history of "women's writing" that I offer here indicates that, even before texts were classified in reference to individual authors, they were organized by gender. The conception of "the woman writer" as a cultural figure whose writing was marked by the social signs of gender difference represents a crucial development in the history of the idea that texts reflect their authors' identities—the hallmark of modern authorship for Foucault. But in the fourteenth and fifteenth centuries, the earliest historical moments of my focus, the notion of a writing located in an individual author was not a sign of a laudatory originality and self-expression but rather one of loss and alienation from the communal structures of authority. In this period the woman writer thus represents both the "first modern author"— as Maureen Quilligan has persuasively argued of Christine de Pizan— and a site of resistance to the very notion of an individuated authorship that she, in her modernity, embodied.[55] The cultural ambivalence about individual authorship that settled in the figure of the woman writer becomes visible in the circulation of Christine's works in England, which I discuss in my second chapter, when Christine's models of an individuated female authorship were adapted to a culture that continued to valorize writing as a communal practice but removed it to the new collective structures of aristocratic patronage.

If the promises and dangers of individuated authorship were explored, disavowed, or desired through the figure of the woman writer, that figure also became pivotal for the development of the idea of English literary history as a coherent cultural category. Classic and still-influential accounts such as René Wellek's hold that a self-conscious notion of English literary history as such emerges only in the eighteenth century, before which time notions of a native literary tradition and its development were unknown: as Wellek insists, "there was no literary history in the Middle Ages."[56] But by uncovering the cultural significance of the woman writer to early discussions of authorship, vernacular writing, and literary tradition, I find, contrary to Wellek's model, that medieval and early modern readers and writers such as Chaucer, Bale, and Puttenham first explore the possibility of English literature as an entity outside of classical and patristic models through their various constructions of the category of women's writing. By reading for notions of English literary history not just in literary texts but also in the paratextual apparatus that shapes their circulation—in the work of selection by printers and patrons, the private notes of readers, and the seemingly invisible decisions of translators and editors—I trace the development of a notion of English literary history in the material traces of early English texts' transmission. I thus seek to construct what Fredric Jameson calls a "literary history of objects," which stresses the levels of mediation between literary and social domains that shape a particular text's significance within a particular moment of its reception.[57] The material shapings of texts reveal a constellation of judgments about the nature of literary value, the changing milieux of literary consumption, and the particular qualities that mark a text at a given point as the work of a woman or a man. In this process, paratextual signals about the woman writer take their place among the other markers of literary meaning—genre, intended readership, visual display—as ways of signaling to readers its particular uses and significance. Such moments are crucial to the understanding of how the figure of the woman writer signifies to a larger literary culture. Thus I find that literary history is shaped not only on the broad and abstract level by its theorists but also on the material, local level of the book, when a work and its author are made meaningful within a specific social moment.

Against the backdrop of current debates about the woman writer's place in the English canon, the conjoined history of "the woman writer" and "English literature" in the late medieval and early modern periods assumes particular relevance. The relation that texts by women bear to the authoritative, male-authored texts of English literary tradition has always been in question for feminist literary criticism, which has debated whether texts by women should be integrated into that authoritative tradition or, alternately, whether they constitute a discrete tradition of their own.[58] Rather than seeking to establish an autonomous female tradition or arguing for the canonization of women's writing *tout court*, *Lost Property* finds that the representation and circulation of writing by women destabilizes the notion of "tradition" by giving shape to the forms and acts of writing that it forcibly expels. "The woman writer" thus haunts medieval and early modern considerations of canon formation as a figure of the canon's excluded other. While I do not claim to offer a comprehensive account of all representations of women writers across the two hundred years of my focus, the particular cases I examine here support the larger point that "the woman writer" was not an unthinkable anomaly during this period; nor was she automatically excluded or absented from a literary culture and history that were de facto exclusively masculine. Rather, *Lost Property* argues that the very instability of the category of "English literature" during this period made "the woman writer" an unexpectedly central figure within early English literary culture.

The process by which the woman writer becomes an embodiment of loss is captured in my title, *Lost Property*, which is the British equivalent of the American term "lost and found." Where "lost and found" suggests a narrative of loss and recovery similar to the Freudian narrative of *fort-da*—an object is lost and then is found again—"lost property" suggests a different narrative, not so much one of recovery as a process by which objects become designated and gain their identity as embodiments of loss.[59] Loss, then, becomes their defining property, and the term "lost property" turns them into palpable emblems of alienation. Likewise, this book argues that the woman writer in medieval and early modern England became a "lost property" insofar as she was defined through her exteriority to literary tradition. But in the proccess, she gave shape to new models of writing and authorship that became foundational to English literary history.

One

FOLLOWING CORINNE

Chaucer's Classical Women Writers

"Evir wemenis frend"

"For he was evir, God wait, wemenis frend."[1] Gavin Douglas's well-known judgment of Chaucer offers one of the earliest reflections on what Jill Mann calls "the woman question" in Chaucer's work—the heightened importance assigned to women and their stories from the early *Book of the Duchess* to later works like *Troilus and Criseyde* and *The Wife of Bath's Tale*.[2] For readers of Chaucer, the status of women has been an abiding focus, and Douglas's remark has become a critical touchstone for an ongoing debate as to whether or not Chaucer truly was a friend to women.[3] But to return Douglas's remark to its original context is to reveal the broader significance of "the woman question," not only as a comment on Chaucer's female characters but as an early effort to place Chaucer in a vernacular literary history that had not yet been written.

An early Scots poet who translated the *Aeneid* in 1513, Douglas was one of the first British writers to elevate the vernacular to the same level of authority and cultural prestige as the classical canon.[4] His remark about Chaucer emerges in the *Eneados*'s first preface, which meditates on the circuit of masculine alliances binding living writers to their distinguished predecessors. After establishing Virgil as "the king of poetis" and acknowledging his cultural debt to him, Douglas turns his attention to Chaucer, a poet who was no less concerned about the relation that vernacular writing bore to the classical canon. In later generations Chaucer would come to be seen as the poet who installed a vernacular canon in line with the classical and thereby fulfilled the ambitions that Douglas would express. After Spenser anointed Chaucer the English Virgil, Dryden could proclaim him the inaugural figure in a classically modeled English canon, claims that owe much to Chaucer's own objectifications of the classical canon in moments such as the well-known homage to "Virgile, Ovide, Omer, Lucan, and Stace" at the end of *Troilus and Crisyede* (TC 1792).[5] But for Douglas, Chaucer's vernacular *auctoritas* falls disastrously short of its promise, a charge he substantiates by citing *The Legend of Good Women*'s "Legend of Dido." According to Douglas, Chaucer initially pledges to follow Virgil's example—"saying he follwit Virgillis lantern to forne." However, he breaks this pledge when he turns away from the canonical story of Aeneas to take up instead the story of Dido, which Aeneas's story abandons; in so doing, Douglas charges, "my maister Chaucer grettlie Virgil offendid." If this "offense" disqualifies Chaucer from becoming Virgil's vernacular heir, Douglas attributes it to Chaucer's excessive sympathy for women: "For he was ever, God wait, wemenis frend."[6] What Douglas calls Chaucer's "friendliness" to women—his compulsion to tell their side of the story—is noteworthy, in other words, because it disrupts the continuity of literary authority from the classical canon to the vernacular.

If Douglas presents women as the site at which canonical authority falters, his selection of Dido as an example is especially fitting. In ways that Marilynn Desmond has made clear, the medieval Dido already called into question the notion of canonical continuity that Douglas would champion.[7] When Douglas blames Chaucer for betraying Virgil in order to tell Dido's story, he represses the classical precedent for that betrayal in Ovid's *Heroides* 7, which retells the *Aeneid* from Dido's perspective.[8] Where Virgil's narrative makes Dido's abandonment necessary to Aeneas's imperial destiny, Ovid's Dido pens a righteous complaint from the epic's margins. Chaucer approaches the story of Dido and Aeneas with the aim of extending the classical literary tradition to English; but instead of eliding Ovid's Heroidian challenge to Virgil, as Douglas does, he allows Dido to emerge in his own work as a counterpart to Virgilian *auctoritas*. In light of his expressed interest in literary canons, it is significant that Chaucer, like Ovid, makes Dido a writer. In the two texts in which Dido appears, *The House of Fame* and *The Legend of Good Women*, Chaucer offers

Dido's story as a difficult object of textual recovery. Purporting to take Dido as his "auctour" in *The House of Fame* (314) or to present the "lettre" that she "wrot" in the "Legend of Dido" (1354), Chaucer makes Dido's letter into a "lost" text retrieved from the margins of the *Aeneid*. If the *Aeneid* upholds the promise of canonical stability and continuity, Chaucer's Dido, as Douglas realizes, represents forms of writing that Virgilian canonicity leaves out.

After Spenser and Dryden installed him as the *fons et origo* of English poetry, Chaucer was widely held to be, in A. C. Spearing's words, "the first English poet to conceive of his work as an addition, however humble, to the great monuments of the classical past."[9] But Douglas's words can illuminate a different side of Chaucer's imagined relation to the classical canon, which reflects the perspective not of one who inherits it through a direct line of succession but of one who writes from its margins. In this, Douglas can help to historicize the project of vernacular canon formation of which Chaucer would later be adopted as head. As A. J. Minnis and M. B. Parkes have shown, the concept of literary history as an autonomous list of named authors may have been applicable in the late Middle Ages to classical or patristic *auctores*, as in *Troilus and Criseyde*'s homage to "Virgile, Ovide, Omer, Lucan, and Stace," but there was a great distance between these models and those available to the vernacular writer, whose works emerged within what Ralph Hanna III characterizes as "a literary culture constructed without a single central canon and without the constrictions of a hegemonic sense of national identity."[10] Chaucer rarely acknowledges Middle English literary precursors or contemporaries—thereby helping to construct the impression, as adopted by post-Renaissance readers, that he stood alone in an otherwise barren literary field. Nonetheless, he shows an acute interest in the problem of the noncanonical: that is, the condition of those texts that lack the authorial presence and cultural permanence of the classical works.[11] In so doing, he emerges as an important theorist of literary canons not so much through his self-installation in a literary line of descent as through his ongoing exploration of literary tradition's limits, represented in the acts and forms of writing that are consigned to that tradition's margins.

Douglas's judgment of Chaucer as "evir wemenis frend" feminizes this position of literary marginality as it emerges in Chaucer's work. This is in contrast with the consistently masculine terms in which Chaucer's own canonicity has been theorized by his later readers: if Thomas Usk praises Chaucer's "manliche speche," Dryden famously names him "father of English Poetry," envisioning Chaucer's canon-

icity as a form of literary paternity.[12] Within Chaucer's own work, as
Carolyn Dinshaw notes, literary authority is continually conceived as
a masculine attribute.[13] But this masculine language of literary authority can obscure the important role played in Chaucer's work by
women writers, who emerge into positions of unexpected centrality
in figures such as Dido, Criseyde, and Anelida, all of whom are shown
in the act of writing, as well as in a number of more marginal figures
who haunt Chaucer's *oeuvre*. Moreover, these women writers surface
within broader discussions of writing and literary tradition in ways
that make them central to those works' interrogation of the problem
of canon formation as Chaucer conceives it.

Chaucer's representations of women writers bring to the foreground the problems of literary canon formation and vernacular writing that recur throughout his works but are suppressed in the more
familiar, masculine images of literary tradition embodied in the classical male authors. Furthermore, in ways that would trouble Douglas and that this chapter will examine further, Chaucer seems hardly
able to consider literary tradition without also invoking figures of
women writers. While it has now become commonplace to see "the
woman writer" and "literary tradition" as mutually exclusive categories, Chaucer's works offer an opportunity to historicize this opposition by tracing it to a moment in which notions of vernacular authorship and national literature were under construction. Rather than
appearing timeless and self-evident in their opposition, the categories
"the woman writer" and "literary tradition" as they appear in Chaucer's work are reciprocally formed and symbiotically interconnected.
If literary tradition has come to be represented as an "unflawed capacity for patriarchal communication and instruction through time," to
cite a memorable formulation by Thomas Greene, it achieves that
imaginary unity through its exclusion of the category of "the woman
writer."[14] But just as "the modern" defines "the traditional" by delim-
iting its threshold, Chaucer's representations of women writers show
how in a similar way "the woman writer" becomes necessary to the
definition of an implicitly masculine "literary tradition" by representing a realm outside its borders.[15]

Chaucer's best-known discussion of women writers asserts that
there were none. In *The Wife of Bath's Prologue*, the Wife decries the
misogyny of clerical writing and imagines how literary tradition
would be different if only women wrote:

> Who peyntede the leon, tel me who?
> By God, if wommen hadde writen stories,

As clerkes han withinne hire oratories,
They wolde han writen of men moore wikkednesse
Then al the mark of Adam may redresse. (692–96)

By lamenting the apparent absence of women writers, the Wife defines "the woman writer" as a figure outside literary authority.[16] That outsideness has been easy to equate with nonexistence; it is a small step from the Wife's famous lament to the proposition that there were no women writers in the Middle Ages.[17] However, as a rich vein of recent scholarship has established to the contrary, medieval women wrote texts across a variety of genres, and they sometimes attained a level of visibility that the Wife of Bath might have recalled to mitigate her despair. It is clear, moreover, that Chaucer knew that medieval women writers existed—but so, apparently, does the Wife of Bath: lodged within the very codex that prompts the Wife to lament the unequivocal absence of women writers, Jankyn's "book of wikked wyves," are two historical women writers, "Trotula," the name by which the medical writer Trota was widely known, as well as "Helowys, / That was abbesse nat fer fro Parys" (677–78).[18] In addition to these named women writers, the passage may well contain a third, lurking beneath the surface of the resonant line with which the Wife famously raises the question of women writer's absence: "Who peyntede the leon, tel me who?"[19] About the source of the reference, the *Riverside Chaucer* asserts that while the story itself is from Aesop, "the painting of the lion (rather than sculpting, as in Aesop) suggests Marie de France's version of the fable as the source of the allusion."[20] If we accept this suggestion, the very line that has been taken to articulate women writers' absence from literary history actually contains a woman writer, Marie de France, at its core.[21]

Bringing these women writers to the surface reveals a striking contradiction at the heart of the Wife of Bath's famous lament about women writers' absence, by showing that women did in fact write; it also reveals the gap between the activities of historical women writers and a discourse about "the woman writer" that developed in Chaucer's works. Heloise, Trota, and Marie de France each demonstrate, in different ways, how some historical women writers attained unexpected levels of authority and influence within medieval literary culture, despite the authority of "clerkes . . . withinne hire oratories." Moreover, in the diversity of their work, they also show how medieval women's writing resists unification under any single, autonomous notion of a "female tradition."[22] At the same time, the Wife of Bath's famous lament shows how "the woman writer" could emerge as a culturally significant figure whose symbolic function was not in any simple way descriptive of, or coterminous with, women's historical literary activities.[23] Rather than reflecting women writers' literal "absence" from literary history, this famous moment in *The Wife of Bath's Prologue* shows how "the woman writer" could be conceived within literary history as a figure of absence and marginality. Instead of taking the Wife of Bath's statement about medieval women writers' "absence" at face value, I want to consider how that absence becomes central to the definition of both "the woman writer" and the "literary tradition" that she was conceived to stand outside.

Throughout Chaucer's works female characters occupy conspicuous positions as writers: among the more prominent examples that this chapter will take up are Anelida in *Anelida and Arcite* and Criseyde in *Troilus and Criseyde*, as well as Dido in *The House of Fame* and *The Legend of Good Women*. At the same time, each of these texts insists in various ways that women are not writers—not, at least, in the sense of the named *auctores* and male writers who populate these same works. Yet rather than holding the woman writer to be therefore either eliminated or absent from a Chaucerian model of writing, these works show that representing the woman writer's "absence" from literary tradition is a way of representing tradition itself. Despite the existence of historical medieval women writers such as those who unexpectedly lurk beneath the Wife of Bath's famous lament, the Chaucerian woman writer is repeatedly conceived as a figure of loss, whether in terms of literal loss, as an elegiac or suicidal figure, or of textual loss, as one whose writing is impaired by illegibility, misapprehension, or disappearance. It is my argument that by representing the woman writer as the embodiment of loss, Chaucer concentrates in her a range of dreaded losses—the loss of linguistic meaning over time, the loss of texts through carelessness or material decay, the loss of literary tradition to a collective amnesia—that destabilize the concept of canonical continuity that a writer like Douglas will invest in the figure of Virgil. Even as Chaucer expels the figure of the woman writer to the margins of authorized literary production, therefore, his representations of women writers assign shape and form to the qualities and practices that are disallowed from that realm of canonicity. The category of "women's writing" as it emerges in Chaucer's work exemplifies what Terry Eagleton calls "the tradition of the dispossessed," which is revealed to be "not a parallel, autonomous narrative which 'ghosts' [the dominant history] and can be plucked out and recounted whole and entire . . . but nothing less than a set of crises or spasms *within* that hegemonic history."[24] Such a point can help to explain the unexpectedly central role that women writers play within the discussions of canonicity and writing that recur throughout Chaucer's work.

The twin problems of literary canon formation and the woman writer in Chaucer's work come together most urgently around the issue of the vernacular's relation to the classical canon, the very issue on which Douglas found Chaucer so dubious an exemplar. On the one hand, Chaucer clearly aspires to follow Dante in raising the authority of the vernacular to that of the classical languages.[25] Yet it is telling to compare Dante's measured consideration in *De vulgari eloquentia* of the diverse forms of spoken Italian with Chaucer's expressed anxiety in *Troilus and Criseyde* that the "gret diversite / In Englissh and in writyng of our tonge" (5.1793–94) will threaten the continued survival and even intelligibility of his work.[26] "Tradition," as modeled in Chaucer's work in the classical lineup of "Virgile, Ovide, Omer, Lucan, and Stace," posits a level of cultural stability and permanence that is opposed to, and potentially undone by, the social and material conditions of vernacular textual transmission. Where "tradition" posits an autonomous history of authors, transmission opens up a much broader field of writing that challenges the autonomy of authors and literary works. In ways that Ralph Hanna III has recently demonstrated, the very idea of a literary canon lifts texts and authors out of the social contexts that historically gave them meaning, contexts that, if examined through the evidence of early books, appear much more fragile and unstable than the notion of canonical continuity and stability permits.[27] To consider literary works not as part of an autonomous canon but as material artifacts belonging to specific cultures reveals the multiple ways in which texts gain meaning and significance through circulation within particular textual communities, rather than through the abstract transferral of authority from one author to another.[28] If this focus undermines theories of canonical stability, it brings to light the conditions of vernacular writing in the fourteenth century, which, as Hanna points out, constituted a "prenational literature" of great diversity in its generic and cultural affiliations, for which unified notions of "the author" or "the literary work" were notably foreign.[29] Even as Chaucer appears to disown this vernacular field in favor of classically derived models of canonical stability and permanence, the problem of writing in "Englissh" continually raises the question of what it means to create texts without the assurance of a permanent, unifying tradition, subject to the vagaries of transmission over which the writer has little control.

Concern about the instabilities of the vernacular forms a constant backdrop in Chaucer's work but rises to the fore in the "classical" texts he produced in the middle of his career. After the early, courtly *Book of the Duchess,* Chaucer wrote a series of texts—*The House of Fame, Anelida and Arcite, Troilus and Criseyde,* and *The Legend of Good Women*—that take place in classical settings and retell, at least obliquely, the stories of the classical canon.[30] As many readers have recognized, these texts represent an effort to imagine a vernacular literary model that could approach the authority of the classical canon; however, they also repeatedly articulate uncertainty about the applicability of classical modes of writing and literary authority to the vernacular poet. In these works, women writers emerge to play unexpectedly central roles. Springing, like Dido, from the margins of the classical canon, these women writers represent authorial positions that are both contiguous with and peripheral to the literary authority of the classical "poetes." They thus represent a model of writing that departs from the idealized lines of paternal transmission and inheritance that, for a poet like Douglas, underwrite the continuity of the classical tradition. Together, these classical women writers become focal points for the urgent questions that Chaucer poses in his early work about the disjunction between writing in the vernacular and the classical canon. If Chaucer's work continually invokes the classical authors as figures of the transcendent stability of literary tradition, it also invokes the woman writer as a figure of the contingent processes of transmission that the very model of tradition represses. Within this context, "the woman writer" as she emerges in Chaucer's classical works represents the problem of writing with neither a visible past nor a certain future, from a position that was contiguous with but marginal to the classical canon. As such, she makes it possible to objectify and hence to analyze the instability of the category "English literature" itself, while also absorbing that instability into an explanatory model of sexual difference.

An example will illustrate this point. *The House of Fame,* Chaucer's dream vision that repeatedly takes up the anxious mismatch between vernacular writing and literary authority, contains a passage that has long puzzled its readers.[31] Early in Book 3, within the House of Fame itself, the narrator encounters Orpheus, the classical figure of vatic authorship, who is surrounded by legions of lesser poets, "smale harpers," who would imitate him, "countrefete hem as an ape" (HF 1209, 1212)—an example that almost parodically anticipates Douglas's vision of vernacular *imitatio* of classical literary authority. In this company is a figure named "Marcia" who has been punished for her unauthorized literary ambition:

> And Marcia that lost her skyn,
> Bothe in face, body, and chyn,
> For that she wolde envien, loo,
> To pipen bet than Appolloo. (HF 1229–32)

The reference is to Marsyas, a satyr from Dante's *Commedia* and Ovid's *Metamorphoses* who is famous for challenging Apollo to a singing contest, for which he is flayed as punishment.[32] Given Marsyas's masculinity in the sources, however, Chaucer's decision to re-gender him as the female "Marcia" has struck readers as an inexplicable misinterpretation. Alfred David ascribes "Chaucer's curious notion that Marsyas was female" to a possible scribal interpolation in a source text, while A. C. Spearing hypothesizes that "Chaucer did not know who Marsyas was" and therefore was uncertain about her or his gender.[33] In my reading, however, Marcia's femininity is not an unimportant detail but is rather consistent with Chaucer's broader practice of embodying problems of authority, writing, and the classical tradition in women writers.

The episode with Marcia in *The House of Fame* culminates an increasingly anxious meditation about the dangers of poetic ambition that begins with the narrator himself reflecting on his own literary aims. At the beginning of Book 3 he invokes the same Apollo who will flay Marcyas/Marcia to come to his poetic aid:

> O God of science and of lyght,
> Appollo, thurgh thy grete myght,
> This lytel last bok thou gye! (1091–93)

But having asked for Apollo's guidance, the narrator immediately disclaims the ambition that the invocation suggests by backtracking: "Nat that I wilne, for maistrye, / Here art poetical be shewed" (1094–95). Rather than seeking the lofty goals of mastery or "art poetical," he expresses the hope merely to mitigate the embarrassment of writing in the "lewd" vernacular: "but for the rym ys lyght and lewed, / Yit make hyt sumwhat agreable" (1096–97). Acting out of a fear that is never fully identified, he thus disowns his earlier ambition: from the desire for vatic inspiration, he descends to the more humble wish that his writing be "somewhat agreeable."

Chaucer's address to Apollo forms an incomplete citation of Dante in *Paradiso* 1.13–27, who similarly invokes Apollo but compares himself to Marsyas (here masculine) when he calls for inspiration:

> Entra nel petto mio, e spira tue
> sì come quando Marsïa traesti
> de la vagina de le membre sue.

(Enter into my breast within me breathe
the verys power you made manifest
when you drew Marsyas from his limbs' sheath.)[34]

In this passage inspiration is a divine force that will ravish the poet
from his flesh—"de la vagina de le membre sua"—by casting Marsyas's flaying as a liberation of the spirit from a feminized, carnal
body, here arrestingly imaged as the spirit's "vagina."

While Chaucer likewise invites Apollo to "entre in my brest
anoon!" (1109), he delays the reference to Marsyas for over a hundred
lines, when he elects to represent the satyr as a figure not of inspiration but of dangerous ambition, and this time not as a man but literally as a woman. If Chaucer's fearful invocation of Apollo suggests
that "maistrie" and "art poetical" are not fit objects for the vernacular
poet's aspiration, Marcia's punishment illustrates the horrible fate of
one who did presume to match the heights of classical poetic achievement, thus giving form to the narrator's fears. Marcia's flaying, and
thus her continued association with the corporeal, brings to mind the
actual animal skin of which manuscripts are constructed, reminding
us that in medieval literary culture, as Carolyn Dinshaw points out,
"literary production takes place on bodies."[35] The desire to be free of
the skin that Dante expresses could be seen to reflect a philological
desire to liberate literary production from its material circumstances
in manuscript circulation.[36] In Chaucer's text, however, Marcia is
disavowed as a model of poetic inspiration, a disavowal that is reinforced by the figure's seemingly gratuitous feminization. By turning
Marcia into a female figure, this passage in *The House of Fame* draws
a prophylactic distinction of gender between her and the male poet
that would appear to shield him from the very dangers in his own
work that he projects onto her. While as a poet she is a figure of anxious identification for the narrator, as a woman she can contain those
anxieties in a gendered narrative that still leaves open the possibility
that a male poet might fare better. I thus read the feminization of
Chaucer's Marcia as part of an effort to concentrate in the figure of the
woman writer all that appears debased and corruptible about vernacular manuscript culture, and thus all that prevents the living writer
from aspiring to the timelessness and idealized classicism that is represented by Apollo.

The episode with Marcia writes small a larger dynamic that informs the roles of the women writers who unexpectedly populate
Chaucer's classical works. Through these women writers, Chaucer
explores what it means to write from a position that is both contigu-

ous with yet marginal to classical literary authority, a position he invests with equal measures of desire and danger. As we shall see, a woman writer like Dido creates a model of female authorship that is notably different from that of Marcia; yet like Marcia in this reading, she also becomes the focal point for a set of related concerns about the material processes of writing, literary authority, and the vernacular's relation to the classical past. In their marginality to literary tradition, Chaucer's classical women writers embody and objectify the paradoxes that underlie Chaucer's own relation to the classical canon. While Chaucer's works present frequent images of such a tradition as an assembly of male poets—for example, in a gallery of classical authors in *The House of Fame,* or a procession of similar figures at the end of the *Troilus*—it remains a pressing question whether or not this tradition can be extended to the vernacular poet. On the other hand, in contrast to such personifications of classical *auctoritas,* Chaucer's women writers continually express awareness of their own alienation from any such time-honored lineage, since, unlike the "poetes," they claim no illustrious ancestors and will leave no cultural legacy of their own.

Furthermore, where the classical poets are represented by permanent literary monuments that are seemingly autonomous of the field of writing, Dido, Anelida, and Criseyde write letters, which emphasize through their very form the fragile and material processes of composition and circulation that are repressed by the transcendent category of "poetrie." In this, letters reduce writing to what Janet Gurkin Altman calls "losable words."[37] Unlike the lasting works of the classical *auctores,* the writing of Chaucer's classical women is subject to mistransmission, misunderstanding, and above all, loss. Where the classical authors represent a line of authority that will never be clearly extended to the vernacular poet, the women writers who populate Chaucer's classical works become the focal points for an ongoing exploration of writing that takes place without tradition, authority, or assured survival. In so doing, they absorb and objectify the distance that Chaucer's works continually posit between the late-medieval vernacular writer and the classical model of tradition to which he aspires but continually falls short.

Dido's Poetics of Absence

The two texts from Chaucer's corpus in which Dido's letter appears, *The House of Fame* and *The Legend of Good Women,* both offer extended meditations on the relationship between the "old books" of the literary past and a vernacular literary culture that is devoted to pleasing but ephemeral novelty. The narrator of *The House of Fame* is initially berated for his preference for "[sitting] at another book" rather than seeking "reste and newe thynges" (658, 654); this criticism leads him to seek out "newe tydynges" (1886) in the House of Fame.[38] The *Legend of Good Women* similarly opens on a narrator who is enthralled by the authority of "old bokes" (F 25), but who is forced by an indignant God of Love to redirect his literary work to a new requirement, the "makyng of a glorious legende / Of goode wymmen, maydenes and wyves" (F 483–84). By staging the encounter between a tradition of "old books" and a living, literary culture that produces "newe thinges" (HF 1887), the two works continually examine what it means to write literary texts from a position that derives from, yet is fundamentally distinct from, a literary tradition of "old books." This question finds a particularly charged focal point in Dido, who stands both outside and within classical literary culture with all the precariousness of Chaucer's narrators in *The House of Fame* and *The Legend of Good Women*. In this, she comes to embody and objectify the dangers of literary discontinuity that plague both projects.

As much as *The House of Fame* explores, in Jesse Gellrich's words, "the nature of tradition (that is, 'fame') itself," it also explores the distances that separate that same fame and tradition from the vernacular writer.[39] Turning from books to "newe thinges" as the source of literary knowledge, the poem's narrator, "Geffrey," emphasizes his distance from the classical authors in Fame's house who, presided over by Calliope, the Muse of epic poetry, embody a literary fame that is as contrastingly permanent and authoritative as Geffrey's "tydynges" are novel and fleeting. Those authors include Statius ("The Tholosan that highte Stace / That bar of Thebes up the fame / upon his shuldres" [HF 1461–63]) as well as Virgil ("That bore hath up a large while / The fame of Pius Eneas" [1483–85]), whose monumental fame coincides with that of their literary achievements. Dido, in contrast, recalls the stories and forms of writing that the classical model of fame represses. Unlike the monumental figures of classical tradition in Fame's house, Dido's appearance in *The House of Fame* highlights the place where influence and tradition break down. Writing between the lines of the *Aeneid*, Dido produces a text that exists both within and outside the traditional matter of the classical *auctores*.[40] But her "writing"—the letter that she is said to have composed on the brink of suicide—also poses a fundamental problem of recoverability that represents the threatening inverse of classical fame.

If Dido's "authorship" exists in the gaps between and among the accounts of the classical *auctores*, her writing forms a negative mirror image of the classical author's epic matter. Proceeding from the position of abandonment rather than conquest, Dido's writing produces an etiology of loss. While the authors in Fame's house seek to magnify their names, Dido laments the "loss" of her own name: "thorgh yow is my name lorn," she complains in a line that takes on extra resonance, as Elaine Tuttle Hansen points out, in a poem that constantly worries about the durability of the personal name.[41] In her complaint, Dido insists that the mechanisms by which her name is lost are directly connected to those by which Aeneas's name is celebrated—not just because Aeneas has wronged her but because the production of epic, masculine fame is strangely contingent upon the seduction and abandonment of women: a man will seduce a woman, she bitterly asserts, simply because "he wolde haue fame / In magnifyinge of his name" (305–6). Not only does men's pursuit of fame lead them to seduce and abandon women, in other words, it appears to require it.[42] The same argument is repeated later in the House of Fame by a group of men who seek fame for the perception "that wommen loven us for wod" (1747), in the absence of any actual success in erotic conquest:

> Thogh we may not the body have
> Of wymmen, yet, so God yow save,
> Leet men gliwe on us the name—
> Sufficeth that we han the fame. (1759–62)

To the extent that it is grounded in the "body . . . of wymmen," then, the "magnifying" of men's names leads to the loss of women's, suggesting that as long as men seek fame, women will be fame's casualties. Likewise, just as male heroes build their reputations on the seduction and abandonment of women, so epic, the canonical genre of male fame, generates female complaint as its by-product.

Women's writing, coming from a position of loss and abandonment, represents the inverse of male poetic fame: in place of immortality, the product of epic, the female complaint such as Dido's produces mortality. In Ovid's Heroidian model, the female letter of complaint is written at the point of the woman writer's suicide and is literally premised on the death of its author. Ovid's Dido opens her letter by invoking the dying swan and comparing her own letter to the swan song: "Sic ubi fata vocant, udis abiectus in herbis / ad vada Maeandri concinit albus olor" (Thus, at the summons of fate, casting himself down amid the watery grasses by the shallows of Maeander, sings the white swan).[43] If the letter begins by announcing her incipient death, Dido herself analogizes her impending suicide with her act of writing:

> adspicias utinam, quae sit scribentis imago!
> scribimus, et gremio Troicus ensis adest,
> perque genas lacrimae strictum labuntur in ensem,
> qui iam pro lacrimis sanguine tinctus erit.

> (Could you but see now the face of her who writes
> these words! I write, and the Trojan's blade is ready
> in my lap. Over my cheeks the tears roll, and fall
> upon the drawn steel—which soon shall be
> stained with blood instead of tears.)[44]

This analogy is fulfilled in the final line of *Heroides* 7, which emphasizes that the hand with which Dido wrote her letter became the instrument of her death: "Ipsa sua Dido concidit usa manu" (from the hand of Dido herself came the stroke by which she fell).[45] Dido's linkage of writing and suicide recalls other female letter writers in the *Heroides* who similarly bring together the two actions analogically. The letter from Canace to Macareus, for example, explicitly compares the woman writer's pen to the sword with which she will kill herself:

> Siqua tamen caecis errabunt scripta lituris,
> oblitus a dominae caede libellus erit.
> dextra tenet calamum, strictum tenet altera ferrum,
> et iacet in gremio charta soluta meo.

> (If any of what I write is yet blotted deep and escapes
> your eye, it will be because the little roll has been
> stained by its mistress' blood. My right hand holds
> the pen, a drawn blade the other holds, and the paper
> lies unrolled in my lap.)[46]

Canace's posture, holding the pen in one hand and the blade in the other, echoes that of medieval writers of manuscripts, who are conventionally depicted holding a pen and a blade, which is used to scrape out mistakes.[47] Here the blade becomes the instrument of erasure not only of the female-authored text but also of the female author herself, since the letter is blotted with Canace's own blood. In this as in many others of Ovid's *Heroides*, the delivery of a letter implicitly signals its author's death, since it is only after her suicide that the text will be read. This model is one that Chaucer picks up in his own representation of Dido, to suggest that if men's writing confers immortality, women's writing is literally suicidal.

While *The House of Fame* presents Dido as a writer, it falls short of delivering her actual letter and in its place describes her suicide. Here, a woman's writing leads not only to its writer's death but to its own disappearance; unlike Ovid's heroines, Chaucer's Dido writes in invisible ink. In the absence of Dido's text, Chaucer's narrator rushes to substitute two canonical male poets, Virgil and Ovid, ostensibly seeking narrative stability in classical tradition:

> When that this was seyde and doo,
> She rof hirselve to the herte
> And deyde thorgh the wounde smerte.
> And al the maner how she deyde,
> And alle the wordes that she seyde,
> Whoso to knowe hit hath purpos,
> Rede Virgile in Eneydos
> Or the Epistle of Ovyde,
> What that she wrot or that she dyde.
> And nere hyt to long to endyte,
> Be God, I wolde hyt here write. (377–80)

But as many readers have pointed out, Virgil and Ovid cannot both provide the true version of Dido's dying words, because they offer completely contradictory accounts of them. While Ovid's Dido writes a sympathetic lament as she stands at the brink of a pitiful suicide, Virgil's Dido curses Aeneas and Rome before killing herself in spite and rage. Many have therefore taken Chaucer's reference to Ovid and Virgil to be an ironic comment on the disjunction between poetry and truth, and on the unstable authority of the literary source. As Jesse Gellrich notes, this moment in Chaucer's text unsettles the ideal of a unified literary tradition by revealing the internal conflicts that inhere in it.[48] Furthermore, as both John Fyler and Carolyn Dinshaw read it, the episode presents that tradition as divorced from a knowable reality, since "the relationship between [Ovid's and Virgil's] accounts and . . . what really happened" is fundamentally uncertain, urging the conclusion, as Fyler puts it, "that poets are liars."[49] The passage thus engages issues that will recur throughout *The House of Fame*, as it questions the relationship between truth and poetry and the nature of literary authority itself.

But at the center of this dilemma of masculine textual authority is the question of Dido's own writing. While Chaucer's narrator promises to deliver Dido's exact words in a faithful transcription, he is unable to recover the actual text of "what that she wrot" (HF 380) and instead directs the reader to Ovid and Virgil. This episode therefore represents women's writing—that is, the truth of what Dido said or wrote—as fundamentally uncertain and its texts inaccessible. If the absence of Dido's text allows both Ovid and Virgil to present themselves as speaking in her place, it also means that we will never know which of them, if either, to believe. The instability of female authorship is thus both what allows male authors to put words in women's mouths and what calls the truth-value of those authors' writing into question.

To recall Terry Eagleton's terms, Dido's "lost" letter is a dispossessed text that represents a "crisis or spasm" threatening classical tradition from within. As the complaint of an abandoned woman, it emerges between the lines of the epic's story of masculine fame and empire. Furthermore, as a text that exists in a state of radical instability and loss, it reverses the myths of continuity and permanence on which the very notion of classical tradition is founded. In a work in which questions about the nature of literary tradition and canonicity are omnipresent, Dido establishes "the woman writer" in *The House of Fame* as a figure of the canonical repressed.

In "The Legend of Dido," Dido's letter again becomes central to a broader meditation on the problems of canon formation, since *The Legend of Good Women* is built on an act of textual recovery that begins with the premise of women's absence from literary tradition. Drawing as they do on Ovid's *Heroides*, Chaucer's "legends" recover their women's stories from the margins of the "olde appreved stories." But in the case of "The Legend of Dido," the object of recovery differs from that of *The House of Fame;* where the earlier text recovers Dido's letter as a literal absence, "The Legend of Dido" offers the actual text that Dido produces when "she wrot a lettre anon" (1354). By "reproducing" the text of Dido's letter, Chaucer allows Dido to articulate the state of loss and abnegation that in *The House of Fame* is reproduced as a textual blank space; in doing so, she produces a text that explores the outer limits of the discourses of fame and tradition represented by the classical canon.

Dido's letter begins by recalling Ovid's *Heroides* 7, Dido's self-elegiacal swan song that again links the act of writing to her incipient suicide:

> Ryght so, quod she, as that the white swan
> Ayens his deth begynnyth for to synge,
> Right so to yow make I my compleynynge. (1355–57)

The text that Chaucer's Dido writes is conditioned, as in Ovid, upon the death of its author: as the swan's song proceeds from its dying moments, so too Dido's writing measures the approach of her suicide. Dido's writing is not only expressive of loss; it is also productive of it, as she reveals when she reflects on the act of writing itself:

> But syn my name is lost thourgh yow, quod she,
> I may wel lese on yow a word or letter
> Al be it that I shal ben nevere the better. (1355–61)

One who has already lost her name can only write from a position of loss, and for Dido the very act of writing reenacts that loss by "losing" words: "I may wel lese on yow a word or letter." If to write is to lose— to send texts to an uncertain destination, outside the writer's control, where they will have an uncertain effect ("Al be it that I shal ben nevere the better")—it embodies in textual form the loss of control that Dido suffers as an abandoned woman. The state of loss that she comes to inhabit is therefore given form in the letter that she writes.

Developing the exploration of gender and writing in *The House of Fame*, which presents women's loss as a by-product of men's search for fame, in "The Legend of Dido" women's loss gives rise to a kind of writing that is the inverse of fame. Where the classical figures in Fame's house are made immortal through their texts, Dido's writing in "The Legend of Dido" takes place on the brink of mortality, securing not fame but self-loss. And where the classical poets survive through the textual monuments of "old books," Dido's letter is a fragile text of uncertain circulation and doubtful survival itself.[50] In the earlier *House of Fame*, Dido's writing reflects her loss in its invisibility; where Chaucer promises to deliver her letter, he instead delivers a description of her suicide that displaces "what that she wrot" (HF 380). In contrast, Dido's letter in *The Legend of Good Women* turns loss into a text that reflects the author's state of abnegation, whereby to write is to "lese" words rather than to preserve them. In this, Dido presents a model of writing that reverses classical models of fame and tradition and that also exposes the qualities of writing that those models repress by embodying the textual instability that underlies an idealized model of tradition but that is also hidden from view.

Following Corinne: Anelida and the "Lost" Woman Writer

The woman writer who emerges as an emblem of textual loss becomes the organizing figure of *Anelida and Arcite*, whose own textual instability makes it a fitting exemplar of the very dangers Chaucer takes as his perennial subject. Concerns about the conflict between literary tradition as represented by the classical canon and the

problems of textual transmission in a manuscript culture find prominent and especially unsettling expression in *Anelida and Arcite*.
These concerns are announced in the poem's opening stanzas, in
which the narrator declares his intent:

> With pitous hert in Englyssh to endyte
> This olde storie, in Latyn which I fynde,
> Of quene Anelida and fals Arcite,
> That elde, which that al can frete and bite,
> As hit hath freten mony a noble storie,
> Hath nygh devoured out of oure memorie. (AA 11–13)

From the beginning, the poem establishes an antagonism between
"memorie," an idealized form of cultural inheritance, and "elde," the
passage of time that deteriorates the very artifacts, manuscripts, and
linguistic models that are memory's vessels. This opposition between
memory and time is a pervasive concern in the poem, which continually sets up the desire for recovery against the material threat of loss.
Such doubleness is also, as Louise Fradenburg has notably pointed
out, one that pervades modern medieval studies, which is similarly
driven by the desire for the restoration of the archaic object in its
wholeness while simultaneously haunted by the spectre of its degen-
eration and loss.[51] This tension between recovery and loss becomes
the defining drama of humanism as it is articulated by Petrarch. The
desire to speak with the dead, as his *Familiares* to the classical authors show, breaks down when Petrarch encounters the corrupt Greek
manuscripts of Homer's corpus, which drive him to meditate, like
Chaucer, not only on the loss of texts to devouring time but also on
the futility of believing that any of one's own writing will survive:
"How many things perish! How little survives of all that our blind
activities have accomplished under the revolving sun!"[52] In *Anelida
and Arcite* such questions of textual loss and instability will be redirected onto the "lost" woman writer, who comes to figure a range of
broader anxieties about textual transmission and impermanence in
both the poem itself and the history of its subsequent transmission.

If *Anelida and Arcite* opens by worrying about old texts whose
wholeness is lost to devouring time, the story of its own complicated
transmission has borne out this concern. As Vincent J. DiMarco has
pointed out, the poem has attracted little critical commentary, and
much of what exists hardly progresses beyond affirmations of the
poem's technical virtuosity.[53] Yet these attempts to ground the poem
in Chaucer's controlling genius obscure the real technical problems
that affect it; as A. S. G. Edwards asserts in an important analysis of

the poem's transmission, the unity of the poem is by no means certain, since its three parts, now called the Invocation, the Story, and the Complaint, are arranged in radically different orders in the manuscripts, which call into question the poem's design and even, Edwards asserts, how much of it may be considered authentic.[54] Modern editors' presentation of *Anelida and Arcite* as a unified object manifests the desire to recover the wholeness of the past that Fradenburg identifies as the driving fantasy of medieval studies. But to insist on the unity and wholeness of *Anelida and Arcite* is not only to ignore the text's instability throughout its transmission history, it is also to read against the central concern of the poem itself, that time destroys the wholeness of memory. Moreover, critical appeals to Chaucer's poetic mastery as a unifying thread in the poem elide the text's own concern that "mastery," conceived as the expression of the authority of the "poete," is helpless against such predations of time and instabilities of manuscript circulation.

For its early readers, *Anelida and Arcite* was clearly a problem. Its three parts, as Edwards points out, are not explicitly related in form or content: the Invocation, with its expressed concern about textual survival, asks for Mars's guidance in a way that suggests that it should come in the middle, rather than at the beginning of a poem: "be present and my song *contynue* and guye" (6; my emphasis). The Story that follows introduces its characters, the false Arcite and the faithful Anelida, so abruptly that even editors who never question the poem's order wonder if some intermediary stanzas of explanation are missing; and the Complaint that follows it, which is usually identified in rubrics as "The Complaint of Annelida to Þe false Arcyte," departs from the preceding poem in tone and structure so dramatically that Edwards concludes that it deserves to be considered a discrete work, as indeed the poem sometimes was, circulating on occasion independently of the rest of the text.[55] In the manuscripts that do include all three parts, their order is unclear. Only five of the existing twelve attestations offer Invocation, Story, and Complaint in the order that is now canonical; in three of the remaining seven, the Complaint actually precedes the Invocation, which would make sense of the latter's plea to "continue" the song.[56] While the poem is clearly unfinished, a tagged-on conclusion, which Edwards believes to be almost certainly not Chaucer's work, has Anelida rising from her Complaint to offer sacrifice in the Temple of Mars. The scene seems to point back to the beginning of the Invocation and the phrase "Thou ferse god of armes, Mars the rede," as if leading back to what is now read as the beginning of the poem, making Anelida the speaker of these lines and turning the text itself into a kind of literary Möbius strip. The one element that connects its disparate parts is an ongoing effort to describe and differentiate a special category of women's writing, which runs through the opening sections, the Introduction and Story, and Anelida's Complaint itself. This idea of women's writing, in turn, became the text's organizing principle for the early readers and editors who shaped its circulation.

The manuscript and printed collections that reproduce *Anelida and Arcite* lodge it in groups of texts that could supply imaginary beginnings and endings as well as thematic contexts in which the poem could make sense. In Bodleian MS Tanner 346 the poem is preceded by *The Legend of Good Women*, which follows *Anelida and Arcite* in Fairfax 16 and Bodley 638, suggesting that Anelida's Complaint should be read among those of Chaucer's bereft women.[57] Furthermore, in British Library MS Add. 34360, the poem is followed by the apocryphal *Assembly of Ladies*, a dream vision with a female narrator that is structured around the production of female complaint.[58] This pairing, furthermore, establishes a linkage between *Anelida and Arcite* and *The Assembly of Ladies* that is observed in the later printed *Works* of Chaucer of 1532 and 1561, indicating a connection between the female complaints that make up *The Assembly of Ladies* and Anelida's Complaint from *Anelida and Arcite*. It also suggests that the persistent practice in print of assigning Chaucer authorship of the female-voiced *Assembly of Ladies* reflected his early modern reputation as a poet who wrote not only to women but as a woman. Thus the very characteristic that struck Gavin Douglas in 1513 as evidence of Chaucer's counter-canonical leanings—his compulsion to follow and present the woman's story—became an organizing principle for the manuscript and printed versions of his work. The textual evidence of its circulation suggests that it was within this context that *Anelida and Arcite* was first read, as a reflection of Chaucer's abiding interest in representing women as writers. These contexts emphasize the concern that *Anelida and Arcite* manifests throughout its disparate parts for what becomes identified as women's writing, not only in Anelida's Complaint, whose female narrator connects it to Chaucer's other female-voiced texts, but also in what I will argue is a broader problematic that finds the woman writer central to understanding the conflict between writing and literary tradition that I have been tracing in Chaucer's classical texts. Reading *Anelida and Arcite* within this context, I suggest, not only recovers the elements that Chaucer's earliest readers found most noteworthy about his work; it also illuminates the ways in which those later readers attempted to resolve the textual problems the poem poses by appealing to the very category of women's writing that the poem works to develop.

The Invocation itself begins by framing the problems of textual loss and obscurity that form its pressing concerns as attributes that are specific to women's writing. Among the other textual and interpretive challenges that *Anelida and Arcite* poses for readers, one of the most persistently troubling has been its identification of its sources. In the opening stanzas the narrator claims, "First folowe I Stace, and after him Corynne" (AA 21). The first source is easily identified as Statius, who makes an imposing presence in *The House of Fame* by bearing up "of Thebes the fame / upon his shuldres, and the name / Also of cruel Achilles" (HF 1461–63). Similarly, in *Troilus and Criseyde* Statius becomes one of the poet's illustrious classical ancestors when the narrator praises "Virgile, Ovide, Omer, Lucan and Stace" (TC 5.1792). Statius's influence is apparent in the first stanzas of the Story, which cite lines from Statius's *Thebaid* concerning Theseus's return from conquering the Amazons, which Chaucer recounts in his opening stanzas. In contrast, the reference to "Corynne" has been harder to place. What we know about Corinne, or Corinna, as a historical author is very little, and it is likely that Chaucer knew even less. We know that she was a renowned poet in her native Thebes and that Plutarch records her defeat of Pindar in a poetry competition; thus she was successful in challenging a famous male poet, whereas *The House of Fame*'s Marcia failed when she challenged Apollo. Some of Corinne's poetry even survives in fragments, which show her to have been less experimental than the better-known female classical poet, Sappho, but accomplished nonetheless in challenging verse forms, although these would not have been known to Chaucer.[59] Skelton would later praise her in "Phyllyp Sparowe," recording that "docta Corinna fuit" (Corinna was learned), and Juan Luis Vives would single her out in his *Instruction of a Christian Woman* as an exemplary learned woman; but Chaucer may well have known only two things about Corinne: first, that she was a woman poet, and second, that in all but name she was lost to literary-historical oblivion.[60] Chaucer's naming of "Corynne" as his source has struck his readers as a deliberately obscure reference, leading one to ask in exasperation, "Why should Chaucer insist on giving us an authority, Corinne, whom he apparently never followed?"[61] The question is an apt one in the contexts of *Anelida and Arcite*, returning us to the problem of textual loss that the opening stanzas of the Invocation raise with such anxiety. If "following" Statius pays homage to a well-known Latin author, what does it mean to "follow" Corinne?

Far safer to follow Statius, who established the pattern for such a model of literary succession in his own work. At the end of the *Thebaid*, Statius instructs his work to follow its famous predecessor, Virgil, bidding it to "follow from afar and evermore / Worship its steps" (12.816–17). Dante picks up the same trope when he describes himself walking behind Statius and Virgil: "Those two were in the lead; I walked alone / Behind them." (*Purgatorio* 22.127–29).[62] This image of authors following one another in succession, which recalls Thomas Greene's model of literary tradition as an "unflawed capacity for patriarchal communication and instruction across time," is also one that Chaucer deploys throughout his work to describe the bonds that connect writers to their literary ancestors.[63] It surfaces, for example, at the beginning of "The Legend of Dido," where the narrator pledges that he will "folwe" Virgil: "I shal, as I can, / Folwe thy lanterne, as thow gost byforn" (LGW 926). But as Gavin Douglas points out, Chaucer was no good follower: despite "saying he followit Virgillis lanterne to forne" at the beginning of "The Legend of Dido," Chaucer immediately diverges from this promise to pursue Dido's story at the expense of Aeneas's. The model of poetic "following" produces similar ambivalence throughout his *oeuvre*. The trope resurfaces at the end of the *Troilus*, when the narrator famously bids his own poem to "kis the steps wheras thou seest pace / Virgile, Ovide, Omer, Lucan and Stace" (TC 1791–92), but the expressed wish to follow his literary ancestors here only invokes, in the next stanza, the tenuousness of textual transmission that undermines the very possibility of continued literary influence. The very image of literary tradition as a succession of male poets itself attests to a continuity of influence in its repetition from Statius to Dante. While Chaucer invokes the same model in a seeming bid for inclusion in this literary-historical succession, he continually undercuts it by recalling the textual contingencies that subvert the continuity on which this idealized model of tradition rests. Similarly, in *Anelida and Arcite*—a poem that announces at the beginning that "tradition," like memory, is a term under question—the pledge to "follow" Statius is immediately undercut by Chaucer's invocation of his second source, "Corynne." Where Statius represents tradition as an unbroken continuity across male poets, "Corynne" stands in for those textual elements that Statius's model of literary influence represses—textual loss, and with it the danger of falling into literary-historical obscurity, dangers that pervade *Anelida and Arcite* itself thematically as well as becoming manifest in its later transmission. If, as Lee Patterson argues, Corinne serves as "an alternative and a counterpart to Statius," the contrast between the two poets is also clearly a gendered one.[64] Where Statius represents an idealized male fame, Corinne represents its opposite in the specter of a feminized literary-historical obscurity. In an Invocation that announces its concern about the opposition between memory and loss in its first stanza, this opposition is embodied in the two "sources" it names in its final lines: if to follow Statius is to uphold the continuity of memory, to honor literary ancestors and to assume a place in their tradition, to follow Corinne is to take the opposite route, to fall victim to the predations of devouring time and to expect not continuity but textual loss.

But Chaucer will not follow Statius—at least not for long. The Story, which follows the Invocation in all the manuscripts that contain it, opens by quoting from Statius's *Thebaid* on the homecoming of Theseus after conquering the Amazons. After narrating in furiously abbreviated form the story of the seige of Thebes and Creon's tyrannical rule over the city, the Story quickly shifts to a narrative that has no antecedent in Statius: that "of quene Anelida and fals Arcite" (49). The narrative of their doomed affair establishes the details that will explain Anelida's spectacular shows of grief, which are presented as a lesson to "thrifty wymmen alle" (197) and establish a setting for Anelida's subsequent action, as reported in all manuscripts that contain the combined texts of the Invocation and the Story:

> She caste her for to make a compleynynge,
> And of her owne hond she gan hit write,
> And sente hit to her Theban knyght, Arcite. (208–10)

Both the Invocation and the Story end, then, with figures of women writers: where the Invocation closes by invoking "Corynne," the Story closes by picturing Anelida picking up her pen and preparing, like Dido, to write a missive "of her owne hond."

The Complaint that follows the Invocation and Story in five manuscripts differs from the poem's first half in tone, style, and subject, shifting from a classical history to a conventional, if technically proficient, female complaint.[65] But readers of the text in the print and manuscript anthologies that lodged it alongside *The Legend of Good Women* and *The Assembly of Ladies* are prepared for the linkage between the two parts, as well as the order that they follow, by reading it in the context of an ongoing concern about women's writing in Chaucer's works (even if, in the case of *The Assembly of Ladies*, there is nothing to indicate Chaucer's authorship beyond the text's "Chaucerian" concern with women's writing). The amalgamated *Anelida and Arcite*, following the order of Invocation, Story, and Complaint, abandons the Virgilian and Statian mode of epic to take up instead the Ovidian genre of female complaint, just as *The Legend of Good Women* also abandons the epic invocation of Virgil in the opening lines of "The Legend of Dido" ("I shal, as I can, / Folwe thy lanterne" [LGW 925–26]) to take up instead the story of Dido's "compleynynge" (1357). Here again the promise to follow a classical, epic poet is betrayed in order to follow a woman writer, as Statius's story of Thebes is abandoned to set the stage for Anelida to take up her pen. We are prepared for such an abandonment of poetic "following" in the Invocation itself, where the narrator's pledge to "follow Statius" is followed by the promise to follow "after him Corynne."

The versions of the poem in which the Complaint follows the Story suggest in their organization that if Chaucer follows Statius in retelling a radically abbreviated and fragmented version of the *Thebaid* in the Story, in the Complaint he follows Corinne. Thus Statius forms the acknowledged source of the epic, classical narrative, while Corinne becomes the imaginary source for the female complaint that succeeds it. This organization suggests that the generic conflict that divides the Complaint from the Story—as a division between the female complaint and the work of imperial history and epic—is prefigured in the Invocation by the opposition between the text's two named sources, Statius and Corinne. As the fictitious production of the "lost" female poet Corinne, Anelida's Complaint also becomes the object of textual rescue that the Invocation's opening stanzas describe so plangently:

> That elde, which that al can frete and bite,
> As hit hath freten mony a noble storie,
> Hath nygh devoured out of oure memorie. (12–14)

While Statius's *Thebaid* is well established in textual culture and has no need of rescue, Corinne, by embodying such textual loss, frames the Complaint as the object of the kind of recovery that texts written by women in Chaucer's classical poems both inspire and defy. But to "recover" Anelida's Complaint from literary-historical oblivion also reveals the ways this text writes itself into such oblivion, thus posing what Fradenburg terms "the unsolved problem of theorizing the recovery of the irrecoverable."[66] If the hope of recovery rests on the fantasy of literary-historical plenitude—embodied in the image of the succession of authors stretching across time—Anelida's Complaint shows that the process of textual loss begins with the act of writing.

Despite the textual, thematic, and stylistic discontinuities that divide the Invocation and the Complaint, the two parts are united in their construction of "women's writing" as a classification for texts that fall outside the models of literary tradition and continuity that are embodied by Statius. Where "Corynne" appears to be the casualty of textual instability and loss that the Invocation raises as a central concern, Anelida's Complaint envisions the kind of writing that proceeds from such problems. If Corinne's writing is lost, Anelida's explains how it came to be that way by presenting a text that writes itself, as well as its author, into literary-historical oblivion. Anelida thematizes the poem's initial concerns about the loss of texts and memory, and does so in a complaint, which is, after all, the genre of loss. In this genre, as Patterson observes, "the poet's relation to the world is . . . one of exclusion, even alienation: rather than participating, he stands to the side, claiming the privilege of irony because he lacks the efficiency of power."[67] Yet in Chaucer's work, the writer of complaint—as self-cancelling, excluded, marginal, and powerless—is nearly always female.[68] Indeed, it is significant that when Ovid writes a complaint as an autobiographical subject, as he does when he complains about his painful exile in the *Tristia*, as Linda Kauffman points out, he occupies a position of loss and grieving that he sees as contiguous with a woman's position.[69] Chaucer, too, chooses the female complaint as a medium through which to voice forms of alienation and dislocation that for him are specifically textual problematics, expressing them as problems belonging to women's writing.

Where the Invocation hopes to recover texts that time has "nygh devoured out of oure memorie," Anelida's Complaint opens and closes by suggesting that recovered memory deals its own wounding blow to its subject:

> So thirleth with the poynt of remembraunce
> The swerd of sorowe, ywhet with fals plesaunce. (211–12)

Like Dido's letter, Anelida's Complaint emerges from the shadows of the classical canon to lament the state of a woman abandoned by her duplicitous lover. And like Dido, Anelida is also poised on the brink of suicide. By presenting herself transfixed with a "swerd of sorowe," Anelida calls to mind Dido's own suicidal poetics, which Anelida explicitly invokes by suggesting that her Complaint, like that of Dido, will also be her swan song:

> But as the swan, I have herd seyd ful yore,
> Ayeins his deth shal singen his penaunce,
> So singe I here my destinee or chaunce. (346–48)

By recalling Dido, Anelida suggests that, like her, she is dying even as she writes. While Arcite's betrayal "slays" her—"Verrayly ye sleen me with the peyne" (288)—she brings about her own death by recreating her abandonment in writing: "For thus ferforth have I my deth [y-]soght? / Myself I mordre with my privy thoght" (290–91). If Arcite's abandonment of her provides the context for Anelida's death, in other words, she herself carries it out through her Complaint. Anelida's handwritten Complaint is not only a suicide note, it is a suicidal act.

Anelida's fatal "remembraunce" offers a bitterly ironic reflection on the Invocation's attempt to summon a "vois memorial" and to rescue the "noble storie" of Chaucer's sources from the ravages of time. If Chaucer's act of textual retrieval aims to restore to "oure memorie" those stories lost to oblivion, Anelida produces a kind of writing that invites oblivion upon itself and its author. "Thirled with the poynt of remembraunce" (350), Anelida writes herself into self-extinction; it is not forgetting that kills her, then, but memory. Read as a continuation of the conflict between memory and time in the Invocation, Anelida's Complaint gives form to the very qualities of loss and instability that are the opposite of tradition. Where the "vois memorial" of the muse produces the name of a male poet, Statius, as a mark of immortality, it also produces the name of "Corynne" as the sign of textual loss that is embodied and given a textual form in Anelida's Complaint. The example of Anelida, in other words, enables us to imagine how a woman writer such as Corinne produces that obscurity, by developing the possibility that the loss of her texts is in some way attributable to the femininity of their author.

If Corinne signifies textual loss and obscurity, Anelida's Complaint proceeds out of the narrator's attempt to "follow Corinne"—that is, to write outside the lines of permanent literary tradition that are embodied in Statius. At the same time, the figures of Corinne and Anelida also capture and embody the dangers that this kind of writing poses to the nonclassical author. Rather than securing durable fame and status, Corinne and Anelida write themselves into obscurity, showing that the only alternative imaginable to classical authority is the absence of that authority—that is, loss and literary-historical oblivion. By recovering women's writing as an artifact that gains identity in loss, Chaucer's poem upholds the fiction of literary influence represented by Statius by imagining its opposite: first, by embodying in the woman writer those textual dangers that such a fiction of literary influence excludes, and second, by holding out the possibility that the male author can escape the very dangers to which the female author falls victim.

Refiguring Criseyde

The figure of the woman writer concentrates the broad questions about writing, authorship, and literary tradition that emerge from Chaucer's ongoing analysis of the relationship between vernacular writing and the classical canon—an analysis that comes to the foreground in *Troilus and Criseyde*. The poem has long stood as a landmark in the history of the idea of English Literature; it is the first time that Chaucer imagines the possibility that English poetry could, in A. C. Spearing's words, "[possess] something of that potentiality for permanence that in England had hitherto been associated only with Latin writing." [70] As such, it marks a turning point in the development of what Spearing characterizes as "a history of literature in which a work in English may have a place, however modest, alongside the great writers of antiquity." [71] The idea has, however, a difficult birth. While later writers would hail *Troilus and Criseyde* as the model and point of origin for an English literary tradition that could rival the classical canon, such a developmental narrative represses the considerable misgivings that Chaucer's text expresses about the very possibility of such a project. The poem's effort to insert itself into a classical model of canonicity famously comes to a head in its envoy, when the poet closes his "litel book" by sending it to pay homage to the great figures of "Virgile, Ovide, Omer, Lucan, and Stace" (5.1792)— who represent, Spearing notes, a model of "literature conceived as a single continuum of great works." [72] However, the stanza that follows immediately on the heels of this envoy seriously questions whether such a model could ever embrace the English writer. Where the classical authors appear frozen in time, enshrined forever in an unchanging language, the writer in English can be confident of no such enduring legacy:

> And for ther is so gret diversite
> In Englissh and in writyng of oure tonge,
> So prey I God that non myswrite the,
> Ne the mysmetre for defaute of tonge;
> And red wherso thow be, or elles songe,
> That thow be understonde, God I biseche! (TC 5.1793–98)

If Chaucer is the first poet to dare to place English writing alongside the classical canon, this placement also reveals their incommensurability. Not only the changeable nature of a living language but also the contingency of manuscript culture make the English text an eminently unstable entity. [73] While the classical canon rests on a notion of a transcendent tradition embodied as "a single continuum of great works," the English work brings to mind a material substratum of textual culture that resists such transcendence. The problems of literary survival that English writing here embodies indicate that it is not "tradition" that causes texts to be read by future generations so much as the social, contingent processes of textual transmission that can as easily preserve texts as deform or lose them.

This expressed concern with literature's ability to withstand time is one that *Troilus and Criseyde* shares with earlier "classical" works like *Anelida and Arcite* and *The House of Fame*. Furthermore, in ways that echo and develop those earlier texts, *Troilus and Criseyde* explores and plays out this concern within a narrative that makes gender and textual production into parallel problems. For example, textual transmission becomes a gendered process in a passage from Book 2, which opens by articulating the poem's ongoing concern about the instability of language in time:

> Ye knowe ek that in forme of speche is chaunge
> Withinne a thousand yeer, and wordes tho
> That hadden pris, now wonder nyce and straunge
> Us thinketh hem . . . (TC 2.22–25)

Anticipating the anxious meditation on "diversite / in Englisshe and in writing of oure tonge" that will come to a head in Book 5, the passage's metaphor of monetary circulation captures the poet's fear of linguistic devaluation across time; words that hold value and "pris" to one age will lose significance in a later one. However, this stanza deflects this fear of linguistic mutability by turning its attention in the lines that follow to the contrasting immutability of language's object, the pursuit of love:

> . . . and yet thei spake hem so
> And spedde as wel in love as men now do. (TC 2.25–26)

Despite linguistic difference, the stanza insists, the words that seem antiquated to the current age were once put to the same uses as are those words that "men" use today: to "speed well in love." While language changes, the passage insists, "love" stays the same. Love's status as an unchanging pursuit posits the immutability of the differentiated roles of men and women in heterosexual courtship, an activity that, as this passage reminds us, regulates who has the power to use language—namely "men," a point that willfully represses the historical women writers who did manipulate the language of love, from Marie de France through the *trobairitz*. But in this passage gender difference secures the notion of language as an unchanging erotic field. Just as men wielded language in the past to win love, according to this model, so will men continue to wield it to the same end through all time. Against a vision of complete, annihilating change, suggested in the poet's admission that "in forme of speche is chaunge," the poet offers a reassuring image of permanence in a literary system that appears to be predicated on women's silence.

However, an image that presents love as a safeguard against change sits uncomfortably in a poem about the infamously disastrous love affair of Troilus and Criseyde. There are no successful lovers in *Troilus and Criseyde,* including the narrator: claiming that he cannot "dar to love, for myn unliklynesse" (1.16), he invites reflection on how the pursuit of love interlinks with the pursuit of poetry, and how a crisis in one produces a crisis in the other. The passage's assertion that men's use of language to "speed in love" guards against the threat of change renders Troilus's eventual failure in love symptomatic of both men's loss of prerogative over language and the broader linguistic and historical mutability against which this early passage attempts to guard. If gender is called on to secure linguistic and textual stability, it is also given explanatory value, in the drama of love and writing that *Troilus and Criseyde* constructs, for the instability to which language and texts become subject in the poem.

Troilus and Criseyde tells the story of two lovers who are both writers, and the poem's broader concerns about writing and gender are plotted microcosmically in the letters that pass between them. Troilus's letters have attracted literary and critical attention for some time: the *litera Troili* of Book 5 was interpreted by manuscript tradition as a lyric set piece that was detached and circulated independently of the rest of the poem, and it has been taken to exemplify a medieval epistolary genre with claims to high literariness.[74] In contrast, Criseyde's letters have been easier for criticism and literary history to ignore. While John McKinnell identifies Troilus's letters as an important "formal type" in the poem, he finds Criseyde's so anomalous and enigmatic that he questions whether "we are meant to take [them] seriously."[75] But if Troilus's letters call on the continuity of medieval literary and rhetorical traditions and thus reinforce the high-literary aspirations of *Troilus and Criseyde* itself, Criseyde's letters perform a no less important meta-literary function as pieces of writing that are unassimilable into such traditions; as such, they become focal points for the concerns about writing, language, and the material text that are repressed to create the notion of tradition as a transcendent cultural inheritance.

The letter has always occupied an ambiguous place in literary history. Sometimes a medium for rhetorical performance of the highest levels, like Petrarch's *Familiares,* it more often served the quotidian functions that one glimpses in the actual medieval letters that survive in archives or collections like the Paston and Stonor letters. Historically, its writers have held an uncertain claim to literary authorship, which is perhaps why the letter was a genre particularly favored by medieval women writers, as a number of studies have suggested.[76] But by the same token, the conviction that "letters did not count," as Virginia Woolf dismissively put it, has helped keep those texts marginal to the more authoritative literary canons.[77] As material texts that find their meaning in exchange, letters give form to ephemeral and transitory qualities that depart from, and threaten to undermine, those more permanent values enshrined by literary tradition; if tradition idealizes textual transmission as a continuous line of influence across time, letters recall the palpably fragile forms in which texts travel, as marks of ink on paper or parchment that thereby become (in Janet Gurkin Altman's memorable term) "losable words."[78]

Together, Troilus's and Criseyde's letters activate the contrasting registers of the epistolary mode, the high-literary and the ephemeral, while also exploring the relationship between them. In this, they show that if in such high-literary moments as the *litera Troili, Troilus and Criseyde* stakes a new claim for vernacular literary authority, it does so by both invoking and feminizing its opposite in the letters of Criseyde. The hierarchy of literary values that the lovers' letters represent is evident in the incongruent treatment and levels of attention that they receive in the narrative.[79] Troilus's writing is self-expressive, proceeding from his desire to "telle his woo" (2.1082). Following Pandarus's advice, Troilus creates his first letter as a written surrogate of himself, shaping his words with an effectiveness that will evade him when the lovers meet in person, and sealing it with his own tears before directing it, as if in his place, to Criseyde: "lettre, a blisful destine / The shapyn is: my lady shal the see!" (2.1091–92). In so doing, he calls on a literary convention that cast love letters as physical extensions of the lovers themselves.[80] In contrast to Troilus, for whom letter writing is a medium of self-expression, Criseyde finds it one of self-alienation. "I nevere dide thing with more peyne / Than writen this," she insists upon completing her first letter (2.1231–32), making writing a process that fragments and violates the self rather than revealing and asserting the writer's inner state. The self-estrangement that Criseyde experiences in writing is reflected in the texts she produces, which are opaque and nearly incomprehensible to her readers.

Troilus initially finds her letter a cypher—"al covered she tho wordes under shield" (2.1327)—and there is no indication that the narrator can offer any further insight into its meaning. While Troilus's first letter attracts three stanzas of description that detail its careful rhetorical construction and "pitous" affect, Criseyde's response is summarized in a pedestrian five lines, when the narrator offers to give "th'effect" of Criseyde's letter, "as fer as I kan understonde" (2.1220). It will not, he hints, be an easy job. Likewise, in the fifth book, the *litera Troili* occupies fifteen stanzas of what is widely held to be some of the poem's most finely crafted verse; in contrast, Criseyde's response is again only summarized in its "effect" (5.1423), this time in just four lines. When the full text of a *litera Criseydis* is finally presented, it is an exercise in textual opacity, which Criseyde pathetically excuses: "I dar nat, ther I am, wel lettres make, / Ne nevere yet ne koude I wel endite," she claims, concluding, "Th'entente is al, and nat the lettres space" (5.1626–27, 1630). But Criseyde's "entente" is illegible, leaving only a "lettres space" that resists interpretation. That material letter, as Criseyde frets, holds the power to betray its writer through its potential for misinterpretation or misdirection once it leaves her hands: she protests her fear "lest that this lettre founden were" (5.1602). If Troilus upholds John of Salisbury's assertion that letters should "speak voicelessly the utterances of the absent," Criseyde's letters instead call attention to their writer's absence from any direct circuit of communication.[81] In the end, Criseyde's letters become "a kalendes of chaunge" (TC 5.1634)—a significant problem in a poem that foregrounds language change as a major concern and barrier to the transmission of literary tradition.[82] They thereby illustrate the poem's broader concern that "in forme of speche is chaunge" by embodying precisely the danger that the narrator associates with textual transmission in a vernacular, manuscript culture to show just what a text looks like when it cannot be understood by its readers.

The contrast between Criseyde's and Troilus's letters upholds a distinction that the poem establishes between "good" writing and "bad." If Criseyde excuses her indeterminate writing by claiming that "nevere yet ne koude I wel endite," Troilus exemplifies just the opposite quality: "Thow kanst wel endite" (5.1292), Pandarus compliments him, significantly selecting the very term—"enditing"—that Anne Middleton shows to be key to Chaucer's construction of vernacular authorship.[83] And if Criseyde finds writing to be an untrustworthy medium, Troilus's letters are always artful compositions, as when he "rolleth in his herte to and fro / How he may best descryven hire his wo" (5.1313–14). Troilus manipulates the terms of courtly address in his letters so skillfully that he impresses Criseyde with his literary ability, as when she "avysed word by word in every lyne, / And fond no lak, she thoughte he koude good" (2.1177–78).

   Troilus and Criseyde thus produces a gendered taxonomy of writing in order to differentiate the material, "losable" textuality of Criseyde's letters from Troilus's self-expressive, lyrical ones. Where Criseyde finds her "entente" threatened by "the lettres space," Troilus works in a medium that appears to evade the dangers of a material textual culture. Like the Petrarchan *Canticus Troili*, Troilus's letters appeal to models of composition that seem more vocal than textual.[84] When Pandarus first instructs Troilus in the art of writing, he invokes the musical example of "the beste harpour upon lyve" (2.1030), while stressing that Troilus must avoid being "scryvenyssh" in his writing (2.1026), thus differentiating the Troilan letter from the famously unstable manuscripts of "Adam Scriveyn."[85] Accordingly, Troilus appropriates vocal terms to describe his acts of writing—as, for example, when he refers to his final letter as *my song, in pleynte of myn adversitee* (5.1375, emphasis added), and the very tears that "biblotte" his page, we are told, aspire to "speke" and "pleyne" (5.1337). Troilus's letters thereby fall under the definition of what Sylvia Huot calls "lyric writing"—that is, writing that claims the status of song.[86] By taking on the characteristics of vocal productions, Troilus's "lyric writing" participates in what Derek Pearsall remarks as "the myth of delivery that Chaucer cultivates so assiduously in the poem."[87] Where the written letter signals the writer's absence when it circulates outside his or her control, voice is immediate, controllable, and clearly connected to the body of its producer. Seeming to sing his letters rather than to write them, Troilus evades the materiality of textual production. His "good" writing thus appears to escape the subjection that *Troilus and Criseyde* associates with the act of circulating texts in a manuscript culture, an association that is represented in Criseyde's letters.

   Criseyde, like Anelida, writes letters "of her hand," and the materiality of her handwriting is linked to her letters' alienability, their dangerous tendency to betray their writer's "entente" through "the lettres space." That textual "space" is consistently feminized in *Troilus and Criseyde*.[88] Early in the narrative Troilus associates the act of reading Criseyde's letters with the visually exciting experience of beholding her physical "shap":

> The lettres ek that she of olde tyme
> Had hym ysent, he wolde allone rede

An hondred sithe atwixen noon and prime,
Refiguryng hire shap, hire wommanhede
Withinne his herte. (5.470–74)

In this passage, Chaucer selectively revises his Boccaccian source for
this passage in order to emphasize the materiality of Criseyde's letters. For both Chaucer and Boccaccio, Troilus's private scene of reading invokes an imaginary representation of Criseyde. What differs is
the fantasy itself: while Boccaccio's Troilo imagines Criseida delivering her words orally, by envisioning her face ("bel viso") and speech
("parole"), in Chaucer's text Troilus's loving perusal of the letters
summons fantasies not of Criseyde's speech but of "hire shap, hire
wommanhede." Troilus's act of reading thus locates a resolutely
physical and gendered image in the visual space of Criseyde's handwritten letter.[89] But what does it mean to locate "wommanhede" in
a written letter? If Troilus's act of erotic reading aims to repair Criseyde's absence with a fantasy of her physical presence, it also recalls
us to the various ways in which Criseyde's "wommanhede" is figured
in Troilus and Criseyde as a site of perpetual loss and deprivation that
is manifested in her writing.

The first descriptions of Criseyde's physical appearance present
her as a visual symbol of deprivation, clad head to foot in black widow's weeds. But this outward sign of her bereavement is what makes
Criseyde visually appealing to Troilus, when he is suddenly thunder-
struck by the sight of the black-clad woman: "she, this in blak, li-
kynge to Troilus / Over alle thing, he stood for to biholde" (1.309–10).
Criseyde's black clothes, the sign of her deprivation, are continually
linked to the visual, inky aspect of written language. For example, the
narrator's description of Criseyde's appearance in mourning compares
her to the written alphabet:

Among thise othere folk was Criseyda,
In widewes habit blak; but natheles,
Right as oure first lettre is now an A,
In beaute first so stood she, makeles. (1.169–72)

Similarly, when Pandarus delivers Criseyde's first letter to Troilus, he
draws attention to its physical appearance by directing Troilus, "Have
here a light, and loke on al this blake" (2.1320)—recalling, in its reference to the visual effect of ink on parchment, Troilus's first love-
struck gaze at Criseyde in mourning, "she, this in blak." If Criseyde's
beauty makes the narrator think of a letter, the blackness of her letters makes Pandarus and Troilus think of Criseyde's body.

Criseyde's appearance in Troilus and Criseyde, I am arguing, is associated with the materiality of writing. But that materiality is also held to interfere with the processes of signification. When Pandarus presents Criseyde's letter to Troilus, he emphasizes its "black" appearance over any intended meanings it might convey, suggesting that Troilus will take more pleasure in the text as a visual object than as a communication. Where Criseyde's "blak" letter refuses to yield ready significance to Troilus's perusal—"al covered she tho wordes under sheld"—this veiled language increases Troilus's desire, rather than dampening it: "So thorugh this letter which that she hym sente / Encresen gan desir, of which he brente" (2.1336–37). Similarly, throughout the narrative Troilus's desire for Criseyde is fueled by his inability to deduce her intentions, as the erotic exchanges between them are metaphorized in images of writing that resist interpretation. In the pivotal consummation scene, for example, Troilus expresses desire for Criseyde by comparing her "eyen clere" to an unintelligible text:

> Ye humble nettes of my lady deere!
> Though ther be mercy writen in youre cheere,
> God woot, the text ful hard is, soth, to fynde! (3.1354–57)

Criseyde's eyes are beautiful to behold as long as they remain unreadable ("the text ful hard is, soth, to fynde!"). Like the insistently material texts she writes "of her hand," Criseyde's body, which is constantly compared to texts, produces desire by rendering meaning irrecoverable.

In making this argument, I am not suggesting that Criseyde's "textuality" is a reflection of her femininity *tout court*; nor do I intend to argue that Criseyde is herself merely a "text" to be read, interpreted, and circulated by men.[90] Rather, by stressing Criseyde's position as a writer, this reading makes her a central figure within *Troilus and Criseyde*'s larger analysis of gender, writing, and canon formation. By embodying a set of dangers associated with writing and circulating texts in a manuscript culture, Criseyde's letters also absorb these dangers to a model of a specifically "womanly" writing. But if the feminization of Criseyde's writing distances it from the masculine models of literary authority and tradition that otherwise seem to rule *Troilus and Criseyde*'s classical frame of reference, it also masks a level of identification that tinges the narrator-poet's descriptions of her letters. Criseyde's unstable letters exemplify the linguistic instability that the narrator first names as a major concern in Book 2, when he considers how "in forme of speche is chaunge." Where that passage initially expresses fears about the vernacular project of *Troilus and Criseyde* itself, that fear is redirected onto Criseyde's letters, which become "a kalendes of chaunge" (TC 5.1634) and thereby absorb the worst dangers of vernacular textual culture, which renders texts unintelligible to their readers.

Criseyde's palpably material letters thereby come to embody a set of anxieties that Chaucer's narrator elsewhere associates with the failure of *auctoritas* to provide a sustaining model for the living writer. While the classical canon represented by "Virgile, Ovide, Omer, Lucan, and Stace" forms a repeated touchstone throughout the "classical" works such as *Anelida and Arcite, Troilus and Criseyde, The House of Fame,* and *The Legend of Good Women,* these poets are never shown, as Anne Middleton points out, in the act of writing.[91] In contrast, the poet-narrator of *Troilus and Criseyde* constantly pictures himself writing: indeed, as Gerald L. Bruns is not the only reader to suggest, Chaucer's writing narrator resembles no one so much as a scribe, and "in the work of the scribe," Stephanie Jed notes, "the material effects of corruption can be felt."[92] It is precisely in the extent to which he calls attention to his own act of writing that Chaucer's poet-narrator in *Troilus and Criseyde* marks his distance from the *auctores.*

This contrast comes into focus in the stanza that immediately follows the narrator's paean to the *auctores* when, in contrast to the autonomous realm of *auctoritas* in which "Virgile, Ovide, Omer, Lucan, and Stace" "pace" in an unbroken line, the narrator confronts the fear of textual corruption that he sees as inextricably linked to textual transmission. Addressing his "litel bok," the narrator confesses a great fear for its survival in the passage I cited earlier in this section, worrying about the "gret diversite / In Englissh and in writyng of oure tonge" that affects his text's transmission and offering the anxious prayer, "That thow be understonde, God I biseche!" (5.1793–94, 1797). By its end the poem is decidedly a product of writing; and, as Susan Schibanoff points out, "as the narrator-poet begins to conceive of us as reading rather than listening to his words, his authority diminishes, and his uncertainty about his poetic abilities grows."[93] By situating his poem within the material conditions of textual transmission, the narrator's outcry reveals the extent to which the fiction of literary authority is propped up on contingencies of writing and being read, contingencies that are represented throughout the poem most cogently in Criseyde's letters.

Despite the many ways in which Chaucer's narrative appears to marginalize them, Criseyde's letters share many of the concerns central to Chaucer's investigation of literary authority by embodying a set of anxieties about textual transmission that permeate *Troilus and*

Criseyde. While Troilus's letters may represent an idealized form of textual communication that resembles song in its transmission and seeming transparency, they represent a model for textual transmission that Chaucer's narrator decisively sheds. Instead, the most detailed discussions of literary authority in *Troilus and Criseyde* call to mind Criseyde's own anguished meditations on writing. To write a poem in English, *Troilus and Criseyde* suggests finally, is to be less like Troilus—and much less like "Virgile, Ovide, Omer, Lucan, and Stace"—than like Criseyde, for whom writing is associated with uncertain transmission and self-loss, and for whose texts the process of being read confirms the failures of written communication, as well as the impossible remoteness of the literary authority represented by the *auctores.*

The conflict between literary tradition and textual transmission that I read throughout these classical works is narrated as a gendered drama that pits a masculine and heavily patriarchal model of classical canonicity against the dispossessed figure of the woman writer, as Anelida, Criseyde, Dido, and even the ghostly Corinne are both implicitly and explicitly contrasted with male figures of literary authority. While male *auctores* such as Statius or Virgil draw on models of continuous influence that uphold their perpetual fame, Chaucer's writing women are dramatically vulnerable to the contrastingly unstable conditions of textual production that form Chaucer's anxious focus in the Invocation to *Anelida and Arcite* and the closing stanzas to *Troilus and Criseyde.* If writing women such as Criseyde, Anelida, and Dido represent the limitations of medieval theories of *auctoritas,* the self-loss, immobilization, or abjection in the narratives that they experience as a consequence of their writing reflects Chaucer's failure to envision a model of writing outside literary tradition. As a consequence, if the literary authority exemplified by the classical "poetes" is shown to be an unattainable ideal for the writer, the only alternative is textual uncertainty and loss. By projecting these anxieties onto the figures of Dido, Anelida, Criseyde, and even Corinne, Chaucer offers the figure of the woman writer, such as he depicts her, as the embodiment of the literary-historical instability afflicting the vernacular author in the later Middle Ages.

In considering the importance and the function of the writing woman in Chaucer's classical works, I mean to revisit these works' reputation as sites in which the notion of a vernacular literary history comes into being. As texts that continually engage questions about the relationship between the vernacular traditions and the classical past, the forms of writing that are permanently preserved and those that will be lost forever, these works presage the dynamic that mutually shapes the categories of "canonical" and "noncanonical" as terms for English literary history. But, as I have argued, by focusing these questions around figures of writing women, these works assign gender a crucial taxonomic function for upholding notions of difference that continually inform and shape models of literary history. This is not because men's and women's writing is inherently different, but because drawing distinctions between men's and women's writing naturalizes a broader network of textual differences that can be organized under this taxonomy—differences, for example, of genre, language, and canonicity. Given the important role that Chaucer's classical texts played in the narratives that English literary history would tell about itself, I have also aimed to bring to light the ways in which writing is not an unproblematically masculine pursuit from the start; nor is the woman writer in any simple way absent or "lost" in these texts. Rather, these texts show how the notion of "literary tradition" and "the woman writer" come to define one another by exclusion, a point that can illuminate the unexpectedly central role that representations of women writers play in Chaucer's discussions of literary history and its problems. But if "the woman writer" represents forms of writing outside the borders of tradition, she also becomes the focal point for precisely those qualities that Chaucer perceived to exclude "English literature" itself from "literary tradition." The woman writer thus becomes a figure of anxious identification and disavowal for the writer who aims to explore what it means to write outside classical literary tradition, and in forms of textual transmission that appeared to threaten cultural instability and loss. In these works Chaucer establishes a model by which "the woman writer" could take shape as a figure who is outside literary tradition but also contiguous with the culturally uncertain place of "English literature." This would be important for the later conception not only of "the woman writer" but also of Chaucer. If later readers, shaping English literary history as a classically modeled canon, would adopt Chaucer as the "father of English poetry," for readers like Gavin Douglas or the nameless compilers of the manuscripts of *Anelida and Arcite,* Chaucer was more notable as a poet who identified—and identified with—the figure "woman writer."

Two

THE CITY OF LADIES IN THE

LIBRARY OF GENTLEMEN

Christine de Pizan in England, 1450–1526

Lost in Translation

The most widely read woman writer in fifteenth- and early sixteenth-century England was Christine de Pizan, the French author of numerous works across the varied genres of instruction, courtly entertainment, and the defense of women.[1] During Christine's lifetime (c. 1364–c. 1431), a number of deluxe manuscripts of her works, some of whose production she oversaw herself, found their way into the libraries of French-speaking English aristocrats.[2] A generation after her death, her works continued to appeal to English readers in translation: between 1450 and 1550 there appeared at least nine different translations of her works into English, with some, like *L'epistre d'Othea* (The letter of Othea) and *Le livre des faits d'armes et de chevalerie* (The book of deeds of arms and chivalry), circulating in more than one translation in both manuscript and print. Interest in those works carried deep into aristocratic and royal centers of power: among the translators, patrons, and owners of these works were noblemen prominent in the service of Lancastrian, York, and Tudor monarchs. Furthermore, translations of Christine appear alongside the poetry of Chaucer and Lydgate in several important manuscript collections and printed editions produced during this time, establishing her presence in the foundational edifices of English literature. Yet if Christine's works achieved a level of influence in fifteenth- and sixteenth-century England that was unprecedented for a woman writer, her name and identity as the author of those works became increasingly contested. While the French manuscripts in English libraries announce Christine's authorship in dedicatory epistles and illuminations, the English translations of the same works—sometimes based on those very manuscripts—almost universally reassign authorship of her works to men. The fifteenth-century translators of *Le livre des faits d'armes* and *L'epistre d'Othea* devised elaborate fictions to claim that the texts were written not by Christine de Pizan but by male clerks; as if following suit, later English printed editions of *L'epistre* and even *Le livre de la cité des dames* (The book of the city of ladies) reascribed the works to the men who were in fact their translators, while one text, *Les proverbes moraulx* (Moral proverbs), was reassigned without basis to Chaucer. Thus Christine de Pizan's circulation in fifteenth- and sixteenth-century England is marked by a troubling paradox: at the very zenith of her works' influence among English readers, Christine's status as author of those works was thrown into question.

As one of the few known women writers whose works circulated widely in late medieval and early modern England, Christine offers a rare opportunity to examine questions that are of chief concern for feminist literary history today: namely, how was it that women writers who were known—and even celebrated—in their own age later fell into obscurity, apparently lost from the canon? Most importantly, Christine offers the chance to ground this question in a specific literary-historical milieu. The translation and circulation of Christine's works took place within a relatively concentrated historical period spanning the mid-fourteenth century to the first quarter of the sixteenth, and the individuals involved belonged to a relatively small and identifiable social group connected with aristocratic and courtly literary centers. Christine's translation coincided with a major reorganization of vernacular literacy and literate institutions in England in the face of several interrelated key events: the emergence of a highly literate, book-owning aristocracy in the fifteenth century, the Lancastrian promotion of English as a national language, and the development of print in the 1480s by William Caxton and his followers, all of which helped to establish a secular, English culture of the book.[3] These events, as has been widely recognized, influenced contemporary understandings of authorship, patronage, and the makeup of literate communities. Christine de Pizan's circulation during this time reveals that the same events, along with the literary culture to which they gave rise, both shaped and were shaped by ideas about the woman writer.

P. G. C. Campbell, who first noted the paradox of Christine's English reception in a still-important article of 1925, attributes the contests over Christine's name in the English books to a general indifference to authorship that, he argues, proves that the producers and readers of early English books were more interested in written works than in the names of those works' writers.[4] Given the instability of the early textual conventions that designated authorship—an instability that has been further illuminated by recent work on the history of the late medieval and early modern book—Christine's name, by this argument, was quite simply lost in translation.[5] Representing a converse critical perspective, recent readers have argued that what appears to be Christine's deprivation of authorship through the English fifteenth and sixteenth centuries resulted less from general negligence than from a deliberate suppression—even censorship—of a female author by the male agents of literary culture.[6] These two lines of argument implicitly advance opposing historical models of authorship in the fifteenth and sixteenth centuries.[7] For those who see Christine's name as lost simply through negligence, authorship was so unformed in this period that the question of who wrote a text was inconsequential to its producers; in contrast, those who see Christine as the victim of a more deliberate suppression implicitly hold that authorship was not only fully in place but also so thoroughly masculinized that a female author would seem anomalous and even threatening enough to require erasure. The textual evidence surrounding Christine's circulation in fifteenth- and sixteenth-century England, however, indicates the limitations of both arguments, as well as demanding a modification of the models of authorship that support them. While some English translations of Christine's texts do suggest that their author's identity may have been uncertain to readers, they also manifest a reworking of Christine's authorship that is more deliberate than simple carelessness would explain; indeed, the fact that Chaucer was elevated to the position of ideal English author at the very moment that Christine's works were translated indicates that authorship was both a growing concern among English book producers and a category under active construction.[8] But rather than concluding that the figure of the English author had a stable, and fully masculinized, existence prior to Christine's translation and circulation in England, which the contests over her authorship were meant to protect, I see those acts of translation and circulation, together with the contests they produced, as themselves defining moments for the invention of English authorship.

I develop this argument by examining the books within which Christine's works circulated from the perspective of what Gérard Genette calls the paratext: the titles, prefaces, dedications to patrons, and other pieces of textual apparatus that together "[enable] the text to become a book and to be offered as such to its readers and, more generally, to the public."[9] The paratextual apparatus framing the earliest English translations of Christine's works evinces a broad effort by those works' translators, editors, and printers to make them and their female author meaningful within a new and distinctly English literary milieu. Rather than attempting to censor Christine's writing and authorship, the paratexts show the cultural encounter between Christine's texts and their English readers to have been dynamic and reciprocal in unexpected ways. Editing and translation are above all acts of interpretation, and those who adapted Christine's texts to English contexts show themselves to be responsive, if not always faithful, readers of their French originals. At the same time that the paratexts reveal the historical bases of English readers' interest in Christine's works, they also throw into relief the specific aspects of those works that resisted assimilation into English contexts. The problem with which the paratexts most strenuously contend is Christine's self-identification as a woman writer. Unlike the early French editions of Christine's texts, which calculatedly expunged all mention of their female author, the paratexts of the early English manuscript and print editions continually return to the figure they name "Dame Christine" or simply "Crystine," indicating that the female author's identity was considered significant to the texts' circulation.[10] At the same time, the paratexts' struggles to explain and represent this figure also indicate that it posed an interpretive quandary for the texts' producers. The contradictory evidence of the paratext indicates that Christine's definition of "the woman writer" in part accounted for her works' appeal for fifteenth- and early sixteenth-century English literary culture, because it enabled a new perspective on the nature of literary authorship and its social functions. But at the same time, the editors' and translators' struggles to reshape and redefine Christine's identity as a woman writer reflect the social uncertainties that attended the literary novelty of these works. Thus "the woman writer" becomes a crucial point of both identification and disavowal for these fifteenth- and early sixteenth-century English books and for the broader invention of "English literature" in which they participated. Throughout Christine's works, the woman writer is a figure of omnipresent concern, surfacing in her many moments of self-representation both in the texts themselves (in which she explicitly identifies herself as "Je, Christine") and in Christine's own paratexts, the prologues she addressed to patrons and the illuminations whose production she supervised to craft a carefully wrought authorial self-portrait. Moreover, the texts themselves continually take up the question of what it means to write as a woman, and in their representations of women writers they show "the woman writer" emerging as a historically coherent category. In Christine's works the carefully crafted figure of the woman writer challenges the institutions of medieval literacy by redefining not only who may read and write but also the place and significance of reading and writing as social acts. As she is for Chaucer, "the woman writer" for Christine is a strikingly modern figure, defined, as Maureen Quilligan and Kevin Brownlee have pointed out, through her disconnection from traditional literary institutions.[11] But where for Chaucer the woman writer's similar disconnection results in her self-abnegation and textual loss, for Christine the same position upholds the contrasting promise of a new literary practice.

Like Chaucer's Anelida and Dido, Christine marks her own initiation into writing through the loss of her beloved, when her husband's death first drives her to become "a recluse/ Beaten down, mournful, alone and weary" ("comme recluse, / Mate, morne, seule et lasse"), as she describes in her autobiographical *Chemin de long estude* (The path of long study).[12] As captured in the titles of her first lyrics such as "Je suis vesve, seulete et noir vestue" (I am a widow, alone and clad in black) and "Seulete suy et seulete vueil estre" (Alone am I and alone would be), Christine constructs the figure of the "seulete" as a woman whose experience of loss becomes a defining point of her identity, as the loss of her beloved results in her loss of the social protection of marriage. Although her solitude is initially unsought, that loss also becomes an enunciatory position that is an important part of her authorial self-construction. The opening scene of *Le livre de la cité des dames*, for example, stresses Christine's solitude, when Reason praises her "for your great love of investigating the truth through long and continual study, for which you come here, solitary and separated from the world" ("pour la grant amour que tu as a l'inquisicion de choses vrayes par long et continuel estude par quoy tu te rens ycy

sollitaire et soubtraitte du monde").[13] Here the state of being "sollitaire et soubtraitte du monde" becomes a privileged position of literary knowledge and an enabling stance of Christine's authorship. As
Jacqueline Cerquiglini points out, Christine crafts herself in her own
writing as "une étrangère," a female stranger whose oblique relation
to social institutions allows her to develop a new literary individu-
ality.[14] Christine's construction of solitude, rather than group or institutional affiliation, as a position of writing notably departs from the
medieval theories and practices of communal authorship that A. J.
Minnis and M. B. Parkes find dominant; if to write in the Middle Ages,
as Roger Dragonetti puts it, is to enter "a tradition in which texts
write themselves within one another," Christine writes from a position of self-conscious alienation from tradition.[15] But the woman
writer's alienation from traditional literary communities also gives
her a privileged vantage point from which to critique them, and that
critique becomes the chief pursuit of Christine's writing.

Throughout her *oeuvre* Christine challenges the supremacy of the
medieval institutions of *clergie* and *chevalerie*, the opposing poles,
according to Simon Gaunt, of masculine identity in the Middle Ages.[16]
Excluded from active participation in the sex-segregated literary communities of both *clergie* and *chevalerie*, Christine developed through
her work a new sphere of secular literary production that owed allegiance to neither. In texts such as *L'epistre d'Othea* and *Le livre des
faits d'armes et de chevalerie*, Christine works to dislodge chivalry
from its medieval associations with courtly love, which she attacks
as a misogynist cultural edifice.[17] *L'epistre au dieu d'amours* (The letter to the god of love), for example, demystifies the medieval courts of
love as "gatherings / at which ladies' honor is stripped away" ("[les]
assemblees / ou les honneurs des dames sont emblees").[18] Christine's
critique of courtly love turns the tables on the conflict between love
and knighthood as exemplified in the works of Chrétien de Troyes;
where a romance like *Erec et Enide* insists that women compromise
the knight's martial vocation, Christine aims to create a model of
chivalry that does not confine women to its margins. By distinguish-
ing chivalry from courtly love, she also broadens the definition of
chivalry beyond martial activity in a way that allows those who do
not have direct experience on the battlefield—including women—to
become its practitioners, just as she claims the authority to write
about chivalry herself even though, as a woman, she has never fought
in a battle.[19] Rather than martial prowess alone, Christine's notion of
chivalry is marked by the pursuit of virtuous behavior and literary

learning. Thus in *L'epistre d'Othea*, study and learning are seen to be
as strenuous and demanding as the arts of war; in comparison to the
soldier's arduous physical training, Christine stresses the equally arduous process by which the student achieves learning when she describes, in lines that would be translated into English by Stephen
Scrope, "the peyne and the travayle that a stodiere most [master] ere
that he gete connyne" ("la peine et travail quil convient a lestudiant
dompter avis quil ait science acquise").[20] The model of chivalric virtue is Othea herself, who represents "the vertu of prudence and of
wisedome . . . [which] vertues be necessarie to good policie" ("la vertu
de prudence et sagece . . . soient neccessaire a bonne pollicie") and
who thereby shows that the challenges of learning are unrestricted by
gender.[21] By redefining the knight as a figure of learning and prudence,
Christine establishes a place for a new chivalric agent, the prince's
counselor, who works as an intellectual and moral guide for this new,
politic *chevalerie*. As epitomized by Othea, the office of prince's counselor escapes the gender restrictions of the exclusively masculine
fellowship of medieval *chevalerie*, representing instead a job ideally
suited to the learned woman at court.

By making secular learning an avenue for women's occupation at
the prince's court, Christine removes literate activity from the monastic or university settings that, as popularly known sites of anti-
feminist discourse, were no less exclusionary of women than was the
traditional all-male fellowship of chivalry. As Christine's *L'epistre
au dieu d'amours* asserts, women have cause to complain "of many
clerks who lay much blame to them, / composing tales in rhyme, in
prose, in verse, / In which they scorn their ways with words diverse"
("de plusieurs clercs qui leur surmettent blasmes. / Dictiez en font,
rimes, proses et vers, / En diffamant leurs meurs par moz divers").[22]
Recalling the Wife of Bath's assertion that "no womman of no clerk
is preysed" (706), Christine calls on cultural conventions that made
clerks the traditional enemies of women and thus positioned women
at the exterior of the literate, tradition-bound authority inhabited by
the medieval clerisy.[23] Christine both cites and reverses such cultural
antinomies when she imagines a new form of literary culture embodied in the figure she calls a *"clergesce,"* a female *clerc* who represents
a level of learning and literary activity that is removed from the ecclesiastical, institutional settings of medieval antifeminism.[24] Rather
than seeking authorization in the church, the province of the *clergesce* is the court, in which she presides as a moral and philosophical
authority over a new courtly culture of prudence rather than erotic

entertainment. Christine's revisions of the traditionally masculine sites of *clergie* and *chevalerie* thus make literature a secular place of cultural authority and in the process open a place for learned women to serve as what Diane Bornstein calls "a new priestly caste, the teachers and arbitresses of culture."[25]

To the extent that it revises medieval institutions of literacy and constructs a new literary practice in their place, Christine's model of "the woman writer" resonated with the aims of fifteenth- and sixteenth-century English readers who likewise sought to dislocate reading and writing from the courtly setting of medieval secular literature on the one hand and the Latinate, scholastic settings of the medieval monastery and university on the other. But when Christine's works were adapted to English contexts, they were produced by, and packaged as models for, not literate women but gentlemen. After the end of the Hundred Years War with France, the second half of the fifteenth century in England saw the emergence of what might be termed a new literature of the English aristocratic household, encouraged by an increasingly literate aristocracy and a growing lay secretariat in that aristocracy's employment, who together established new networks of literary patronage and community.[26] Such networks formed the condition of Christine's circulation in England. Those responsible for the translation and production of Christine's texts from 1450 to 1526 comprised a set of overlapping groups of literate men from the aristocracy and the newly secular administrative class that R. L. Storey names "gentlemen-bureaucrats."[27] In the mid-fifteenth century, the Norfolk household of Sir John Fastolf, which included his stepson Stephen Scrope and secretary William Worcester, formed an unlikely but important center for translating and circulating works by Christine de Pizan; later in the century, Anthony Woodville, the Earl Rivers and the owner of the sumptuous manuscript of Christine's collected works, British Library MS Harley 4431, oversaw the publication of one of those works by William Caxton, serving as its translator and patron; in the sixteenth century, Christine's works found new editors and translators in the Henrician court, where a later generation of literate aristocrats, including Woodville's nephew, Richard Grey, authorized their later circulation.

The line of cultural descent from John Fastolf and Anthony Woodville in the fifteenth century to Richard Grey in the sixteenth follows the growth of literary patronage as an exercise of aristocratic masculinity, while the parallel line from Worcester to Caxton and later, Henrician editors and translators follows the related growth of the professional man of letters who benefited from this patronage. To these new groups of readers, the medieval literary conventions of *clergie* and *chevalerie* were equally irrelevant. Representing a new secularization of literacy, the new household and courtly literary communities rejected the formerly dominant aristocratic literatures of love and inwardness that had defined the imaginary but culturally powerful *cour amoureuse.*²⁸ For these communities the works of Christine de Pizan, with their reworking of clerical and chivalric conventions, exerted a particular, and historically specific, appeal. The private libraries of the aristocratic households increased in number and volume, and as they did, they contained works such as Christine's *Epistre d'Othea* and her *Faits d'armes et de chevalerie.*²⁹ If these works refashioned the medieval warrior-knight, they also established a new model of secular learning and literary production that was appropriate to the new English secretariat and literate aristocracy, for whom the activities of translating and circulating learned works like Christine's represented an ideal form of intellectual labor.

That Christine's texts were translated at all attests to what Susan Crane calls England's "curiously intimate as well as adversarial contact with France" in the years during and following the Hundred Years War.³⁰ While England had maintained an aristocratic, francophone culture through the late Middle Ages, as evidenced by Henry IV's invitation to Christine herself to join his court, the manuscripts of Christine's works that formed the basis of later translations came to England as a kind of literary spoils of war, when the noblemen who had fought in France with Henry V and established English political outposts following their victory either carried back French manuscripts or commissioned their own copies. The most famous of Christine's manuscripts, the collected works dedicated to Isabeau of Bavaria and now housed as British Library MS Harley 4431, fell into the possession of John, Duke of Bedford, then regent in France, who later took it back to England for his French wife, Jacquetta of Luxembourg, whose signature appears on the flyleaf along with that of their son, Anthony Woodville, Earl Rivers.³¹ The same manuscript formed the basis of Woodville's translation of Christine's *Proverbes moraulx,* printed by Caxton in 1478. Likewise, Sir John Fastolf, who had also accompanied Henry V to France and served as Bedford's master of the household, came into the ownership of a French manuscript of *L'epistre d'Othea,* which would form the basis of Stephen Scrope's 1450 translation.³² These examples reveal that French literature continued to be valued by the English aristocracy after the Hundred Years War, and English ownership of Christine's manuscripts by literate men like Bedford and Fastolf could be seen to reflect broader belief in the English claim to France and things French that was consistent with the will to conquer; as Shakespeare's Henry V claims, "I love France so well that I will not part with a village of it, I will have it all mine."[33] As much as they attest to their owners' French tastes, the translation of those same texts also helped advance Henry V's well-known policy to promote English over French as the official language of government and state business.[34] This policy was supported by an ideological opposition between French as the language of excessive sophistication and duplicity and English as that of truth and plain speaking; the engineered shift from the former to the latter had the effect of redefining the terms on which fifteenth-century English aristocratic culture was constructed.[35] Where the earlier, Ricardian court was vilified by the Lancastrians and their supporters for what was seen as its Francophilic taste for ornament, luxury, and love poetry, the new aristocratic culture of English gave rise to what David Lawton calls the literature of "dullness" in the fifteenth century, which eschewed rhetorical complexity and the genres of love and private sentiment in favor of a literature of public edification that was "parallel to and connected with the structures of power."[36] Christine's texts, with their emphases on public instruction and critiques of courtly love, appealed to this emerging English literary culture—indeed, they shaped it in important ways, by defining a new literature of public edification. But their translation from French also represents a cultural appropriation that claims the qualities of edification and prudence on which Christine's texts were based as the hallmarks of a new English literature.

The terms in which Christine imagined a new class of female counselors in the court—by presenting literary activity apart from the monastery or university, and courtly behavior apart from the *cour amoreuse*—came to define the men who edited, translated, and eventually published her works, who projected themselves into the place that Christine reserved for "the woman writer." But if Christine's construction of "the woman writer" outside the medieval institutions of *clergie* or *chevalerie* provided a new literary model to which the new gentleman bureaucrat could aspire, the actual figure of Christine herself, as continually inscribed in her texts, was clearly problematic to those who translated, edited, and circulated her texts. Rather than trying to do away with the female author, the texts I examine in this chapter attempt to explain the figure they call "Dame Christine," who is vestigially present both in the texts themselves and on the paratextual level as editors, translators, and readers attempt to represent her relationship to the books they circulate. In so doing, they remove her to a position outside the masculine networks of textual circulation in which they construe literary culture, in which the circuits of masculine patronage and literary service become the salient markers of a book's social identity. This I take to be the central paradox of Christine's English reception: although her construction of her own female authorship establishes an enabling model for this new literary culture, the figure of "Christine" as represented on the paratextual level absorbs those aspects of female authorship that were unassimilable into the new English literary culture. Thus if Christine's conception of the female author's marginality to *clergie* and *chevalerie* was adapted by English readers and writers to theorize the novelty of their own cultural position, her conception of the woman writer's solitude and social alienation was not. In contrast to Christine, the English translators and adaptors of her work defined the literary community of the aristocratic household on the model of the medieval university and chivalric masculine communities that they replaced.[37] Where Christine presents herself as the harbinger of a new courtly world in which women become "the priestly caste, the teachers and arbitresses of culture," to recall Bornstein's formulation, the new male readers of the fifteenth-century aristocratic household analogize their authority to that of the masculine literary community of clerks, in order to make the aristocratic household culture into a new, secular, and largely vernacular university, defined, like the medieval clerisy, through its exclusion of women.

The Learned Knight and the Fiction of "Dame Christine"

The fifteenth-century household of Sir John Fastolf shows that the bonds of administrative and domestic service supported the production of a new English literary culture; in the process, this household also became an unlikely center for the translation and circulation of the works of Christine de Pizan. Fastolf, who fought the French in the battles of Harfleur and Agincourt, returned to England after the Hundred Years War and consolidated his wealth and position in his later life through ownership of land, establishing his principal residences at Castle Combe in Wiltshire and, after 1454, at Caister in Norfolk.[38] He shared his household—but little of his wealth—with his stepson, Stephen Scrope, and his secretary, William Worcester, who represented a new generation of gentlemen with refined literary skills and high levels of education but without military careers or land-

holdings of their own.[39] Both Scrope and Worcester produced translations of Christine de Pizan: Scrope of *L'epistre d'Othea* and Worcester of selections from *Le livre des faits d'armes et de chevalerie* in
his manuscript compilation *The Boke of Noblesse*. This selection of
texts is not in itself unusual, since the two were well known to noble
readers: the library of Sir John Paston, for example, contained an
Othea pistill and a *Tretys of Werre*, which may be Christine's *Livre
des faits d'armes*.[40]

That these particular texts found a receptive readership in mid-
fifteenth-century England reflects their readers' interest in Christine's
broader effort to rewrite the medieval institutions of chivalry. The
Hundred Years War redefined martial activity on both sides of the
channel. The advent of new technologies of war such as artillery
and the longbow widened the gap between medieval ideals of chivalry
and modern fighting practices, demanding a new code of practice in
which the traditional manly virtues of the knight errant could be replaced by the new virtues of diplomacy and strategy.[41] Christine's
writings on chivalry, such as *L'epistre d'Othea* and *Le livre des faits
d'armes et de chevalerie*, would become standard texts for this new
order of knighthood because they replace the medieval ethos of individualistic prowess with one of "good policie," as articulated in
Othea's words to Hector. But where Christine's texts are written from
the perspective of a woman writer wishing to establish a new class of
female counselors, Scrope and Worcester approach the texts with
greater interest in the possibilities they offered for refiguring aristocratic masculinity.

Scrope translated *L'epistre d'Othea* into English sometime around
1450 under the new title *The Boke of Knyghthode*, a work that bears
the marks of the household literary culture in which it was under-
taken.[42] In a prefatory letter to Fastolf, Scrope presents the book as
an exemplar of masculine virtue. Appealing to Fastolf's "good ffadyr-
hode," he commends the book because it is "exempled vpon the grete
conceytys and doctrine off fulle wyse pooetys and philosophurs . . .
which materis, conseytys and resons be auctorised and approued vpon the textys and dictes off the hold [sic] poetys and wyse men called
philosophurs."[43] Implicit throughout Scrope's dedication—as well as
in his choice of texts—is the belief that the teachings of poets and
philosophers can benefit the knight as much as physical training in
the acts of war. Scrope therefore follows Christine in the desire to define knighthood as an exercise of learning as well as of martial skill,
as when he argues in his dedication to Fastolf:

Ye schal fynde here in this seyde Boke off Cheuallry how and in whatte maner ye, and all other off whatte astate, condicion or degree he be off, may welle be called a knyght that ouercomyth and conqveryth hys gostly ennemyes . . . and most [truly] he is to be renommed in worchip & callid a knyght that dothe exercise hys armes and dedys off knyght-holde in gostly dedys in conqveryng his gostly ennemees and ouyr-comyng Þe peple and aventure off the world.[44]

In this, Scrope projects the traditional acts of chivalry—the overcoming of enemies, the exercise of arms, and the winning of "worchip"—into the immaterial realm of "gostly dedys," which derive from the virtue and wisdom that one can encounter in books. Scrope thus displaces the chivalric realm onto the literary, and thereby broadens the definition of knighthood to imply that what knights do in their libraries repeats on an immaterial level what they do on the battlefield on a physical level. This argument represents a significant attempt to reshape the definition of aristocratic masculinity from the medieval understanding of *chevalerie* to a new model that will comprise literate, book-owning men like himself.

In the process of reframing Christine's book for the benefit of aristocratic men, Scrope both acknowledges and deflects its earlier association with a female author. Immediately following his discussion of "gostly dedys" in his preface, Scrope writes:

This seyde boke, at the instaunce & praer off a fulle wyse gentylwoman of Frawnce called Dame Cristine, was compiled & grounded by the famous doctours of the most excellent in clerge the nobyl Vniuersyte off Paris.[45]

This charge that Christine's works were written by clerks is contradicted by the very manuscript that Scrope used as a source, identifiable by its dedication to the Duke of Berry, which contains a lengthy prologue explicitly identifying Christine as the work's author.[46] Nonetheless, Scrope's confected biography of Christine de Pizan as a benefactress of male authors but not technically an author herself is consistent with his broader effort to shape literary practice into a sphere of masculine activity that could capture the cultural prestige of martial exercise. While Scrope's aim to redefine chivalry is advanced by Christine's own elevation of "prudence and wisedome" as virtues that are "necessarie to goostli knyghthood," he secures the analogy between the immaterial knighthood of literature and the physical knighthood of battle by creating them both as essentially masculine spheres from which women are separated.[47] Thus the imaginary "doctours of the most excellent in clerge the nobyl Vniuersyte off Paris" become plausible analogues for "goostli knyghthood" because they bring together the learned and the spiritual—hence "goostli"—realms under a sphere that is, like Fastolf's army, an exclusively masculine realm.[48] It is significant that Christine is not excised from the manuscript entirely; rather, Scrope's effort to explain—and perhaps explain away—the figure of "Dame Cristine" also assigns her an identity that stands to the side of those qualities that Scrope claims for literate men. If Scrope's new knightly readers are joined in a masculine fellowship that recalls those of the clerical and chivalric communities it replaces, "Dame Cristine" helps to define that fellowship and solidify its common bond with its literary ancestors in her exclusion from it, thereby constituting the borders of the masculine literary community through gender difference.

The fiction of "Dame Christine" resurfaces in a manuscript that also originated in Fastolf's circle around the same time as Scrope's. Fastolf's secretary, William Worcester, produced *The Boke of Noblesse*, a title that echoes Scrope's *The Boke of Knighthode* and announces its similar preoccupation with the institutions of aristocratic masculinity.[49] The manuscript, a treatise in English on the arts of war, now in the British Library, continually draws on Christine's *Le livre des faits d'armes et de chevalerie* as a source for its central contention that wars should be shaped by policy and good counsel rather than unchecked violence and force. This notion of a war fought by policy entails a self-conscious redefinition of medieval masculinity, as Worcester shows by citing no less an "autor" than Sir John Fastolf himself to support a distinction between the "hardy man" of violent force and the "manly man" of counsel and policy. The "hardy man" commits acts of individualistic courage and strength but does so without advice or counsel ("the hardy man . . . sodenly, [without] discreccion of gode avysement, avauncyth hym yn the felde to be halde courageuse"), while in contrast the "manly man" acts out of "policie," discretion, and concern for his collective "felyshyp" above his own reputation for valor.[50] Thus "manliness" becomes coterminous with prudence and policy, rather than strength; it is a virtue that is taught and cultivated rather than deriving from an innate virility and display of physical force. This elevation of policy over individualistic hardiness is consistent with Christine's new order of chivalry, as *The Boke of Noblesse* reveals by frequently citing from Christine's text, whose author it identifies familiarly as "Dame Cristyn." The book thus shows the extent to which Christine's writings on chivalry and knighthood had come to structure fifteenth-century definitions of these topics. However, in the margin of one such citation, a note in Latin—presumably by Worcester, who is known to have annotated his own writing—provides the following identification of "Dame Cristyn":

> Notandum est quod Cristina [fuit] domina praeclara natu et moribus et manebat in domo religiosarum dominarum apud Passye prope Parys; et ita virtuosa fuit quod ipsa exhibuit plures clericos studentes in universitate Parisiensi, et compilare fecit plures libros virtuosos, utpote *Liber Arboris Bellorum*, et doctores . . . attribuerunt nomen autoris Christinae, sed aliquando nomen autoris clerici studentis imponitur in diversis libris.[51]

> (It is to be noted that Christine was a famous lady who was born, died, and lived in a religious house in Poissy near Paris; and this woman was so virtuous that she employed many clerks in the University of Paris, and made them compile many virtuous books. . . . And learned men . . . gave the name of author to Christine, but otherwise the name of author was given to the clerks in many books.)

In its effort to explain Christine's identity, the note once again replaces Christine with a company of nameless clerks from the University of Paris, while adding the fiction that she was cloistered from birth until death in Poissy, the religious house to which Christine in fact retired at the end of her life. The note thereby advances a step beyond Scrope's by separating Christine physically and institutionally from the network of men presumed to be responsible for the book, differentiating the communal setting of male literary production from the private, cloistered space to which Christine is relegated.

In separating Christine from the imaginary scene of the book's authorship, the note appears to confuse Christine's text with one of her sources, the *Liber arboris bellorum*, or *L'arbre des batailles*, by Honoré Bonet, while at the same time obscuring the fact that the text she did write, *Le livre des faits d'armes*, was the actual source for *The Boke of Noblesse*. The confusion of Christine's *Faits d'armes* with its source, *L'arbre des batailles*, may well reflect an inconsistent attribution to Christine in the manuscripts. While major manuscripts such as Harley 4431 are clearly attributed to Christine, as Cynthia J. Brown has recently shown, a number of fifteenth-century French manuscripts and printed editions of Christine's *Faits d'armes* assign authorship to its sources; in the process, they also went so far as to excise all references to Christine within the texts themselves and to change her pronominal self-references from female to male, in what can only be taken as a concerted effort to rewrite Christine's authorship as masculine.[52] However, the reference to "Dame Christine" suggests the presence of an attributed manuscript source; rather than eradicating this name and thereby allaying confusion about the authorship of these texts, both Worcester and Scrope undertake considerable imaginative effort to explain how Christine's name might have come to be associated with the text—and, importantly, they retain it in the text—while also doing so in ways that reserve the category of true authorship for men.

The fiction of "Dame Christine," as Scrope and Worcester produce it, indicates that authorship was more consequential in late fifteenth-century literary culture than P. G. C. Campbell, in his seminal article on Christine's literary afterlife in England, suggests when he ascribes such inaccurate attributions to a widespread indifference about authorship.[53] Were authorship merely a matter of indifference, both Scrope and Worcester would have simply ignored whatever contradictory evidence their own source texts may have provided. At the same time, their readiness to adopt the fiction of "Dame Christine" suggests that they were not driven to seek out evidence of who wrote a text before assigning authorship either. Rather, the ascription of authorship appears to serve primarily as a means of classifying texts, a point that supports Julia Boffey's observation that authorial ascriptions in manuscript collections serve the purpose of "placing" texts by designating, through the author's name, the larger contexts in which they are to be received.[54] Such early uses of authorial naming recall Foucault's argument that "the author's name," by assigning texts to individuals, "indicates the status of this discourse within a society and a culture"; at the same time, the English translations of Christine's works also offer a historical correction to Foucault's well-known thesis about the development of "the author function."[55] Where Foucault holds that "the author function" first emerged as a method for individuating authorship by assigning texts to single speakers, authorship for Scrope and Worcester serves less to distinguish an individual writer than to set a text in a complex of relationships—between patron and client, text and source, compiler and translator. For Scrope and Worcester the salient facts about a book's authorship concern the relationships of patronage that authorize it. "The author" as they use the term, then, designates less an individual than an authorizing relationship that is characterized by service and reward.[56] And that relationship is above all one of gender, in a way that recalls Teresa de Lauretis's observation that "the term *gender* is, actually, the representation of a relation, that of belonging to a class, a group, a category. . . . so gender represents not an individual but a relation, and a social relation."[57]

By the *nomen autoris*, "the name of author," Worcester designates the authorizing lines of patronage and service in which books were produced, rather than a single author identified with the writer, a point confirmed in the text of *The Boke of Noblesse*, which refers to Sir John Fastolf as "myn autor," making the "author" in this case not the originator, but rather the head of the household literary community in which the text was produced. This communal notion of authorship, evident in medieval conventions of textual production, would continue in the early modern period, of which Peter Stallybrass and Margreta de Grazia observe that "the authorial name ties the work not to a sole agent or 'onlie begetter' but to a productive and reproductive network."[58] If Worcester thereby produces authorship as a communal activity of men, his marginal note explaining the identity of "Dame Christine" indicates that the name was given to her as an honorific in such a way as to distinguish her from the imaginary clerical community of writers, implying that she is not a true "autor" in the same way that Fastolf is in Worcester's text—that is, one who authorizes and secures a textual community. Thus "the name of author," this example suggests, secures textual communities of men while also exiling the female author to the periphery of those communities.

The notion that Christine de Pizan's texts were written or compiled by men under her name, as William Blades points out, "is unsupported by a single known instance."[59] Nonetheless, the fiction of "Dame Christine" appears to have been readily adopted as an explanation of Christine de Pizan's identity, and it found acceptance well into the sixteenth century. So much is evident from a reader's note on the flyleaf of a manuscript copy of *L'arbre des battailles* belonging to the sixteenth-century bibliophile John, Lord Lumley. Recalling the notes of Scrope and Worcester, this later note invokes the figure of "Dame Christine" specifically to deny that she was the author of the book:

Note [that] in some Authors this Booke is termed Dame Christine of [the] tree of Battayles; not that she made yt; But bicause she was

a notable Benefactour to Learned men and perchaunce to [the] autor
of this Book And therefore diuers of them sette furthe their Bookes
under her name. See [the] Booke of Noblesse in englishe.[60]

In this case, at least part of the assertion is correct: *L'arbre des battailles* was not Christine's book but her source.[61] According to the
catalogue of his personal library, Lumley owned not only this book
and *The Boke of Noblesse*, which the note mentions, but also a copy
of "Christine of Pise hir booke of the feates of armes and chivalrie."[62]
This was presumably a copy of an edition of Christine's text that William Caxton brought out in 1489 as *The Boke of Fayttes of Armes and
of Chyualrye*, which he attributed, unlike Worcester, clearly to Christine: as the colophon reads, "Thus endeth this boke whiche Xprystyne
of pyse made & drewe out of the boke named vegecius de re militari
& out of tharbre of bataylles."[63] Lumley thus would not have had to
search long in his own library to confirm Christine's actual relation
to *L'arbre des battailles*; however, his note indicates that for at least
this sixteenth-century aristocratic book owner, Christine was less famous as an author than she was as a woman who was *not* an author,
suggesting that the fiction of "Dame Christine," as Scrope and Worcester constructed it, appeared more reasonable than Caxton's more
straightforward account of female authorship. If "Dame Christine"
was concocted in part to explain the variations of attribution in Christine's texts, the fiction takes hold because it upholds a gendered
model of authorship that makes masculine communities into the
centers of authorized textual production and displaces literate women
to their margins.

The revision of Christine's authorship in these works needs to be
understood within the expectations English readers held about themselves and their literary communities within the changing institutions of pre-Reformation aristocratic masculinity. The shifting nature of those institutions is visible in the generation gap between Sir
John Fastolf on the one hand and Stephen Scrope and especially William Worcester on the other. While Fastolf excelled in the traditional
spheres of aristocratic masculinity, war and landownership, his stepson Scrope and secretary Worcester, who lacked both inherited wealth
and military careers, sought in literature an avenue of patronage and
an alternative arena for the development of aristocratic masculine
identity.[64] Worcester benefited from the kind of education that in an
earlier age would have suited him for holy orders; indeed, the expec-
tation that a man of such literate accomplishment should be a cleric

is reflected in Fastolf's uncertainty about how best to reward his labors. As Worcester reports in *The Paston Letters,* Fastolf once expressed the wish that he had been a priest, so that he might have given him a beneficed living.[65] By instead serving as a secular administrator in Fastolf's household, Worcester participates in what R. L. Storey identifies as an emerging lay class of gentleman bureaucrats in the fifteenth century.[66] Called by K. B. McFarlane "the father of English antiquaries" and by Colin Richmond "the founder of modern English history," Worcester represents a new man of letters for the fifteenth century.[67] Although Worcester's major professional undertaking was in his administrative function as Fastolf's secretary, he turned his skills as a cataloguer and self-directed scholar to other activities, as is witnessed not only in his *Boke of Noblesse* but also in his extensive *Itineraries,* which record his visits to historical sites in a form that anticipates the work of the later antiquarians John Leland and John Bale, and the now-lost *Acta domini Johannis Fastolf.*[68] In his education and his dedication to Fastolf's service he bridged the medieval divide between *clergie* and *chevalerie* by making secularized learning a new site of noble masculinity.[69] His literary proclivities were well known to his contemporaries, and the *Paston Letters* report of Worcester that "he wold be as glad and feyn of a good boke of Frensh or of poetre [sic] as my Master Fastolf wold be to purchase a faire manoir"—thereby showing the desire to substitute literary accomplishment for landownership as a mark of masculine refinement, in a way that resembles Scrope's desire to cast the act of reading as a spiritual equivalent to the physical acts of warfare.[70]

This promotion of secular learning as a new site of aristocratic, and even chivalric, masculinity participates in what Gordon Kipling identifies as a rising vogue in the late fifteenth and early sixteenth centuries in England for Burgundian models of "learned chivalry," which upheld literature as a means of exercising the political and social virtues necessary to the maintenance of the modern state.[71] According to an earlier model, the consumption of literature was understood to be an idle pleasure, anathema to the martial work of the knight, as Thomas Walsingham instances when he charges the courtiers of Richard II with being "armed with words rather than weapons, prompt in speaking but slow in performing the acts of war."[72] In contrast, "learned chivalry" defined literary practice not in opposition to the office of a knight but in concert with it; and in so doing, it facilitated the emergence of a new class of gentlemen who, like Worcester, aspired to serve the state not through military but through literary efforts. These new literati thereby respond to Christine's own call to expand chivalry's cultural prestige to a new class of courtly readers and writers.[73] But while Christine envisioned this class as an avenue by which women would become "the teachers and arbitresses of [courtly] culture," as Bornstein puts it, to Scrope and Worcester this "priestly caste" would be filled not by women but by male literary functionaries: educated secretaries, translators, and bibliophiles like themselves. Scrope's and Worcester's substitution of clerks for Christine as the true authors of *L'epistre d'Othea* and *Les faits d'armes et de chevalerie* reflects their beliefs about the medieval literary past they were both inheriting and reshaping. If the Burgundian model of "learned chivalry" shifted the place of textual learning from the monastery or the university to the aristocratic household, making the latter the new site of masculine learned community, the position to which Scrope and Worcester aspired in Fastolf's household was the secular equivalent to that of the university clerks with whom they replaced Christine de Pizan in their reattributions of her texts. At the same time, by transforming Christine herself into a cloistered, religious woman, Scrope and Worcester separate her both from the medieval university and the early modern aristocratic household in order to analogize the medieval university and the aristocratic household as all-male preserves.

If the fiction of "Dame Christine" that emerges in Scrope's and Worcester's paratexts solidifies textual communities of men, it does so by creating a female outsider who embodies the characteristics that are exiled from those communities. Where Christine's works theorize a literate practice outside the traditional medieval collectivities of *clergie* and *chevalerie* and thereby supply the terms by which the new textual communities of men like Worcester and Scrope were formed, they do so by associating that literate practice with a female space of exclusion.[74] English readers like Scrope and Worcester adapt Christine's reworkings of *clergie* and *chevalerie* to theorize and justify their own literate activities, but they conceive their activities as continuations of the medieval masculine textual communities from which Christine herself was so self-consciously alienated. Instead of adopting the pose of "l'étrangère" by which Christine authorized her own writing as an individual enterprise, Scrope and Worcester consider textual production still an essentially communal activity, but one that has changed place, from the monastic and university settings of medieval literacy to the patronage-based setting of the aristocratic household. Where Christine sees her isolation from traditional textual communities as an authorizing position, Scrope and Worcester refigure it as a sign of alienation from the institutions of literary authority by banishing Christine's authorizing model of female solitude and marginality to the periphery of their translations under the figure "Dame Christine." In her very isolation, "Dame Christine" embodies the qualities that continue to be repellent and threatening about the modern author as Christine invents the figure. What was for Christine the very condition of her authorship—her alienation as a woman from masculine literate communities—becomes, in the fifteenth-century English translations of her texts, a sign of her marginality to the authorial structures of the aristocratic household.

Christine's transformation into a cloistered woman displaces her from her historical place of writing—the French court. Instead, in her imagined religious enclosure, removed from the political sphere, she presides over but does not participate in the communities of men who are imagined to be the true creators of her books, from the imaginary clerks at the University of Paris to the men in the Fastolf household at Caister and Castle Combe. The fiction in Worcester's marginal annotation that Christine was a cloistered nun rather than a worldly counselor and courtier makes her embody the qualities of medieval monasticism that the new household literary culture decidedly rejected: its separation of scholarly, literate activities from the worldly setting of government and bureaucratic *negotium*. The removal of "Dame Christine" to a space of privatized piety supports Ruth Kelso's hypothesis that women in the early Renaissance were ideologically called on to take up the religious practices and social positions that men discarded in favor of secular pursuits. Ann Rosalind Jones elaborates Kelso's thesis to argue that "as men turned more and more to secular, civic ambitions, the residual virtues of humility and retirement from the world were displaced onto women."[75] In the case of "Dame Christine," a woman's displacement to a position of religious retirement literally enables men to step into the space—of secular counsel and civic commitment—in which she had defined herself.

From "Aucteresse" to *Auctor: The Morale Proverbes* of Caxton and Pynson

The lines of patronage and service that structured the production of manuscripts in the aristocratic household continued in, and aided the development of, a new culture of print. The first printed books that William Caxton introduced into the English literary culture of the late fifteenth century manifest the influence of the same Burgundian tastes that shaped the libraries of the English nobility, and Caxton's cultivation of noble patrons for these works reflects his effort to insert the printing press into the lines of aristocratic textual production that were already in place for manuscript production and circulation.[76] At the same time, Caxton also attempted to adapt the administrative and civic-minded literary models that are exemplified by William Worcester to the new social structures of print patronage, an enterprise that brings him into polite, but significant, conflict with the older social protocols that governed manuscript production and circulation in courtly contexts. While the first printed books physically imitated their manuscript counterparts, the press altered the social circuits of textual production by introducing into literary culture the new figure of the printer, who made book production into a public and commercial venture, rather than a private and personal one.[77] This shift in the social milieu of book production was reflected in new paratextual conventions such as the printer's prologue and epilogue, which typically record details about the texts' production and patronage. The editorial paratext superseded the function of the colophon, the short tag at texts' end that recorded their authors, titles, and details of their production. As a convention for situating a text specifically within the contexts of its reproduction and dissemination rather than its writing, the printer's prologue and epilogue had the effect of placing patrons where authors had been.

The paratexts that frame Christine's texts as they appeared in print recall Natalie Zemon Davis's description of the printed book as a "carrier of relationships," since, in ways that are visible in its paratextual conventions, it calls on multiple agents to bring it into production.[78] Christine's books, like other books in early print, register the combined and sometimes competing interests of printer, patron, translator, and projected reader in the paratextual apparatus in which these different agents leave their mark. Among these various interests, Christine, as the absent author, is the one agent least able to assert her claim on the text. Instead, the representation of her identity and name in the text becomes another paratextual element that is subject to, and produced in the clash between, the competing interests of the text's makers. William Caxton's 1478 edition of Christine de Pizan's *Les proverbes moraulx* registers his effort to create a new protocol of print that adapts the textual conventions of the gentleman bureaucrat of the aristocratic household to a commercial culture of print, at the same time that it contends with an earlier model of courtly book production that is upheld by its aristocratic patron and translator, Anthony Woodville. Printer and patron each assert their competing visions of textual production through their representations of Christine de Pizan.

Les proverbes moraulx has not been popular with modern readers, but, as a text that resonated with fifteenth- and early sixteenth-century interests, it can illuminate the historical significance of "the woman writer" that Christine constructed as an enunciatory posture. A collection of edifying couplets that affect a platitudinous, universal voice, *Les proverbes moraulx* exemplifies Christine's effort, as seen in other works such as *L'epistre d'Othea*, to fashion herself as public teacher. The text appears to have been written originally as a sequel to Christine's book of advice to her son, the *Enseignemens moraulx*, and it is clearly directed at fashioning virtues befitting a young man at court.[79] But its emphasis on the importance of prudence and good counsel to the well-governed state also makes it a handbook for the new courtly bureaucrat that emerges in *L'epistre d'Othea* and the *Faits d'armes*, Christine's other most popular works in England at this time. The work continually affirms the office of the counselor and governor and its importance to the prince, as in couplets such as the following, as translated in Caxton's edition: "A pryncis court withoute a gonverneur / Beyng prudent can not leste in honneur" ("Court de seigneur sans prudent gou[ve]neur / Estre ne peut maintenue en honneur"), or "A mighty prynce that wole here his consaille / Paciently / to prospere cannot faille" ("Prince poissant a qui destre repris / Ne lui desplait est signe de grant pris").[80] While the work counsels the prince to heed his governor, it also counsels governors to develop "prudence," "vertue," and "gentillesse"—all qualities that the text affirms to be learned, rather than innate, virtues.

If *Les proverbes moraulx* is directed at men, it affirms the importance of the woman counselor as represented in both the figure of Othea and Christine's own career: the femininity of the speaker is stressed in the illumination that accompanies the text in British Library MS Harley 4431, which presents Christine, in her characteristic dress, instructing a group of men from behind a desk (Figure 1). The same manuscript would form the basis of the text's first translation into English by its owner, Anthony Woodville, Earl Rivers. Woodville's translation was printed by Caxton in 1478, and it would be followed half a century later by an edition that Richard Pynson published in 1526. Unlike the earlier, manuscript translations of Christine's work, Caxton's edition fully acknowledges her authorship, entitling

Figure 1. Christine de Pizan, from the opening of *Les proverbes moraulx*. Illumination, British Library MS Harley 4431 fol.261 ᵛ. Reproduced with permission of the British Library.

the work "The Morale Prouerbes of Christine" and printing an epilogue by Woodville that identifies and lavishly praises the work's "aucteresse":[81]

> Of these sayynges Christyne was aucteresse
> Whiche in makyng hadde suche Intelligence
> That therof she was mireur & maistresse
> Hire werkes testify thexperience
> In frenssh languaige was writen[n] this sentence
> And thus Englished doth hit rehers
> Antoine Wideuylle therl Ryuers

In the model of literary production that Woodville presents here, texts become "mirrors" that reflect the personal qualities of those who write them: Christine's "werkes testify thexperience" of their "aucteresse" and thereby augment the authority of their maker. Portraying himself as a translator whose work "rehearses" the original by "Englishing" Christine's own "frenssh languaige," Woodville assumes a position that is decidedly secondary to his female author.[82] In this, Woodville's epilogue enacts a courtly show of deference to a female figure of literary authority, a gesture that repeats what Richard Firth Green calls "the polite fiction of female sovereignty" that upheld the fictional but powerful model of the medieval *cour amoureuse*.[83] With its emphasis on love debates and literary diversions, the "court of love" actively produced a ceremonial model of female literary authority that was also decidedly French in its ambience. As the owner of the famous French mansucript of Christine's works that is now British Library MS Harley 4431, Woodville himself was known for his French tastes. He was also known for his courtly solicitude toward women, as Caxton acknowledges in the epilogue to another book for which Woodville was translator and patron, *The Dictes or Sayengis of the Philosophres* (1477); the epilogue gently chides Woodville for "the very affeccyon, love and good wylle that he hath unto alle ladyes and gentylwomen."[84] If such attitudes were a mark of courtly manners, Caxton's remark suggests that by the late fifteenth century they were also beginning to seem outdated.

In his edition of *The Morale Prouerbes* Caxton appends a second stanza to his patron's verse that differs sharply from Woodville's in tone and focus, reflecting a new perspective on the sources and shapes of literary authority in England's changing literary culture. Where Woodville pays tribute to Christine de Pizan as the source of his text's authority, Caxton's verse redirects his tribute from the female author to the relationship between printer and patron:[85]

> Go thou litil quayer / and reco[m]maund me
> Unto the good grace / of my special lorde
> Therle Ryueris, for I haue enprinted the
> At his co[m]andement, followyng eury worde
> His copy / as his secretaire can recorde.[86]

This stanza employs the conventional envoy formula familiar from Chaucer's closing stanzas in *Troilus and Criseyde*. However, while Chaucer directs his poem, "Go, litel bok," to pay obeissance to "Virgile, Ovide, Omer, Lucan, and Stace," Caxton sends his printed "quayer," or quire, not to the author or the text's literary ancestors but rather to Anthony Woodville, his "special lorde," the text's male translator and patron. Caxton thus finds in Chaucer's recollection of the literary past a suitable posture of deference to frame the relationship of printer to patron. Moreover, his claim to have "follow[ed] eury worde" of Woodville's text recalls the tropes of literary servitude that are embedded in medieval translation, while also adapting these literary conventions of *translatio* to endorse the reproductive mechanism of the printing press. The imitative function that Caxton establishes in "followyng" Woodville's every word is less poetic than it is bureaucratic, or literally secretarial; he has "followed" the Earl's copy "as his secretaire can recorde," Caxton claims, suggesting not only that the secretary bears witness to the transaction between printer and patron but also that in the act of "recording" Woodville's words typographically, Caxton himself is acting "as his secretaire."[87] While appropriating the conventional postures of medieval literary production to describe his own press, Caxton locates the work of the printer within the bonds of patronage and service that upheld an emergent coterie of court functionaries responsible for overseeing and authorizing the production of texts. He thus portrays himself in a relationship with Woodville that is parallel to Worcester's relationship with Fastolf.

If Woodville advances the authority of the woman writer above his own, decidedly secondary work as translator, for Caxton, in contrast, literary authority is the product not of an originary act of writing but of the circuits of textual reproduction. This is apparent, for example, in Caxton's later reference to *The Morale Prouerbes* in the epilogue to his edition of *Cordial* (1479), which, like the verses concluding *The Morale Prouerbes*, also narrates the story of the book's patronage. Anthony Woodville translated *Cordial* from French to English and delivered it to him, Caxton recounts, "for to be enprinted and so multiplied to goo abrood among the peple."[88] Praising his patron's industry and "vertuous disposicion," Caxton recalls the other "diverse bookes" that Woodville has similarly translated, of which he elects to name *The Morale Prouerbes* as an example: "Emong other passid thurgh mynn honde [are] . . . the wise and holsomm proverbis of Christine of Pyse, set in metre."[89] Whatever wisdom and wholesomeness Caxton ascribes to Christine here are meant as a tribute not to her but to Anthony Woodville, whose selection of the proverbs for translation and publication reflects his own "vertuous disposicion." For Caxton, *The Morale Prouerbes* is culturally significant because of its transmission through the patronage relationship, rather than in its reflection of female authority. As Caxton puts it, the text is remarkable for having "passid thurgh mynn honde": he thereby makes it a form of currency that circulates between patron and printer and secures an alliance based on textual exchange. From there, the *Cordial* epilogue continues, it carries on to form a broader network of alliances after it is "enprinted and so multiplied to goo abroad among the peple." The book exists to be endlessly circulated, where it will reproduce within the commonwealth the lines of alliance initially established in the book's patronage. This I take to be the function of Caxton's envoy at the end of *The Morale Prouerbes:* by redirecting the focus away from Christine de Pizan, he sends the text to Woodville instead and thereby establishes the text's value within a circuit of exchange that will extend from patron and printer to a broader community of readers of the printed book.

Caxton's 1478 *Morale Prouerbes* represents the text's first appearance in print; its second is in 1526, in an edition published by Richard Pynson, "the King's Printer." Where Caxton's verses displace authority from the female author to the figure of the male patron, the *Morale Prouerbes*'s later appearance in print displaces the female author still further, in ways that help to construct the male author as a cultural figure that was newly authorized in the structures of royal patronage centralized in the Henrician court. When Pynson reprinted *The Morale Prouerbes* in his 1526 three-volume edition of Chaucer's works, he was concerned less with Christine than with his subject, Chaucer, and his renowned predecessor, Caxton. In his editions of *The Canterbury Tales* in 1478 and 1483 and of *The House of Fame* (as *The Book of Fame Made by Geffrey Chaucer*) in 1483, Caxton established the pattern for publishing Chaucer's works, and when Pynson brought out his own edition of Chaucer he both adopted Caxton's text as his source and invoked Caxton directly as his cultural and professional ancestor. In his edition of *The Canterbury Tales* Pynson proclaims his fidelity to Caxton through his fidelity to Chaucer:

> Whiche boke diligently ouirsen & duely examined by the pollitike reason and ouirsight of my worshipful master Will Caxton accordinge to the intente and effecte of the seide Geffrey Chaucer, and by a copy of the seid mastr Caxton [do I] purpose to imprent.[90]

Pynson thus presents himself as a servant of two masters. Locating his authoritative source in "my worshipful master Will Caxton" as much as in Chaucer, Pynson situates printers in relations of mastery and servitude to one another that resemble those in which Caxton describes patronage relationships in his verse epilogue to *The Morale Prouerbes*; he thereby substantiates Alice Miskimin's point that early modern editors tended to take one another's texts, rather than manuscripts, as their sources.[91]

Yet if Pynson demonstrates his fidelity to Caxton through his reproduction of Chaucer, his reproduction of *The Morale Prouerbes* strikingly departs from Caxton's earlier edition. Christine's text appears in the third (and last) volume that Pynson published of Chaucer's collected works, which is entitled, following Caxton's 1483 edition, *The booke of fame, made by Geffray Chaucer: with Dyuers other of his Workes*. Together with *The House of Fame* and several of Chaucer's short poems, the volume includes a number of apocryphal works presented as Chaucer's, exemplifying the principle of editorial inflation that led to the expansion of the Chaucer canon in the sixteenth-century editions.[92] Among the apocryphal works that Pynson prints is Christine's *Prouerbes*, introduced thus: "here foloweth certayne moral p[ro]uerbes of the foresayd Geffray Chaucers doyng."[93] Under this heading fall Chaucer's short poem "Truth" or the "Balade de Bon Conseyl," and after it a set of verses entitled "Morall prouerbes of Christyne."[94] Pynson thereby retains Caxton's title, *The Morale Prouerbes of Christyne*, but rewrites the text's authorship.[95] Instead of crediting Christine as "aucteresse," as had Woodville, Pynson causes "Christyne" to be subsumed under the authorial name of Geoffrey Chaucer by classifying *Christine's Prouerbes* as Chaucer's work. With no indication of separate authorship—the verses' end is merely signaled "Thus endeth the morall proverbes"—readers are invited to read them as "of the foresayd Geffray Chaucers doyng." The figure of "Christyne" named in the title appears less as an author than as a female voice produced by Chaucer, in much the same way that "the compleynt of Anelida" is manifestly of Chaucer's making in *Anelida and Arcite*. In Pynson's *Morall Prouerbes*, the name "Christine" remains in the work's title as a residue of female authorship in much the same way that the name "Dame Christine" in Scrope's and Worcester's translations marked an absence where earlier Christine had inscribed herself.[96]

As the text's title indicates, Pynson clearly used Caxton's 1478 edition of Christine as his source and thus had more than ample evidence that Christine de Pizan, and not Chaucer, was the author of *The Morall Prouerbes*; but in his reascription of the text Pynson further shows that the construction of authorship in early print culture had less to do with the evidence of who wrote a text than it did with an effort to shape the figure of the author as the text's organizing principle. The early sixteenth-century editors' practice of expanding the Chaucerian canon by incorporating ever-greater numbers of apocryphal texts into his published corpus has been dismissed by modern editors as a mark of their carelessness or greed, as each tried to market a larger text than his predecessors or rivals. But more recently the Chaucerian apocrypha have been seen as part of a larger effort to fashion Chaucer's place in literary culture and history and have been therefore read for the ways in which they shape Chaucer as an authorial figure.[97] Similarly, Pynson's absorption of Christine de Pizan into Chaucer's works shows how the making of Chaucer into an exemplary English author was built, on the local level of Pynson's text, upon the unmaking of Christine de Pizan.

Pynson's three-part edition of Chaucer in 1526 offered the first comprehensive collection of Chaucer's works, and as such it initiated a new model for Chaucer in print. Presenting in a bibliographical form the idea of a Chaucerian canon as a coherent whole, Pynson's edition constructs the figure of the author as the work's principal source of unity; but the task of shaping Chaucer as a figure of textual unity forced Pynson to reconcile the numerous and contradictory versions of Chaucer already in circulation. Before 1526 Chaucer maintained a divided literary-historical reputation; while poetry such as "Truth" appealed to Henrician literary tastes for moral and edifying work, his other works like *The House of Fame* seemed to disclaim the very position of public authority that the sixteenth-century English readers craved from the figures of their national literary past.[98] As "the King's printer," Pynson showed an interest in humanist texts and works of instruction that reflects his sensitivity to Henrician tastes.[99] At the same time, in this office Pynson himself was called on to print the royal edicts that throughout the 1520s increasingly restricted the circulation and printing of works in English, thus contributing to a new and increasingly anxious awareness of the powers and dangers of vernacular literary culture. Pynson's edition of Chaucer participates in what I take to be a larger cultural effort to redirect English literary production and consumption to a broader realm of social utility by fashioning Chaucer in the model of the public teacher. But accomplishing this also forced Pynson to confront Chaucer's sometime reputation as a love poet, which compromised his ability to function as a voice of morality.[100]

In his effort to build a monumental Chaucer for a Henrician readership, Pynson addresses Chaucer's divided reputation in the volume that is dedicated to *The House of Fame*—the work in which

Chaucer's literary authority is most visibly unstable—by both invoking and containing Chaucer's associations with what *The House of Fame* itself calls "tydynges of love." In the pages that follow *The Booke of Fame,* Pynson reprints a number of apocryphal works that bear out Julia Boffey's suggestion that the Chaucerian apocrypha might be seen as "responses to, or extensions of, the main themes in the canonical works."[101] As well as the "Morall prouerbes of Christyne," this section includes "The Letter of Dydo to Eneas," which Boffey persuasively reads as an extension of Chaucer's meditation on Dido in *The House of Fame,* and, immediately preceding "The Morall prouerbes," "La Bele Dame Sans Mercy," a love debate actually written by Alain Chartier and translated by Richard Roos, although Pynson frames it as Chaucer's translation. "La Bele Dame Sans Mercy" would appear to confirm Chaucer's early modern reputation as a love poet grounded in French genres and conventions, as it looks back to a model *cour amoureuse* that is notably distanced from the public and edifying genres expected of an English national poet.[102] But in Pynson's edition it is extended and, I suggest, contained by what is labeled "lenuoy de limprimeur," in which the printer steps back to frame the text not as a courtly erotic entertainment but as a warning against the dangers of love:

> And ye ladyes / endued with hye prudence
> Whan these diceitfull louers labour styll
> With their fayned and paynted eloquence
> Their carnall lustes to cause you to fulfyll
> Many a huge othe / depose they wyll
> yet for all that / take hede aboue alle thyng
> It is no loue they shewe / but blandisshyng. (sig. Ciii)

This envoy, as James E. Blodgett points out, appears to be original to Pynson and differs entirely from the conclusion of the poem in the manuscript versions.[103] Its accomplishment is to reframe the text from a love poem to a warning against love and, by extension, to reshape Chaucer from an alleged love poet to an anti-love poet, who writes instead warnings to ladies to eschew love and its dangers.

If the poem does not sound like Chaucer, the writer it does sound like, in the moral critique it wages against courtly love, is Christine de Pizan. And indeed, the end of this section leads directly into "certayne moral p[ro]uerbes of the foresayd Geffray Chaucers doyng," in which Chaucer's short poem "Truth" is followed by "The Morall prouerbes of Christyne," just as "La Belle Dame Sans Mercy" is followed by Pynson's own "Ienuoy de limprimeur." The effect of the textual packaging of "Chaucer's" works is the same: in both cases, Pynson frames works presented as Chaucer's in order to depict him as a poet of public morality, an effort whose intended cumulative effect is to counteract and contain Chaucer's dubious reputation as a love poet.

Given the fifteenth- and early sixteenth-century taste for poetry addressing issues of public morality, it is not surprising that the short, Boethian poem "Truth" was one of Chaucer's most widely attested poems during this period, presenting Chaucer in an uncharacteristic mode of public address well suited to a Henrician male poet.[104] As George Pace and Alfred David describe it, "its counsel is for Every-man, [but] is especially appropriate to the man of affairs or states-man, that is to say, a man engaged very much like Chaucer himself in public life."[105] Highlighting the poem's moral stance, Pynson assigns "Truth" the central position in his edition of Chaucer's *House of Fame;* moreover, by appending the restyled *Morall Prouerbes* to "Truth" as the work of Chaucer, Pynson's edition offers a resolution to potential contemporary uncertainty about the public utility of poetry in general and about Chaucer's own authorial identity in particular by reforming his reputation as a poet of love and recrafting him instead as one dedicated to the public edification of men. The twenty-one lines of Chaucer's "Truth" present an author whose counsel to seek truth despite adversity delivers a level of moral certainty attractive to the model of public poetry. But despite the poem's injunction to "know thy contree," the "Truth" that it counsels its reader to seek is largely to be found outside the court: "Flee fro the prees [i.e., "crowd"] and dwelle with sothfastnesse," it advises, for "Prees hath envye" (1, 4). The addition of *The Morall Prouerbes* raises the short poem's focus to a more explicitly public and politic level. Where "Truth" counsels the reader to "Reule wel thyself" (13), *The Morall Prouerbes* suggests that self-rule will lead to self-advancement: "Grete diligence with a good Remembrance / Dooth a man ofte to hygh honneur auance" ("Diligence grant soing et souuenir / Homme souuent fait a grant bn venir"). And where "Truth" addresses the individual, *The Morall Prouerbes* reminds individuals that they belong to a larger social structure, are subject to a prince's rule, but are also capable, through study, of playing a part in the state's diplomatic machinery. Such a message is calculated to appeal to the Henrician court for which Pynson packaged his edition of Chaucer, as well as making a case for the utility of literature to the state. The text thereby contributes materially to Chaucer's reshaping as an author of public edification by making him into the model of the new courtier, the gentleman administrator who flourished in the royal household.[106] By incorporating *The Morall Prouerbes* into his edition of Chaucer, Pynson confronts and redirects early modern perceptions of medieval English poetry, transforming it, through the newly canonical figure of Chaucer, into work befitting the public and moral instruction of men.

The elevation of vernacular literature as a site of aristocratic, secular learning that takes hold in the Fastolf household of the mid-fifteenth century was solidified in the court of Henry VIII, which installed Chaucer as its figurehead. Authorizing the work of printers such as Pynson as well as a new generation of aristocratic book owners and poets, the early Henrician court could be considered, as James A. Blodgett suggests, "an unofficial center for Chaucer studies."[107] Once carefully aligned with the interests of the monarchy over potential agents of religious or baronial dissent, Chaucer would become an emblem of linguistic and national purity; as such, he attained special, protected status from the repeated attempts to ban or restrict works printed in the vernacular in the early years of Tudor censorship before and after the Act of Supremacy.[108] Chaucer's adoption as a state poet was promoted by early editions by Pynson and William Thynne, which were both produced under Henry's direct patronage. Such editions helped establish Chaucer as the first poet of an officially sanctioned English literature not only by bringing his work into line with public interest, but also by bringing the model of textual patronage and community initiated in the aristocratic household into the royal court as a new mechanism of state control.

But if Pynson promotes a form of literate, noble masculinity on behalf of the English state in his edition of Chaucer, he betrays its French, female origins in his reprinting of "The Morall prouerbes of Christyne."[109] If this new courtly literacy would settle in the state-sanctioned figure of Chaucer, the vestigial name of "Christine" that remains in Pynson's title recalls that it was invented by Christine de Pizan. Making Chaucer into a poet of the English state meant at one level appropriating to him the critical stances and enunciatory postures that had been crafted by Christine de Pizan to describe the place of the female counselor. If the mention of "Christyne" in the title recalls Christine's literary-historical importance to the development of this discourse, the text's embeddedness in the edition of *The House of Fame* emblematizes Chaucer's emergence in her place.

Les proverbes moraulx followed the fortune of Christine's other works in being absorbed into a textual community of men, even as it, like her other works, helped to define the new masculinity that shaped its reception. Pynson's absorption of *The Morall Prouerbes* into his edition of Chaucer thus participates in a gradual but decisive shift in Christine's reception in England. Christine's fortune in early English print culture follows an opposite tack from Chaucer's: while early editions expanded Chaucer's corpus to include texts that he never wrote, Christine's corpus contracted as editors and translators attempted to reconcile the evidence of her textual practice with an increasingly masculinized literary culture that her works were seen to address. In Pynson's edition, the emergence of Chaucer's masculine authorship into fully sanctioned, cultural centrality is supported by the appropriation of Christine's construction of "the woman writer" in the *Proverbes moraulx* as a literate counselor speaking from outside medieval clerical and courtly milieux. At the same time, Christine's name remains in the title as a vestigial reminder of its origins. Like the marginal figure of "Dame Christine" that haunts the paratexts of Scrope's and Worcester's translations, the name of "Christyne" in Pynson's edition marks the space where Chaucer's formation as a moral, public poet was shaped by Christine de Pizan, even if Christine herself would be thereby reduced to the status of a paratextual ghost.

The City of Ladies in the Library of Gentlemen

In 1521 the London printer Henry Pepwell published an English translation of what is perhaps Christine's best-known work today, *Le livre de la cité des dames,* as *The Boke of the Cyte of Ladyes.*[110] The translation is unusually faithful to Christine's original, and Pepwell appears to have made no efforts to disguise the work's female authorship within its body: the text retains Christine's name throughout, and it features a specially commissioned woodcut of Christine at work in her study that recalls the book's by now well-known opening scene (Figure 2). In it, Christine is at work in her study, "sollitaire et soubstraitte du monde," when she happens upon a book about women by a certain Mathéolus. Sampling its contents, she discovers it to be a misogynist satire and puts it aside; but even closing the book will not put it out of her mind, and she finds herself overwhelmed by the pervasive antifeminism that the book shares with the work of "solemn scholars, possessed of such deep and great understanding." ("si sollempnelz clercs de tant hault et grant entendement").[111] In despair, she is suddenly visited by the three allegorical female figures of

Figure 2. Christine de Pizan in Her Study, *The Boke of the Cyte of Ladyes* (London: Henry Pepwell, 1521). Reproduced with permission of the British Library (C.13.a.18).

Reason, Rectitude (or "Droiture"), and Justice, who console her by rebuking clerical misogyny and guiding her to construct a revisionary history of women in the City of Ladies.

In its resurrection of women's stories that have been forgotten by traditional historiography, Christine's *Cité des dames* resonates with the project of women's history today. And there is evidence that the book was interpreted at least in visual iconographical traditions as a strong support of female power, inspiring a set of tapestries that were owned by early modern queens, as the recent work of Susan Groag

Bell shows.[112] But Pepwell's edition of the book also gives evidence of another line of reception that was consistent with the work of Christine's other early English readers, who adopted her works as guides for a new class of literate gentlemen. In a verse prologue to the 1521 book that commends it to his potential readers and his noble patron, Pepwell situates *The Boke of the Cyte of Ladyes* within a model of aristocratic literary culture that self-consciously recalls both the conventions of masculine alliance and service promoted by writers such as Scrope and Worcester within the Fastolf household, as well as those conventions for representing patronage that Caxton established in his paratextual addresses to Woodville. Negotiating the Henrician courtly print culture with what were by 1521 increasingly dated versions of aristocratic masculinity, Pepwell's prologue once again renders Christine herself marginal to the lines of masculine textual exchange deemed central to the book's production:

> The kyndly entente / of euery gentylman
> Is the furtheraunce / of all gentylnesse.
> And to procure / in all that euer he can.
> for to renewe / all noble worthynesse.
> This dayly is sene / at our eye expresse.
> Of noble men / that do endyte and rede.
> In bokes olde / theyr worthy myndes to fede.
>
> ¶ So nowe of late / came in my custodye.
> This foresayd boke / by Bryan Anslay.
> Yoman of the seller / with the eyght kynge Henry
> Of gentylwomen / the excellence to say
> The whiche I lyked / but yet I made delay
> It to impresse / for that it is the guyse.
> Of people lewde / theyr prowesse to dyspyse.
>
> ¶ But then I shewed / the foresayd boke
> Unto my lorde / the gentyll Erle of kente
> And hym requyred / theron to loke.
> With his counsayle / to put it in to prente
> And he forthwith / as euer dylygente
> Of ladyes (abrode) to sprede theyr royall fame.
> Exhorted me / to prynte it in his name.
>
> ¶ And I obeyenge gladly his instaunce
> Have done my deuoyre / of it to make an ende
> Prayenge his lordshyp / with others [that] shall chaunce
> On it to rede / the fautes for to amende

> If ony be / for I do fayne intende
> Gladly to please. and wylfully remytte
> This ordre rude / to them that have fresshe wytte.
>   Thus endeth the prologue[113]

Pepwell's prologue situates the book within a narrative of textual circulation among men: the text is made to be *"by* Brian Anslay," who is in fact the book's translator, but Anslay shares responsibility for the book's production with the other men who authorize it through the bonds of patronage. Just as Anslay serves the king as "yoman of the seller with the eyght King Henry," Pepwell himself is similarly bound to serve "my lorde / the gentyll Erle of kente."[114] If Pepwell's courtly subservience to Richard Grey, the Earl of Kent, seems deliberately to court comparison to Caxton's relation to his own "Earl Rivers" in tone, it most certainly does in genealogy: Woodville was Grey's uncle.[115] And where Woodville was the owner of Christine's magnificent manuscript, British Library MS Harley 4431, and the translator of her works, Pepwell invites Grey to reproduce the literary tastes of his famous relative by offering his patronage to a latter-day edition of Christine's works. While the prologue seems directly to cite the conventions of male patronage and textual exchange that were earlier authorized by Fastolf or Woodville, here the sheltering figure of Henry VIII indicates that such patronage circuits have been effectively centralized and contained within the royal court, which has become the new center of gentlemanly literary practice.[116]

Strikingly, Pepwell's narrative prologue makes no mention of Christine de Pizan but instead effectively displaces women from any potential position of control in literary production. Relocating Christine's books within masculine textual communities follows a practice that Scrope and Worcester established in their manuscript translations by displacing their female author, as "Dame Christine," to the margins of their texts and the communities of men—from the imaginary clerks to the Fastolf circle—held to be responsible for them. Similarly, Pepwell, by resituating the text's genesis in a community that binds patron, translator, and printer, also displaces Christine to the margins of the text's production. But unlike *Le livre des faits d'armes,* *L'epistre d'Othea,* and even *Les proverbes moraulx,* which could more easily be appropriated for masculine literary circles, *Le livre de la cité des dames* seems a singularly illogical choice of text to package for gentlemen readers, given the overtly feminine title and the subject, a monumental history of women directed against clerical misogyny. Despite his effort to market the text to "every gentylman" in the prologue, Pepwell did not try to disguise its female authorship, unlike the French manuscripts and editions that excised every reference to Christine's femininity; instead, both the opening woodcut and the book's table of contents foreground Christine's importance to the text by picturing or naming her directly. That the book's female authorship was evident at least to one early reader is attested by an annotation in the British Library's copy of *The Boke of the Cyte of Ladyes*, which glosses a reference to "Xpine" thus: "The auctors name. w[hich] was a woma[n]."[117] It is my argument here that Pepwell self-consciously invokes the conditions and positions that Christine associated with female authorship, but does so in order to arrogate them to the gentlemen readers to whom he directs his book. Pepwell's aim in the prologue is to convince a new breed of courtiers of the utility of printed texts like his own for their advancement. He thus promotes and fulfills a pattern of reception whose development runs from Scrope and Worcester through Caxton and Pynson, by taking the literature that Christine shaped for a new community of literate women and turning it into the basis of a literary culture of men.

The story that Pepwell recounts in his prologue concerning the book's production directly invokes and revises Christine's own narrative of her book's genesis, captured in the woodcut that opens the 1521 edition. Where the *Cité des dames* depicts Christine alone in her study perusing ancient books when she comes across one concerning the reverence of women ("la reverence des femmes"), Pepwell sets up a similar scenario, describing himself in perusal of "bokes old" when he finds diversion in a book that, like Christine's, concerns the "excellence" "of gentylwomen."[118] Both Christine and Pepwell are then led to muse on the politics of reading and writing about women in a literary culture that is ruled by misogyny. For Christine, of course, this narrative forms the pretext of *Le livre de la cité des dames*, the three books of which will go on to establish an alternative history of women to counter the misogyny of clerks. Pepwell too declares himself to be an enemy of misogyny; but in his prologue, Christine's critique of clerical misogyny is transformed into a meditation on printing, class, and patronage. Having discovered *The Book of the City of Ladies* ("this foresayd boke . . . Of gentylwomen / the excellence to say"), Pepwell maintains that, while he approved of the text, he initially hesitated to print it for fear of popular disapprobation: "it is the guyse // of people lewde / theyr [i.e., women's] prowesse to dyspyse." Where Christine targets clerical misogyny, Pepwell targets the misogyny of popular printed works such as *The Gospeles of Dystaves*, printed by Wynkyn de Worde in 1510, which found wide circulation for their satirical portraits of women's vices.[119]

If "lewde" people blame women, however, it will take Pepwell's noble patron to intervene in their defense, since he is "euer dylygent / of ladyes." The claim recalls Caxton's earlier comment on Anthony Woodville and the "affecyon, love, and good wylle that he hath unto alle ladyes and gentylwomen." But where Caxton views Woodville's solicitude toward "all Ladyes" as a mark of outdated courtliness, Pepwell invokes Grey's similar solicitude—with a hint of nostalgia—as a sign of cultural refinement. The defense of "ladyes" becomes for Pepwell a marker of a specifically literary taste that distinguishes the "lewd" genre of antifeminism from the "gentle" genre of the defense of ladies—a distinction that appears not to have been observed among book owners—to make the act of reading and writing about women into an index of class positions among men.[120] Where Christine sees the defense of women as a necessary precondition for women's entry into literary culture, for Pepwell that defense becomes primarily an act of publication and textual circulation that takes place within an aristocratic masculine community. Thus where Christine frames *La cité des dames* as a work of female literary self-assertion, Pepwell frames *The Cyte of Ladyes* as an intervention in a battle between a high and low culture of the printed book.

This aristocratic phobia against the popular press and its cultural contaminations anticipates the "stigma of print" of the later sixteenth century that drove Elizabethan aristocratic writers to the private circulation of coterie manuscripts instead.[121] While records of book ownership show that readers did not themselves observe distinctions between "popular" and "elite" genres in distribution among readers of different classes, Pepwell's attempt to create such a distinction, even where none may have existed, reflects his effort both to follow Caxton in his cultivation of aristocratic patrons and to offer aristocratic readers like Grey a literature of nobility—as well as to extend such a literature to potential nonaristocratic readers who wished to model their literary tastes and purchases on the habits of their social betters.

By making literature the point of definition for aristocratic masculinity, Pepwell recalls Scrope's earlier efforts to redefine knighthood, on the model of Christine's redefinition of chivalry, as an exercise of learning and virtue. Where Scrope's model of "ghostly chivalry" made the consumption of books into the spiritual equivalent of the

performance of martial acts, for Pepwell "the furtheraunce / of all gentylnesse" is achieved not through fighting or landownership but
through study.[122] This model of gentleness as a social rather than an
inherited virtue, familiar from the Wife of Bath's conception of "gen-
tilesse," recalls Christine's own words about "gentillece vraye" from
her *Proverbes moraulx*: "Gentillece vraye nest autre chose / Fors le
vaissel our vertue se repose" ("Trewe gentillesse can be noon other
thing / But the palais where honneur is dwellyng": significantly,
Woodville's translation removes "gentillesse" to a courtly architec-
tural setting, by placing it in a "palais").[123] But for Pepwell, the preeminent site for the cultivation of gentleness is the private library or
study, where men apply their minds to "bokes olde." Pepwell's reference to the "noble men / that do endyte and rede // In bokes olde /
theyr worthy myndes to fede" could be imagined to hold a special va-
lence in Henry VIII's bookish court. At the same time that the Henrician court offered a highly developed literary culture under a king
who was himself an accomplished poet, the aristocracy itself underwent changes both within and without that demanded modification
of the traditional avenues of knightly activity and made them particularly receptive to the notion of a revised chivalry of the book.[124] Pepwell's patron, Richard Grey, was present with Henry VIII at the Field
of the Cloth of Gold in 1520, the ultimate demonstration of chivalry's
transformation from a martial to an ornamental social practice.[125] But
the Henrician aristocracy underwent changes that were demographic
as well as cultural. In 1521, men like Grey faced particular hardship
under the more traditional avenues of aristocratic self-perpetuation.
Like many Henrician aristocrats, he was threatened by insolvency
and the lack of a male heir; indeed, after Grey's death in 1524, three
years after Pepwell's *Cyte of Ladyes*, Henry VIII dissolved the earl-
dom.[126] In the face of the dissolution of Grey's name and title—a fate
that awaited many of his peers from old families—Pepwell's offer to
print his book "in his name" gave him a way to perpetuate his name
and influence through the mechanical reproduction of the press, despite his failure to do so himself through biosocial means. And by
grounding the production and dissemination of texts in the service of
"the furtheraunce / of all gentylnesse" and the "renew[al]" of "all noble worthyness," Pepwell describes his work as a printer by using the
tropes of patrilineage and aristocratic succession. These tropes might
have been imagined to appeal to a court that was as aware of the problems of biosocial reproduction as Henry VIII's was—indeed, by 1521
the king was deeply concerned about his own reproductive troubles

and lack of a legitimate heir, making the Henrician court a site in which patrilinear reproduction was in crisis.[127] By offering the press as a means of perpetuating noble names and influence, Pepwell creates books in place of patrilineage as the site of English cultural renewal.

But Pepwell's promotion of his book in the service of "the furtheraunce / of all gentylnesse" established a special appeal to the new ranks of nobles who came to join the aristocracy, thanks to Henry's willingness to replenish its dwindling ranks by creating new titles at an unprecedented rate.[128] To these new aristocrats, Pepwell's lesson in gentleness calculatedly suggests that the refinement and social conduct of the nobility were functions less of birth than of correct reading material, assuring readers that through books "noble men" are able "to procure / in all that euer [they] can // for to renewe / all noble worthynesse." Reading defenses of women such as *The Boke of the Cyte of Ladyes* allows this new nobility to participate in the cultural practices that distinguished the old aristocracy, like Grey and Woodville. Therefore, the mixture of social conservatism and nostalgia that pervades Pepwell's prologue, together with the suggestion that it is possible to tell a nobleman from what he reads, wage a careful appeal to the new aristocratic readers of Henry's court eager to establish themselves in their titles. Pepwell thus frames Christine's defense of women within the textual conventions of the book of instruction for gentlemen that was popular in the sixteenth century among a new generation of literate knights. In this context, *The Boke of the Cyte of Ladyes*, as Pepwell presents it, forms a late outpost of the model of literate, aristocratic masculinity in which Scrope and Worcester present their earlier translations of Christine's *Faits d'armes* and *Epistre d'Othea*, a model dedicated both to teaching knights how to uphold the social functions of their calling and to convincing them of the importance of literature to this undertaking.[129] Where Scrope and Worcester aimed to convince their would-be patron Fastolf that chivalry could be as well exercised in the library and in the act of moral education as on the battlefield by analogizing the two experiences, for the nobility and newly created aristocrats to whom Pepwell addressed his book, the library took the place of the battlefield as the proving ground of knightly virtue.

As with Scrope's and Worcester's translations, in Pepwell's edition Christine's displacement to the margins of this masculine textual community does not elide her presence entirely but rather gives it a new form. If the woodcut opening Pepwell's *Boke* invokes the terms of the original's initial scene, which Pepwell's prologue would appropriate to gentlemen readers, it also enforces Christine's own distance from that gentlemanly community through iconography. While the woodcut appears to visually cite the illumination of the same subject from Harley 4431, it replaces Christine's trademark *cotehardie*, the headdress denoting upper-class status in which she appears in all the book's illuminations, with a widow's barb and veil, which, as Martha Driver has pointed out, closely resembles the iconography of religious women from woodcuts that Pepwell had previously printed of Saints Bridget and Catherine of Siena, who are likewise depicted in solitary scenes with books, dressed similarly in veils (see Figures 3 and 4 in Chapter 3).[130] By picturing Christine as a religious woman, the woodcut recasts her opening position, "sollitaire et soubstraitte du monde," as one of religious confinement, recalling Worcester's confected biography of Christine as a woman who was born, lived, and died in the cloister of Poissy. Where Worcester's account of "Dame Christine" removes her from the scene of masculine textual production, represented by the communities of the imaginary clerks on the one hand and the Fastolf household on the other, Christine as pictured in Pepwell's opening woodcut is removed from the scene of gentlemanly reading and textual exchange that Pepwell invokes in his prologue. In contrast to Pepwell's study, which he depicts as a place of self-fashioning that opens out into the larger social world of the court, Christine's study as depicted in the woodcut is a space of religious enclosure that separates her from that world.

The distinction that Pepwell's edition establishes in its opening pages between the study of the literate, courtly gentleman and that of the religious woman, Christine herself, displaces the debt that Pepwell's definition of literate, courtly masculinity owes to Christine's own discussions of female literacy and wisdom. But that debt explains his otherwise puzzling decision to print Christine's text at all; moreover, it helps to illuminate how a book like *Le livre de la cité des dames* could have been read in the contexts in which Pepwell directed it. If Christine's other texts such as *Les proverbes moraulx* seek to fashion "l'homme prudent" (the prudent man), while advocating to princes the importance of a "prudent gou[ve]neur" (prudent governer), *La cité des dames* undertakes a thorough exposition of the value of "prudence" through examples and discussion. Crucially, prudence underlies women's claim to intellectual equality with men, as it does as well Christine's response to clerical misogyny: while "clercs" may have mastered the formal institutions of learning, this in no way is to be equated with prudence, she insists: "I am baffled when eminent scholars—including some of the most famous and learned—exhibit so little prudence in their morals and conduct in the world" (87) ("toutesvoyes a maint, en y a meismes de plus reputtés, grans clers et plains de science, voit on aucuneffoiz assez petite prudence en meurs et en gouvernement mondain, dont j'ai grant merveille" [762]). On the other hand, prudence ("which is called 'natural sense,'" as Reason defines it [87]), is a gift that is not restricted to those of formal learning, and it is one of which women are in ample possession. Christine prompts Reason into a long discussion confirming as much when she asks her whether women are "clever in those matters which prudence teaches, that is, whether women can reflect on what is best to do and what is better to be avoided, and whether they remember past events and become learned from the examples they have seen, and, as a result, are wise in managing current affairs, and whether they have foresight into the future. Prudence, it seems to me, teaches those lessons" (87) ("Si [l'entendement de femme . . .] est autresi prompt et habille es choses qui prudence enseigne. C'est assavoir que elles ayent avis sur ce qui est le meilleur a faire et ad ce qui doit estre laissié, souvenance des choses passees, par quoy soyent plus expertes par l'exemple que ont veu, sages ou governement des choses presentes, qu'elles ayant pourveance sus celle a advenir. Ces choses, comme il me semble, enseigne prudence" [762]).

If prudence is the defining characteristic of Christine's heroines in the *City of Ladies*, it is also a notably practical virtue that demonstrates women's aptitude for intellectual public service of the kind that Christine saw herself to be offering in her writing. Where prudence indicates a knowledge of past events, current affairs, and even foresight into things to come, it is fulfilled in Christine's text by the sibyls, who hold pride of place in Book 2. The sybils, as Christine describes them, are not only supremely knowledgeable in all such areas, they demonstrate the importance of this knowledge to monarchs and rulers. The sybil Delphica "foretold long in advance the destruction of Troy" ("predit longtemps devant la desruccion de Troye"), while Erythrea, "at the Greeks' request, . . . described [in song] their struggles and battles" ("a la requeste des Grieux descript tante clerement en dittiez leur labours [et] les battailles"), which she recorded in twenty-seven poems.[131] The sybil Almathea produces books of her prophecies, which she offers to Tarquin of Rome; when he refuses to pay her asking price, she destroys them three at a time until he relents, and her books subsequently become treasured guides that are

consulted by all subsequent emperors. From the example of Almathea
Christine presents this lesson, which encapsulates Christine's model
of the female courtier-counselor: "consider how God bestowed such
great favor on a single woman who possessed the insight to counsel
and advise not only one emperor during his lifetime but also, as it
were, all those who were to come into Rome as long as the world lasts,
as well as to comment upon all the affairs of the empire" ("prens cy
garde, doulce amye, et vois comment Dieux donna si grant grace a
une seulle femme que elle ot scens de conseiller et adviser non mie
seullement un empereur a son vivant mais si comme tous ceulx
qui le monde durant estoyent a avenir a Romme et tous les faiz de
l'empire").[132] The sibyls thus represent forms of knowledge that are
above all politically expedient, producing what Helen Solterer calls
"visionary advice," offered in the form of "a type of civic ethics."[133]
As figures who are gifted with "foresight into the future" ("pourveance"), the sibyls exemplify the virtue of prudence that is articulated
in the *Proverbes moralx:* "He is prudent that maketh pourveyance /
For thing to come before er falle the chance" ("Cil est prudent qui au
temps futur vise / Sil y pourvoit et son meilleur avise").[134] And as they
show in the examples that Christine cites, that knowledge is most
valuable of all when it can be put in the service of princes' counsel.

Maureen Quilligan notes that the sibyls in Christine's text fulfill
the crucial function of "manifesting by their appearance to Christine
the previously secret, hidden wisdom of female power in the world,"
and it is clear that the sibyls crucially help to authorize the model
of female literacy that Christine attempts to shape throughout her
work.[135] But Pepwell's 1521 edition suggests that the sibyls also represented a set of qualities that were desirable for the class of literate,
courtly gentlemen Pepwell addresses in his prologue. Like these gentlemen, the sibyls are royal counselors who secure patronage for their
intellectual labor without holding office themselves. Their model of
influence from the margins reiterates Christine's ongoing project to
validate a new class of counselors who could wield power not directly but through their influence on those inhabiting official positions of power. They thus complete Christine's self-fashioning in
texts like the *Epistre* or the *Proverbes moraulx* as a female teacher
and arbiter of a new class of courtly literati by embodying prudence as
the virtue of good governance. But the model that the sibyls present
also addresses the interests of the new class of English aristocrats and
courtiers who were brought into Henry's court to influence those
in positions of power from the margins.[136] To these men Pepwell's
Boke of the Cyte of Ladyes offers a primer in seeing the office of the

subordinate as one that, while not revolutionary or radically threatening to social structure, could take its place within that structure.[137] Thus Christine's story of gender becomes for Henrician readers a story about class that shows how hierarchy need not bring silence to those who are subjugated by it, as well as demonstrating the utility of learning and rhetorical skill to those unable to secure their social status through the traditional avenues of male privilege.

If the sybils help to illustrate the political uses of prudence, they are also cogent emblems of the woman writer's modernity as she is crafted throughout Christine's works. They are able to see into the future because they are profoundly displaced themselves and literally stand outside of time. As Christine reports, although they were born pagans, they were able to foresee Christianity: "they prophesied quite clearly Jesus Christ and His coming, just as has been said. And yet they were all pagans and did not follow the law of the Jews" (100) ("Toutes prophetisierent grans choses a avenir et par especial de Jhesu Crist et son avenement tres clerement, si que dit est. Et toutesvoies furent elles toutes payennes et non mie de la loy des Juyfs" [780]). In this they resemble the female saints of Book 3, whose sufferings mark the historical passage out of a pagan past into a Christian future. As time-travelers, the sybils are inevitably misunderstood in their own age, as is Cassandra, whose father and brother attempt to shut her away and so to silence her prophecies: "if they wanted to have any peace, they had to shut her up in a room far away from people in order to get her racket out of their ears. However, it would have been better for them if they had believed her, for everything which she had predicted happened to them, and so finally they regretted not having listened, but it was too late for them" (107) ("se paix vouldrent avoir, qu'en une chambre longtaine de gens l'enffermassent pour oster sa noyse de leurs oreilles. Mais mieulx leur vaulsist l'avoir creue: car tout ce leur advint que predit leur avoit; si s'en repentirent a la parfin, mais ce fu trop tart pour eulx" [799]). In this, the sybils become modernity's scapegoated messengers: if they can foresee the destruction of the present in the future, they also attract the fear and violent denial that attend historical change.

As figures of a literary modernity, the sybils promise a new form of literate work in service to the state that in Pepwell's edition speaks directly to the position of the literate gentlemen of the prologue, who attempt to carve out new positions of influence in the Henrician court that are neither clerical nor courtly in the traditional, medieval sense. The same terms by which Christine authorizes the woman writer, then, become in Pepwell's *Cyte of Ladyes* guides for self-fashioning offered to a new literary community of gentlemen.[138] But Pepwell's absorption of Christine into his masculine, Henrician setting is by no means complete: indeed, we might see the mismatch between Christine's and Pepwell's literary aims to be registered in the marginal comment cited earlier from the British Library copy, which notes of "Xpine," "the auctors name. w[hich] was a woman." While Pepwell's prologue contains no mention of the historical Christine de Pizan, Christine is everywhere in this book, which, as many scholars have noted, asserts its author's name and identity to a degree unusual in a late medieval text.[139] Pepwell's woodcut of Christine in her study both acknowledges the book's female authorship and removes it to a setting that is markedly distant from the masculine study in which Pepwell sets his prologue to gentlemen readers. As I have argued, the iconography of Christine's presentation locates her in the monastic, cloistered setting that Pepwell's new gentlemen readers reject when they fashion themselves as literate but distinctly secular figures in the new Henrician court. "The woman writer" as Christine defines her thus becomes in an important way the enabling figure for the movement of literary production into the early Tudor court, which would become a key site of literary and textual production for the sixteenth century. But if "the woman writer" defines the role of those lay administrators and courtly literati, the uncomfortable representation of Christine, as in the woodcut of Pepwell's edition, demonstrates the ways in which the actual woman writer resisted assimilation into this new cultural milieu and still had to be maintained in a position marginal to it. As Pepwell's prologue shows, the new courtly literati defined the bonds of authorship as essentially communal, marked in circuits of patronage. To this model, Christine's self-defined marginality, "sollitaire et soubtraicte du monde," represents a threat to be contained and absorbed by the figure of "Dame Christine." Where for Christine "the woman writer" begins as an essentially solitary figure, the early English translations that proffer her representations of "the woman writer" to gentlemen readers render Christine herself, in the shape of "Dame Christine" or Pepwell's woodcut, an embodiment of qualities that must be banished to the margins—solitude, femininity—if these new gentlemen readers are to constitute themselves as a coherent masculine community.

Yet Christine de Pizan did not disappear completely from literary history. As these printed books show, she was woven into the fabric of late medieval and early modern English literary history, while her fashioning of "the woman writer" as a figure of prudent, literate counsel helped to facilitate the emergence of a new class of secular, literate gentlemen in England. It is a fitting coda to this chapter to recall the example of a text that was later ascribed to Christine de Pizan in a way that would erroneously, but suggestively, return her to English literary history as Chaucer's source. A manuscript now housed at the Pierpont Morgan Library, which Martha Driver has recently brought to light, contains a fifteenth-century French text, *Le roman de Melibee et de Prudence,* which is collated with excerpts from Chaucer's *Melibee.*[140] Those excerpts appear to have been supplied by the book's eighteenth-century owner, the English antiquarian Peter Le Neve, under the assumption that this *Roman de Melibee et de Prudence* was the source for Chaucer's text. Whether by Le Neve or a later reader, the French text was attributed to Christine de Pizan, an attribution that was perpetuated by generations of bibliographers including Seymour de Ricci, and that remains in the Morgan Library catalogue.[141] Despite its mistakenness, the attribution follows a logic that recalls the terms of Christine's earlier English circulation. Christine did in fact write *Le roman de prudence,* the text with which the ascriber appears to confuse *Le roman de Melibee et de Prudence.* Moreover, a printed edition of *Le roman de Melibee et de Prudence,* also in the Morgan, is bound with, and immediately preceded by, a French text entitled *L'ordre de cheualerie.* Given that in their afterlife in publication and translation Christine's texts were reascribed to men, it seems just compensation that a later bibliographer would ascribe to her a text that she did not write. But the ascription of *Le roman de Melibee et de Prudence* to Christine de Pizan also recalls the circumstances in which Christine's texts were read in the fifteenth- and sixteenth-century contexts that I have traced here. As in those contexts, this false ascription acts on the knowledge that an important component to Christine's later circulation was her invention of a concept of prudence, which would later become key, as I have argued, to her reception in English literary communities centered in the aristocratic household and the court. Similarly, her association with *L'ordre de cheualerie* recalls her historical refashioning of chivalric institutions in works like the *Faits d'armes* and *Epistre d'Othea,* which were no less important to her reception in fifteenth- and sixteenth-century England. The misascription points to the fact that Christine de Pizan did not disappear entirely in the course of her English circulation, despite the ways in which she was clearly made a marginal figure in the translations in which her texts were disseminated. Instead, her unexpected reappearance in the Morgan manuscript in the form of what Driver calls "a pseudo-Christine" represents a return of the textual repressed. Where Scrope and Worcester reassigned authorship of

Christine's *Epistre d'Othea* and *Faits d'armes* to nameless clerics, where Pynson's 1526 edition evacuated Christine from *Les proverbes moraulx* in all but the title to reassign authorship to Chaucer, and where Pepwell's *Cyte of Ladyes* replaced the scene of female authorship with one of gentlemanly patronage, the mistaken ascription of the Morgan manuscript belatedly acknowledges the cultural debt that early modern England owed to Christine, as the woman writer who revised medieval literary institutions to enable new modes of secular authorship, by making her the author who taught prudence to Chaucer.

Three

THE REFORMATION OF THE
WOMAN WRITER

English Literary History and the Pious Woman

Between 1520 and 1580, the religious, political, and cultural conflicts that attended the English Reformation brought together "English literary history" and "the woman writer" as parallel, and newly urgent, concerns. In historiographical terms, the Reformation has been seen more often as an interstitial period marking the end of one culture or the beginning of another than as a cultural moment in its own right. Viewed as the beginning of early modernity, it signals the rejection of the Roman church in England, the construction of a new religion of inwardness in its place, and the emergence of a new sense of distance from the historical past. Conversely, viewed as the end of the Middle Ages, the period represents a narrowing of cultural practices: the destruction of monastic centers of literacy and the cessation of England's link to the intellectual life of the continent.[1] Defined thus as a break between two cultures, the Reformation becomes a cultural vacuum itself, a period that "made an iconoclastic holocaust of the culture which already existed" (as Patrick Collinson paraphrases a prevailing view) and created nothing of its own but ruins.[2] Yet in a broader sense the Reformation can also be seen to have invented the very idea of English culture. The iconoclastic movement of the 1530s was motivated by the imperative to differentiate licit from illicit cultural practices and forms, and to separate strains of native English culture from the perceived taint of Rome. This imperative gave the period a new degree of self-consciousness about the uses and meanings of cultural objects and the complex relationship between past and present that they carried. Moreover, the cultural models that resulted were strongly dependent on notions of literacy and the book. For all its emphasis on visual icons and idols, the Reformation's preoccupation with the uses of books, the English vernacular, and popular literacy made it, as Brian Cummings has recently argued, a "pre-eminently literary event," in which books and literature became the ground on which new models of "Englishness" were formulated.[3]

The religious woman writer became a pivotal figure in Reformation efforts to shape and define English literary culture. Throughout what has been called "England's long Reformation," women's religious writing formed the subject of ongoing struggles between the agents and the opponents of reform to define orthodox religious practice and national identity.[4] At various points, both sides enlisted women's religious writing on their behalf, reflecting the liminal position that "the woman writer" had come to occupy within the discourses of medieval devotion. As a number of studies have recently shown, pious women in the Middle Ages could be alternately made figures of heresy or orthodoxy: in late medieval England the literate, pious woman was especially vulnerable to accusations of heresy, given the heretical Lollards' support of female literacy.[5] On the other hand, she could also be drafted as a powerful cultural symbol into the anti-Lollard campaign: one of the most calculated acts of Henry V, as part of his effort to strengthen the political ties of the church and wipe out Lollard heresy, was his foundation of Syon Abbey, the famous center of female literacy. This ambivalent medieval legacy made the religious woman writer a potential figure of both orthodoxy and dissent during the Reformation. Moreover, as the relative meanings of these terms shifted, so too did the meaning of the religious woman writer, making her a flashpoint within the debates that surrounded the spread of vernacular literacy and book ownership, the distinctions between licit and illicit cultural practices, and ultimately, I will argue, the contruction of an English literary history to ground a new national identity.

This chapter follows several editors of women's religious writing over the contentious decades from 1520 to 1580, whose work reflected and intervened in the broader cultural struggles of the English

Reformation. Common among them is an interest in shaping the devotional genre of female prayer. Prayer was a privileged literary genre for women before and after the Reformation, not only as a form of devotional reading but also as a form of writing that, by virtue of its origin and destination in the divine, allowed women to disclaim the forms of worldly self-interest that other forms of authorship involved.[6] Thus the majority of surviving texts written by late medieval and early modern Englishwomen take the form of prayers or pious meditations, from the anonymous female author of the Middle English prayers called *The Feitis and the Passion of Our Lord Jhesu Crist* (c. 1450), written for her "religious sister," to Catherine Parr, the royal author of *Prayers Stirryng the Mynd unto Heavenlye Medytacions* (1545), written within the Queen's coterie of Protestant women, and Elizabeth Tudor herself, whose translation, *The Miroir or Glasse of the Synnefull Soule* (1548), was dedicated to Parr and later published by John Bale.[7] But over the period of Reformation such devotional writing by women became the subject of a larger debate about the meanings and uses of prayer in religious life, which was played out as a struggle to define not only the cultural place of the woman writer but also, and in interrelated ways, the uses of the book as a religious object.

The changing fortunes of the pious woman writer over the contentious decades of the English Reformation show how the seemingly private writings of women—especially in the genre of female prayer—could carry meanings of the highest political significance. To those who sought to mediate those writings to a broader reading public, the task of representing the woman writer advanced the larger task of shaping England's past, present, and future. Endowing the publication of women's writing with a heightened level of importance, these editors produced key terms to describe their work and its subjects that have continued to define women writers—among them, the notion of a "lost" history of women writers, the "recovery" of that history from cultural darkness, and the centrality of "experience" to the truth of women's writing. In the process, they not only give new form to the figure of the woman writer, they reveal that figure to have been instrumental to the production of England's literary and religious identity during the Reformation.

The Fifteen Oes and the Reformation of Devotion

The history of "the woman writer" across the contentious period of the English Reformation is inseparable from the history of the book during this time. Central to the period's broader conflicts over heresy and doctrine were questions about the meanings and uses of books—which books could be read by whom and in what languages, what kinds of control printers had over their lists and the physical format of their books, and the proper attitudes and postures that devotional readers were expected to observe. A measure of the book's power during this period can be glimpsed in the numbers of official struggles that involved books: where the period began with the first mass book-burnings in opposition to Lutheran heresy, the spread of religious reform was marked by the dissolution and destruction of the monastic libraries, as well as the printing of the first English Bible and works such as John Foxe's *Acts and Monuments.* In these and related events, the reformation of England's religious identity was a reformation of the book.[8]

Of the contemporary narratives that were produced to support the cause of religious reform in England, one of the most resonant and durable was the claim that Protestantism emerged more or less directly from the printed book, a story whose most energetic proponent was John Foxe. Praising "The Invention and Benefit of Printing" for the Protestant cause, Foxe famously declares that through the press "tonges are known, knowledge groweth, judgment increaseth, books are dispersed, the Scripture is seen, the doctors be read, stories be opened, times compared, truth discerned, falsehood detected . . . through the light of printing the world beginneth now to have eyes to see, heads to judge."[9] Foxe's conviction that the printed book would lead directly to mass enlightenment and hence to religious reform reflects a teleological view of the Reformation as a natural outgrowth of the spread of literacy and book ownership, a view that has been echoed by modern accounts in which the rise of print is presented as organically interconnected with the rise of Protestantism.[10] However, to accept this narrative is to ignore the important role that the early press played before the Reformation in the service of Catholic religious practice, which suggests that the link between print and Protestantism was far from inevitable and had rather to be carefully engineered.[11] In the years between the introduction of the printing press into England and the Reformation, printers' book lists attest to the continued popularity in print of the books of hours and devotional works that were the staples of medieval manuscript culture; even after 1500, for example, Wynkyn de Worde is recorded to have printed three editions of Walter Hilton's *Scala Perfectionis,* eight editions of Richard Rolle's *Contemplacyons* and *Devoute Medytacyons,* three editions of *The Myracles of Oure Blessyd Lady,* two indulgences, and twelve books of hours.[12] Similarly, Richard Pynson, who printed Christine de Pizan's *Moral Proverbs* in his 1526 edition of Chaucer, established a flourishing career before the Reformation producing popular saints' lives, including those of St. Margaret (1493), St. Francis (1515?), St. Bridget (1516), St Thomas à Becket (1520?), St. Werburgh (1521), and St. Radegund (1521?).[13] Protestant printers, editors, and writers did not eschew the influence of their Catholic predecessors. The reformed primers that replaced medieval books of hours mimicked their textual ancestors in form and, to a surprising degree, content; indeed, even as unimpeachable a Protestant classic as Foxe's own *Acts and Monuments* shares some iconography with the detested *Legenda Aurea,* the immensely influential work of pre-Reformation hagiography that appeared in eight editions before 1527.[14] Rather than initiating a new culture of print where none had existed previously, the agents of Protestant print culture were forced to engage, appropriate, and reshape the conventions and expectations already established by those who had found the press to be a receptive medium for Catholicism.

A crucial cultural legacy of the pre-Reformation press with which Protestant printers would contend was its association with the textual practices of female devotion. The feminization of devotion as an English genre had begun in manuscript culture generations before the coming of print, as reflected in the frequency with which devotional treatises are addressed to women. Cultural associations linked women readers and devotional works, such as books of hours or saints' lives.[15] This gendering of the devotional genre may have some basis in the demography of devotional books' readership and patronage, as some studies have suggested.[16] The Bridgettine house of Syon Abbey, whose nuns were known to be avid consumers of such material, fostered the production of a number of Middle English devotional works, while records of patronage and book-giving indicate that these works were also popular among lay and noblewomen and formed the center of what Felicity Riddy calls a female literary subculture in the late Middle Ages.[17] While Caxton complained about the "gentyl yong ladyes and damoysellys" who "occupye theym and studye ouermoche in bokes of contemplacion," others of his colleagues were quick to capitalize on this perceived female market for devotional printed books.[18] Lady Margaret Beaufort headed a coterie of pious noblewomen who supported the printing of vernacular works of devotion such as the *Scala Perfectionis,* in recognition of which Wynkyn de Worde called himself "Prynter vnto the moost excellent Pryncess my lady the Kynges mother."[19] And, recording the names of less illustrious female owners and readers, books of hours and collections of English prayers suggest that the devotional genre found a widespread lay, female readership.[20]

It is difficult to gauge the actual female readership of devotional texts, given the uncertainty of measuring female literacy rates—and, indeed, the added complication that these texts' "readers" may have rather been listeners to texts read aloud.[21] Clearly men as well as women read these texts; yet so linked was the genre of devotion to a female readership in the literary culture that even authors who hoped to address a mixed-gender readership had to assure their male readers that their words applied to them as well. As one writes, "Þouȝ þis treatis and writyng after þe maner of spech be made to women allonly and þat for certeyn causys, yet every man hauyng discreccioun þat redis þerin may also take well hys lernyng and spirituall availe þerby as it had been written to hem also specially as it is written to women."[22] As well as attesting to women's historical importance in the development of vernacular works of devotion, the figure of the pious woman as represented in printed books also reflects printers' awareness of the spread of devotional book ownership and the privatization of religious textual practices.

Spurring the spread of devotional texts among religious and lay readers was the belief that the act of reading was an efficacious form of prayer. The readers of *The Ancren Riwle* are told that "reading is good prayer," while *The Myroure of Oure Ladye* informs its readers that "the devout redyng of holy bokes ys called one of the partes of contemplacyon."[23] The idea of reading as prayer undergirds the use of the medieval book of hours, with its sets of prescribed prayers to God, the Virgin, or the saints, as well as additional vernacular prayers that were sometimes also included in books of hours to be applied to quotidian needs, such as "when one rises in the morning," or "for the rain."[24] This model of prayerful reading was shared by women religious as well as laywomen, as the author of *Le ménagier de Paris* shows when he composes, along with directions in household management, a set of prayers for his young wife to read daily.[25]

Among the most ubiquitous of all devotional texts that the sixteenth century inherited from late medieval manuscript culture was a work by a woman—or one that was believed to be. *The Fifteen Oes*, a set of fifteen prayers in both Latin and vernacular so named after the vocative "O" with which each begins, invokes the Passion in emotional, visual terms—"O Jhesu heuenly leche haue mynde of thy langour and blewnes of thy wou[n]des and sorowe that thou suffredest in the heyght of the crosse"—and petitions Jesus for the speaker/reader's protection and health.[26] According to a legend that circulated widely with them, the prayers were believed to have been revealed to a "woman solatarie and recluse" when she wished to know the number of Christ's wounds.[27] That woman became identified, probably apocryphally, as St. Bridget of Sweden, whose *Revelations* were popular in England and whose order at Syon Abbey formed a center of devotional literary culture; consequently, *The Fifteen Oes* came to be known simply as "St. Bridget's prayers."[28] *The Fifteen Oes* gained a wide circulation and came to form a staple of late medieval devotion, appearing widely in private prayer books and books of hours, particularly of the Sarum use, as well as in a versified translation by Lydgate and an edition printed by Caxton (despite his earlier complaint about the proliferation of devotional books among women readers) under the patronage of Elizabeth of York and Margaret Beaufort in 1491.[29]

Contributing to the popularity of *The Fifteen Oes* was a large indulgence that the prayers carried. Rubrics that routinely accompanied the prayers promised readers that anyone who recited them every day for a year would deliver fifteen family members' souls out of purgatory, convert fifteen sinners to a good life, encourage fifteen others to maintain a good life, and secure themselves any wish.[30] Similar examples abound in late medieval devotion: a prayer believed to have been revealed in gold letters on the breast of the Virgin Mary could, when spoken every day, warn the devotee of the exact day of his or her death.[31] Another had the power, if recited regularly, to protect the prayerful reader from sudden death or, if the written text was laid on the womb of a woman in labor, to bring her to a safe and swift delivery.[32] And woodcuts of the wounded Christ that were bound into some devotional books were thought to have the power, if gazed at in combination with the right number of prayers, to deliver the reader many thousands of years of pardon.[33] Such uses of prayer promoted the notion of books and reading as carrying talismanic significance and extending direct powers of salvation. Books of hours, which frequently reproduced indulgenced prayers such as *The Fifteen Oes*, were held to be not just aids to devotion but also, as Claire Sponsler points out, "ritually efficacious" objects in their own right.[34] Likewise, books of saints' lives could carry the thaumaturgic powers of saints' relics.[35] Literacy and book ownership, as a result, took their place alongside a set of other devotional rituals with salvific benefits, such as praying the rosary, fasting, or wearing a hair shirt. The advent of print did not stanch such textual practices but promoted them further: Caxton's edition of *The Fifteen Oes* carries an indulgence, as do the printed books of hours that were widely disseminated before the Reformation.[36]

Such devotional textual practices associated with the preReformation book belie the now-familiar historical paradigm that defines Protestantism as a culture of the book against medieval Catholicism as a culture of the image.[37] While the image held a privileged place in medieval contemplative practices, the visual was not necessarily a replacement for the textual, despite St. Gregory's famous dictum that images could serve as books for the unlettered; rather, located in books as woodcut prints or illustrations, the image could serve as a map for reading.[38] In the woodcuts illustrating devotional texts that were associated with Syon Abbey, books become the vehicles of visionary and contemplative practices: in one woodcut of St. Bridget, the female saint gazes at a vision of the Trinity while writing in an open book before her, while in another of St. Catherine, the saint looks up from her open book to a vision that surprises her in the midst of her reading[39] (see Figures 3 and 4). In both, the textual and the visual experience share the same space. The culture that produced books of hours and embraced reading and writing as key devotional practices was not one that devalued texts in favor of images, but one that endowed books and reading with salvific power. It was this use of texts, and not only the use of images per se, that would attract specific condemnation in the Reformation.

The wide-scale cultural reform that was conducted under the Reformation campaign against idolatry applied to and affected a broader range of practices and beliefs than is appreciated when "idolatry" is narrowly defined to apply only to the visual realm. When the Protestant writer Edward Dering attacked what he called "the idolatrous superstitio[n] of the elder world," he took as his chief target not images but books "which Satan had made, Hell had printed, and were warranted unto sale under the Popes priuiledge, to kindle in mens hartes the sparkes of superstition."[40] The charge of idolatry, as Michael Camille points out, has historically been wielded as a means of separating licit from illicit cultural forms and practices.[41] Rather than simply replacing a culture of the image with one of the book, the Reformation campaign against idolatry contested the specific ways in which books were used and evaluated within medieval devotional culture. If the forms of devotion surrounding indulgenced prayer like *The Fifteen Oes* made reading into a salvific ritual, sixteenth-century Protestants, in attacking such forms, also attempted to redefine the use of books for a new culture. Given, moreover, the central importance of the female reader to medieval devotion, the Reformation's

Figure 3. St. Bridget, *The Dyetary of Ghostly Helth* (London: Henry Pepwell, 1521). Reproduced with permission of the British Library (C.21.c.3).

¶ Here foloweth dyuers doctrynes deuoute & frupt=
full / taken out of the lyfe of that gloryous vyrgyne / &
fpoufe of our lorde Saynt katheryn of Seenes. And
fyrst thofe whiche our lorde taught & fhewed to her=
felfe / and fyth thefe whiche fhe taught and fhewed vn
to others.

Figure 4. St. Catherine of Siena, *Here foloweth a very devoute treatyse (named Benyamyn)* . . . (London: Henry Pepwell, 1521). Reproduced with permission of the British Library (C.21.a.4).

refashioning of books would have a significant impact on the cultural place of female literary practice.

An immensely popular text that exemplified the indulgenced prayer and textual ritual of pre-Reformation book culture, *The Fifteen Oes* was singled out for condemnation in the Reformation as an example of precisely the kind of idolatrous superstition that Dering attacks. William Marshall's *Certen Prayers and Godly Meditacyons Very Nedefull for Every Christian* (1538) enjoined readers to "henseforth . . . forget suche prayers as saynt Brigittes & other lyke / whiche greate promyses and perdons have falsly auanced," calling them "pestilent infections of bookes" that seduce readers "with infinite erroures / & taught prayers . . . by cause they were garnyshed with glorious titles and with redde lettres promisinge moche grade and pardon (though it were but vanyte) have sore deceyved the unlerned multitude."[42] Likewise, *Certeyne Sermons or Homilies, appointed by the Kynges Majestie* (1547) lists the ".xv. oos" among the most blameworthy "papisticall supersticions and abuses, as of Bedes, or lady psalters and Rosaries, of .xv. oos, . . . of pardons, with suche like merchaundise which were so esteemed & abused to þe great preiudice of Gods glorye and commaundements, that they were made most high & most holy things, whereby to attaine to the eternal life, or remission of synne."[43] These attacks, by bringing *The Fifteen Oes* together with indulgences, rosaries, and books (such as "lady psalters," or books of hours), reveal that written prayers were counted among the idolatrous "merchaundise" that made up the material culture of medieval devotion.[44]

Against the belief that salvation could be secured through the use of such holy objects, the Protestant belief in faith over works reshaped the theological value of prayer and thus rejected a central tenet of late medieval devotional practice. William Tyndale articulates this opposition when he contrasts "superstitious prayers, and pope-holy deeds" with "the prayer of faith, and the deeds thereof that spring of love."[45] The latter he condemns as "belly-prayers," rituals that replace spiritual with material desires, which he derides as ultimately economically driven (thereby echoing Luther's attack against indulgences), in contrast to the "prayer of faith" that replaces prescribed rituals with an expression of inner belief.[46] The belief that prayers could not in their very utterance win salvation or escape from purgatory entailed a radical revision not only of the act of prayer, by stripping it of the power of indulgence, but also of religious books themselves, which had been the vehicles of indulgenced prayers.

Accordingly, the reformed primers that replaced late medieval books of hours presented themselves as fundamentally different models of textuality, beginning by explicitly revoking the indulgences that were attached to *The Fifteen Oes*. The Marshall Primer of 1538 admonishes its reader to disregard prayers that are "garnyshed with glorious titles, and with redde letters, promysyng moche grace, and many yeres, dayes, and lents of Pardon, whiche they coude never in dede p[er]form, to [the] great decept of the people, and the utter destruction of theyr soules."[47] Likewise, the 1535 *Goodly Prymer in English Newly Corrected and Printed* condemns the "goodly glorious titles, that promyse innumerable dayes, & yeres of pardon" that accompany prayers like *The Fifteen Oes*.[48] The official attempt to eliminate the indulgences attached to *The Fifteen Oes* is reflected in the books of prayer that were kept in private libraries during the Reformation. One such book, now in the Bodleian, contains numerous indulgenced prayers to the Virgin along with *The Fifteen Oes*, which is preceded by the conventional rubricated preface explaining the prayers' origins with St. Bridget and the indulgence they carry.[49] Throughout this book the indulgences are systematically crossed through with pen marks, as if to fulfill the new primers' directions to readers to disregard indulgenced rubrics. Curiously, however, while the indulgences are defaced, the prayers themselves remain intact. Moreover, the book shows evidence of having remained in the family well after the Reformation: it belonged to the Sidney family, and notations in the book's calendar indicate that it was in continuous use throughout the religious upheavals of the sixteenth century.[50] Another manuscript collection of indulgenced English prayers, now in the British Library, shows a similar pattern of defacement: as in the Sidney prayer book, the indulgences, including those that accompany *The Fifteen Oes*, have been largely rubbed out. But here too the prayers themselves are allowed to remain, and the book likewise bears evidence of continuous ownership through the late sixteenth century.[51] The defacement of these indulgences, then, does not destroy the books that house them but rather surgically corrects them in a way that redefines their use.

These "corrected" manuscript prayer books reflect the reception of *The Fifteen Oes* after the Reformation: while condemning the pardons that were attached to them, many primers still retain the prayers themselves, allowing that good remains in them independent of the indulgences they formerly bore. The prologue to the 1535 *Goodly Prymer in English* asserts, despite its broad condemnation of "superstitious prayers," that the prayers themselves retain some virtue: as the author allows, "I do not conde[m]pne every worde in every [one] of them."[52] Likewise, Bishop Hilsey's primer of 1539 warns readers not to give credence to any "goodly printed prefaces, promisinge to the sayers therof many things both folyshe and false" that they may have seen attached to *The Fifteen Oes*; still it reprints the prayers, maintaining "Yet are the prayers [them]selfe ryght good and vertuous, yf they be sayde without any such superstitious trust or blynde confydence."[53] In this insistence, Hilsey maintains that the offense lies not in the actual prayers but in the parameters of their use: uttered without "superstition," they shift from being "folyshe and false" to being "good and vertuous." And indeed, the prayers were reprinted in other books and found a large post-Reformation readership. While some of the more strikingly "papist" elements were dropped—a meditation on the Eucharist in the eighth prayer, a veneration of the Virgin Mary in the fifth—*The Fifteen Oes* continued to be reprinted in the primers and other major works of Protestant devotion, including Thomas Becon's *Pomander of Prayer* (1558) and Richard Day's *Christian Prayers* (1578).[54]

To Helen C. White, *The Fifteen Oes*'s continued popularity throughout the decades of Reformation in England "affords fresh confirmation of the extraordinary substratum of continuity through all the changes of the period."[55] And indeed it does refute the notion that the Reformation represented a complete break with or a total immolation of the cultural practices of the past. However, rather than seeing the prayers' cultural persistence as a sign of continuity across the Reformation, I see it as a product of careful adaptation and selective modification that was performed on cultural artifacts to bring them into conformity with changing definitions of licit cultural practice, which allowed particular objects or practices to survive by dramatically redefining their meanings. By this argument, the circulation of *The Fifteen Oes* reflects an alternative model of historical change to those of recent historians who have debated the meanings of Reformation iconoclasm. Eamon Duffy, for whom the Reformation was a "violent disruption" from a still-vigorous "traditional religion," emphasizes the literal violence that the Reformation inflicted on medieval culture by including in his book *The Stripping of the Altars* copious illustrations of medieval religious artifacts that suffered destruction or defacement, apparently at the charge of Reformation agents like Thomas Cromwell, thereby suggesting that the Reformation meant to eradicate the medieval past.[56] On the other hand, Christopher Haigh stresses the tentative and discontinuous nature of the Reformation, pointing to evidence that many cultural artifacts and practices from England's Catholic past continued to find uses well past the period of official Reformation, which he takes as an indication that the population retained Catholic beliefs long after the official break with Rome.[57] In ways that modify the accounts of both Duffy and Haigh, the continued circulation of *The Fifteen Oes* indicates the limitations of a binary of "continuity" against "change" as an explanatory model for the cultural developments that marked this period. Rather, *The Fifteen Oes* supports Tessa Watt's argument that on a cultural level the Reformation involved not merely "conflict and displacement" but also adaptation.[58] The prayers and the books that contained them were not destroyed but rather continued to circulate after the Reformation, at the same time that official and private efforts to remove the indulgences suggest that their meanings and uses were renegotiated.[59] That renegotiation involved a major shift in thinking about the religious significance of cultural artifacts. Hilsey's insistence that *The Fifteen Oes*, uttered without "superstitious truste or blynde confidence," could be recuperated for a new Protestant devotion attempts to define a social place for prayer beyond the salvific ritual, in a culture for which faith alone, not works such as indulgenced prayer, could secure salvation. Given the centrality of indulgenced prayer to late medieval textual culture and its practices, the attempt to circulate prayer without indulgence effectively remakes the book as an object of devotion. Once stripped of their indulgence, books lost their ritual efficacy; if they could no longer secure salvation, it became necessary to reconsider what devotional books were for.

While Foxe holds that Protestant book culture emerged fully grown from the printing press, it is more accurate to see it as the result of a major engagement with and renegotiation of the textual conventions of the pre-Reformation period. The number of major skirmishes in the Reformation that centered on books and their distribution indicates the degree to which, perhaps even more than the image, the book was the major target of cultural reform. Official concern about the need to govern books' content produced new institutions of textual discipline, such as the Stationers' Company, the practice of licensing, and the office of the royal printer, institutions that Roger Chartier and Joseph Loewenstein find fundamental to the development of modern notions of proprietary authorship.[60] The refashioning of *The Fifteen Oes* shows that the agents of Reformation book culture were concerned not only with books' content but also with their uses as objects. Medieval devotional book culture—and in particular, its advancement of indulgenced prayer—made the book into a material object of salvific power and a vehicle of miraculous presence. Conversely, the Reformation repudiated such books as "idols," not only because they upheld the belief that prayers would purchase salvation but also because such beliefs overemphasized the book's value as a material object. Thus when *The Seconde Tome of Homelyes* (1563) attacks medieval books of hours as "idols," it is because they are held to be precious objects in their own right, and thus become "graven bookes, and paynted scripture of the glorious gylt ymages and ydolles, all shynynge and glytteryng with metal and stone, and covered with precious vestures."[61] Shaping a Protestant culture of the book meant displacing books' value from the material realm to a symbolic one. Thus Bishop Hilsey's attempt to distinguish the superstitious use of prayers like *The Fifteen Oes* from the virtuous use of the same prayers implied a wide-ranging revision of medieval textual practice. Where Tyndale differentiates between the "belly-prayer" that is falsely held to purchase salvation and the "prayer of faith" that is only an expression of the Christian's inner religious state, Hilsey's discussion extends the contrast between instrumentality and expression to the act of reading. In contrast to the "superstitious" reader, who approaches the written prayer as a ritual practice endowed with salvific power, the "virtuous" reader will approach it as the expression of faith.

This contrast between superstitious and virtuous forms of reading directs the Reformation's revision of the pious woman writer and the genre of female prayer. Protestants who attacked the medieval devotional culture of the book singled out for particular critique its dangerous attractions for women readers. As the author of *The Seconde Tome of Homelyes* writes, continuing his attack on the medieval book of hours, "Be not these thinke you pretie bokes, and scriptures for simple people, and specially for wyves and yonge maydens to loke on, reade on, and learne such lessons of?"[62] In this, he appears to recall medieval tendencies to associate books of hours with women, such as Eustache Deschamps's satirical attack on women's overly material desires for such books:

> A book of hours, too, must be mine,
> Where subtle workmanship will shine,
> Of gold and azure, rich and smart,
> Arranged and painted with great art.

> (Heures me fault de Nostre Dame . . .
> Qui Soient de Soutil ouvraige,
> D'or et d'azur, riches et cointes,
> Bien ordonées et bien pointes.)[63]

In the literary-cultural imagination, reforming the Catholic book meant reforming female literary practice, a project that would hold important implications for the representation of women writers as well as readers in a Protestant England.

The medieval legacy of female prayer found a charged focal point in the figure of the Virgin Mary, who was adopted as both the object of prayer, as in the indulgenced "Ave rose sine spinis" that was ubiquitous in books of hours and prayer collections, and also as a figure of female authorship herself, in "The Magnificat," the song of praise she utters in Luke 1:46–55. The prayer formed a privileged part of the medieval Psalter, which formed the textual basis of the later medieval books of hours.[64] In the Hours of the Virgin, "The Magnificat" featured among the prayers offered at Vespers.[65] When English Protestants confronted the medieval books of hours, they were particularly eager to strip away the excrescences of Mariological prayer and indulgenced ritual that they found there. William Marshall's *A Goodly Prymer in Englyshe, Newly Corrected and Printed* (1535) attacks the indulgenced rubrics that routinely accompanied prayers to the Virgin like the "Ave rose sine spinis" and the "Obsecro te" for advancing the false belief that prayers to the Virgin could carry salvific benefits (a belief encouraged by texts such as the incipit "Here foloweth many devout prayers / petitions / and requestes necessary for all persons / to our sauyour Jesu cryst / et to his glorious mother saynt Mary. To the whiche is graunted grete gyftes of grace," which opens a Sarum primer from 1532[66]). Likewise, Bishop Hilsey's *Manual of Prayers, or the Prymer in Englyshe* (1539) explicitly repudiates the "many Scriptures dystorted unto oure Lady, whyche in theyr owne natyue sence are nothynge mente of her" and worries "least the youth shuld learnd to take such scriptures to be of our Lady, whyche are of God, and to geue such prayse to her as shulde onely be geuen to God."[67]

As Susan Schibanoff has shown, Italian humanists downplayed Mary's authorship of "The Magnificat" by stressing its origins in divine revelation.[68] But in Protestant countries, ascribing the poem to divine revelation did not minimize the cultural problems associated with the female author but rather multiplied them, by calling to mind the most offensive practices of indulgenced prayer—namely, the claim that such prayers derived from a privileged relationship with the divine. Marshall specifically distances himself from the model when he attacks the "Ave rose sine spinis": "But the most fondnes or madnes of all, is that they made our lady to gyue and delyuer the sayd prayer by reuelation."[69] What made the prayer by revelation particularly noxious was the belief that its miraculous origins conferred special benefits on those who recited it, as opposed to the rehearsal of faith that Protestant prayer was held to be.

Luther himself attempted to reshape this legacy of Mariological prayer when he undertook a thorough exposition of "The Magnificat" in 1521 (published in England in 1538) to model how the Virgin Mary and her prayers could be reincorporated into a Protestant culture.[70] Luther's chief tactic in Protestantizing Mary is to ground her prayer not in revelation but in experience, arguing that "in order properly to understand [it] . . . , we need to bear in mind that the blessed Virgin Mary is speaking out of her own experience."[71] His discussion of Mary thus attempts to de-transcendentalize her by presenting her life as that of an ordinary, pious woman whom he imagines "milking the cows, cooking the meals, washing pots and kettles . . . and performing the work of a maidservant." By historicizing Mary as a woman who milks cows and cooks meals, Luther articulates a model of female "experience" to counteract the practices and beliefs associated with female prayer of revelation. Likewise, the 1535 *Goodly Prymer in Englyshe* attempts to recuperate "The Magnificat" from late medieval Mariolatry by fashioning Mary as an undeserving subject of God's grace and favor who does not differ from any Christian, "euyn as she her selfe dothe knowledge in the songe Magnificat." In the model of Luther's revision of the Virgin's prayer, it asserts of a prayer to Mary like the "Ave Maria," "here thou seist that in these wordes no petition, but pure prayses and honours are conteyned."[72]

The process of recuperating the Virgin Mary for Protestant readers required a redefinition of the textual practices that surrounded her cult. Just as *The Fifteen Oes* was recuperated into Protestant book culture once the indulgences that accompanied it were discarded, allowing it to be transformed from "folyshe and false" to "good and vertuous," the prayers surrounding the Virgin Mary could be preserved once purified of the indulgences and petitions that had accompanied them. Redefined, they were transformed from supernatural objects of revelation to human testaments of faith. This redefinition of prayer held profound implications for the production of female piety in the post-Reformation sixteenth century. If revelation authorized medieval female authorship, as it does in the woodcuts of Saints Bridget and Catherine or in the legend that accompanied *The Fifteen Oes*, Luther's revision of "The Magnificat," along with the 1535 primer's revisionary treatment of Mary, shows how, in order to counter the medieval discourse of miraculous revelation, petition, and indulgence, such female-authored texts were regrounded in experience.

The category of "female experience" has held an important place for practitioners of women's history. As Joan Scott has productively observed, "female experience" itself is a historical category that needs to be interpreted within the various contexts of its ongoing construction.[73] Luther's and Hilsey's revisions of "The Magnificat" illuminate how the category of female experience, as the source of women's writing, emerged as a Protestant antidote to the Catholic category of female revelation. By reinterpreting the Virgin's text as a work of "experience," Luther breaks its charm, making it an artifact not of indulgence and revelation but of faith and biographical understanding. The move is one we might see as inaugural to the modern notion of the woman writer, whose writing is grounded in the expression of a subjectivity or experience; but, as well as allowing us to see how "the woman writer" is historically contingent, Luther's and Hilsey's interest in the Virgin Mary's "Magnificat" can also remind us that she was also implicated in a struggle of the highest political stakes.

Margery Kempe as "Devout Anchoress": Henry Pepwell's Edition of 1521

Reformation attacks on and revisions of iconic women's prayers like *The Fifteen Oes* and the Marian prayers reflect the cultural and political importance that these texts had come to have in England by the sixteenth century. Despite their appeals to the otherworldly and timeless, women's written prayers became potent ideological weapons during periods of religious controversy; and in the contentious early years of the Reformation, editions of these prayers showed that they could be wielded by the opponents as well as the agents of reform. In 1521, the same year that he printed Christine's *Boke of the Cyte of Ladyes,* the London printer Henry Pepwell produced a book of vernacular devotion that contained a short selection from *The Book of Margery Kempe.* The same selection had first been published two decades earlier by Wynkyn de Worde as *A shorte treatyse of contemplacyon taught by our lord Iehesu Cryste, or taken out of the boke of Margerie Kempe of Lynne.*[74] Only four leaves long, it omits many of the autobiographical details that have become most familiar since the discovery of the manuscript: gone are Margery's pilgrimages and references to daily medieval domestic life that often form the focus of selections from *The Book of Margery Kempe* in today's anthologies.[75] Instead, the "shorte treatyse" focuses exclusively on scenes of private revelation or prayer, turning a sprawling and strikingly worldly narrative into a short and intensely inward-looking work of devotion. So many of the details pertaining to Margery Kempe's historical existence are missing, and so shifted is its emphasis toward private prayer, that when Pepwell reprinted de Worde's text he amended its colophon to call his author "a deuoute ancres," a designation that would be unthinkable of the peripatetic Margery Kempe who appears in the manuscript. But until the manuscript's rediscovery in 1934, this short edition offered the only textual evidence by which Kempe was known, allowing earlier readers to surmise not unreasonably, like Edmund Gardner in 1925, that its author was "a woman of some wealth and social position, who had abandoned the world to become an ancress, following the life [of enclosure described in] . . . the *Ancren Riwle [The rule for anchoresses]*."[76]

Given the manuscript's evidence of Margery Kempe's extensive travels and material engagements with her early fifteenth-century English world, the early printed version's emphasis on prayerful inwardness, compounded with Pepwell's designation of Kempe as an "ancres," appears to be a drastic and willful misreading of *The Book of Margery Kempe*. Accordingly, what little discussion the printed "shorte treatyse" has attracted since the manuscript's discovery has tended to view it as the product of censorship: Sue Ellen Holbrook argues that by favoring private acts of prayer over "public and physical acts," the extractor "has left behind all that is radical, enthusiastic, feminist, particular, potentially heretical and historical" from the original *Book of Margery Kempe*.[77] Similarly, Anthony Goodman argues that "when Henry Pepwell came in 1521 to reprint the brief, anodyne selection from the Book issued by Wynkyn de Worde, he transposed Margery to where the secular world always wants to put spiritual dissidents—out of it. He entitled her 'a devout ancres.'"[78] Yet while the printed Margery Kempe is markedly sanitized of the social disruptiveness and eccentricity that continue to trouble and fascinate many of Kempe's modern readers, the printed text also offers a new avenue for reading Kempe's work and authorship historically, by shedding light on the particular meanings Kempe held for readers in the early sixteenth century, as well as the particular historical circumstances in which her text was understood—and to which, I will argue, it was shaped to respond.

If the printed version reduces *The Book of Margery Kempe* to a "shorte treatyse" of private prayer, the text it produces is by no means anodyne, apolitical, or ahistorical; nor does removing Margery herself to an imaginary anchorhold, as Pepwell does by designating her "a deuoute ancres," necessarily mean removing her from the world. Though physically isolated, medieval anchoresses were not isolated from religious and political controversies of late medieval England; as

Nicholas Watson has recently argued of Julian of Norwich, "neither Julian nor her book was impervious to history."[79] If Julian sought "to respond preemptively" (as Watson argues) to potential charges of Lollardy in her written visions, Claire Cross has shown that anchoresses were subjects of suspicion during periods of anti-Lollard persecution.[80] Indeed, *The Fifteen Oes* demonstrates that the prayers of a "woman solatarie and recluse" were not considered removed from the world but could become the object of intense, public struggle to define the nature and meanings of popular religious practice more broadly. Likewise, I will argue, the printed text of Margery Kempe, and in particular Pepwell's fashioning of Kempe as a "deuoute ancres," does not remove the work from the political or historical realms but rather situates it and its author within them, in a way that calculatedly activated the most controversial meanings of female devotional authorship in the first decades of the sixteenth century.

Pepwell's edition of Margery Kempe places her text squarely in the conventions of pre-Reformation devotion that were embodied in *The Fifteen Oes*, as well as demonstrating the tactically important role those conventions played at a critical moment in the early history of the English Reformation. The anthology in which the selection of Margery Kempe appears is introduced by this incipit: *Here foloweth a veray deuoute treatyse (named Benyamyn) of the myghtes and vertues of mannes soule /⁊ of the way to true contemplacyon* (hereafter *Benjamin*), announcing the selection with which it opens, a text based on Richard of St. Victor's *Twelve Patriarchs*.[81] Like its titular text, the other selections in the volume are likewise concerned with the practice of contemplative devotion: following Richard of St. Victor is a set of meditations by St. Catherine of Siena, extracted from *The Orcherd of Syon*, which is in turn followed by *A shorte treatyse of contemplacyon taught by our lorde Jhesu cryst / or taken out of the boke of Margery kempe ancresse of Lynne*. Following the selection from Margery Kempe are four shorter texts: Walter Hilton's *Song of Angels* and three works associated with the author of *The Cloud of Unknowing: The Epistle of Prayer, The Epistle of Discretion in Stirrings of the Soul*, and *A Devout Treatise on the Discerning of Spirits*.[82] Although, unlike Richard's *Benjamin*, these shorter texts do not appear to have been originally intended for a lay readership, nonetheless they are joined by similar emphases on the importance of prayer and contemplation over strict ascetic practices.[83] As the *Epistle of Discretion in Stirrings* asserts, true devotion does not require a life of strict observance "in grete scylence / i[n] singuler fastyng [and] in onely-dwellynge [i.e., solitude]"; likewise, Hilton's *Song of Angels* insists that "reuerent affeccyoun," rather than ascetic practice, is most pleasing to God: "This onely by itselfe / without ony other maner of doynge (As is fastynge / wakynge sharpe werynge / with all suche others) onely by itselfe pleaseth almyghty god / and deserueth to haue mede of hym."[84] Pepwell's choice of texts recalls the literary contexts of Bridgettine devotion: the selection from St. Catherine had previously appeared in de Worde's *Orcherd of Syon*, a text he dedicated to the "religious modir and devout sustren . . . at the hous of Syon," and works by Richard of St. Victor and Walter Hilton both appeared in Syon's library.[85] But the book's message, grounding devotional practice in prayer and contemplation over acts of strict discipline or enclosure, has special application for laypersons, who formed a significant readership for devotional works such as Pepwell produced.

The most striking feature of Pepwell's *Benjamin* is the woodcut that appears on its title page (Figure 5). Known as an Image of Pity, it depicts a risen Christ displaying his wounds, surrounded by the instruments of the Passion. At the image's feet appears a short verse: "O man unkynde / Bere in thy mynde / My paynes smerte. // And [you] shalt fynde / Me true and kynde / Lo here my herte."[86] And around the sides of the image runs the text of an indulgence: "The pardon for .v. pater [nosters] .v. aves / & a crede w[ith] pyteous beholdynge / of these armes is .xxxii.M. & .iv. yeres." Pepwell's image resembles single-sheet woodcut indulgences that were sold at Syon and other sites of pilgrimage, to be used alone or sewn or pasted into books of hours.[87] Like others of the type, its distinctive appearance and use are grounded in the legend of the Mass of St. Gregory, in which Christ was said to have appeared in bodily form at the altar in order to refute the doubts of a woman who questioned the verity of transubstantiation: to celebrate the miracle, Gregory authorized its reproduction, accompanied by a lavish indulgence, and the image became a staple of late medieval devotion.[88] It thus exemplifies in its form and prescribed meaning a religious practice that valorizes images, together with the books in which they appear, as objects of devotion and ritual.

Combining image, prayer, and indulgence, the Image of Pity inscribes a religious practice that is familiar from the devotional landscape of *The Book of Margery Kempe*. In church one day, the book recounts, Margery was ravished into contemplation by gazing at an image "clepyd a pyte. And thorw the beholdyng of that pete hir mende was al occupyed in the Passyon of owr Lord Jhesu Crist."[89] If Margery's response to the image epitomizes the affective stance of "pyteous beholding" that the viewer of Pepwell's woodcut is invited to take, elsewhere Margery also confirms the doctrine of indulgence on

Figure 5. Image of Pity, *Here foloweth a very devoute treatyse (named Benyamyn)* . . . (London: Henry Pepwell, 1521). Reproduced with permission of the British Library (C.21.a.4).

which the Image of Pity is grounded.[90] Throughout her book Margery
tallies the value of her prayers and devotional acts in terms of the
"pardon" they secure for her: on pilgrimage in Assisi she obtains "gret
pardon of plenyr remyssyon, for to purchasyn grace, mercy, & for-
ӡevenes for hir-self, for alle hir frendys, for alle hir enmys, & for alle
Þe sowlys in Purgatory" (79). Undergirding the practice of pilgrimage,
the promise of indulgence drives Margery to travel great distances; yet
she also learns that she can obtain the same indulgenced benefits
through prayer alone. She learns this lesson in "Rafnys" (Ramleh),
when she desires to return to Jerusalem "for to purchasyn hir more
pardon. And Þan owyr Lord comawndyd hir for to gon to Rome, & so
forth hom in-to Inglond, & syd vn-t hir, 'Dowtyr, as oftyn-tymes as Þu
seyst or thynkyst, 'Worshepyd be alle Þo holy placys in Ierusalem Þat
Crist suffyrde bittyr peyn & passyon in,' Þu schalt haue Þe same pardon as ӡyf Þu wer Þer wyth Þi bodily presens bothyn to Þi-self & to
alle Þo Þat Þu wylt ӡevyn it to" (75). She is subsequently instructed
that prayer and contemplation are more effective than physical acts of
religious discipline: "Dowtyr, Þow xalt han as gret mede & as gret
reward wyth me in Heuyn for Þi good seruyse & Þe good dedys Þat Þu
hast don in Þi mynde & meditacyon as ӡyf Þu haddyst don Þo same
dedys wyth thy bodily wittys wyth-owtyn-forth" (203). In her preoccupation with the practices and benefits of indulgence, Margery
shows an affinity with the readers who helped to make indulgenced
prayers like *The Fifteen Oes* tremendously popular in the late Middle
Ages.

That contemplation and prayer alone could win the same indulgenced benefits as physical disciplines and pilgrimage seems to have
been the most important lesson of *The Book of Margery Kempe* for
the early sixteenth-century context in which it was received. The
selections that are preserved in the printed version are united in
their interest in indulgences, and the story they recount emphasizes
Margery's lesson that prayers and contemplation can replace more
arduous physical deeds of devotion for gaining "mede & reward in
heuen." The first selection from Pepwell's 1521 *shorte treatyse of
contemplacyon . . . taken out of the boke of Margery kempe* opens by
stating that Margery "desyred many tymes that her heede myght be
smyten of with an axe vpon a blocke for the loue of our lorde Ihesu."
But she is told that she need not suffer actual martyrdom to gain divine favor, and that the thought alone is worth the rewards of the
deed: "as often as thou thynkest so thou shalte haue the same mede
in heuen / as yf thou suffredest the same dethe." Likewise, Jesus advises her that silent prayer and meditation will please him more than

bodily acts: "yf thou ware the habergyon or the heere / fastynge brede and water." Repeatedly the selections stress that "thou shalte haue mede & rewarde in heue[n] for þe good wylles & good desyres / as yf thou haddest done them in dede." The benefits of such "rewarde" are measured in indulgences. In what might be seen as the climax of the short text, selections taken from the twenty-ninth and seventy-third chapters of *The Book of Margery Kempe* are brought together to re-count the story of Margery's lesson at "Rafnys," where she learns that she can win the same pardons of pilgrimage for herself and for those who share her belief through prayer alone:

> ¶ Doughter he sayd / as oftentymes as þu sayest or thynkest wor-shypped be all the holy places in Iherusalem / where cryst suffred bytter payne and passyon in / thou shalte haue the same pardon as if thou were there with thy bodely presence / both to thyselfe and to all those that thou wylte gyue to.
> ¶ The same pardon that was grau[n]ted the aforetyme / it was con-fermed on saynt Nycolas daye / that is to saye / playne remyssyon / & it is not onely graunted to the / but also to al tho that beleue, & to all tho that shall beleue unto the worldes ende / that god loueth the. . . . Be [they] sorye & heuy for that they haue done and wyll do due penaunce therfore / they shall haue the same pardon that is graunted to thyselfe / and that is all the pardon þat is in Jherusalem / as was granted þe / whan thou were at Rafnys.[91]

The salient message of these passages is not only that Margery can gain the same indulgence through thought and prayer that she could through the physical acts of pilgrimage, but that this same benefit can extend to all those who read this selection of her book. The language of Christ's promise that those who read the text with belief and con-trition for their sins will gain pardon reinforces the promise of the indulgence that surrounds Pepwell's Image of Pity, which offers an enormous pardon to all those who gaze "piteously" upon it. Signifi-cantly, this Image of Pity, printed on the opening page of the anthol-ogy, is repeated in the body of the text on the page that immediately precedes the selection from Margery Kempe. In this position, the woodcut directs the reader in the proper attitude and practice with which to read the *shorte treatyse of contemplacyon;* as well as func-tioning as a powerful icon in its own right, the Image of Pity thus serves as a map for reading. If the Image of Pity at the opening of Pep-well's book announces to prospective readers that its central focus will be indulgence, that promise is fulfilled in the *shorte treatyse of contemplacyon . . . taken out of the boke of Margery kempe ancresse of Lynne,* which brings together the other selections' shared interest in a devotional practice grounded in prayer over acts and further-more announces that prayer itself is worthy of significant indulgenced benefits.

In printing this selection of Margery Kempe along with the Image of Pity that accompanies it—and, I argue, shapes its use—Pepwell creates a text on the model of *The Fifteen Oes* that will excite readers' belief in the ritual efficacy of reading and the salvific power of the book. The connection with *The Fifteen Oes* is heightened in Pep-well's colophon announcing that the text's author and subject is "a deuoute ancres called Margery Kempe of Lynne." By making Margery Kempe into "a deuoute ancres," Pepwell invites readers to draw an analogy between his anchoress and the "woman solatarie and re-cluse," St. Bridget, who was associated with the authorship of *The Fifteen Oes.* In the process, Pepwell produces Margery Kempe as a fig-ure of nationalistic interest, by offering the detail that she is a native daughter, "of Lynne," and thus grounding the practice of indulgenced prayer in English soil.[92]

Pepwell could have expected to find a lay readership for his book, as did many similar works of vernacular devotion by the late fifteenth and early sixteenth centuries; as S. S. Hussey points out, evidence of ownership indicates that even devotional texts that were originally composed for recluses or those in enclosed orders found their way, through the circuits of print and manuscript transmission, "into the hands of devout, moderately well-off London tradesmen and mer-chants" or aristocratic laywomen.[93] The indulgence promoted in Pep-well's representation of Margery Kempe seems calculated to appeal to a new devotional reader who seeks the benefits of indulgence without having to undergo the physical disciplines or actual pilgrimages that might have been expected of him or her at an earlier time.[94] To such readers, Pepwell's Margery Kempe offers a promise that is reinforced in the other selections brought together in the anthology: that heav-enly reward can be sought and won through prayer alone. The book itself is an important conduit in this lesson, driving home through the Image of Pity the notion that a devotional book can allow the pious reader to obtain significant indulgenced benefit without having to abandon the domestic space for the far-flung pilgrimage or the rigors of monastic enclosure. Pepwell's anthology, *Benjamin,* offers devo-tional readers a model of the book that is similar to that promised in the prologue to *The Boke of the Cyte of Ladyes* to would-be gentlemen; just as the gentlemen readers of the *Cyte of Ladyes* find that they can attain class status through reading rather than through birth or through martial acts, so too the readers of *Benjamin* learn that they can attain even greater heavenly rewards than those purchased by physical, disciplinary acts through prayerful acts of reading. In both cases, the printed book asserts its own centrality to the social and devotional practices that shape its readers.

Pepwell's decision to frame Margery's text in the late medieval conventions of indulgenced prayer held specific political meanings in 1521. The doctrine and practice of indulgence had been contentious in England ever since the Lollards and John Wyclif criticized them in the fourteenth century.[95] In the 1520s the controversy raged again, but this time from a new source. In 1520 Martin Luther published *The Babylonian Captivity*, which intensified the attack that his earlier *95 Theses* had leveled against the practice of indulgences (its full title being *A Disputation on the Power and Efficacy of Indulgences*).[96] Spurred on by Leo X, Henry VIII and the English Bishops launched a counterattack against Luther: in January 1521 Cardinal Thomas Wolsey banned the sale and possession of Luther's books in England, and in May John Fisher delivered a sermon against Luther at St. Paul's Cross that was dramatically staged against a bonfire of Luther's books—the first major act of censorship against printed books in England.[97] In June of the same year, 1521, Henry himself attacked Luther in a work published under his name, *Assertio Septem Sacramentorum*. Pepwell published his edition of Margery Kempe in November 1521, after months of controversy over indulgences and printed books. Within these contexts it was significant that he chose to bring out a book that featured prominently and repeatedly an indulgenced woodcut, along with a text that asserted indulgenced prayer as a native, English practice. Pepwell's reprinting of the "shorte treatyse of devotion" represents a powerful intervention in the debate, demonstrating how both the printed book and the genre of female prayer could be wielded for polemical purposes on behalf of indulgences. By presenting Margery Kempe as a "deuoute ancres" and thereby courting association with St. Bridget of *The Fifteen Oes*, Pepwell pointedly recalls earlier instances when Bridget had been wielded on behalf of English political and religious interests: where Bridget's *Revelations* were frequently called on during the Hundred Years War to support English victory, Henry V offered special indulgences and endowed the Bridgettine Syon Abbey as part of his effort to consolidate church and state power and to combat Lollard heresy within England.[98] Pepwell's interest in presenting Margery Kempe as a prayerful anchoress, this context suggests, was less to remove her from the political than to wield her as an agent of inoculation against Lutheran heresy.

What is known about Pepwell's professional life and work suggests that he was, in the observation of the antiquarians Joseph Ames and William Herbert, "attached to the Roman Catholic religion all his days."[99] The 1520s marked an early stage in Pepwell's career: four years after publishing this devotional anthology he went on to become warden of the newly formed Company of Stationers, a position that charged him with the responsibility of examining and disciplining printers suspected of publishing heretical works.[100] John Foxe attacked Pepwell's patron, the conservative Bishop of London, John Stokesley, for his role in bringing about the martyrdom of a number of early Protestants; this same Stokesley commissioned Pepwell to publish works like those of John Eck that supported the English campaign against Lutheran heresy. Against Foxe's assertion that printing was the natural tool of reform, Pepwell's career shows how the press could be made to serve the opposing side.

The anti-Lutheran campaign in England is associated with the first major crackdown on the freedom of the press, initiated by the ban on and burning of Luther's books during the spring and summer of 1521. Where other printers worked under suspicion of heresy, Pepwell secured his own safety and established what would be a successful career as an enforcer of orthodoxy—which he did in part through his publication of Margery Kempe, who allowed him to assert a native book culture of indulgenced prayer in support of textual orthodoxy. In so doing, Pepwell resembles the "theologians and prelates" whom Carolyn Walker Bynum cites—such as Jacques de Vitry, hagiographer of Mary of Oignies—who deployed female mysticism "in the thirteenth-century fight against heresy."[101] So too Margery Kempe enables Pepwell to assert the orthodoxy of indulgence after the anti-Lutheran bonfires of 1521—and in the process, to assert his own usefulness as an instrument of a print culture that was increasingly called on to combat heresy within its own ranks.

If Pepwell intended his *Benjamin* anthology, together with the *shorte treatyse of contemplacyon . . . taken out of the boke of Margery kempe ancresse of Lynne* that it contains, as a work upholding the power of indulgence, the textual evidence suggests that this is how it was received. What was orthodox in 1521 was soon subject to rapid reevaluation when England officially split with Rome and repudiated the doctrine of indulgence, and Pepwell's support for indulgences put him on the losing side of the new orthodoxy.[102] And the British Library copy of his book bears the marks of a later, private iconoclast: Pepwell's Image of Pity has been defaced with pen marks that score through the text of its indulgence. This pattern of deface-ment is likewise visible in nearly all surviving Images of Pity from England, which are similarly scored through the texts of their indul-gences, with pen marks that sometimes concentrate only on the final word, "pardon" (see Figure 6). If Pepwell's book appropriates the in-dulgenced reading conventions that were associated with *The Fifteen Oes,* the reception of the former appears to be patterned after that of the latter, in which post-Reformation readers privately took it upon themselves to "correct" the books with their pens.

But, as in the case of *The Fifteen Oes,* what is significant about this defacement is not so much the fact of its occurrence—after all, the 1550 *Act against Superstitious Books and Images* required that "su-perstitious books and images" be "openly burnt or otherways defaced and destroyed"[103]—but that the text has suffered so little. The image itself remains untouched, and the book is otherwise unharmed; in-deed, the text of the indulgence itself remains partly legible under the pen marks. The survival of Pepwell's book contradicts Tessa Watt's assumption that "the 'images of pity' disappeared around 1535, burnt up in the first fires of the Reformation," since the text and image are remarkably well preserved.[104] Eamon Duffy, who examines similar patterns of defacement, contends that the lightness with which the offending text is scored through indicates the defacer's reluctance to destroy the artifacts of Catholic culture and to embrace the new Prot-estantism.[105] But I read it differently, not as an act of half-hearted de-struction but as a correction whose near-surgical precision recalls the calculated reshaping of *The Fifteen Oes* through the excision of its indulgence. In a similar vein, the marks that score through Pepwell's indulgence come out of an effort, I suggest, to reshape the medieval cultural heritage of the indulgenced prayer and thereby to redefine the uses of its texts for a new, reformed book culture.

This defacement writes small a pattern of Reformation response to religious books and especially the literary genre of women's prayer. As the English agents of Reformation reconsidered the artifacts and prac-tices of late medieval religion, they likewise reconsidered the iconic figure of the female writer of indulgenced prayer. But here again, the woman writer was not censored so much as reshaped: and the process of reshaping women's prayer meant reshaping as well the cultural and textual practices that it embodied. The pen marks scoring through Pepwell's indulgence, like those that score through the rubrics of *The Fifteen Oes* in the Sidney prayer book, Bodley 850, destroy the indul-gence but preserve the text. Again, what is being attacked is not the

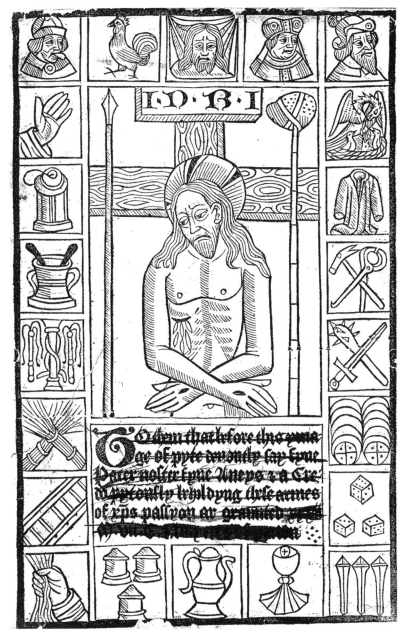

Figure 6. Image of Pity, Bodleian MS Rawl. D. 403, fol. 2ᵛ. Reproduced with permission of the Bodleian Library, Oxford.

book itself but the indulgence that directs how that book will be used and valued. Stripped of the indulgence, the book's charm is broken, and it is thus recuperable into Protestant culture. The examples I have discussed here—the refigured *Fifteen Oes* in manuscript prayer books and printed primers, the surgically altered Image of Pity in Pepwell's edition of Margery Kempe—challenge what Patrick Collinson characterizes as the "widespread prejudice" that holds that the new English Protestantism "produced no culture of its own but made an iconoclastic holocaust of the culture which already existed." [106] In contrast, I see in that iconoclasm not simply an effort to destroy but also one to reshape, redeem, and thus recuperate the artifacts of the past. I therefore want to consider how the fragments, scorings, and textual effacements are the signs not so much of a violent eradication of medieval culture as of a broader cultural transformation. In the place of a Catholic religious book culture of ritual prayers and images, these acts of recuperation help construct a Protestant literary culture of the fragment.

John Bale's Protestant Bibliography and the Lost History of Women

One of the few life records of Pepwell that survives from contemporary sources comes from a Protestant polemic, *Yet a Course at the Romysche Foxe* (1543), written and published pseudonymously by the Protestant polemicist, bibliographer, and editor John Bale. [107] In it, Bale laments the destruction and censorship of Protestant books under the direction of Pepwell's patron, Stokesley, whom Bale further attacks for supporting the publication of Catholic works like "the enchyridion of Eckius" which "co[n]tayneth [in] yt all doctryne of deuylyshness, as the popes . . . worshyppynge of Images rodes and rellyques . . . hys purgatorye pardons and pylgrimages . . . and all of soche fylthynesse" (54ᵛ). For promoting this book culture of idolatry Bale blames the work's publisher, whom he excoriates by name and affiliation as "harry pepwell stokyslayes prouider" (55ʳ). This swipe against Pepwell reveals the obverse of Foxe's famous statement crediting the printing press with responsibility for religious reform: those who helped to develop a Protestant print culture, as Bale would, did not establish it on barren ground but rather had to wrest control of the press away from a Catholic culture of print that was already vigorous and powerful. As an editor himself and a careful manipulator of the press, Bale attacks Pepwell's work in the service of "purgatorye pardons" in part as a way of establishing his own editorial work in an

oppositional model. Yet Bale's work as an editor in many ways continued to revisit the genres and subjects that occupied Pepwell's press in
the 1520s. Like Pepwell, Bale would also become an editor of women's
religious writing. Where Pepwell offered Margery Kempe as an English St. Bridget in 1521, in 1546 and 1548 Bale edited texts by Anne
Askew and Elizabeth Tudor. Where Pepwell's "devout anchoress" asserted the Englishness of Bridgettine-modeled female devotion, Bale
too sought to fashion his female authors as examples of native female
piety, which he, like Pepwell, also sought to ground in a preexisting
history of pious women in England. In writing this history, however,
Bale was forced to redefine not only the English tradition of female
piety that Pepwell embodies in Margery Kempe but also the cultural
understandings of reading, prayer, and above all, books, on which that
tradition was grounded.

Bale has attracted renewed critical attention because of his work as
a bibliographer; in the wake of the Reformation, he compiled a set of
massive catalogues of British writers that has been seen, following
René Wellek, to inaugurate the very idea of English literary history.
For Wellek, however, the originality of Bale's literary-historical project is compromised by the fact that it never significantly moves beyond "the medieval tradition of the catalogue of writers" to develop a
coherent literary-historical narrative or principles of selection and
evaluation such as later literary historians would do.[108] Yet I suggest
that Bale's contribution to the developing notion of English literary
history comes not from his catalogues alone, as important as they
are, but from the intersection of his bibliographical work with the
literary-historical project he developed as an editor of women's writing. Where the catalogues favor an exhaustive accumulation of authors' names and the titles of their books, Bale's productions of
women writers meditate more abstractly on the meanings of literary
history for a new Protestant culture of the book. The woman writer
would occupy a prominent role in Bale's work as both a historical
and a symbolic figure. His catalogues display a surprisingly detailed
knowledge of the role that women played in England's literary landscape, recording the names of women writers both recent, like Askew,
and historical, from Claudia Rufina, the legendary British writer commended by Martial, to Juliana Berners, the reputed English author of
the little-known *Book of Hunting* (1486). But it is in his editions of
Anne Askew and Elizabeth Tudor in particular that Bale allows himself to speculate more broadly on the shape that a literary history of
women might take. In tracing these imaginary literary histories, Bale

attempts to wrest control over the representation of women writers from editors like Pepwell, thereby showing that if "the woman writer" was an instrument in the battle for Catholic orthodoxy, she could be transformed into an equally powerful figure of religious dissent. Bale's career shows how the task of fashioning "the woman writer" and that of fashioning English literary history came together as preeminent sites for the Protestant redefinition of the English past. Where the post-Reformation struggle to redefine *The Fifteen Oes* reveals that the written works of pious women became focal points of reform, Bale harnesses this controversy to rethink material book culture, thus giving rise to a new model of literary history in which the figure of the woman writer becomes an unexpectedly central player.

As a bibliographer as well as an editor of women writers, Bale sought to rewrite England's national, cultural heritage through its books. Following the first Acts of Dissolution, Bale accompanied John Leland as he toured the monastic libraries and witnessed the dispersal of their contents, which Bale records in *The Laboryouse Journey and Searche of Johan Leland* (1546). In an effort to preserve what he called the textual monuments of England's literary heritage, Bale attempted to identify and catalogue all English books and authors in his "A Regystre of the names of English wryters" (1549) and the *Illustrium Majoris Britanniae Scriptorum* (1548), works that trace a preliminary map of English literary history and represent what Trevor Ross calls "the first full-scale objectifications of the canon of British letters."[109]

Bale's bibliographical project is haunted by his conflict-ridden desire to construct a new, Protestant culture out of the fragments of a repudiated, Catholic past. In responding to this challenge, Bale hazards a difficult balance between supporting the aims of the Reformation and rescuing a model of English literary history and cultural identity from its ravages.[110] As a Protestant agent of reform himself, Bale applauded the "utter destruccyon" of the monastic libraries, "whyche God then appoynted for their wickednesses sake;" moreover, he openly endorsed the destruction of so-called "papist" books, as he put it, so "that all kyndes of wicked superstycyons, and . . . sophystycall doctrynes myghte be remoued hens."[111] But the aim of reform was not to separate from the Catholic past wholesale so much as to "reform" it, implying that a version of history could be retrieved that would authorize the present. Accordingly, even as Bale excoriates "superstitious" books, he also seeks to recuperate the contents of the former monastic libraries as what he calls "library monumentes" of supreme cultural importance. But he seeks to do so in ways that will separate those books from their former setting while also supporting those in his own party who authorized their destruction.

Bale finds a partial solution to these conflicts in the practice of bibliography. Arising from the humanist disciplines of textual scholarship that developed around the study of classical manuscripts, bibliography offered a methodology and a set of terms for assigning value to textual objects that were already destroyed, defaced, or lost.[112] As a bibliographer, Bale was able to survey the material remains of medieval libraries without contesting directly the causes of their destruction at the hands of his fellow reformers. Instead, recreating medieval literature as a culture of fragments, Bale's bibliography shares with the discourse of humanist antiquarianism a will to transform the texts and objects of a former culture of religious idolatry into a transcendent cultural patrimony.

Bale's overriding project is thus to redefine the cultural value of books for a society that appeared to him to be bent on their destruction. On the one hand he laments the practices of monks who hoarded their books and kept them "tyde up in chanes, and hydden undre dust in the monkes and fryres libraryes."[113] Bale characterizes this hoarding of books as a form of avarice, charging that "avarice . . . hath made an ende both of our lybraryes and bokes"; in this formulation, he recalls St. Paul's association of avarice with idolatry, developed in *The Parson's Tale*, which holds that "an avaricious man is [in] the thraldom of ydolatrie," because he "loveth his tresor" as an idol.[114] If the monastic librarians offend by idolatrously hoarding bibliographical treasure, Bale charges reformers who sacked the libraries with undervaluing cultural objects. After witnessing the despoliation of the libraries, Bale reports that men used the leaves of manuscripts to clean their boots, or worse: "I have bene also at Norwyche . . . And ther all the library monumentes are turned in the use of their grossers, candlemakers, sope sellers and other worldly occupyers, so studyouse have we bene ther for a common wealthe and so careful of good lernynge."[115] What the monastic librarians have in common with their iconoclastic opponents is a tendency to overvalue books as material objects. In hoarding books as treasures and reducing them to the value of their materials, both monks and iconoclasts miss the source of books' truer, immaterial value as bearers of "good lernynge."

By casting the Dissolution's destruction of the monastic libraries as a misrecognition of cultural value, Bale displaces the political and theological elements of the conflict in order to suggest that the medieval libraries were destroyed not through the excesses of the zealous reformers of his own party but through the ravages of a culture of consumption. When consumption becomes the key determinant of cultural value, books are reduced to "commodytees," Bale asserts, neatly bringing together terms that Peter Stallybrass has explored in his review of Marx's concept of commodity fetishism. Against a common reading that uses Marx's term as a critique of capitalism's overvaluation of the object, Stallybrass asserts that Marx coined the term intending to argue the opposite, that by reducing objects to commodities capitalism robs them of value: thus "the triumph of the commodity betokens the death of the object."[116] Similarly, when Bale faults iconoclasts for reducing books to "commodytees," it is to point out the inability of a consumer society to appreciate and conserve objects of cultural value:

> We sende to other nacyons to have their commodytees . . . we drynke the wynes of other landes, we bye up their frutes & spyces, yea, we consume in aparell their sylkes & their velvets. But alas our own noble monumentes and precyouse Antyquytees, whych are the great bewtie of our lande, we as lyttle regarde as [the] parynges of our nayles.[117]

Wines and spices, silks and velvets—those objects that the English value most highly are those that come from other nations. They are also luxury, consumer goods that emphasize the pleasures of the evanescent. Such pleasures define the national culture, Bale charges, earning the English a reputation abroad for overvaluing "things which lasteth not, as in bankettes and late suppers," while also undervaluing those "thynges lastyng & durable."[118] In a similar vein, he charges those who brought ruin to "so many noble monumentes of Antiquite" with caring for "nothyng els . . . but theyr bellyes," as if their destruction of the libraries literally reduces manuscripts to consumables.[119]

Bale's distinction between what is material and impermanent on the one hand and what is immaterial but lasting on the other projects the terms of a Protestant critique of idolatry onto the realm of the book. Where Bale critiques the misuse of books as "commodytees," the Protestant *Certayne Sermons or Homilies* issues a standard critique of Catholicism's idolatry by dismissing its ritual objects as "merchandise," which form the basis of "papisticall supersticions and abuses, as of Bedes, or lady psalters and Rosaries, of .xv. oos, . . . of pardons, with suche like merchaundise which were so esteemed & abused to þe great preiudice of Gods glorye and commaundements," all of which overinvest in the material value of objects. If Catholicism reduces Christianity to "merchaundise," Bale similarly charges that the Dissolution reduced books to merchantable objects: "in those un-circumspecte and careless dayes, there was no quickar merchaundyce than lybrary bookes."[120] Bale's bibliographical project thus shares with the Protestant critique of idolatry the aim of differentiating faith from superstition by inventing new ways of assessing the value of cultural objects that can transcend the level of material value.

For Bale the antidote to such objects' reduction to "commodytees" or "merchandyce" is their enshrinement as "noble monumentes and precyouse Antyquytees," which endows them with a value that is contrastingly permanent and immaterial. In his use of this language to define transcendent cultural value, Bale borrows from the vocabulary of the new discourse of antiquarianism that emerged in the sixteenth century. In the aftermath of Reformation iconoclasm, the formerly sacred artifacts of the medieval church were recuperated into new uses as objects of secularized, historical interest. Books formerly housed in monasteries formed the basis of secular libraries like the Royal and Cottonian collections, the building blocks of the British Library.[121] Similarly, the relics and objects of sacred art were preserved as examples of native exoticism in collectors' cabinets, which replaced reliquaries as furniture for the collection, display, and visual delectation of precious objects.[122] To suspicious contemporaries, the antiquarian fascination with the artifacts of medieval culture suggested a kind of Catholicism *manqué*. Certainly to the contemporary authorities it did: the antiquarian (and great editor of Chaucer) John Stow was charged with being a papist, and his colleague Anthony Wood, the book collector, was held and examined in connection with the Popish plot.[123] In a climate of suspicion that followed on the heels of religious reform, the antiquity resembled the medieval relic: "a broken statue would almost make [the antiquarian] an Idolator," John Earle joked in 1628.[124] But there are crucial differences between the broken statue and the "idol": as D. R. Woolf points out, the relic was a fragment talismanically invested with life-giving properties, metonymically representing the wholeness of the saint's body. The antiquity, by contrast, bore physical witness to the temporal and transient and derived value through its connection to the historical. Where the relic became a vehicle of presence, the antiquity bore silent witness to a no-longer-present reality. The transformation of the object of idolatry into the object of historical memory meant replacing a discourse of miraculous presence with one of historical absence, a task that would become central to the Reformation's cultural and theological project.

The transformation of idols into memorial objects underwrote

Reformation debates over the nature of that most denigrated "idol," the Eucharist itself, whose continued use in the Protestant service exemplified a contemporary's observation of the Reformation in England, "that many of the popish ceremonies were still tolerated; but . . . new significations were put on them."[125] While the Catholic doctrine of transubstantiation considered the host to be a literal embodiment of Christ on the altar, the reformed English church retained the Eucharist but reinterpreted its meaning, holding it to be not Christ's body itself but a holy "memorial" of the Passion.[126] Thus in 1539 the reformed service enjoined English men and women to understand that "neither holy bread nor holy water . . . be the workers or works of our salvation, but only be as outward signs and tokens whereby we remember Christ and its doctrine."[127] While the Act of Six Articles enforced a return to Catholic doctrine on the Eucharist and contested the assertion that the host was merely a "remembrance," the Reformation critique of Catholic ceremony, *The Rationale of Ceremonial* (c. 1540–43) reinstalls the Eucharist as a memorial by asserting that it, like other church ceremonies, should be "taken for tokens and signs to put them in remembrance of things of higher perfection."[128] If the theory of transubstantiation implied the cultural centrality of a theory of signs, then the Reformation's transformation of the Eucharist represented an attempt to reformulate that theory by substituting for the language of substantial presence an alternative language of remembrance, which stressed the distance between the past and the present celebration of it.[129]

While the Protestant revaluation of the Eucharist produced the host as a memorial object, the first antiquarians employed a similar memorial vocabulary to ascribe value to the ruins newly littering the English countryside. The destruction of the monasteries was hastened by those who pillaged the ruins for objects of material value— lead was the first to go, but doors and bedding were sold profitably to householders.[130] In their visits to these ruins, Bale and Leland renamed the broken buildings "monuments," thus assigning them a value that resided not in their physical presence but in their connection to the broader, immaterial realms of heritage, history, or posterity which were largely founded on memory. The primary meaning of the monument, as a sepulchre or memorial, grounds its value in its ability to safeguard public memory by standing in for an object, person, or event from the past. In the sixteenth century, the monument was protected from the charge of idolatry because it did not claim value for its own material presence but rather for the lost thing for which it stood.[131] This crucial distinction was institutionalized in the

Proclamation Against Breakinge or Defacing of Monumentes of Antiquitie, beyng set up in churches or other Publique Places for Memory, and not for Supersticion (1560), which attempted to halt the destruction that zealous iconoclasts visited on churches by asserting the difference between idols and memorial objects. Monuments, the proclamation asserts, should not be destroyed as objects of idolatry but should rather be preserved as memorials erected "only to shewe a memory to the posteritie of the persons there buryed . . . and not to noryshe any kind of superstition."[132] The monument transforms loss into memory, and memory into posterity: in this, it forms the grounding point for a Protestant culture that emerged out of iconoclastic destruction. If church monuments memorialized the dead, ruins became monuments to the past, and foundations of a cultural heritage born out of a collective loss.

Bale's bibliography extends this memorial function to books by transforming the formerly idolatrous objects of late medieval devotional book culture into "library monuments" that carry transcendent, historical value. Bale's aim in so doing is, as he puts it, "to holde thynges in remembraunce, whych otherwyse had most wretchedly peryshed."[133] His choice of the word "remembrance" here resonates with Protestant reworkings of the Eucharist, which substitute historical memory for miraculous presence as the basis of collective belief. Yet the reason it becomes necessary to hold things in remembrance is precisely because they have perished in substance. As Bale admits of his "A Regystre of the names of Englysh wryters," the catalogue can only ever be a work of fragmentation. While it records authors by their "names, their actes, their ages, and the tytles of their bokes," the catalogue cannot comprehend the works themselves, as Bale remarks with regret: "yf ye had their whole workes in dede, as they were in substaunce and fashyon, whych now for the more part are peryshed, ye shoulde have seane most wonders of all."[134] What bibliography preserves, in other words, is not books but bibliographical records that manifest books' loss, since "in substaunce and fashyon" the books "for the more part are peryshed." Thus for Bale, the catalogue is a bibliographical graveyard that monumentalizes texts that have been lost in all but name and title, as Bale indicates when, quoting Erasmus, he laments: "So oft as I in readynge the catalogues of olde writers, do beholde what profyghtes, yea, what pusaunce, ayde, and confort we haue lost."[135]

Destruction and loss are elementary to Bale's model of literary history. If Bale's bibliography preserves not books but the record of their destruction, this destruction enables him to produce the catalogue

itself as a record of a transcendent cultural heritage, whose function
is to create monuments of texts that as material objects would be vulnerable to misuse as idols or commodities. In so doing he advances
the claim that the cultural value of books and authors resides not in
their substance but in their connection with a realm of durable, immaterial value that enables them to prove their worth beyond the
sphere of "godless materiality."[136] The province of this immaterial
value is what Bale calls England's "Elected Heritage," a Protestant English literary history written through books that have undergone, and
have been redeemed through, acts of destruction.

There are parallels between Bale's bibliography, which is premised
on the destruction of the material book, and the gesture that I read in
the anonymous readers' desecrating marks through the indulgences
that frame the texts and images of pre-Reformation devotion. The
scoring-through of the indulgence, as I argued above, was not simply
a gesture of destruction but an attempt to redefine the material book
as it was shaped by medieval devotion as a vehicle of salvific power.
The desecrating mark works to refashion the book from an object of
superstition and idolatry into one that is, to recall Bishop Hilsey on
The Fifteen Oes, "ryght good and vertuous"—an expression of immaterial faith rather than an object of veneration in its own right. In
a similar vein, Bale also works to refashion books that had been the
objects of abuse as material artifacts, but that, as fragments, could
become "monuments" to the immaterial realm of "posterity" and
"heritage," terms that transform English books into tokens of a transcendent category of cultural value. In both cases, a Protestant book
culture defines itself in opposition to an "idolatrous" Catholic book
culture by virtue of its elevation of the immaterial above the material,
and the transcendent above the object; but it signals its distance from
the idolatrous overinvestment in the object by giving symbolic value
to objects that are broken. Where the devotional woodcut is recuperable into Protestant culture because its indulgence has been scored
through and therefore its charm as an object broken, Bale's literary
history of England is made up of books that, we are continually told,
have been lost.

If the catalogues are premised on the loss of material books,
though, what we find in their contents is an index of medieval writers
that includes not only secular writers like Chaucer and Skelton but
also religious ones, from "Ricardus Hampole, heremita" (Richard
Rolle), "Gualtherus de Hilton" (Walter Hilton), and "Joannes Lydgate,
monachus Buriensis" (John Lydgate), to the detested Duns Scotus and

Thomas à Becket.[137] But these writers are not "lost"; rather, they constitute a significant portion of England's surviving, native literary culture. And what Bale's catalogues attest again and again is the extent to which England's literary past, especially as represented by those texts that were preserved in print, was a Catholic one.[138] Thus the catalogues manifest the conflict at the core of Bale's project: at the same time that he shares the Dissolution's aim to eradicate "wicked superstycyons" and "sophystycall doctrynes," he still believes that he can recover a native literary history of dissent to which religious reform can return the nation. But, as long as he preserves the dream of recovering the literary past in its totality, that desire will not be fulfilled by the actual names of authors he is able to retrieve. Bale's turn to the humanist discipline of bibliography, which offers a discourse that balances a desire for recovery with a melancholic acceptance of loss, allows him to resolve this dilemma at least in part. The bibliographical entries in evidence in Bale's catalogues can only record texts' titles and authors in the most fragmentary forms; thus this format allows Bale to recover—and revere—those texts as lost objects. Far easier to mourn the loss of such textual figures than to attempt a comprehensive literary history that could accommodate them.

If Bale struggles in his catalogues with the problem of how to write a Protestant literary culture out of the fragments of a Catholic past, he transforms this problem in his work on women writers by raising cultural loss and destruction to the level of its defining features. Where the catalogues show Bale's familiarity with medieval women writers, his editions of Anne Askew and Elizabeth Tudor of 1546–47 and 1548 attempt to develop a coherent, English literary history in a way that his catalogues could not. The two-volume *Examinations of Anne Askew* collects a young Protestant noblewoman's account of her trials for Protestant heresy, which "she wrote with her owne hande," the text reports.[139] A year later Bale published Elizabeth Tudor's *Miroir or Glasse of the Synnefull Soule,* a translation of Marguerite de Navarre's *Le miroir de l'âme pécheresse* (1531) that the eleven-year-old princess made for her Protestant stepmother, Catherine Parr, in 1544, as *A Godly Medytacyon of the Christen Sowle* (1548).[140] Both texts are important not only as examples of women's writing in print but also as key moments in the production of "the woman writer" as a significant figure for a post-Reformation literary culture. In the bulky editorial matter that he uses to frame and present the two texts, Bale consistently stresses his two authors' femininity, in ways that distort Elizabeth's and Askew's representations of their own gender:

where Askew cites her femininity as a strategic effect that allows her to slip into and out of roles during her interrogation—a point that has been developed recently by Megan Matchinske—for Bale, Askew's gender is a mark of her frailty, as he continually calls her "a woman, frayle, tendre, [and] yonge" (107). Likewise, when the young Elizabeth asks her reader to "behold rather the matter and excuse the speech, considering it is the work of a woman which hath in her neither science nor knowledge," she quickly moves on to compare her frailty with that of all mankind; but when Bale paraphrases the passage, he takes its meaning to be gender-specific, as he writes in his conclusion, recalling and reshaping Elizabeth's own words: "If the homely speech here do too much offend, consider it to be the work of a woman, as she in the beginning thereof hath most meekly desired" (39ʳ).

Bale's point in emphasizing Askew's and Elizabeth's femininity is not to downplay or preclude the two women's authorship, but rather to figure them as "women writers" in a way that positions them as the inheritors of a literary history of English women. "No realme under the skye hath had more noble women, not of more excellent graces, than have thys realme of Englande," Bale insists in a lengthy conclusion to his edition of Elizabeth's translation (42ᵛ). And he goes on to list numerous learned English women who are Elizabeth's forerunners—for example, "Claudia Rufina, a noble Briton, witty and learned in both Greek and Latin" and "much commended in Martialis the poet for the epigrams and poems which she then compiled in both those tongues" (44ʳ). Likewise, "Helena Flavia," Bale writes, "excelled all other in the diverse speeches of nations" and "made a book of the providence of God, another of the immortality of the soul, with certain Greek poems, epistles, and diverse other treatises" (44ᵛ).

England's learned women have been so plentiful, Bale reports, that they could be gathered in a lengthy catalogue, yet this has never been done: "none in this land have yet done as did among the Greeks Plutarch and among the Latins Boccaccio . . . that is to say, left behind them catalogues or nomenclatures of famous and honorable women, yet hath it not at any time been barren of them" (46ʳ). Where Bale's own catalogues of English authors produced a bibliographical site of mourning, the nonexistent catalogues of learned Englishwomen are themselves *objects* of mourning for what was never written. As such, the imaginary history of women responds to and transforms the conflicts that dogged Bale's catalogues. Where Bale's bibliography recovers as lost the texts of medieval Catholicism, the history of women embodies loss from the start and offers Bale the imaginary basis for constructing a literary history in the image of Protestant national identity.

The reason that the history of women has never been written, Bale contends, is the misogyny of medieval clerics, who have unjustly ignored or belittled the intellectual achievements of women. Thus in his *First Examination of Anne Askew*, Bale singles out for attack "that blynde popysh worke whych Walter Hunte a whyte fryre, wrote iiii. score yeares ago, Contra doctrices mulieres, agaynst schole women, or els some otherlyke blynde Romysh beggeryes" as an example of the Catholic clerks' hostility to women (30–31). Against the misogynist clerks who erase the contributions of women from their chronicles, Bale imagines a lost history of learned women that would form a shadowy legacy of dissent against the official church. This imaginary history, in turn, establishes the background and precedence for the examples of Protestant, female piety he locates in Anne Askew and Elizabeth Tudor. The exemplary ancient women whose names he recalls in his discussions of Askew and Elizabeth are notable for struggles against Roman tyranny that prefigure those of their sixteenth-century inheritors against the Roman church: thus Bale compares Anne Askew's martyrdom to that of Blandina, martyred by the Roman emperor in the second century, while he recalls in comparison to Elizabeth's text an ancient example of English, female political rulership in "Voada . . . a woman of wonderful force and heart [who] strongly armed herself, her two daughters, and five thousand women more of the Briton blood, in battle against the furious fierce Romans to suppress their tyranny and execrable filthiness in abusing maids, wives, and widows" (43ᵛ). In Bale's account, these exemplary women's struggles against the misogynist Romans are continued by medieval religious women's parallel struggles against the established church in England: Bale cites the examples of Bede's Abbess Hild, who "openlye dysputed in [scriptures] agaynst the superstycyons of certen byshoppes," and Eleanor Cobham, persecuted as a witch in the early fifteenth century, "whom Antichrist's grand captains, the bishops then of England, in hate of her name and belief, accused of sorcerous enchantments and experiments of necromancy against their holy horned whorish church" (46ᵛ). In cases such as these, women's religious practices are naturally opposed to those of the misogynistic, established church. Positing a timeless enmity between women and the agents of Rome, Bale envisions in the lost history of women a narrative of dissent that prefigures and grounds the history of English Protestantism. Where Foxe identifies Lollards as proto-Protestants to the extent that they form a native, vernacular dissidence against the Church of Rome, Bale locates a parallel dissident legacy in the unchronicled history of women.[141] Bale's imagined history of women does not constitute a "female tradition," since in Bale's account tradition per se is the suspect invention of ecclesiastical custom, which he sneeringly dismisses as "the myre of mennys tradycyons" (21). Rather, the history of women represents to Bale what is lost from tradition—and as such, fills a place of historical and political mourning. Bale's history of women proves in its incompleteness the efforts of the misogynist, Roman clerisy to obliterate the traces of the native, female past. By extension, to reconstitute that history around the figures of Anne Askew and Elizabeth Tudor, as Bale does, frames these sixteenth-century women writers and their work as the return of England's dissident repressed.

If Bale's bibliographical project of recovery makes the destruction and loss of books into the foundation of a new literary history, his recovery of a "lost" history of learned women and women writers as the groundwork for his editions of *The Examinations of Anne Askew* and Elizabeth Tudor's *Godly Medytacyon of the Christen Sowle* likewise produces a Protestant national and literary history by revaluing the "lost" objects of historical memory. For the young Elizabeth Tudor, Bale's "recovery" of a "lost" history of female precursors serves a specifically political function. In his introduction to the *Godly Medytacyon*, Bale begins by recalling the various claims that nations and peoples have made to ground their legitimacy in tradition, all of which Bale dismisses as false: just as "the haughty Romans set not yet a little by themselves that they have risen of Aeneas and Romulus," so "the Romish clergy" base their authority in scholastic writers whom Bale dismisses with characteristic energy. In contrast, Bale claims that true nobility comes from the qualities and inner virtues that he finds exemplified in learned women, of whom he presents Elizabeth as representative:

> Of this nobility have I no doubt (Lady most faithfully studious) but that you are, with many other noble women and maidens more in this blessed age. If questions were asked me how I know it? my answer would be this: By your godly fruit, as the fertile tree is none otherwise that thereby known (Luke 6). I received your noble book . . . (7ʳ)

This argument is fulfilled in the "nomenclature or rehearsal of names" he offers of learned women of the past. Such an argument is calculated to appeal to Elizabeth; given that tradition in the form of genealogy or royal history had been produced to declare her a bastard and to support her mother's execution, Bale's argument that dominant traditions are inevitably bogus and self-serving could not fail to resonate with her own predicament. Moreover, by locating an alternative site of nobility in a collectivity of studious women, Bale appears to uphold the cultural importance of the literary and religious circle of Catherine Parr, the immediate context for Elizabeth's production of her manuscript translation, which she dedicated to her stepmother and presented in a cover she had embroidered with the queen's initials (see Figure 8 in Chapter 4). Within this context, Bale's citation of women such as Eleanor of Aquitaine and Margaret Beaufort as examples of learned royal women constructs an alternative royal female identity that is grounded above all in the studious use of letters.

But Bale's assertion that this history of learned women has gone unrecorded by historians, while learned women themselves were condemned by misogynistic monks, allows him to construct a history that is as meaningful for its lacunae as for the fragmentary evidence that Bale is able to present. In its absences, the history of learned women reveals the biases of historians; it thereby resembles the sacred histories produced by the "papist" church, which repress, as Bale charges, the stories of the "true" martyrs, which include those put to death "for heresy and lollerye, they saye. These Christen martyrs were never solempnysed of them" (78). In *The Examinations of Anne Askew*, Bale brings together the "lost" history of England's learned women with that of its "true" martyrs to redefine the historiographer's goal of recovery by creating a history of absences.

Absence is the defining trope of *The Examinations of Anne Askew*. In words that resonate with Bale's bibliographical project, Askew defends her views on the Eucharist by insisting that the bread of the sacrament is not the actual body of Christ, which is absent: rather, she holds that Christians are meant to "receyve the bread in remembraunce of Christes deathe" (93). Where Askew recreates the Eucharist as a remembrance of an absent body rather than the experience of a substantially present one, Bale's edition of Anne Askew both draws from and refigures medieval hagiography by revising the thaumaturgic textual models that he inherits from late medieval religious book culture.[142] In the process, he also shows that the task of reforming English literary history and its artifacts would require a reformation of the popular images of female piety that were grounded in pre-Reformation books. The woodcut that opens both volumes of Bale's edition presents Anne Askew overcoming a papal dragon, holding a martyr's palm in one hand and the Bible in the other (Figure 7).[143] Depicting Askew as a figure of a new female sanctity, this woodcut recalls but pointedly revises the iconographical conventions established by woodcuts of Saints Bridget and Catherine in books of late medieval devotion such as Pepwell's. Where those earlier woodcuts pictured books as the material basis for a female devotion grounded in visionary experience and penitential ritual, Askew's piety, culminating in her martyrdom, is founded on the explicit refusal of such models. Where the woodcuts of Saints Bridget and Catherine indicate that the book shared a conceptual space with the visionary experience, in the woodcut of Anne Askew, the book is The Book, the Bible, which is closed in her hand, as she gazes out of the picture's frame to an unpictured source of light. And in place of the pen that Bridget holds as she transcribes her vision into the open book before her, Askew holds her martyr's palm in her hand like a writing instrument, in a gesture that links her writing with her martyrdom, as if to suggest, like the Heroidian women's analogies between their pens and the swords with which they will kill themselves, that writing will be the means of her destruction.[144]

Askew's appeal to a divinity that does not inhabit the material realm is reinforced in the line that Bale selects from Psalm 116 to accompany her woodcut and frame her story: "The verity of the Lord endureth forever." Her constant differentiation of the permanent and immaterial from the material and ephemeral allows Askew to fulfill Bale's search for the "lastyng & durable" in textual culture. At the same time, the lastingness of Askew's writing is secured through the physical afflictions that bring it about. Bale continually establishes the durability of the truth of Askew's writing in contrast with the physical weakness of her body: "The strength of God is here made perfyght by weaknesse. Whan she seemed most feble, than was she most stronge" (13). While Askew's persecutors believe that in destroying her physical body they can bring her to silence, Bale produces her writing as evidence that the truth will outlast the physical destruction that is visited on Askew's body.

Bale displays a calculated insouciance about the fate of Askew's physical remains: "What was done with the Ashes of Anne Askewe and her companyons, I can not yet tell" (12). His deliberate implication is that she left no relics, a point that differentiates her from the Catholic saints whose stories shape the hagiographical genre. At pains to make a similar point, John Foxe contends that his "monuments of martyrs" differ from the hagiographies of his medieval

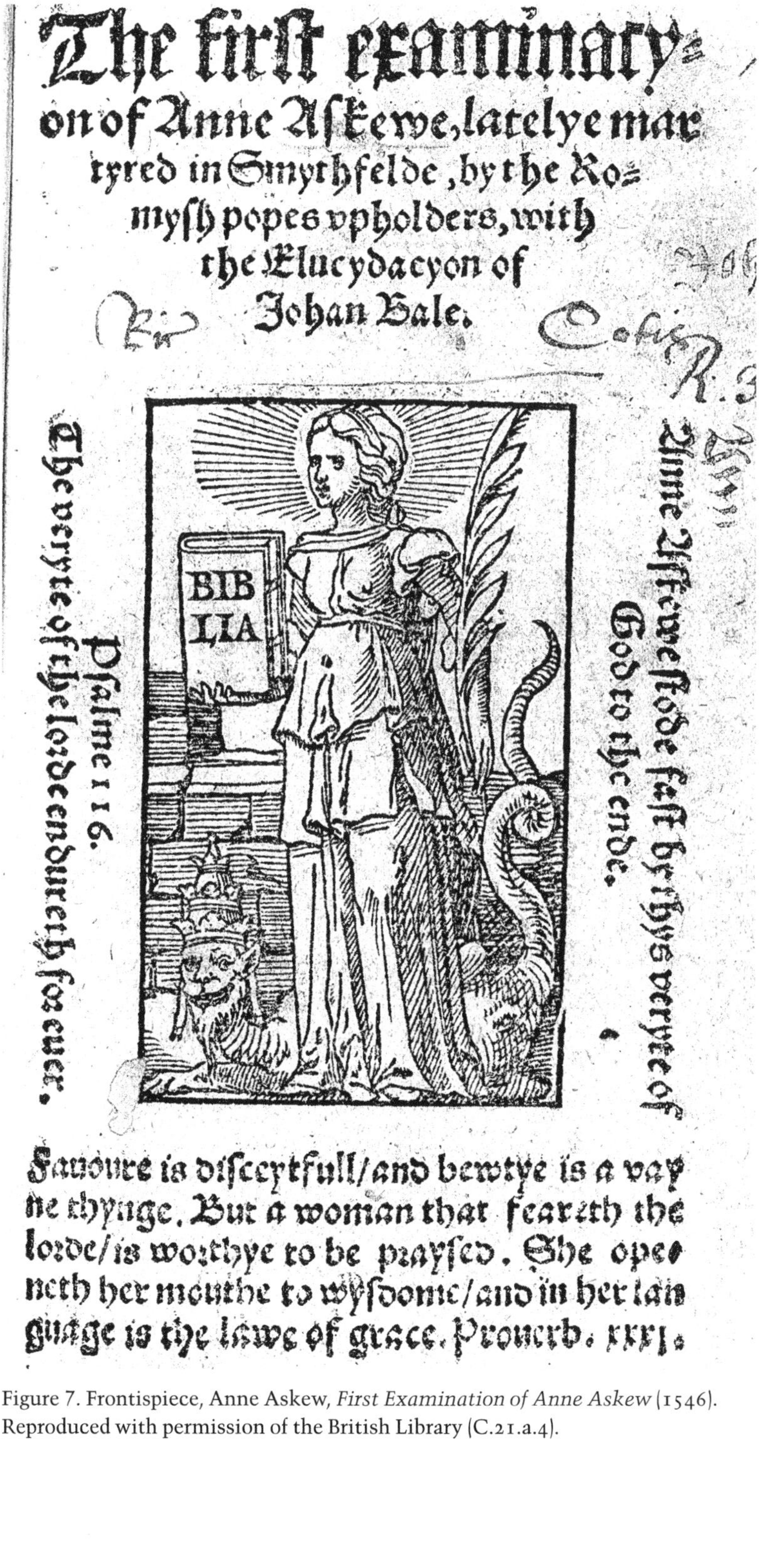

The first examinacy-
on of Anne Askewe, latelye mar
tyred in Smythfelde, by the Ro=
mysh popes vpholders, with
the Elucydacyon of
Johan Bale.

BIB
LIA

The veryte of the lorde endureth for euer.
Psalme 116.

Anne Askewe stode fast by thys veryte of
God to the ende.

Fauoure is disceytfull/and bewtye is a vay
ne thynge. But a woman that feareth the
lorde/is worthye to be praysed. She ope
neth her mouthe to wysdome/and in her lan
guage is the lawe of grace. Prouerb. xxxi.

Figure 7. Frontispiece, Anne Askew, *First Examination of Anne Askew* (1546). Reproduced with permission of the British Library (C.21.a.4).

predecessors on the subject of relics: while the earlier saints' lives attest to the "admiration, and almost superstition [with which] . . . the
relics of those good martyrs were received and kept," Foxe insists that
his text offers "commemoration" "in the stead of relics."[145] The Protestant saint leaves behind not relics but books, which differ from the
thaumaturgic medieval saint's life in their refusal to transmit miraculous presence. Instead of being proven through miracles, the Protestant martyr is valorized through the textual labor of editors, who, in
Foxe's words, "at their own charges gave to the world the stories of
the martyrs and other ancient documents."[146] Protestant hagiography
becomes a privileged bibliographical discipline, an effort to collect
"scattered writings" that are themselves vulnerable to abuse and ne-
glect. Continually conflating the abuses that are visited on martyrs'
bodies and their books, Bale implies that the suffering of books produces a kind of parallel, bibliographical martyrdom: "no new thynge
is it, that good men and their bokes are destroyed now a dayes" (42).
But, he asserts, the enemy's hope of consigning books to oblivion
through destruction is as futile as the hope of silencing the saint
through martyrdom; mocking those who hope "by condempnynge
and burnynge our bookes, to put us to sylence," Bale recalls that
physical destruction only strengthens the godly message of the saints
and their books (67). In making this point, Bale emphasizes the material fragility of Askew's writing: the document of her trials is a product of her own handwriting, Bale stresses, and in his edition he inter-
sperses passages from Askew's text with long, explanatory glosses,
which have the effect of making her text into an obscure artifact, like
the manuscript of humanist recovery, that needs to be painstakingly
gathered, transcribed, and glossed in order to be culturally sanctified.

Of course, Bale's imagined history of women commits its own re-
pressions, and its incompleteness is not entirely due to the misogynistic negligence or malice of clerks. In the process of imagining the
literary history of the English woman writer, Bale is forced to acknowledge that not all women in religious history have been figures
of dissent. The practices associated with the Eucharist, Bale charges,
came into being "after the manyfolde revelacyons of dyverse relygy-
ouse women," notably "a sorye solytarye syster or Ankorasse in
the land of Leodium or Luke, called Eva after serten visions" (48).
This reference, to the thirteenth-century Eva of Liege, invokes the female traditions of eucharistic and visionary piety that were fostered
in England at religious houses such as Syon, or through the practices
of anchoresses such as Julian of Norwich and the abundant literature
that addressed them; however, by locating them in the anchoress

Eva, Bale displaces them to a continental source and thereby upholds his contention that the Eucharist is a foreign innovation with no legitimacy in native church practice.[147] The martyrdom of Askew, however, as well as the hagiographic conventions on which Bale draws in its portrayal, derive from and echo earlier English conventions. As Donald Weinstein and Rudolph M. Bell point out in their survey of medieval saints, martyrdom was a conventionally English marker of sainthood, a convention of which the editor of the printed *shorte treatyse of contemplacyon . . . taken out of the boke of Margery kempe* betrays awareness, in repeatedly stressing Margery's prayers for martyrdom.[148]

When Bale presents Askew as an English martyr, he is careful to differentiate her from the English traditions of medieval women martyrs whose colorful examples adorn the history of the English church. Citing the example of Saint Juthwara, a seventh-century Englishwoman who sought her own execution by feigning lactation and hence illegitimate pregnancy, Bale sneeringly asserts: "Saynt Juthwre a vyrgyne was byheaded . . . for layenge fresh chese or cruddes whether ye wyll, to her brestes. The cause of Anne Askew and her other fellawes, conferred with Christes scriptures, semeth a farre other matter" (82). Similarly, Bale recalls the convention of female saints who rebelled against the institution of marriage in pursuit of their faith, manifested in the legends of English Saints Osritha and Winifred, as well as the Scottish Maxentia, only to declare Askew, who likewise left her husband to pursue her faith, superior to her Catholic ancestresses:

> Osrytha runnynge awaye from her husbande, by the intysement of ii. monkes bycame a professed noone, and was murthered of the Danes. Wenefryda by counsell of a prest, dysdaynouslye refusynge the marryage of a prynce chistened, lost her head for it. Maxentia also played a part not all ynlyke to thys. Soch pylde popysh martyrdomes, compared to the martyrdome of Anne Askew and her faythfull cumpanye, is as is rustye yron compared to pure sylver. (82–83)

Askew is superior to these Catholic saints not because her story reverses their examples but because it does a better job fulfilling them. In the process of showing Askew the superior to her Catholic sisters, Bale also demonstrates unwittingly how grounded in their example she is.

To recall these female saints, as Bale does in relation to Anne Askew, is to suggest the contours of a native history of women that has not been simply lost due to the misogyny of clerical chroniclers—

a history of women, moreover, that offers an antecedent to Anne Askew that is not proto-Protestant, as Bale shapes the examples of Hild and Eleanor Cobham to be, but one that is rather grounded in Catholic orthodoxy. These examples further recall that the hagiographer's work of recovery, as he shows the female saint to be a victim of unjust persecution, had historically served as one of the founding moves of Catholic self-legitimation. The examples of Juthwara, Osritha, and Winifred show that the Catholic Church in England, for all its manifest misogyny, did not obliterate the history of women but rather made it the ground of its own legitimacy.[149] To recall this fact is to acknowledge that the practice of "recovering" women's writing has a long political history in England that is linked to larger debates about England's own historical and religious identity. But to "recover" his own "lost" history of English women writers requires Bale to ignore the line of English editors who performed similar acts of recovery before his, but on behalf of Catholic orthodoxy, which places him in a greater literary kinship with Henry Pepwell—who is, as I have argued, an equally polemical editor of religious women's writing—than he would care to acknowledge.

Bale's recuperation of the history of women as an object of loss, fragmentation, and textual obscurity frees him from the more troubling responsibility of recovering a history of women that does not answer to his desire for dissent. Contrary to his assertion otherwise, there was a recent history of women in the church, but that history contains Margery Kempe as well as Hild, St. Bridget as well as Eleanor Cobham—figures, that is, who are much more difficult to assimilate into a narrative of dissent. Imaginarily removing women's history to a shadowy realm of loss enables Bale to abstract it and therefore avoid confrontation with the elements that run contrary to a Protestant historiography, just as his bibliography of absence allows him to mournfully recall "what profyghtes, yea, what pusaunce, ayde, and confort we haue lost" while also saving him from recollecting the Catholic contents of those works. The history of pious English women, in other words, has to be recovered as an object of loss, lest it be acknowledged to have taken the more immediate forms it did.

Protestant bibliography, like Protestant hagiography and historiography, is haunted by the threat of textual loss and historical oblivion: as John Foxe explains in elaborating his guiding rationale behind the *Acts and Monuments*, "I thought it not to be neglected, that so precious monuments of so many matters, meet to be recorded and registered in books, should lie buried by my default, under darkness of oblivion."[150] By recovering the idols of the Catholic past as the monuments of the Protestant present, however, Foxe, like Bale, produces a cultural graveyard; his "monuments" are safe from the charge of idolatry because their subjects are lost, but as such, they recover not presence but absence. Likewise, Bale's contribution to the history of the woman writer is his production of a vocabulary that can recover and repress in the same gesture.

Bentley's *Monument of Matrones* (1582) and the Recovery of Women's Prayer

Bale's imaginary histories of women writers helped to establish the pious woman writer as a privileged figure for the narratives of English literary history that emerged in the later sixteenth century. The next generation of Elizabethan antiquarians shared Bale's interest in women writers from England's past as well as his view that their history was shrouded in obscurity. But where Bale's call for "catalogues or nomenclatures of famous and honorable women" emphasizes the irrecoverability of such a comprehensive history of women, the Elizabethan Thomas Bentley responded to Bale's call almost literally by producing an encyclopedic work that is explicitly founded on the models of Protestant antiquarianism and women's literary history that Bale established. Entitled *The Monument of Matrones* and published in 1582, Bentley's work compiles the pious writings of contemporary, ancient, and Biblical women into a collection so exhaustive that Suzanne Hull finds that it "[comes] close to being an entire female library between two covers."[151] The scope of Bentley's focus is indicated in the book's opening table, captioned "a breefe catalog of the memorable names of sundrie right famous Queenes, godlie Ladies, and vertuous women of all ages, which in their kind and countries were notablie learned." Bentley's debt to Bale is explicit both in the form of his "catalog" and in its prologue, which invokes Bale by name as a chief model: "Thus, good Readers, I haue set downe the names of some notable learned women to your consideration, referring such as desire to knowe further of their severall works to this treatise following, and to Gesnerus, Bale, Ludouicus Viues, the Chronicles, and such other writers of our time" (Prologue). Bentley's book acknowledges a debt to both of Bale's bibliographical projects, his antiquarian catalogues of English writers and his work as an editor on the writing of English women. By combining antiquarian aims with a focus on women's writing, Bentley claims to produce what Bale himself failed to: a catalogue that is also a library in its own right, bringing together a comprehensive anthology of female writers and their work. In so doing, Bentley brings "their manifold workes into one entire volume, and by that meanes, for to register their so rare and excellent monuments, of good record, as perfect presidents of true pietie and goodlinesse in woman kind to all posteritie" (sig. Bi^r).

Like Bale, Bentley presents women's writing as the object of historical obscurity and textual loss. While England has famously spawned a long history of great women writers, he explains, the work of these women has not been collected together in print; hence the rationale for his work rests in the fact that "[women's] excellent and rare works" are "obscured and worne cleane out of print, and so out of practice." Like Foxe, whose *Acts and Monuments* Bentley's *Monument of Matrones* clearly recalls in its title, Bentley presents himself in the model of the heroic Protestant editor who will rescue lost texts from oblivion and thus enable them to be "by some painefull hand collected and reniued [i.e., renewed], or brought againe to their former good and godly use in the church." Here again, the task of editing women's writing involves recovering it from loss to a prior position of religious centrality, a goal that fulfills Bale's identification of women's writing with a native proto-Protestant past. In this, Bentley brings together a Bale-inspired interest in the "lost" history of English women's writing with the vocabulary that Bale develops in his catalogues for defining cultural value by stressing the textual obscurity and fragmentary nature of women's surviving writing.

The "breef catalog" is offered as the contemporary fulfillment of an age-old line of female literary descent, which includes not only the names of women writers from Bale, such as "Anne Askew martyr," Claudia Rufina, and Bale's proto-Protestant Hild, along with Bentley's female contemporaries such as Lady Frances Abergavenny and Anne Bacon, but also classical women such as "Proba Romana" and "Sappho Poeta," thus linking the history of women writers back to the classical age. Bentley's aim in so doing is to create a model of posterity and heritage that is explicitly feminized, as he presents his book "vnto women as one entire and goodlie monument of praier, precepts, and examples meet for meditation, instruction, and imitation to all posteritie" (Epistle); that posterity, furthermore, takes the form of an explicitly female literary inheritance, "that all godlie women . . . may shew themselves daughters woorthie such mothers" (sig. B4^r). It thereby embodies an abstract narrative of cultural inheritance characteristic of modern theories of literary history, in which the past extends to the present in a metaphor of genealogy; but in place of the

more familiar lineage of fathers and sons, Bentley's is a literary genealogy of mothers and daughters.

However, Bentley's list makes it clear why for Bale the catalogue of
women writers was better off lost: as well as comprising a nascent
canon of Protestant women writers, it also includes women who were
icons of Catholic female literacy, including "Saint Bridgitte," "Catherine of Sienna," and even the shadowy but clearly un-Protestant
"Elizabeth, an abbesse." Despite their appearance in the "breef catalog," these are women whose work has not been collected in Bentley's
anthology, showing that his "recovery" of lost women writers has
been more selective than first promised. Despite Bentley's desire to
offer women's writing as a totality that could exemplify Protestant
virtue, his appeal to the textual loss of women's writing ("worne
cleane out of print") enables him to account for the gaps that punctu-
ate his anthology. Bentley follows Bale, then, not only by identifying
Protestant literary history with the recovery of "lost" women writers
but also by producing women writers as "lost" in ways that enable
him to imagine "women's writing" as a coherent category.

Bentley's project has a practical interest as well as an antiquarian
one: the collected literary history of women writers that he presents
in his three volumes is an anthology of female prayer, which he offers
to his readers as a guide for their daily religious practice, "a register of
holie praier for all women generally to haue recourse unto, as to their
homelie or domesticall librarie" (sig. B1 ᵛ). In this goal, Bentley brings
the monumental into the female space of the domestic, by conflating
the history of women's writing with the history of women's prayer. As
a collection of literary history that is also a prayer book, it offers the
writings of the past as exemplars for the women readers of the present.
In the collection itself Bentley's pious women readers will find prayers
from historical women writers such as Anne Askew (under the heading
"Certaine praiers made by godlie women Martyrs" [2:214]) along with
prayers that are presented without named authors for more quotidian
uses, such as prayers to be recited "so soone as ye awake in the morning" (4:363), or prayers familiar from Catholic applications, such as
prayers to be recited at communion ("When ye are about to receiue the
bread" [4:588] and "After you haue receiued the holie communion" [4:
596]), or a prayer to be recited "in time of drought for raine" (4:471).

In its ordering of prayers for daily practice, Bentley's work resembles nothing more than an expansive book of hours, a generic
proximity that Bentley acknowledges, though he is eager to disown
the resemblance; while he offers women prayers for every occasion,
his is not a "superstitious" work, he insists, arguing that the prayers

are not petitions and are not meant to be read in church, as were Catholic books of hours, "unless we would be deemed meere superstitious" (sig. B3 ʳ). What distinguishes Bentley's work from the book of hours, besides size, is the absence of the Virgin Mary as central figure; while she is acknowledged in the book's "catalog" as an exemplary learned woman, she is marginal to the book itself. Instead, the central figure of Bentley's work is Elizabeth I, who fills the place that the Virgin formerly filled in the pre-Reformation book of devotion as both the source and the subject of prayer.[152] Following Bale, Bentley reproduces Elizabeth's *Godly Medytacyon of the Cristen Sowle*. But for Bentley, Elizabeth is not just a princess turned into a Protestant female icon; she is the queen. Her prayers, therefore, are both exemplars of female piety and utterances from the head of the English church, showing how the category of female prayer could comprise both private devotion and public interests.

The queen's prayers cross the boundaries between women's "domesticall" devotion and the public interests of the commonwealth, as Bentley shows when he offers up for the reader's admiration one "praier made by hir Maiestie, when she was in great feare and doubt of death, by murther," or "Another praier and thankesgiuing made by hir grace, as she rode in hir Chariot from the Tower, to be crowned Queene at Westminster" (2:36). Bentley's book includes not only prayers composed by Elizabeth but also prayers composed for her, in which she is called on to "[bind] hir selfe as it were by a solemne oth, vow and promise, to consecrate hir life wholie to the true worship and sincere service of God, in all holie obedience to his lawes, to the glorie of God, and full discharge of hir dutie, both in hir Court and Realme" (3:320). As well as offering the female reader a broad range of prayers, the book also offers "a praier for the Queenes Maiestie," which upholds a heavenly monarchy by appealing to God as "king of kings, Lord of lords, the onlie ruler of princes, which dooest from thy throne behold all the dwellers upon earth" (4:470). In his dedication to Elizabeth, Bentley takes the queen's own writing—"the admirable monuments of your owne Honourable works" (Epistle)—to be the inspiration for the work as a whole, thereby making her work both the example of Protestant piety and the apex of a long history of women's writing beginning with Sappho and Proba and continuing, through Hild, to the Elizabethan present day.

By making Elizabeth I the exemplary author and subject of women's prayer, Bentley's *Monument of Matrones* offers her as the fulfillment of what had been to Bale both the "lost" history of women's writing in England and the history of English letters traceable in the "monuments" of the medieval literary past. Elizabeth's works, in contrast, are living monuments that give a material form to the history that precedes them. They are also, as Bentley never forgets, the writings of both a woman and a monarch; thus they epitomize the political importance that female prayer held since the late Middle Ages and throughout the Reformation. Pepwell's publication of Margery Kempe as a "devoute ancres" in 1521 does not simply remove his subject from the world but rather wields her as part of a larger debate about books, indulgences, and England's religious identity in which female prayer like *The Fifteen Oes* formed a charged focal point. Likewise, Bale's editions of Anne Askew and Elizabeth herself assert that the history of the pious woman writer could be imagined as a history of dissent that prefigures and legitimates the dissenting project of the English Reformation; thus he makes the woman writer a powerful symbol of England's break from religious tradition. Fulfilling this project, Bentley makes his Elizabeth, now queen, into a figure in whom English literary history and the history of the pious woman writer come together to make women's prayer the defining genre of the Protestant commonwealth.

Four

Elizabeth I and the Making of English Poetry

"With Lady Sapphoes Pen"

In the third book of *The Arte of English Poesie* (1589), George Puttenham considers "who in any age haue bene the most commended writers in our English Poesie."[1] According to René Wellek, this represents a pivotal moment in the invention of English literary history: by endowing English poetry with an honorific past, Puttenham enables it to emerge for the first time as "an independent national tradition."[2] The poets he brings together to represent that tradition—among them, Chaucer, Wyatt, Sidney, and Ralegh—create an author-centered literary history that transfers to English letters the classical authority that Chaucer had embodied in "Virgile, Ovide, Omer, Lucan and Stace," thereby fulfilling the project begun by John Bale in the wake of the Reformation to establish a native literary heritage. Puttenham's endowment of English poetry with an authoritative past, as well as the particular names he produces to fill in its outlines, would prove enormously influential for later literary historians, who used Puttenham as a model for constructing a canonical English literary history. What fewer of Puttenham's later readers would notice, however, is the fact that the central figure of Puttenham's literary history is a woman writer. After tracing a history of English poetry from

Chaucer to his present day, Puttenham names the poet at the pinnacle of English literary achievement, who is none other than Elizabeth I: "last in recitall and first in degree is the Queene our soueraigne Lady, whose learned, delicate, noble Muse, easily surmounteth all the rest that haue written before her time or sence" (77). To support this claim Puttenham reproduces in full "The Doubt of Future Foes," a poem Elizabeth wrote in reponse to the threat posed by Mary Queen of Scots, which Puttenham nominates "the most bewtifull and gorgious" of all of English poetry (254).

It is easy to dismiss Puttenham's hyperbole as a piece of courtly sycophancy; among its many meanings, the *Arte* is a treatise about courtly advancement, and Puttenham's praise is surely redolent of his own ambition. But, coming in the midst of the foundational treatise of English literary history, it also serves as an important indication of how the idea of "English literature" was developed around the figure of a woman writer, even if, in this case, that woman writer was the queen. In this chapter I argue that Puttenham's invention of English literary history in his *Arte of English Poesie* pivots on his representation of Elizabeth as a poet, and in particular, her uses of poetry in her struggle with Mary Queen of Scots. As the immediate context of Elizabeth's "Doubt of Future Foes," Mary's captivity and execution provide both subject and setting for a new poetry of politic secrecy, which for Puttenham establishes poetry's utility to the state, as well as demonstrating the topical significance of what he will identify as Elizabeth's womanly writing. An editor as much as a literary theorist, Puttenham resembles earlier writers and editor figures who formulated their ideas about "English literature" in and through figures of women writers. If the woman writer at the center of Puttenham's work differs from previous examples because she is the English queen, that status also enables Puttenham to endow poetry with a new level of cultural and political importance while at the same time establishing it as what he calls an "arte of a ladies penne."

While later criticism of Elizabethan poetry would tend to emphasize the work of Elizabeth's male courtiers while consigning the queen herself to the position of patron or beloved female object, Elizabeth's contemporaries considered her a poet of the highest rank. In 1598 Francis Meres finds Elizabeth "an excellent Poet herselfe, whose learned, delicate and noble muse surmounteth [all], be it in *Ode*, *Elegy*, *Epigram*, or any other kind of Poem *Heroicke*, or *Lyricke*," thus making her the best poet of all genres as well as of all time.[3] Similarly, in "The Teares of the Muses" Spenser praises the queen as a "most peereless Poetresse."[4] Even after her death removed the

incentive to flatter, Elizabeth's reputation as a poet persisted: in 1624
Thomas Heywood praised Elizabeth above all "Women Poets," citing
her "pleasant Fancies, and Ingenious Ditties, [of which] I have seene
some and herd of many," while Edmund Bolton's *Hypercritica* (1610–
17) classifies Queen Elizabeth among "the best Authors for written
English," placing her approvingly in a Puttenham-like list that includes Sidney, Spenser, Drayton, Shakespeare, Surrey, and Wyatt.[5]
What has survived of Elizabeth's poetry may be a fraction of what she
actually wrote, Leah Marcus suggests, and William Camden hints as
much when he reports that the queen "read or wrote something every
day."[6] But whatever Elizabeth's actual output, the comments of her
contemporaries indicate that her reputation as a poet played an important part in her royal self-fashioning; indeed, among Elizabeth's
surviving poetic efforts is her partial verse translation of Horace's *Ars
Poetica.*[7]

To Elizabeth's contemporaries, the art of poetry was coextensive
with the arts of rule. Henry Savile, for one, imagined kings and queens
to be the ideal authors of books, since they so often formed books'
subjects: "As the great actions of princes are the subject, so stories
composed or amended by princes, are not onely the best patterne and
rule of great actions, but also the most naturall registers therof, the
writers being persons of like degree and of proportional conceits with
the doers."[8] In similar terms Puttenham praises the queen's "noble
Muse," which, he claims, "surmounteth all the rest that haue written before her time or since . . . euen by as much oddes as her owne
excellent estate and degree exceedeth all the rest of her most humble
vassalls" (77). In the Elizabethan period, it would appear, poetry was
a language not only of "princepleasers" (in Puttenham's memorable
term) but also of princes: Elizabeth's verse, claims Bolton in his final
analysis, is praiseworthy because it is "princely."[9] In writing, Elizabeth followed the example of other poet-monarchs such as James I of
Scotland and her father, Henry VIII.[10] But where James and Henry use
the tropes of Petrarchanism to craft themselves as male lovers, the
queen's poetic persona was distinctly female.

To the more familiar figurations of her royal persona—Elizabeth
as amazon, Diana, Astraea—we must add one more, Elizabeth as
Sappho.[11] The Epistle prefacing the 1569 translation of Jan van der
Noodt's *Theatre for Worldlings* not only praises the queen for her
"learning, knowledge, counsell, iudgement, and eloquence," but also
claims that she is "so instructed in the divine Arte of Poetrie, that you
may woorthily be called the second *sappho.*"[12] And in the *Partheniades,* the manuscript sequence of his own poems that Puttenham

presented to Elizabeth as a new year's gift in 1579 and to which he frequently refers in *The Arte of English Poesie,* the queen writes "w[ith] Ladye Sapphoes pen / In sweet measures, of poesye t'endite."[13] The comparison to Sappho grounds Elizabeth's writing in a distinctly female literary genealogy, making her work not only the anchor of a new English literary history but also the embodiment of an alternative classical ancestry that runs parallel to the all-male classical canon of Virgil and Homer.[14]

Elizabeth was by no means typical of women writers of her day. It is doubtful whether her example encouraged her female contemporaries' literary pursuits, and it is clear that to at least some of her male contemporaries, Elizabeth's learnedness was a sign of her exceptionality.[15] But if Elizabeth is now recognized to have been a careful manipulator of her public persona, as shown in her strategic performance of a set of postures and roles associated with early modern femininity, it is clear from Puttenham and her other contemporaries that one key facet of that public persona was the position of "woman writer."[16] Representations of Elizabeth as a woman writer, as well as her own careful self-fashioning as one, stand to illuminate the cultural meanings that attached to and defined "the woman writer" in the Elizabethan age. If Elizabeth attained a level of authority and power that was highly unusual for early modern women, she also showed that the position of the female poet was not inconsistent with a position of female authority and power. To the contrary, it enabled her to negotiate the paradoxes and politically delicate dilemmas that came with being both a woman and a ruler.

The humanist models of public authority and rhetorical power that became ideals for educated men by the mid-sixteenth century notably excluded women from active participation, as a number of studies have shown.[17] While humanism encouraged men to craft themselves as orators and rhetoricians in the public eye, it maintained an unabated phobia about female speech. As Leonardo Bruni insisted in his well-known letter to Battista Malatesta, the same rhetorical arts that were glorious for men to pursue were monstrous for women: "For if a woman throws her arms around while speaking, or if she increases the volume of her speech with greater forcefulness, she will appear threateningly insane and requiring restraint. These matters belong to men; as war, or battles, and also contests and public controversies."[18] If speech signified virility and public authority in a man, a woman who dared to speak in public usurped a masculine privilege; this assumption is articulated by the Chorus in Elizabeth Cary's *Mariam:* "Then she usurps upon another's right, / That seeks to be by public language grac'd."[19] Such a linguistic trespass signified a violation of female chastity, as Cary's Herod implies when he attacks Mariam: "she's unchaste, / Her mouth will ope to ev'ry stranger's ear."[20] Thus, as authorities from Sophocles to Vives asserted, silence, like chastity, was counted as "a woman's greatest ornament."[21]

A female monarch who was required to assert her authority in the male-gendered medium of oratory inhabited a paradox-ridden position; yet the numerous speeches that Elizabeth delivered throughout her reign indicate that such standard injunctions were not all-powerful, nor did humanist restrictions of women's speech consign the female ruler to literal silence. Rather, one of the tactics that Elizabeth deployed to authorize her own public speaking was to invoke and perform the very restrictions that humanism would place on her. With disarming frequency Elizabeth refers to herself in her speeches as "a poore weak woman" of whom decency required silence.[22] In one of her first public addresses, a Latin oration at Cambridge University in 1568, Elizabeth claims reluctance to speak in public, since "my feminine modesty might deter me from making a speech and offering these rude, off hand remarks in so great an assembly of most learned men."[23] Likewise, in a parallel oration at Oxford she admits to having been "possessed of long and grave hesitation as to whether I should speak or keep silent. For if I should speak, I would make evident to you how unskilled I am in letters. But if I kept silent, this failure to speak might be interpreted as contempt."[24] And in another speech, to Parliament in 1575, Elizabeth tells her listeners, "Yf any looke for eloquence, I shall deceive their hope. . . . My sex permitts it not."[25] Elizabeth's speeches, as Frances Teague points out, are carefully crafted rhetorical constructions, which Elizabeth made into key sites of her royal self-fashioning.[26] As an orator herself, Elizabeth tacitly acknowledges oratory's cultural status as a masculine art in ways that also allow her to appropriate it for her own uses: thus in her speeches she eloquently disclaims eloquence, and she violates the humanist injunction to female silence in the very act of articulating it.

Humanist constructions of oratory as a masculine practice are well known; they were clearly known to Elizabeth, as she demonstrates through her canny manipulation of them. But it is less clear how such constructions affected women's writing. If humanists wished women to be silent, few wished their daughters illiterate. Indeed, although Leonardo Bruni emphatically discouraged women from learning rhetoric for the purposes of public speaking, he allowed them to do so for the sake of writing.[27] While the terms "silence" and "speech" or "voice" have been used as common critical metaphors in our own

age for discussing women's writing and its circumscription in the
early periods, in practice, writing and speech were far from inter-
changeable categories during this time. Indeed, the wide range of written media and genres that proliferated in the sixteenth century—
when writing might take the form of letters, private commonplace
books, printed books, or plays, among myriad other possibilities—recalls that "writing" itself was hardly a uniform category. As a material
practice, writing inhabits spaces and claims social forms easily over-
looked when it is collapsed under the metaphor of "speech."[28] Unlike
oratory, writing could take shapes that actually upheld the demands
of female modesty, privacy, and chastity.[29] If Elizabeth's speeches cannily manipulate humanism's gendered construction of oratory, her poetry betrays an awareness of a different set of conventions by calling
attention to its own restrictedness and privacy in ways that set it in
opposition to public speech.

From childhood Elizabeth produced texts within predominantly female, household spaces. In her youth, she translated Marguerite de
Navarre's *Le miroir de l'âme pécheresse* as *The Miroir or Glasse of the
Synnefull Soule* (later published by John Bale as *A Godly Medytacyon
of the Christen Sowle* [1548]), which she presented as a gift volume,
complete with a cover she embroidered herself, to her learned stepmother Catherine Parr.[30] (See Figure 8.) The art of embroidery also
identified the then princess with a model of domestic, feminine activity that was held to unite women across all classes, as attested in
*A Booke of Curious and Straunge Inuentions, called the First Part of
Needleworks* (1596):

> This worke beseemeth Queenes of great renowne,
> And Noble Ladies of a high degree:
> Yet not exempt for Maids of any Towne,
> For all may learne that thereto willing be.[31]

Handbooks of embroidery for women contrasted the act of holding a
pen with that of holding a needle, reflecting a cultural commonplace
that contrasted women's sewing with men's writing.[32] But by creating
a book that brought together both embroidery and writing, Elizabeth
made writing and needlepoint into contiguous, rather than opposed,
activities. Moreover, by circulating this book within the devotional
coterie that was headed by Parr, a writer herself, the young Elizabeth
produced writing as an activity that could be performed within the
private and domestic spaces of women.

Elizabeth's *Miroir or Glasse of the Synnefull Soule* emerges within
what John N. King identifies as "a circle of aristocratic women . . .

Figure 8. Embroidered Cover, Elizabeth Tudor, *The Miroir or Glasse of the Synne-full Soule.* Back cover, Bodleian MS Cherry 36. Reproduced with permission of the Bodleian Library, Oxford.

who sponsored humanistic scholarship and patronized the translation and publication of religious works into the vernacular," of which Catherine Parr formed the center.[33] Furthermore, by electing to translate a work by Marguerite de Navarre, Elizabeth associated herself with a work by an important female writer who was admired by Tudor women.[34] As a queen, Elizabeth continued to produce and circulate texts that created intimate networks among women. The image of the queen as a woman who wrote texts for other royal women influenced popular representations of Elizabeth, as reflected in a poem purporting to be an "Epitaph, made by the Queenes Maiestie at the Death of the Princesse of Espinoye," that found its way into print in John Soowthern's *Pandora* (1584); while its authenticity has been doubted, the poem nonetheless promotes Elizabeth's verse as a medium that created intimate bonds with other women.[35]

Although interpretations of Elizabeth's reign have long focused on the queen's relations with men as the central ones in her life, Philippa Berry establishes the importance of women in the Elizabethan court, pointing out that the queen chose to confine her most private activities to female company.[36] If her speeches to the male students and scholars at Oxford and Cambridge present her feminine speech as out of place in these masculine milieux, Elizabeth's writing couches itself in the private confines of real or imaginary female textual communities. The textual milieu of women's private writing offered a set of culturally significant terms that were notably distinct from the terms used to describe the contrastingly masculine domain of oratory. It was within this privatized, feminine domain that Elizabeth's texts circulated; and if they were destined for wider audiences and readerships, the queen's poems and letters nonetheless self-consciously recall the cultural conventions associated with a sphere of feminine literary activity based on the private exchange of texts.

This chapter argues that Elizabeth I consciously crafted herself as a poet, not because the poet occupied a position of masculine privilege but rather because poetry and the conventions associated with its circulation in manuscript allowed a new measure of authority and communicative power that could coexist with the privacy and silence that humanism so stridently required of women. In the process, Elizabeth's poetry offers us the opportunity to rethink the early modern categories of feminine "privacy" and "silence" not as absolute prohibitions but rather as constructs that could allow unexpected degrees of manipulation. Poetry, which was visibly marginal to the public space of oratory or the open proclamation, offered Elizabeth a medium that not only evaded the gendered constructions of speech and silence but also enabled forms of covert communication that were precluded by the overt medium of the public speech. If Elizabeth learned to write within the privatized, female community that surrounded Catherine Parr, she extended the conventions of this practice in the texts she circulated among other women—including the poem that forms the focus of this chapter, "The Doubt of Future Foes," which was positioned within an imaginary female coterie in its various manifestations, both inside and outside Puttenham's *Arte of English Poesie*. In the poem Elizabeth brings the conventions of female manuscript circulation together with a political practice of covert communication in order to negotiate her complicated relationship with her Catholic kinswoman, Mary Queen of Scots, a relationship in which a textual exchange between women was invested with the highest political stakes.

The poetic practice that Elizabeth develops, furthermore, becomes for George Puttenham the centerpiece of a new English literature, which consciously departs from humanist oratory and the dominant, classical models of rhetoric in the mid-Tudor period. One of *The Arte of English Poesie*'s central aims is to redeem poetry from the secondary position it occupied within English humanist thought and rhetorical culture. As Richard Halpern points out, poetry was never incorporated into the university curriculum in England as it had been in Italy, and it thus remained institutionally marginal to formal rhetorical training, which was meant to produce orators rather than poets.[37] William Webbe, whose 1586 *Discourse of English Poetrie* was published three years before Puttenham's work, sets out to contest this marginality, demanding, "why should we think so basely of [poetry]? rather then of her sister, I mean Rhetoricall *Eloquution*?" His strategy is to redeem poetry by establishing its kinship with oratorical eloquence, claiming that "they were by byrth Twyns, by kinde the same, by originall of one descent."[38] But in so doing, Webbe absorbs poetry into the governing medium of oratory—arguing, for example, that rhyme "is proper not onely to Poets, but also to Readers, Oratours, Pleaders, or any which are to pronounce or speake any thing in publike audience"—and thereby effectively acknowledges oratory's cultural dominance.[39] Puttenham's tactic is altogether different. While he echoes Webbe in making "poets . . . the best perswaders and their eloquence the first Rethoricke of the world" (25), in his central discussion of ornament Puttenham asserts that poetry's arts of persuasion differ fundamentally from those of oratory. Quintillian's *Institutio Oratoria* sows the seeds of humanist discomfort with poetry by warning students of eloquence that "the orator must not follow the poets in everything; more especially in their freedom of language and their license in the use of figures."[40] For Puttenham, on the other hand, freedom of language and license with figures become the sources of poetry's particular power, as when he famously defines "figures and figurative speaches" as "abuses or rather trespasses in speach [which] passe the ordinary limits of common utterance," such

as "*allegorie* [which works] by a duplicitie of meaning or dissimulation vnder couert and darke intendments" (166). While Webbe regrets
poetry's fall from cultural seriousness to "lighter deuises alluring
vnto pleasure and delight," Puttenham emphasizes poetry's ornamental, covert pleasures, only to establish those pleasures' centrality to
the function of the state.[41] Puttenham's emphasis on the ornamentality and covertness of poetic language reverses the terms of oratory's
cultural dominance by taking as the basis of a positive, literary identity those very qualities that accounted for poetry's marginality. If he
thereby distances poetry from oratory irredeemably, Puttenham describes more nearly and historically the poetic practice that took hold
in Elizabeth's own court.

Puttenham's *Arte* testifies, as Louis Montrose points out, to "the
failures of Renaissance Humanism" in England by demonstrating oratory's irrelevance to the Elizabethan political life.[42] As an idealized
version of civic discourse, oratory envisions a polis built around open
communication and public debate, qualities incompatible with the
centralized court of the Tudor monarch.[43] Furthermore, by centering
Elizabeth's production of poetry in the Queen of Scots affair—an
event of central importance to *The Arte of English Poesie* in my
reading—Puttenham recalls a particular political moment in which
the public speech and the open proclamation presented less effective
forms of governance than the covert language of poetry. The incident
thus allows Puttenham to redeem poetry from cultural secondariness
by making it instrumental for a new form of governance, one that op-
erates not through open debate or decree but rather through "duplicitie of meaning or dissimulation vnder couert and darke intendments,"
which he finds exemplified in the queen's own poetry.

By construing Elizabeth's position as a female poet to be central
to her royal persona, Puttenham reveals himself to be perhaps the
queen's best reader, illuminating how poetry was able to serve her interests in ways that oratory could not. Moreover, by presenting Elizabeth in *The Arte of English Poesie* as the greatest English poet of all
time, he makes the woman writer's cultural difference from the classical orator into the basis of a new, English poetics. These points beg
a rereading of Puttenham to assess the mutual dependence of the
terms "woman writer" and "English poetry" as they emerge together
and define one another in the *Arte*. If Puttenham is now widely accepted to be a founding figure of English literary history, what does it
mean to take him seriously when he claims that "the art of English
Poetry" is modeled in what he calls, in reference to Elizabeth, "the
arte of a ladies penne" (255)?

"The Arte of a Ladies Penne"

We can start by reconsidering the gender of poetry in Puttenham's *Arte*.[44] For Puttenham, removing poetry from the space of oratory means necessarily removing it from a masculine to a feminine venue. In his chapter "Of Figures and Figurative Speaches," Puttenham traces the split between oratory and poetry to ancient courts, whose judges feared poetry's ornamental duplicity and thus resolved "to forbid all manner of figurative speaches to be used before them in their consistorie of Iustice." Yet Puttenham defends figures by removing poetry from the court of law to a more ornamental and private place:

> But in this case because our maker or Poet is appointed not for a iudge, but rather for a pleader, and that of pleasant and lovely causes and nothing perillous, such as be those for the triall of life, limme, or livelyhood; and before iudges neither sower nor severe, but in the eare of princely dames, yong ladies, gentlewomen, and courtiers . . . and that all his abuses tende but to dispose the hearers to mirth and sollace by pleasant conveyance and efficacy of speach, they are not in truth to be accompted vices but for vertues in the poetical science much commendable. (166–67)

Distancing poetry from the masculine rhetorical sphere of the court-room, Puttenham recalls Leonardo Bruni's dismissal of women from the court because, as Bruni contends, such grave, public forums are not for them:

> Hers is not the task of learning to speak for and against witnesses, for and against torture, for and against reputation; she will not practice the commonplaces, the syllogisms, the sly anticipation of an opponent's arguments. She will, in a word, leave the rough-and-tumble of the forum entirely to men. (244)

In contrast, the feminized space to which Puttenham withdraws poetry disclaims such public interest and grounds literate practice in the production of pleasure rather than the arbitration of serious matters of the state.

Puttenham's poet is distinguished from the orator by the gender of the company he keeps, as Daniel Javitch notes of the *Arte* in observing "the irrelevance of women to the orator's activity as opposed to their decisive influence on the courtier's"; while the orator serves the state in forums of men, the poet, Javitch asserts, frames himself as "a dilettante who uses his versatile gifts to entertain an exclusive and often largely feminine audience."[45] The women whom Puttenham identifies with poetry's ornamental, privatized place are not only the audience of male poets—they are poets themselves. Chief among his readership Puttenham identifies a group he calls "gentlewomen makers" (256), of whom the queen is the most visible representative, as well as other, unnamed "Ladies and young Gentlewomen" who desire "for their own priuate recreation to make now and then ditties of pleasure" (170). Where William Webbe seeks to redeem poetry from its association with "ditties of lighter matters" rather than "grave and necessary matters," Puttenham's *Arte* emphasizes that association by locating these "ditties of pleasure" in a distinctly feminine realm.[46]

Rather than being closed to women, as is the public world of humanist oratory, a Puttenham-defined poetry, with its emphasis on covertness, ornament, and dissemblance, is a womanly art. The femininity of this art is reflected in Puttenham's discussion of poetic figures, which he describes as decorations similar to the "courtly habillements" of "great Madames of honour" (149) and "the crimson tainte, which should be laid vpon a Ladies lips" (150). These comparisons recall Frances Dolan's recent analysis of anticosmetic polemics in the Renaissance, which associate the "colors" of cosmetic ornament with the worst dangers of rhetoric, which counterfeit the natural world and construct an artificial one out of false appearances.[47] But where the anticosmetic debates limit women's creativity to their cosmetic self-adornment, for Puttenham the use of rhetorical ornament seems particularly fitting to women poets. Puttenham warns male poets against the overuse of figurative language, asserting that excessive "surplusage or preposterous placing or undue iteration or dark word[s], or doubtfull speach" is potentially unseemly and counted as a vice; however, he holds that the same uses of figurative language can "passe without any great reproofe" in texts by women (156). Indeed, what he calls "the pretie Poesies and devices of Ladies, and Gentlewomen makers" (256) appear to be poetic ornament's natural locale.

As the highest embodiment of poetic ornament Puttenham presents Elizabeth's "Doubt of Future Foes," which exemplifies the feminine art of beautiful seeming (*"beau* semblant"). Being "desciphered by the arte of a ladies penne," as Puttenham puts it, the poem reflects the beauty of its maker, "her selfe beyng the most gorgious and bewtifull" (255).[48] But if Puttenham thereby seems to promise a "pretie poesie" and a poem of "private recreation," the queen's "ditty" delivers something entirely different. In Puttenham's words, "the ditty is as followeth":

The doubt of future foes, exiles my present ioy,
And wit me warnes to shun such snares as threaten
  mine annoy,
For falshood novv doth flow, and subiect faith doth ebbe,
Which would not be, if reason rul'd or wisdome weu'd
  the webbe.
But clowdes of tois untried, do cloake aspiring mindes,
Which turne to raigne of late repent, by course of
  changed vvindes.
The toppe of hope supposed, the roote of ruth vvil be,
And frutelesse all their graffed guiles, as shortly ye shall
  see.
Then dazeld eyes vvith pride, vvhich great ambition
  blinds,
Shalbe unseeld by vvorthy wights, vvhose foresight fals-
  hood finds,
The daughter of debate, that eke discord doth sovve
Shal reap no gaine where formor rule hath taught stil
  peace to growe.
No forreine bannisht vvight shall ancre in this port,
Our realme it brookes no strangers force, let them
  elsvvhere resort.
Our rusty svvorde vvith rest, shall first his edge employ,
To polle their toppes that seeke, such change and gape
  for ioy. (255–56)

Where Puttenham stresses poetry's "pleasant and lovely causes and nothing perillous, such as be those for the triall of life, limme, or livelyhood," Elizabeth's poem delivers a matter that is "perillous" in the extreme, as well as directly linked to "the triall of life, limme, or livelyhood"—the queen's struggle with her political enemies—but it produces these causes under the cover of pleasing poetic ornament. True to its designation as the exemplum of poetic ornament, the queen's poem pullulates with figures: in its sixteen lines it comprises a shifting allegory of the changes of climate, the travels of a ship at sea, and, in its most pronounced recurring image, the tending of a garden, figures that were conventional in Petrarchan poetry as well as contemporary emblem books.[49] But its subject, clearly visible beneath the thin veneer of figurative language, is one of the most highly charged political dramas of Elizabeth's reign. The "daughter of debate," as Puttenham explains, is the Queen of Scots, who was Eliza-

beth's cousin and Catholic rival for the throne; and as the poem fore-
tells, she was indeed beheaded for treason on February 8, 1587, after
her long captivity in England. This reference is supported by the
poem's textual history: surviving manuscripts of "The Doubt of Future Foes" place its composition at around 1570, within two years after Mary fled Scotland to seek the refuge that she apparently expected
to find in England's borders. Because of fears that she would amass
armies of Catholic supporters and pose a threat to Elizabeth, Mary
was instead imprisoned for nineteen years before she was finally exe-
cuted.[50] "The Doubt of Future Foes" expresses the royal speaker's
"doubt" about the intentions of her "foes" and brandishes an imaginary "swerde" in her protection; it thus appears to wage a threat
against a fellow queen, and to predict future events with deadly ac-
curacy. For Puttenham's readers in 1589 those events would still be
a recent memory. Yet for Puttenham "The Doubt of Future Foes" is
an example of "poeticall Ornament," a "ditty . . . passing sweete and
harmonicall," and "the most bewtifull and gorgious of all others." If
this poem epitomizes the "bewtifull and gorgious" in poetry, it also
forces its readers to reexamine what these terms mean for Puttenham's *Arte*.

"The gorgious," according to *The Arte of English Poesie*, exemplifies the complexity of the art of poetic beauty, "*beau* semblant"—
which means not so much "seeming beautiful" as "beautiful seeming," the beauty of an appearance that is visibly dissembled. The
figure takes its name and meaning from the work of marble polishers,
Puttenham informs us, whose art shears away the outer roughness of
the stone to leave a mirror-like surface, "so smooth and cleare as ye
may see your face in it." At the same time that it clarifies the stone's
surface, the "gorgious" art embellishes the stone's native dullness,
Puttenham continues, just as "rich and gorgeous apparell" embellishes "the bare and naked body" (254). Both dressing up and shearing
away, the figure of "the gorgious" implies an ability to cloak and to
reveal at the same time.

The dialectic of cloaking and revelation is central to the poem itself, whose overriding thematic concern is the danger of others' hidden meanings. The speaker promises to uncloak "aspiring minds," to
clear away "clowdes of tois," to "unseal" eyes formerly blinded, and
to root out "falsehood" and hidden "snares." The poem thereby creates an opposition between outward appearances and inner meanings, as the speaker worries that her "foes" dissemble their threatening intentions under pleasant facades, and then resolves to expose
and eradicate them with a threat of violence, with the sword that the

speaker brandishes in the final lines. The dissembling arts that the speaker ascribes to her "foes" pointedly recall the Elizabethan arts of poetry; poems, after all, were commonly referred to as "toys" and figurative language as a "cloud," as when Spenser describes his *Faerie Queene* as being "clowdily enwrapped in Allegorical devices."[51] Puttenham's *Arte* itself is a map of such poetic dissimulation, which is concentrated famously in its discussion of allegory, "the figure of false semblant" (197):

> As figures be the instruments of ornament in euery language, so be they also in a sorte abuses or rather trespasses in speach, because they passe the ordinary limits of common vtterance, and be occupied of purpose to deceiue the eare and also the minde, drawing it from plainnesse and simplicitie to a certaine doublenesse, whereby our talke is the more guilefull & abusing, for what els is . . . your *allegorie* [but an inversion of sence] by a duplicitie of meaning or dissimulation vnder couert and darke intendements. (154)

By dissecting such figurative practices, Puttenham not only instructs courtiers in the art of courtly dissimulation, he also provides a handbook for the apprehension of such dissimulative strategies, which, for all their pleasantness, also constitute dangerous "abuses" and "trespasses" against order. This argument departs from Louis Montrose's assertion that "to the Queen, Puttenham proposes an art to keep courtiers occupied with idleness. To her courtiers, he proposes an art in which they may pursue their own ends by dissembling idleness."[52] While it presents itself as a guide for writing poetry, taken as a practical handbook Puttenham's *Arte* is remarkably ineffective: after all, real courtiers like John Harington despised it for reducing poetic art to mechanical craft.[53] Rather, my argument is that by laying bare the linguistic productions of "duplicity of meaning," Puttenham's book not only offers the queen's own "Doubt of Future Foes" as the exemplar of poetic dissimulation, it also offers the queen herself an *ars legendi* for rooting out the dissimulations of others, the dangers of which become a major thematic preoccupation of "The Doubt of Future Foes." But the queen's own poem shows that she already knows how to read through others' deceptions; while threatening to uncloak the hidden meanings that are concealed in "clowdes of tois," "The Doubt of Future Foes" does so in a language that is itself glutted with figures, suggesting that the queen can penetrate allegorical obscurity because she understands its operations. In the very act of opposing poetic "falsehood," then, the royal speaker also shows herself to be an aficionada of its language.

At the time of the poem's composition in 1570, the threat posed by the "falshood" of "aspiring mindes" was more than hypothetical. Mary Queen of Scots had recently entered England and threatened to unify the Elizabethan Catholics into a rebellious faction. With Mary residing in England, covert plots—organized through coded letters, secret symbols, and, as we shall see, poetry—threatened to undermine domestic security, but these required a covert, rather than overt, form of management. In Puttenham's discussion, "The Doubt of Future Foes" counters a hidden threat by issuing an equally hidden threat of its own through the use of a figurative language that enables the queen to present both the subject and herself very differently than she could in an open speech. Her aim in the poem, Puttenham argues, is less to make an outright declaration of knowledge than to display her own skill at piercing the dissemblance of others by proving that she is an arch-dissembler herself. This art was particularly suited to the broader contexts of the poem, as Puttenham describes it:

> Our soueraigne Lady perceiuing how by the Sc. Q. residence within this Realme at so greate libertie and ease . . . bred secret factions among her people. . . . The Queene our soueraigne Lady to declare that she was nothing ignorant [of] those secret [practizes], though she had long with great wisdome and pacience dissembled it, writeth this ditty most sweet and sententious, not hiding from all such aspiring minds the daunger of their ambition and disloyaltie, which afterward fell out most truly by th'exemplary chastisement of sundry persons. (255)

In keeping with the doubleness implied by the figure of "the gorgious," "The Doubt of Future Foes" cannily manipulates the appearances of secrecy and disclosure. The poem is not a straightforward declaration of knowledge but rather a declaration of a lack of ignorance: the queen wrote it "to declare that she was nothing ignorant [of] those secret [practices]." It is not an outright revelation but a strategic decision not to hide, in "not hiding from all such aspiring minds the daunger of their ambition and disloyaltie." And it is not so much a denunciation of dissemblance—"though she had long with great wisdome and pacience dissembled it"—as it is an effort to foreground the queen's dissemblance, to show how her "ignorance" is merely a cover. What "The Doubt of Future Foes" reveals is not *what* the queen knows, but *that* she knows—and that she keeps what she knows hidden. This register suits the queen whose motto was "video et taceo," "I see and hold my tongue."[54] Poetry enables the queen to display that she is holding her tongue in ways that are appropriate to the social

NON SINE SOLE
IRIS.

Figure 9. Queen Elizabeth, The Rainbow Portrait, attributed to Marcus Gheer-
aerts the Younger. Reproduced with permission of the Marquess of Salisbury.

requirements for female silence, while also allowing her to maintain
a position of threateningly silent surveillance, as emblematized in
the famous Rainbow portrait, in which Elizabeth wears a dress that
is embroidered with emblematic eyes and ears, the organs of surveillance, while her own sealed lips are pressed into a serene half-smile.[55]
(See Figure 9.) This image embodies Elizabeth's poetics of queenship, by representing her vigilance in signs that are both feminine—

embroidered figures on a dress—and threatening, manifesting the queen's powers of all-seeing surveillance.

The Poetics of Queenship

Puttenham's *Arte,* then, is not simply a guide for poetic dissimulation; it is a key for the decoding of such dissimulation and thus offers itself to the queen as an anti-poetic that is in league with her own aim in "The Doubt of Future Foes." In the closing paragraph of *The Arte of English Poesie* Puttenham makes explicit his own ambition to be of service to the queen by "describing the toyes of this our vulgar art," in a bid for service that pointedly repeats the queen's own paranoid terms from "The Doubt of Future Foes":

> I write to the pleasure of a Lady and a most gratious Queene. . . . Besides finding by experience that many times idlenesse is lesse harmefull then vnprofitable occupation, dayly seeing how these great *aspiring mynds and ambitious heads* of the world seriously searching to deale in matters of state, be often times so busie and earnest that they were better vnoccupied, and peraduenture altogether idle, I presume so much vpon your Maiesties most milde and gracious iudgement howsoeuer you conceiue of myne abilitie to any better or greater service, that yet in this attempt ye wil allow of my loyall and good intent always endeuouring to do your Maiestie the best and greatest of those seruices I can. (314; emphasis added)

By calling attention to "myne abilitie to any better or greater service," Puttenham is undoubtedly petitioning the queen for reward and employment.[56] But what "ability" is he advertising, and for what "service" does the *Arte* prove his fitness? Puttenham frames his suit by employing terms that have been directly lifted from the queen's own poem and thereby presents *The Arte of English Poesie* itself as an extended reading of "The Doubt of Future Foes." By showing that he can "[describe] the toyes of this our vulgar art," he also shows that he knows how to penetrate the "clowdes of tois" that threaten the speaker in the queen's poem. And by condemning "these great aspiring mynds and ambitious heads of the world seriously searching to deale in matters of state," Puttenham recalls the "aspiring minds" that are threateningly cloaked in those "clowdes of tois" in "The Doubt of Future Foes." Similarly, Puttenham's "ambitious heads" makes a darkly joking reference to the last line of "The Doubt of Future Foes," in which the speaker threatens to wield her sword "to polle their toppes that seeke, such change." "Poll" here can signify both "head" and "to cut" (as in to "pollard" a tree); by glossing the line as a reference to "ambitious heads" he signals that he understands the queen's barely hidden meaning. Considering that Mary's head was cut off just two years before the appearance in print of *The Arte of English Poesie*, the line also reads like a retrospective defense of Elizabeth's policy on Mary Queen of Scots.[57]

In this final paragraph, then, Puttenham shows both that he can decipher the courtly dissimulations of others as the queen herself wishes to in "The Doubt of Future Foes," and that he can read the queen's poetry in all the doubleness that she intends and therefore is fit to serve as an interpreter of and apologist for her "covert and dark intendments." This aim is fulfilled in another text that Puttenham wrote on the queen's behalf. Little is known of George Puttenham's biographical existence, beyond his authorship of *The Arte of English Poesie* and the lesser-known sequence of poems, the *Partheniades*, both of which use poetry to proclaim his allegiance to the queen. Puttenham is also the author of a manuscript that appears to share little with his better-known works beyond devotion to the queen and dedication to defending her treatment of Mary Queen of Scots. The manuscript is variously known as "A Defence of the Honorable Sentence and Execution of the Queene of Scotes" and "An Apologie or True Defense of her Ma[jesty's] Hono[r] and Good Renowne," and it proclaims itself to be "writen by GEORGE PUTTENHAM to the servece of her ma[jesty]" to defend Elizabeth's execution of the Queen of Scots against potentially dangerous detractors.[58] If the roughly contemporaneous "Defence" and *Arte of English Poesie* share an interest in Elizabeth's treatment of Mary Queen of Scots, the rhetorical undertaking of the former reflects upon the poetic project of the latter, by reading the incident as the origin of a dark language of hidden significations and secret threats that is produced by the queen and requires Puttenham's gloss.

In *The Arte of English Poesie*, allegory's "covert and dark" language marks it out as the figure of dissemblance ("False Semblant"), a figure that Puttenham argues is especially well suited to rulers: "Qui nescit dissimulare nescit regnare" (Who knows not how to dissemble knows not how to rule) (195). Queen Elizabeth's use of "covert and dark termes" likewise forms the premise of "A Defence of the Honorable Sentence and Execution of the Queene of Scotes," which aims to explain those terms to readers, "to the intent that no part of her Majesty's behaviour or doings therein should be *covered or hidden*" in relation to the Queen of Scots affair (68; emphasis added). Puttenham's aim in the "Defence" is therefore, he explains, "to have laied open and

unfoulded even the most secreat partes of the sayd cause, whiche hath
fallen out from the beginning of this businesse betwene her Maiestie
and the sayd Scottische Quene" (69). The trial and execution of Mary
Queen of Scots are to the "Defence" what "The Doubt of Future Foes"
is to *The Arte of English Poesie*; both the poem and the trial position the queen as the author of a discourse of covert but controversial
meaning that will necessitate a written defense or explanation. And
in both, Puttenham offers his work as the gloss on Elizabeth's dark
text. But while Puttenham promises to "lay open" "even the most
secreat partes of the sayd cause," in the course of the text he admits
that Elizabeth's dealings with the Scottish queen are an open secret:
"Nor this entent of her Majesties was so close or secrete, but that
manie about her haue bene made acquainted with it by her own re-
gall mouthe" (75). Indeed, the queen's "secreats" are coextensive
with those matters "which her Majestie was not unwilling should be
bruted and spred abrode" (74). What makes the queen's secrets "covered or hidden," in other words, does not necessarily keep them from
public knowledge.

  Renaissance discourses of secrecy, as several recent studies have established, manipulated the appearances of public and private knowledge. In the Tudor and Stuart vogue for the "secret" arts of miniatures
and sonnets, Patricia Fumerton discerns the effort to create a private
self both within and beyond the artifice of public spectacle, while
Richard Rambuss analyzes Spenser's poetics of secrecy to conclude
that its primary effort is less to hide a material secret than to craft
that hiddenness as a flagrant display.[59] Such insights can illuminate
the doubleness of Puttenham's "Defence of the Honorable Sentence"
and its promise to "lay open" the queen's secrets. The *raison d'être* of
the "Defence" is not to disclose Elizabeth's secrets, the substance of
which he claims is public knowledge already, but to construct that
public knowledge *as* a secret. The effect is both to make his readers
into privileged insiders and to produce the queen's openly known secrets as objects of desire. This production of public knowledge as private is a function that Horace sees as germane to the art of poetry; in
lines that Queen Elizabeth herself translated into English, Horace instructs the poet, "In private sort the commen thing declare; General
mattar shal be made thy private part."[60] This Horatian model of public knowledge made private forms the basis of Elizabeth's poetics of
queenship, which Puttenham illustrates in both *The Arte of English
Poesie* and "The Defence of the Honorable Sentence": it continually
stages matters of public policy as the stuff of secrets.[61]

If the effect of "The Defence of the Honorable Sentence" is to package Elizabeth's public policy as if it were a secret matter, *The Arte of
English Poesie* shows how poetry enables monarchs to manipulate secrecy to effect public policy. This is the purpose of the poetic form
that Puttenham claims is most suitable to monarchs' use, the emblem. Emblems are hieroglyphic poems that join enigmatic images
with cryptic mottos: as Rosalie Colie points out, they operate through
a "condensation of meaning" that is the opposite of humanist *copia*,
bearing out Daniel Javitch's observation that Puttenham's poetics distinguishes itself from humanist oratory by its interest in "the capacity of figures to convey meaning out of all proportion to words."[62] Yet
while emblems work, as Puttenham asserts, "by secret might," they
also have a public significance, appearing on coins or the monarch's
livery in ways that assert control through intimate means. Their purpose, as Puttenham describes it, is

> to insinuat some secret, wittie, morall and braue purpose presented
> to the beholder, either to recreate his eye, or please his phantasie, or
> examine his iudgement or occupie his braine or to manage his will
> either by hope or by dread, euery of which respects be of no little
> moment to the interest and ornament of the ciuill life. (121)

As an "ornament of the civil life," the emblem shares with the principal "poetical ornament," "the gorgious," the ability to manipulate
the effects of cloaking and revelation in order to produce a realm
of interiorized meaning. From "eye" to "fantasy" to "judgment" to
"will," the emblem produces a series of effects in its reader that is
increasingly internalized; the result is to create in the viewer an advanced state of paranoia, as each "beholder" is given the sense that
the emblem is meant for his eyes, for her eyes, alone, but without
being certain of its exact meanings.[63] As the subject attempts to penetrate the dark meanings of the emblem, the emblem penetrates the
subject. Like the figure of "the gorgious," it begins by beguiling the
eye and ends by transfixing the conscience, as it produces not an image but a mirror that reflects the spectator back to him- or herself, just
as the queenly figure of "the gorgious" creates a surface "so smooth
and cleare as ye may see your face in it." By enlisting each subject as
a private viewer and reader, the emblem becomes an instrument of
public discipline.

In its management of the subject's will "either by hope or by
dread," the royal poetry that Puttenham describes produces an anxiety in its readers that is more familiarly constitutive of the Petrarchan

lover, who is riven with uncertainty about his mistress's true intentions. But the production of this erotic uncertainty is also one of Elizabeth's mechanisms for controlling her courtiers. In one of his own *Partheniades* that he cites in his *Arte of English Poesie*, Puttenham purports to anatomize the queen's production of desire:

> A cheare vvhere loue and Maiestie do raigne,
> Both milde and sterne, &c. (*Arte*, 263)

While the poem in the *Arte* breaks off here, the rest of the "Partheniade" continues in manuscript thus:

> Hauing some secret mighte
> 'Twixte hope and dreede in woe, and w[ith] delighte
> Man's harte in holde, and eye for to detayne;
> Feedinge the one w[ith] sighte in sweete desyre,
> Dauntinge th'other by daunger to aspire. (172)

Where the royal emblem begins by recreating the eye and ends by managing the will, Elizabeth is here credited with "detaining" the eye and "holding" the heart of her subjects, terms suggestive of both erotic fascination and arrest. By thus producing the contradictory Petrarchan effects of hope and dread, delight and danger, she maintains her subjects in a state of continual self-dividedness. If hope and dread are the privileged emotions of the Petrarchan lover kept guessing after the intentions of his aloof mistress, they are also, Puttenham explains, constitutive attributes of the subject's relation to the monarch. Royal poetry, which serves to "manage the will either by hope or by dread," enforces this function. So much is clear in an emblem cited by Puttenham that exemplifies the emblem's status as "ornament of the ciuill life." It depicts

> two strange serpents entertangled in thir amorous congresse, the lesser creeping with his head into the greaters mouth, which words purporting [*ama et time*] love and feare. Which posie with marvellous much reason and subtillity implieth the dutie of euery subiect to his Prince, and of euery Prince to his subiect, and that without either of them both, no subiect could be sayd entirely to performe his liegeance nor the Prince his part of lawfull gouernement. For without fear and loue the soueraigne authority could not be vpholden. . . . All which parts are discouered in this figure: loue by the serpents amorous entertangling: obedience and feare by putting the inferiours head into the others mouth hauing puissance to

destroy. On th'other side, iustice in the greater to prepare and man-
ace death and destruction to offenders. (119–20)

Here the mechanisms of reward—as in the snakes' "amorous congress"—are maintained in an uneasy equilibrium with the mechanisms of punishment—"by putting the inferiours head into the others
mouth hauing puissance to destroy." The ruler's "puissance to destroy"
is also a measure of "love," while the subject's "fear" is also an extension of the desire that compels that subject into such dangerous "amorous entertangling" with the ruler. While the ruler's love for the subject
is, quite literally, all-engulfing, the emblem also warns the subject that
to engage in "amorous congress" with the ruler is to risk decapitation.
The erotic danger and intense intimacy of the scene reflect the ruler's
ability to mobilize each subject's "fear and love" on a distinctly individual level, to give the appearance that the ruler exists for each subject alone, that for "the dutie of every subiect to his prince," there is a
reciprocal and equally individualized duty "of euery Prince to his subiect." It therefore fulfills the function of the emblem—"to manage
[the subject's] will"—by insinuation, as Puttenham puts it, working
not through command and force but by "secret might."

For Puttenham, the key to this "secret might" is the monarch's
manipulation of figurative language, which maintains its reader in a
contant state of uncertainty. By cloaking her meanings, Elizabeth pro-
vokes her reader to look inward and thereby to "examine his iudgement or occupie his braine or to manage his will either by hope or by
dread." Her poetry is the "ornament of the ciuill life" because it reproduces public order on the level of private affect, by making her
subjects into readers who are continually tormented by the desire to
interpret her secrets, knowing that those secrets concern them in intimate ways. Thus the queen is the most important English poet for
the same reason that allegory is the most important figure in *The Arte
of English Poesie:* both use language to the greatest effect by with-
holding meaning.

The Covert Place of Women's Writing

The poetics of covertness that "The Doubt of Future Foes" exemplifies through its use of "covert and dark terms" is abetted by the textual practice of coterie manuscript circulation, the poem's primary
medium of transmission, which makes it a material token of secrecy.
"The Doubt of Future Foes" appeared in print only in Puttenham's
Arte; all of its other contemporary or near-contemporary attestations

are in manuscript, often in commonplace books or the personal anthologies through which Elizabethan readers collected poetry. In the years around and after its composition in 1570, "The Doubt of Future Foes" appears to have been widely circulated, surviving today in eight manuscripts.[64] One is the Arundel Harington Manuscript, which collects courtly poems along with scraps of letters and courtly gossip; in it, "The Doubt of Future Foes" is copied in a careful hand and prefaced by a note, probably by Sir John Harington, which commends the poem to an unnamed woman:

> *Good Madame,*
> Herewith I commit a precious jewel, not for your ear, but your eye; and doubt not but you will rejoyce to wear it even in your heart: It is of her Highness own enditing, and doth witness, how much her wisdom and great learning doth outweigh even the perils of state, and how little all worldly dangers do work any change in her mynde. My Lady Wiloughby did covertly get it on her Majesties tablet, and had much hazard in so doing; for the Queen did find out the thief, and chid for spreading evil bruit of her writing such toyes, when other matters did so occupy her employment at this time; and was fearful of being thought too lightly of for so doing. But marvel not, good Madam, her Highness doth frame herself to all occasions, to all times, and all things, both in business, and pastime, as may witness this her sonnet.[65]

Creating a highly charged dialectic of hiddenness and exposure, Harington stresses the privacy of the poem's composition and circulation. Stolen "covertly" from the queen's private "tablet," the poem is put into circulation apparently against its writer's wishes. But passed from hand to hand in manuscript, it claims value through the very restrictedness of its circulation, becoming "a precious jewel" that its reader will guard intimately "even in [her] heart." Harington emphasizes the poem's privacy by staging its composition within what appears to be an almost exclusively feminine space whose perimeter is defined by the queen, "my Lady Wiloughby," and the nameless "Madame," for whom Harington functions as a go-between.[66] By setting the poem's circulation within the privatized sphere of a female textual community, Harington's narrative calls on the cultural restrictedness of manuscript poetry that is here produced through a nexus of class and gender.

The coterie manuscript played an important role in early modern literary culture, and Arthur Marotti argues that it is no coincidence that "as producers of writing, women were much more active in the system of manuscript transmission than in print," given that "the relative privacy of manuscript transmission" allowed them to circulate their works in a medium that did not violate early modern standards of female modesty.[67] Perhaps as a result, the woman writer in manuscript became a familiar cultural figure. As Jeffrey Masten shows, Lady Mary Wroth's romance *Urania* depicts manuscript circulation between women as "a withdrawal into a privatized discursive space . . . against the making public, the circulation, of a woman's story."[68] This yoking of manuscript, privacy, and femininity recalls the terms in which Elizabeth's tutor Roger Ascham praises the queen's learning as a specifically enclosed and private pursuit, in contrast to the more public forum of masculine education:

> Within the wals of her priuie-chamber she hath obteyned that excellencie of learning, to understand, speak, and write both wittily with head, and faire with hand, as scarce one or two rare wittes in both the universities have in many years reached unto.[69]

Among her other educational accomplishments, it is fitting that Elizabeth's handwriting—her ability to write "faire with hand"—seems a particularly praiseworthy one in a woman, suited to the private site of her learning.[70] The queen's handwriting "within the wals of her priuie-chamber" is thus opposed to the public training in oratory and disputation favored by "both the universities," the milieux from which Elizabeth herself would signal her alienation in her addresses to Oxford and Cambridge.

But if, as Ann Baynes Coiro observes, "manuscript became, in practice, a feminine mode of writing" implicitly opposed to the masculine publicity of print, the example of early modern women writers such as Lady Mary Wroth also suggests that its "privacy" could have public meanings and uses.[71] At the same time that it crafts manuscript circulation between women as "a privatized discursive space," Wroth's *Urania* itself was printed, and its production of a private space of female writing takes place within a female-authored text that aspired to a much wider exposure.[72] It thereby demonstrates the extent to which the boundaries dividing print and manuscript, public and private were not absolute or inevitable, suggesting that we should read representations of the "private manuscript"—as well as the feminization of the manuscript form—less as actual descriptions of historical circulation practices than as rhetorical frames that could be invoked and performed toward particular ends.[73]

It is now commonly understood that aristocratic poets circulated their own poems in manuscript as a way of escaping "the stigma of print," to recall J. W. Saunders's influential term.[74] As Saunders explains, in the Renaissance, print was associated with the common mass of readers, while the more restricted medium of manuscript was favored by both aristocratic poets and their imitators as a mark of privilege. As a matter of course, those poets whose work found its way into print wrote prefaces expressing their horror at the medium and their preference for the privacy of manuscript: as Samuel Daniel avouches in his preface to *Delia* (1592), "I rather desired to keep in the private passions of my youth, from the multitude, as things uttered to my selfe, and consecrated to silence."[75] Yet despite appearances to the contrary, the manuscript medium was far from an entirely "private" one but also had public uses, as Marotti and Harold Love have recently observed.[76] Modifying Saunders's thesis, Jonathan Crewe argues that we should see in these poets' uses of manuscript "neither a strong desire nor a capacity to limit their [texts'] circulation." Crewe sees instead a calculated attempt to create an aura of "privileged insidedness" around the text and its readers. The early modern coterie poet, he argues, attempted "to hide and reveal the secret at the same time; to let the right outsiders become insiders."[77] If Crewe's insight offers us a way of reading the uses of manuscript in the period as part of a larger strategy of textual circulation, it stands to illuminate the different uses of privacy affecting women's writing in the period. By this model, women's apparent preference for manuscript does not necessarily represent an attempt to hide their texts from circulation; rather, manuscript's production of "privileged insidedness" could produce the appearance of hiddenness within the context of a broader circulation. I want to suggest that the privacy to which the female coterie laid claim—and to which Harington refers in connection with Elizabeth's "Doubt of Future Foes"—was not the opposite of public circulation, but rather a strategy that anticipated and even promoted such circulation.

Such an analysis brings together an understanding of the calculated restrictedness of manuscript circulation and the strategic manipulation of public and private in Elizabethan discourses of secrecy to ask how the decorous privacy of women's writing allowed for a wider influence than has been previously imagined. One example that illuminates the conjunction of these three terms is the early modern writer Elizabeth Egerton.[78] Egerton wrote a number of poems, including occasional poetry, verse meditations on scripture, and poems about and addressed to her family. These were all confined to manuscript, and after her death her husband, John Egerton, wrote an epitaph praising his wife for her "modesty in concealing" her verse.[79] Yet

drawing attention to the poems' "concealment" also serves to publi-
cize them. In fact, the poems were hardly concealed, since at least
three separate manuscripts of them currently exist, which suggests
that they were both circulated and recopied by readers outside the immediate Egerton household. The "modest concealment" of Elizabeth
Egerton's poems was thus apparently not inconsistent with their circulation and indeed, may well have played a significant part in it, to
the extent that concealment becomes a marker of value and a stimu-
lant of readerly desire. While the gentlemanly "stigma of print" offered aristocratic poets a chance to signify the restrictedness of their
poetry even while introducing it into public circulation, we might
identify a related but gendered strategy among women writers of
manuscript as a "modesty trope" allowing them to stage the feminine
privacy and concealment of their verses while at the same time sending them into circulation.[80] The common protestation that female-
authored texts are meant to be concealed might be seen as a way of
adhering to humanist injunctions to female privacy while simultaneously constructing their texts as restricted and hence the objects of
elevated value and desire, in the way that Bourdieu defines "restricted
circulation" as a marker of cultural value.[81] Queen Elizabeth shows
an awareness of such postures and conventions in her own poetry,
which invokes the feminine and aristocratic associations of manuscript in order to produce a kind of writing that claims the highest
privilege in its restrictedness at the same time that it maintains an
appearance of feminine modesty in its concealment. Thus the queen's
poetry represented a sphere of literary production in which the privacy and enclosure of women's writing coincided with a sphere of restricted circulation that was endowed with cultural prestige.

The suggestion that the "privacy" of the female-authored text ren-
dered it an object of heightened value and desire is borne out in Harington's narrative of the covert circulation of "The Doubt of Future
Foes." In it, Elizabeth frames the poem within a privatized space that
she wants to distinguish from her public concerns, "the other matters
that did so occupy her employment at this time." But what the poem
reveals for Harington is not the exclusivity of the queen's privacy so
much as the extensiveness of her art—her capacity to "frame herself
to all occasions, to all times, and all things." As Harington observes,
the queen's "privacy" is no less a "frame" than her public self-display.
Indeed, that privacy is constructed retroactively through the narrative
of the poem's exposure: it constitutes less a withdrawal from circulation than a way of representing limitation and restriction as markers
of value that in turn promote circulation.[82] This framing is central to

what I have wanted to call Elizabeth's poetics of queenship. The topic of the poem that Elizabeth would hide, after all, is the very public threat posed by the Queen of Scots. But framed within the conventions of coterie poetry, Elizabeth's poem represents a subject of such public importance as the Queen of Scots affair as a secret more fitting to the private place of a lady's chamber.[83]

By staging the queen's relationship with Mary as a private and not a public matter, the manuscript circulation of "The Doubt of Future Foes" supports Elizabeth's broader strategy for dealing with the Queen of Scots. After Mary's flight into England, the political dilemma of having two queens in one kingdom maintained both captive and captor in a highly charged impasse: once she entered England, Mary could be neither allowed to travel freely nor imprisoned outright, since both would directly threaten Elizabeth's security. But even after Mary was suspected of having plotted to overthrow her, Elizabeth was reluctant to punish her openly, since this could prompt retaliation from forces sympathetic to Mary both in England and in Catholic Europe. Instead of public suppression and punishment, the Queen of Scots required more covert management. In his study of Elizabethan secret services, Alan Haynes argues that it was largely the delicacy of the Queen of Scots affair that gave rise to a powerful domestic espionage network during Elizabeth's reign.[84] Given Mary's own increasingly daring circulation of letters in code to her allies, this network concentrated significant energies on the interception and interpretation of secret texts. Thus Puttenham's observation that "Qui nescit dissimulare nescit regnare" had urgent applications in the relationship between Elizabeth and Mary Queen of Scots: both queens attempted to dissimulate a relationship of sisterly amity, at the same time that each attempted to see through the other's dissimulation to her real motives. The activities of interpretation and dissimulation thus became charged with the highest political stakes.

Puttenham is right to see the conflict between Elizabeth and Mary as the source of a politically urgent language of "covert and darke intendements" that was communicated in and through poetic figures. Poetry played an important role in Elizabeth's attempts to manage the Queen of Scots affair. The two queens never met in the flesh and only communicated directly through the letters, poems, and tokens that passed between them, coded by both the participants and outside observers as the private exchanges of affectionate women, and thus recalling the scenes of intimate textual exchange between royal women that Elizabeth had encountered in the female coterie of Catherine Parr. Elizabeth herself encouraged this coding, which had powerful applications as a diplomatic strategy. While it enabled her to maintain a relationship of apparently sororal intimacy with the Queen of Scots, the medium of poetry offered Elizabeth a degree of ambiguity and deniability that the other media of rulership—the speech or the published proclamation—would not allow. Thus what Puttenham called allegory's "duplicity of meaning" allowed Elizabeth to maintain a correspondence that was both intimate and surveillant, affectionate and threatening, within a medium that allowed both queens to maintain postures that were consistent in appearance with humanist productions of femininity as silent, private, and marginal to the political.

Such a posture became increasingly useful to Elizabeth as she was called on to account for her policy on the Queen of Scots for the public record. Long after her ministers called for Mary's execution, Elizabeth equivocated for fear of reprisal, and even in the two speeches in which she was pressed to pronounce Mary's sentence, she refused to do so openly. In a speech delivered to Parliament in 1586 Elizabeth protests that she cannot speak openly about Mary, using what by then were signature terms for discussing her supposed aversion for public speaking: "I have this day been in greater Conflict with myself than ever I was in all my life, whether I should speak, or hold my peace. If I should speak and not complain, I shall dissemble; if I should be silent, all your labor and Pains taken were in vain."[85] This moment in the speech on Mary echoes Elizabeth's early oration at Oxford, in which she claims similarly to have been "possessed of a long and grave hesitation as to whether I should speak or keep silence." The terms in which, in the earlier speech, Elizabeth protests her unfitness as a woman to speak in a public forum—"for if I should speak, I would make evident to you how unskilled I am in letters. But if I kept silent, this failure to speak might be interpreted as contempt"—are here adapted to describe the impossibility of coming to a conclusion about the delicate situation of Mary Queen of Scots: "If I should speak and not complain, I shall dissemble; if I should be silent, all your labor and Pains taken were in vain." Elizabeth's contemporaries interpreted her delay at imposing Mary's death sentence as female tenderheartedness, as did William Warner in 1597, who ascribed her reluctance to punish Mary to the fact that she was "still pitying her Foe."[86] But her equivocation was also grounded in *realpolitik*, since giving the order for Mary's death risked inviting revenge from outside, but keeping her alive risked internal rebellion. When it came to publicizing Mary's sentence, then, speech and silence were equally untenable.

In the speeches on Mary Queen of Scots, Elizabeth frames the extreme difficulty of her predicament as an abhorrence of public media of expression: if open speech was impossible, then all the more impossible was "publication of the sentence."[87] But one medium that she did find suitable for her relationship with Mary was the private manuscript exchanged between women. In another speech of 1586, Elizabeth frames her relationship with Mary, as well as Mary's betrayal, as a story of women's secret writing:

> As it is not unknowne to some of my Lordes here (for now I will play the blabbe)[,] I secretlie wrote her a le[ter] upon the discou[er]ye of her treasons, that if she would repent her throughlie of her evell course, confesse it and priuatlie acknoledge it by her l[et]res unto me, she neve[r] should be called for it into publique question, nether did I it of any minde to circumvente her, for then I knew as much as she could confesse, and so did I write.[88]

Once again the queen's relationship with Mary Queen of Scots is staged as a drama of female writing, distinguished by the "secrecy" and "privacy" of its texts, which are sharply distinguished from the "public question" of Mary's trial and execution. The boundary between these realms is marked by the shame of exposure, and again Elizabeth brackets this scene of private writing by calling attention to its involuntary, and unseemly, "publication." Significantly, in disclosing the secret of her writing to Mary the queen calls herself a "blabbe." "Blabb" is an early modern term characterizing women's public speech as a sexually improper activity, one that was used pointedly by other early modern women writers to describe their own writing and the shame it would incur through publication. As Lady Mary Wroth asks in *Urania*, "shall I turne blabb?"[89] By crafting herself as a "blabb" in her speech, the queen similarly draws attention to her own feminine modesty by revealing her self-consciousness at the seeming impropriety of her public display. But while it affects a sincere fear of exposure, Elizabeth's use of the term "blabb" is another way of "framing" herself and the topic of that speech. As she notes herself, it is a careful performance: she "plays the blabb." The speech itself was one that Elizabeth carefully edited in preparation for its circulation in print, maintaining all the while her aversion to public exposure. In her revisions, as Allison Heisch points out, "the queen [retains] . . . the section in which she plays 'the blabb,' plainly affecting not to know that her confidential interjection would find its way to a broad international audience."[90] While Elizabeth affected a horror of public exposure, she did so within the public media of the parliamentary speech and the printed forms it later assumed, to the end of enlisting her audience within a position of "privileged insidedness" more familiar in relation to the manuscript document of limited circulation. The effect of the queen's staged disclosure is therefore less to hide the scene of women's writing than to produce it *as* private, while at the same time performing that privacy within the supremely public medium of the speech to Parliament.

Elizabeth's description of this scene of female writing echoes the dialectic of secrecy and disclosure that both Puttenham and Harington take to be central to the circulation of "The Doubt of Future Foes." For Harington the seemingly unauthorized circulation of Elizabeth's poem promises to reveal the queen's secrets but instead reveals only how skillfully the queen "doth frame herself to all occasions, to all times, and all things, both in business, and pastime." Puttenham similarly describes the queen's circulation of the poem as a way of revealing her own dissemblance of ignorance, but masking the substance of her knowledge, by "declar[ing] that she was nothing ignorant of those secret practices, though she had long with great wisdom and pacience dissembled it." In her own description of writing to Mary in her speech, Elizabeth similarly manipulates the appearances of knowledge and disclosure: while she asks Mary to tell all, she reveals that she already knows all: "for then I knewe as much as she could confesse, and so did I write." By claiming to know in advance any secrets Mary might be hiding, Elizabeth attempts to produce an effect similar to that of the emblem, which, Puttenham notes in *The Arte of English Poesie,* induces the reader "to examine his iudgement or occupie his braine or to manage his will either by hope or by dread." Wielding the appearance of knowledge while witholding its substance, Elizabeth attempts to convince Mary that she already knows her secrets, and thereby to entice her into making a full disclosure.

"Chère Soeur": The Queen of England and the Queen of Scots

If only Mary had written to her, Elizabeth insists in her address to Parliament, her life would have been spared. During the nineteen years of her imprisonment, Mary in fact wrote Elizabeth frequently—sometimes in verse—expressing her desire to see her cousin, insisting upon her innocence, and protesting the conditions of her confinement. But in her letters and other writings to Elizabeth, she not only refused the queen the confession that was demanded but also showed herself to be as skillful in the art of poetry and the poetics of queenship as her cousin, while engaging her in a textual struggle of the highest stakes. In Elizabeth's speech to Parliament, whose terms are echoed in Harington's decription of the covert circulation of "The Doubt of Future Foes," the queen appeals to a model of women's writing as a private textual space, autonomous of the public concerns of Parliament, and thereby ostensibly displaces the political from the women's intimate relationship. But the letters and poetry that passed between Elizabeth and Mary demonstrate the ways in which both queens adapted poetic topoi as well as the conventions associated with the private writing of ladies to construct a language of female rulership that expressed the public dilemma of this case in a covert language of figures.

On September 1, 1568, having fled Scotland and newly crossed England's border, Mary wrote to Elizabeth:

> I will beseach you to look upon and treat me as your relative and good friend. . . . entreating you not to let me be lost for want of a safe port; for like a vessel driven by all the winds, so am I, not knowing where to find a haven, unless, taking into your kind consideration my long voyage, you bring me into a safe harbour. . . . Receive me, then. . . . Do not ruin me, I beseech you, for it is my wish to devote my life and heart to you forever.[91]

The image recurs in a poem that Mary sent Elizabeth in 1568, in testimony to her "affection," which concludes by comparing her bad fortune to that of a ship lost at sea:

> Iay ueu la nef relascher par contraincte
> En haulte mer, proche d'entrer au port,
> Et le serain se conuertir en trouble
> Ainsi ie suis en soucy et en craincte
> Non pas de vous, mais quantes fois à tort
> Fortune rompt voille et cordage double?

> (I have seen a ship freed from constraint
> On the high sea, near to entering a port,
> And serene sky turned to storms:
> Likewise, I am troubled and in fear,
> Not because of you, but because Fortune
> Often wrongly rips sails and rigging.)[92]

Echoing her letter, once again Mary compares her relationship with Elizabeth to that of a ship unable to find a safe port. Mary's letter and poem, both of which stress her insecurity and desire, her "affection" as well as her "soucy" and "craincte," find in the ship a symbol of disappointed aspiration, as in the poem's opening stanza which claims: "Amer et doulx, change en mon coeur sans cesse, / Entre le doubte et l'espoir il m'oppresse" (Bitter and sweet, torments my heart without cease, / Between fear and hope it oppresses me).[93]

Mary finds in the Petrarchan ship a means of figuring her own fear and helplessness as effects of desire. This image is conspicuously taken from Petrarch's Canzone 132, "S'amor non è, che dunque è quel ch'io sento?" (If it is not love, what then is it that I feel?) and Canzone 189, "Passa la nava mia colma d'oblivio" (My ship laden with forgetfulness), which were similarly adapted by Chaucer, Wyatt, and Spenser.[94] But if these male poets take the Petrarchan ship as a figure for the male speaker's lovesickness, Mary presents lovesickness and the desire to see the queen as the explanation for her escape from Scotland: "l'affection de vous veoir qui me presse" (the desire to see you oppresses me).[95]

The image of Mary as a lost vessel seems to have appealed to Elizabeth, for in a letter of May 25, 1569, she recycled it as a warning to the queen of Scots about the dangers of her supposed alliance with the Duke of Anjou. Elizabeth writes, "The bark of your good fortune floats on a dangerous sea, where many contrary winds blow, and has need of all aid to obviate such evils, and conduct you safely into port."[96] Here, as throughout their communication, Elizabeth displays an uncanny ability to pick up Mary's confessions of her own vulnerability and to repeat these back to her as threats. Her response, however, echoes Petrarch less than it does Horace's Ode 1.14, to the Ship of State:

> O navis, referent in mare to novi
> fluctus. O quid agis! fortiter occupa
> portum.
>
> (O ship, new billows threaten to bear
> thee out to sea again. Beware! Haste
> valiantly to reach the haven!)[97]

If Elizabeth accepts Mary's characterization of her as a safe harbor, she extends the imagery to comment on Mary's precarious political situation, reinterpreting Mary's self-professed lovesickness as a sign of political instability and danger. Elizabeth further develops this politicized reading of the ship in "The Doubt of Future Foes," which offers what appears to be a direct rebuke to Mary's verses and their request for sanctuary: "No forreigne bannisht vvight shall ancre in this port, / Our realme it brookes no strangers force, let them elsvvhere resort." Steeling her port against foreign ships and "strangers force," Elizabeth appears to assert the inviolability of her body politic against Mary's invasion.⁹⁸ In so doing, she develops terms that she will use again in her own famous speech to the troops at Tilbury, where Elizabeth would assert the image of her own virginity as a figure for England's repulsion of foreign invasion:

> I know I have the body of a weak and feeble woman, but I have the heart and stomach of a king, and of a king of England too. And I think foul scorn that Parma or Spain, or any Prince of Europe, should dare to invade the borders of my realm.⁹⁹

In "The Doubt of Future Foes," however, the "force" that threatens the speaker's sovereignty is not an act of outright violence and war, but rather a mobilization of dissembling figures. "The Doubt of Future Foes" locates the biggest threat to the royal speaker's sovereignty in the uses and abuses of toys—the "clowdes of tois" that "cloak aspiring minds," the "falsehood" that threatens to replace "subiect faith" and produce "dazeld eyes." It thereby expresses a fantasy of clearing away false figures at the same time that it demonstrates the speaker's own mastery of figurative language. So much is evident in the poem's extended allegory of gardening and rulership, which is worth examining further in the contexts of its sources and textual outreaches.

Like the Ship of State, the allegory of the garden in "The Doubt of Future Foes" offers a conventional figure of rulership that likewise becomes the site of a poetic struggle between the two queens. In Elizabeth's poem reason and loyalty ebb and flow like tides ("For Falshood novv doth flow, and subiect faith doth ebbe"), and usurpation is figured as a sudden storm ("clowdes of tois vntried, do cloake aspiring mindes, / Which turne to raigne of late repent, by course of changed vvindes"). Treasonous forces and legitimate ones vie with one another to control reproduction and growth in a garden-like state, until the speaker engages in a bit of poetic saber-rattling: "Our rusty svvorde vvith rest, shall first his edge employ / To polle their toppes that seeke, such change and gape for ioy." This allegory of gardening and rulership, as Frances Teague points out, is similarly adapted in Shakespeare's *Richard II:* "The natural metaphors, which compare treason to bad weather and traitors to barren plants, remind one of the garden scene in *Richard II*, particularly the Gardener's lines, 'Go thou and, like an executioner, / Cut off the heads of too-fast-growing sprays' (III.iv.34–35); the poem and the play have the same topos."¹⁰⁰ Like that more famous scene, Elizabeth's staging of the garden evokes an anecdote that would have been familiar to educated Renaissance readers. In Livy's *History*, Sextus, the son of the tyrant Tarquin the Proud, infiltrates the rival forces of the Gabians and sends a messenger to his father for further instruction:

> To the messenger, presumably because his fidelity was not trusted, no verbal reply was given. The king, as though in deep thought, passed into the palace garden, followed by his son's messenger. The story goes that as he walked there, he silently cut off the heads of the highest poppies with his staff. The messenger, wearied of repeating his question and awaiting a reply, returned to Gabii thinking that his mission was a failure. He reported what he had himself said and what he had seen, remarking that whether through anger or hatred or an inborn arrogance the king had not uttered a single word. When Sextus realized what his father meant and what instructions he gave through his unspoken riddle, he destroyed the leading men of the city.[101]

Like Tarquin's gesture of "silently cut[ting] off the heads of the highest poppies," Elizabeth's "Doubt of Future Foes" offers a deadly message in a coded language. In so doing, moreover, the poem draws on an image that also directly engages a dialectic of spoken and unspoken meaning that is central to the poem's own circulation. "To this messenger, presumably because his fidelity was not trusted, no verbal reply was given," Livy recounts. In the anecdote's other manifestations—chiefly as told by Herodotus, Ovid, and Aristotle—the element that seizes chief significance is this scene of subverbal communication, which distinguishes between the father and son, whom the message's transmission includes, and the uncomprehending messenger, whom it excludes.[102] Elizabeth's manipulation of the gardening image similarly creates circles of insiders and outsiders in a way that an open speech or proclamation could not. Indeed, given the extreme delicacy of the situation, to make an open declaration of what the poem states covertly—that she suspects Mary of treasonous activity and that she intends to "polle" her "toppe"—would be imprudent in the extreme. To issue such sentiments in a poem, however, afford her a crucial level of deniability, by allowing her to frame it as a "private" text recording her secret thoughts and not an official proclamation of political intent.

If poetry enabled Elizabeth to insinuate under "dark and covert terms" what she could not declare in an open proclamation, it further enabled Mary to refigure the queen's meanings through poetry and poetic figures of her own. Like Elizabeth, Mary was an accomplished needlewoman, and at times when her recreation was strictly limited and her correspondence monitored, she asked to be supplied with the

silk threads and needles that would enable her to maintain her needlework, which she framed as a feminine diversion. As a visitor reported to Sir William Cecil in 1569, "I asked hir Grace . . . howe she
passed the tyme within. She sayd that all that day she wrought with
hir nydill, and that the diversitie of the colors made the worke seme
less tedious and continued so long at it till verray payn made hir
to give over."[103] While imprisoned at Sheffield Castle and Sheffield
Lodge, in the company of another gifted needlewoman, Bess of Hard-
wick, Mary produced copious works of needlepoint. She sent some
to Queen Elizabeth in the form of embroidered petticoats or night-
dresses and so, as J. E. Neale suggestively puts it, "she set siege to
Elizabeth's heart."[104] Embroidery was a sanctioned form of female industry and was coded as a private domestic activity; yet Mary's embroidery attracted the suspicion of her jailers because of the use she
made of cryptic emblems. Some of these appeared on a watch that
Mary kept with her, which was seized and studied carefully in 1576.
According to William Camden, it was the discovery of related "emblems" in particular that secured Mary's conviction:

> Suspitions were layd hold on, as if there were a plot already layd to
> set her at liberty: and that, by occasion of certain *Emblems*[:] . . . a
> scien graften into a stock, and bound about by bands, yet budding
> forth fresh, and written about, *Per vincula cresco*, that is to say,
> *Through bands I grow*. A palme tree pressed down, but rising up
> againe, with this sentence, *Ponderibus virtus innata resistit*, that
> is, *'Gainst weights doth inbred vertue strive*.[105]

The mottos themselves convey conventional expressions of piety and
fortitude, familiar from contemporary emblem books. But in Camden's account they also signal rebellion on the highest order. These
emblems directly recall the figurative language of Elizabeth's "Doubt
of Future Foes," which presents similar images: "The toppe of hope
supposed, the roote of ruth vvil be, / And frutelesse all their graffed
guiles, as shortly ye shall see." For Elizabeth, the political struggle for
the crown is like planting upside down, placing the "toppe" where the
"root" should be (to draw on the literal meaning of "the toppe of hope
supposed," as *sub-ponere*, to place below). While the foes attempt to
"sowe discorde," the speaker is self-assured that these efforts will be
"fruteless" because they are "grafted" and unnatural. But Mary's emblems appear to interpret and answer these images from "The Doubt
of Future Foes." Where Elizabeth imagines her enemies' plots to be
"frutelesse" because "grafted," Mary's emblem of the "scien graften

into a stock" envisions such grafting to be a source of fruition ("bound about by bands, yet budding forth fresh"). The battle over the tops of trees "supposed" (*sub-ponere*) is also refigured in Mary's emblem of the palm tree pressed down by weights ("*ponderibus*") but springing back to its full height. As Camden notes, these emblems resonate with subversive potential; they suggest that the same mechanisms through which Mary is oppressed will be the very sources of her strength, like the bonds that enable the grafted plant to bud forth. Where Elizabeth figures her strength in punishment, Mary figures hers in being punished.

Such is the message of an emblem of Mary's making that does survive. Between 1569 and 1571 in the early years of her captivity, Mary completed a work of embroidery that has come to be known as the Oxburgh Hanging. It was therefore made around the same time as the earliest manuscript of "The Doubt of Future Foes." The centerpiece of the hanging is a panel depicting a scene of gardening. In it, two trees are in fruit and along the base of their trunks winds a vine, half in fruit and half withered. Between them a hand with a blade extends from the sky, and above, a scroll displays the Latin motto "Virescit Vulnere Virtus" (Virtue flourishes through wounding) (Figure 10).[106]

Mary appears to have sent a copy of this emblem to Thomas, Duke of Norfolk, which was produced as evidence of treason at the trial that resulted in Norfolk's execution in 1571.[107] While Norfolk's examiners wondered whether the pruning knife was meant as a threat to wound Elizabeth, the emblem seems rather to embrace that wounding from the point of view of the threatened. The motto, however, indicates that it is Mary who is the blade's victim, and the blade itself that is the source of her fruition. Contemporary uses of the emblem suggest as much. One Elizabethan emblem book, Geoffrey Whitney's *A Choice of Emblemes*, assigns the same Latin motto, "Virescit Vulnere Virtus," to the image of a man trampling down a plant, and it glosses the image thus: "The dockes (thoughe troden) growe, as it is dailie seene: / So uertue, thoughe it longe bee hid, with woundinge waxeth greene."[108] Similarly, the vine in Mary's embroidery is wounded and thereby made fruitful. Such a reading of the panel suggests that Elizabeth's wounding causes Mary's virtue to multiply, as the gardener's wounding cut encourages plants to flourish. "It appeared to be a pious exercise on the part of the captive breathing the spirit of Christian resignation," explains Margaret Swain.[109] Yet in so doing, the emblem also elicits a more threatening image of martyrdom.[110]

As such, it reverses the topoi wielded in "The Doubt of Future

Figure 10. Embroidered Emblem, Mary Queen of Scots. Reproduced with permission of the Victoria and Albert Picture Library.

Foes": "Our rusty sworde with rest, shall first his edge employ / To polle their toppes that seeke, such change and gape for joy." If Elizabeth proposes to "polle" the "toppes" of her enemies, Mary's emblem suggests that such a wounding cut will only encourage more growth, just as "virtue flourishes with wounding." If Mary is to fall victim to Elizabeth's blade, that blade will become the source of her fruition. The image thus reverses a warning that John Knox made to William Cecil, later Lord Burghley, about Mary: "Yf ye srik not att the roote, the branches that appear to be brocken will budd again." Knox calls on Job 14:7–9: "For there is hope of a tree, if it be cut down, that it will sprout again, and that the tender branch thereof will not cease. Though the root therof wax old in the earth, and the stock thereof die in the ground, yet through the scent of water it will bud, and bring

forth boughs like a plant."[111] Like the emblems in Camden's description, the Oxburgh Hanging produces a conspicuously covert code
that demands to be deciphered. And the meanings that it encodes
are threatening enough: it hints at the retributive forces that might
gather to revenge Mary's "wounding," for example—not so empty a
threat if we recall that the Spanish Armada was motivated by Mary's
execution. In unexpected ways, both the Oxburgh Hanging and "The
Doubt of Future Foes" anticipate Mary's trial and execution in 1587,
even suggesting that both queens used poetic figures to write their
own scripts in this historical drama. The suggestion that in 1570 Elizabeth already envisioned beheading Mary, the "daughter of debate,"
and declared as much in a poem, is only slightly less shocking than
the suggestion that around the same time Mary anticipated such a
fate and even dared it to come about—and did so, moreover, in an
embroidery. As a poet and a rival queen, Mary both appropriates and
reverses the same poetic topoi, postures, and meanings that formed
the basis of Elizabeth's poetics of queenship. Through her use of poetry Elizabeth attempts to reveal her mastery of the art of beautiful
and false appearances. But instead of offering Elizabeth a confession
and disclosing her secret guilt, Mary offers more figures. Mary's response to Elizabeth's poetics of queenship was to assert herself a superior practitioner of both. The covert, figurative language of poetry
thereby becomes a medium for producing female power on the highest level.

  "The Doubt of Future Foes" and its circulation show how women's
writing and its representations could be manipulated to signify supreme cultural privilege and even ruthless cruelty. When she attempts
to assert her own authority in the face of Mary's threat, Elizabeth
rhetorically withdraws into a position of feminine enclosure, only to
issue from within this position a deadly threat of force. And further,
Mary's manipulation of poetic topoi shows how proclaiming a position of subjection might pose a threat so dangerous as to be seen to
justify arrest and even execution. Mary and Elizabeth both sanction
their work under prevailing cultural models—Elizabeth by appealing
to the conventions of the female coterie, and Mary by writing through
that most feminine of media, embroidery. Yet they also show how textual communication between women is far more open to public uses
and conflicts than these models are often held to allow. Elizabeth I
presents a striking example of how the early modern woman writer's
culturally enjoined privacy and enclosure could be cultivated and deployed to ends not normally associated with the "chaste, silent, and
obedient" figure of popular conception.[112] Rather, Elizabeth's use of

poetry suggests that the covert terms and restricted circulation associated with coterie manuscript poetry offered a means of manipulating the privacy that humanism famously demanded of women in order to produce the public effects on which the queen's authority as a monarch depended. A poem like "The Doubt of Future Foes" thereby offers an example of how supposedly private women's writing could be manipulated to signify supreme cultural privilege, or to issue the deadliest of threats, or finally to uphold the execution of another woman. And, by extension, Mary's own manipulation of poetic topoi shows how proclaiming a position of piety and subjection—even in feminine embroidery—could be taken as a threat so deep as to justify that execution. Women's postulated exclusion from humanist oratory, therefore, did not necessarily exclude them from the realm of the political but, in the case of both Elizabeth and Mary, such constructions of gender formed the backdrop for a new poetics that reframed the public world of the political in the privatized language of women's intimate textual community.

For Puttenham, the conflict between Elizabeth I and Mary Queen of Scots generated a new poetics of covertness that suited the political exigencies of their relationship by providing a private language of double meanings and mutual deniability in place of the open proclamation of public record. As the center of the broader, English poetics that Puttenham details in *The Arte of English Poesie,* that poetics of queenship offers a context for reading the "covert and darke intendements" and "duplicity of meaning" within Puttenham's famous discussion of allegory as linguistic strategies that developed out of a particular political event. Moreover, it explains the prominent position that Puttenham assigns to women writers and their work in his *Arte*—from Elizabeth's "arte of a ladies penne" to the "prettie poesies of devices of Ladies, and Gentlewomen makers"—a position that has remained invisible as long as the text is assumed to be directed exclusively at male courtiers. To the contrary, reading Elizabeth's "arte of a ladies penne" at the center of "the arte of English poesie," where Puttenham himself places it, reveals that Puttenham's decision to exchange the humanist rhetoric of oratory for a new, ornamental rhetoric of poetry is grounded both in the history of the English state and the history of gender. If Puttenham feminizes English poetry to emphasize its marginal status, by naming Elizabeth I its figurehead, he also makes it the basis of a new national literature.

Afterword

LITERARY HISTORY

WITHOUT WOMEN

Where Queen Elizabeth's stature as a female poet enabled George Puttenham to reject a classically inspired humanist oratory in favor of a contrastingly ornamental and covert English poetry, Elizabeth I subsequently became the target of those who rejected in turn what they perceived to be the literary effeminacy of the Elizabethan age to return to a more classicized and metaphorically masculine literary model. For the Jacobean Richard Flecknoe, the literary style "of Queen Elizabeths dayes" was "flaunted and pufted like her Apparell," a judgment whose equation of Elizabethan poetry with the queen's feminine ornament both recalls and repudiates Puttenham's association of poetic ornament with the queen's "gorgious" person.[1] Similarly, Samuel Daniel disapprovingly notes Elizabethan poets' exchange of "viriliti" for more "subtile" arts; yet he cautions, "ornaments . . . doe but decke the house of a state," thus exiling poetic ornament to the margins of the political and calling for a literature of contrastingly virile *gravitas*.[2] The desire to cure English literature of its perceived effeminacy seized literary theorists even during Elizabeth's reign: in 1598 George Chapman advances his translation of Homer to redress what he calls "all the unmanly degeneracies now tyranysing amongst us," a comment that appears directed against Elizabeth as both a ruler and a model of a feminized literariness.[3]

These writers repudiate what they perceive to be Elizabethan poetry's literary effeminacy by rejecting the very terms that allowed Puttenham to elevate Elizabeth I's "arte of a ladies penne" to the pinnacle of English letters in *The Arte of English Poesie*. In the process, they establish the way for a new model of English literature that took hold in the seventeenth century. Where Puttenham and Bale, as prominent sixteenth-century theorists of English literature, stressed the category's marginality to and independence from the authoritative traditions of the literary past, later theorists would stress continuity over marginality, as they reinvented English literature to give it its own tradition, defined in alliance with the classical past. Chapman's promotion of Homer as an antidote to poetic effeminacy echoes Gavin Douglas's earlier promotion of a paternal Virgil and fulfils the earlier poet's desire to uplift the vernacular to a position of cultural authority on the level with the classical canon. Later in the seventeenth century, Dryden conceives English literature's historical and cultural identity in language that is marked by gender: English writing, he insists, manifests a "masculine vigour," which is upheld by the writers he installs as the touchstones of its past, such as the "father" Chaucer and "manly" Shakespeare.[4] The newly imagined tradition of English literature accordingly took shape as a succession of male poets, forming the basis of the all-male canons by which medieval and Renaissance literature would be known.[5]

Inventing a tradition of English letters significantly shifted the relative meanings of "English literature" and "the woman writer." In the examples that we have followed in the preceding chapters, the woman writer's perceived alienation from an authoritative literary past made her a focal point for the parallel alienation of English letters. The earliest writers to imagine English literature as an abstract cultural entity—Chaucer, Skelton, Bale, and Puttenham—made women writers emblems of both the dangers and promises of writing outside an established but remote tradition. But when English literature was endowed with a tradition of its own, that tradition was modeled on the classical past, which was conceived as a succession of exclusively masculine poets. By extension, the tradition of English literature that emerges in the seventeenth century is likewise defined through its exclusion of women.[6] This point may account for the paradoxical fact that even though there were numerically more women writing and publishing in the seventeenth century than ever before, "the woman writer" became a near-contradiction in terms.[7] A cultural denial that women writers could or ever did exist, even in the face of increasing numbers of writing women, could be seen as the legacy of a new consolidation of English authorship and literary history. When these terms became identified with named individuals who were endowed with proprietary rights and seen to transfer literary authority from the past to the present, they also became associated with social definitions of masculinity and paternal authority. Paradoxically, then, even though fewer women wrote in the fourteenth through the sixteenth centuries, the greater fluidity of the concepts of authorship and literary history in relation to English writing made the term "woman writer" less anomalous and unthinkable than it would become in later periods.

If in the seventeenth century "the woman writer" was excluded from new definitions of English literary tradition, that exclusion also established a discourse for valorizing individual women writers by making historical uniqueness the basis of their identity. The posthumous 1667 edition of the poems of Katherine Philips is prefaced by a set of elegiac verses by contemporary poets. Some of these verses begin by meditating on Philips's death but seamlessly become meditations on the historical loss of women writers more generally. For Abraham Cowley, that loss determines Philips's cultural status as a unique woman poet:

> Of Female Poets who had names of old,
> Nothing is shewn, but onely told,
> And all we hear of them, perhaps may be
> Male Flattery onely, and Male Poetry.[8]

Cowley's comments on the lost history of women writers recall those of Richard Brathwait in 1641, with which my Introduction opens. For both, the process of honoring women writers means evacuating them from literary history and then turning their absence into an object of mourning. And furthermore, for both, the literary-historical absence left by the loss of women writers is filled by male poets: where Brathwait cites "the testimony of our approvedst Authors" as the source of the literary history of women writers, Cowley wonders whether "Female Poets" ever indeed had any historical existence independent of "Male Flattery" and "Male Poetry." It is an unlikely statement for an elegy that purports to praise a recently deceased female poet. But to Cowley what is at stake is the need to affirm not only his own authority as a male poet but also the masculinity of the literary tradition of which he claims part. This he does by making Katherine Philips both the latest entry in a history of lost women writers and a unique figure who stands alone and without precedent. Thus Cowley insists that Philips deserves praise because she worked alone, unlike men, who work within a community and tradition of male poets: Philips, as Cowley writes, "Does all the Business there Alone which we / Are forced to carry on by a whole company."[9] But the effect of this praise is to affirm the status of English literary culture and history as exclusively masculine realms.

The paradoxical historical position of the woman writer valorized for her historical uniqueness is repeated in and around the works of Margaret Cavendish, the seventeenth-century woman writer who most clearly made uniqueness into an authorial stance.[10] In the preface to the 1662 edition of her plays, Cavendish both acknowledges a newly consolidated English literary tradition and establishes her own alienation from that tradition:

> But noble Readers, do not think my Playes
> Are such as have been writ in former daies;
> As *Johnson, Shakesper, Beaumont,* Fletcher wit:
> The Latin phrases, I could never tell,
> But *Johnson* could, which made him write so well.
> Greek, Latin Poets, I could never read,
> Nor their Historians, but our English *Speed.*[11]

Cavendish's separation of herself from Jonson and Shakespeare, Beaumont and Fletcher, betrays her awareness of an English literary tradition that is conceived as a succession of male authors from the past ("former daies") that transfers classical literary authority to English letters, as when she commends Jonson's mastery of "the Latin phrases . . . which made him write so well." By singling out Jonson as the apogee of a classicized English literary authority, Cavendish also recognizes the founding figure of a new English authorship, which Jonson established by overseeing the publication of his 1616 *Workes.*[12] But, as Jeffrey Masten points out, in the contrast that she draws between these male authors and herself, Cavendish also establishes her own originality.[13] In the lines that follow those cited above, Cavendish stresses that, since she claims no sources in literary tradition, she alone is the origin of her works: "I could not steal their wit, nor Plots out take; / All my Playes Plots, my own poor brain did make."[14] Cavendish's self-conscious alienation from a classically inspired literary tradition recalls but tellingly rewrites the terms by which Skelton's Jane Scrope also remarks the woman writer's distance from the classical literary past ("these poetes of auncyente / They ar to diffuse for

me"). But Jane's exclusion from classicism makes her a figure of identification for an English literature that Skelton perceives to be similarly excluded from classical authority; in contrast, Cavendish finds
herself excluded from both the classical past and the recently consolidated English literary tradition that claims that past as its model.

Cavendish's originality requires the absence of any female poetic
predecessors. Where Cowley valorizes Katherine Philips by emphasizing her literary-historical uniqueness, Cavendish likewise trades
on the same uniqueness to valorize herself as a woman writer. In a
poem prefacing Cavendish's *Poems and Fancies* (1664), Elizabeth Top,
Cavendish's former maid, praises Cavendish's originality by stressing
her historical singularity: "Madam, you are not only the first English
Poet of your sex, but the first, that ever wrote this way."[15] But the
claim that Cavendish is the first must elide any trace of the women
writers who had preceded her. This elision is one that Cavendish herself admits to making willingly. As she writes in her "Epistle to my
Readers" in *Nature's Pictures:* "I have not read much History to inform me of the past Ages, indeed, I dare not examin the former times,
for fear I should meet with such of my Sex, that have out-done all the
glory I can aime at, or hope to attain."[16] Here the possibility of foremothers is incapacitating, since it would undermine Cavendish's own
desire for uniqueness. This desire is reflected in the fantasied title
with which she refers to herself, "Margaret the First," a title that both
glances at, but similarly elides, the historical precedence of Elizabeth I.[17] But despite Cavendish's claim to willful ignorance of women's
history, nonetheless that history intrudes in her writing in a figure
Cavendish recurrently cites as a model of female learnedness, the anchoress. The anchoress figures centrally in Cavendish's novella, "The
She-Anchoret," whose titular figure is both an enclosed woman and
a respected authority on natural philosophy; she also becomes a figure of identification in Cavendish's autobiography, in which Cavendish expresses the fantasy of "enclosing myself like an anchoret."[18]
The figure suggests that Cavendish found predecessors in the learned
women from England's past and styled herself as a secular, latter-day
Julian of Norwich. But rather than suggesting the shared authority of
a female tradition, the appeal of the anchoress lies in her isolation,
which Cavendish reproduces as the condition of her own writing.
The ghostly figure of the anchoress therefore embodies the alienation
and solitude that formed the paradoxical legacy of the history of the
woman writer.

With Margaret Cavendish, we are a long way from Virginia Woolf's model of women's literary history as the search for "mothers to think back through." Indeed, when Woolf surveys the literary past in search of the foremothers she would declare nonexistent, she can only express bewilderment over Margaret Cavendish, whom she calls "a vision of loneliness."[19] In *A Room of One's Own*, Woolf articulates the most enduring modern version of "the lost woman writer." Lamenting the absence of women writers from the literary-historical record, she proposes a partial explanation for that absence by constructing the now-iconic narrative of Judith Shakespeare, whom the irreconcilable conflicts between being a woman and being a poet drive, finally, to suicide. For Woolf, Judith Shakespeare gives an imaginary presence to that absence, by explaining why there were no women writers in the Elizabethan age. In so doing, Woolf offers a ghostly woman writer who can still serve later generations as a fictitious foremother: "Now my belief is that this poet who never wrote a word and was buried at the crossroads still lives. She lives in you and in me . . . for great poets do not die; they are continuing presences; they need only the opportunity to walk among us in the flesh."[20] But Woolf's premise that women writers need "mothers to think back through" is strangely reversed in the case of Margaret Cavendish. Where Woolf emblematizes the lost history of women writers in the "empty shelves" at which she despairingly gazes, Cavendish conjures the image of literary history's shelves barren of women writers in order to imagine herself the first and sole occupant. Cavendish's production of her own uniqueness, and her "recovery" of lost women writers in the form of the anchoress who only further reinforces the woman writer's cultural and historical isolation, indicate the need for new understandings of the ways in which women writers were historically produced as "lost," as well as the imaginary relation that they bore to "tradition."

Recent scholarship on early women writers has, of course, proven Woolf wrong in her assertion that there were no women writers before the mid-seventeenth century; furthermore, as Margaret Ezell has shown, the assumptions about the nature of authorship that underlie Woolf's account—for example, her emphasis on publication as the sole form of literary authorship—seriously limit the kinds of women's writing that are visible to her. Such scholarship can indicate the limitations of Woolf's argument without discounting the tremendous importance that *A Room of One's Own* has had in defining the field of women's writing—in the first place, by suggesting that the search for women writers before Jane Austen was a worthy enterprise. Not only does Woolf define the enterprise, she also defines its terms— and particularly its founding term, the lost woman writer. But it has been my point here to argue that, despite their cultural prevalence, representations of women writers as lost are by no means reliable descriptors of women writers' actual absence from literary history. Rather, I have aimed to show that "the lost woman writer" has a complex history that participates in the broader histories of authorship and English literature, and indeed creates the conditions under which women's writing was circulated and interpreted as such, precisely by defining "the woman writer" in opposition to the notion of "literary tradition." Margaret Cavendish writes by disavowing literary tradition—and even the available predecessors that the recent history of women writers might have offered her—but her claim to uniqueness and radical historical isolation might be seen as a late development in the literary history of the "lost woman writer" from earlier periods, which defined "woman writer" as a figure without a history. The same posture that enables Cavendish to write—historical alienation—also renders a literary tradition of women writers irrecoverable. A similar point might be made of Cowley, who could only praise Katherine Philips by evacuating literary history of women writers. If these seventeenth-century writers recall an earlier association of "the woman writer" with historical alienation and loss, they also take that association one step further, by imagining the history of women writers as an empty shelf.

In this book I argue that before the seventeenth century the woman writer is not absent from the earliest conception of English literature; rather, I find that representations of writing women are present in the major sites in which English literary history begins to be defined as such, but present in ways that signify dispossession, marginality, and absence. In this, the woman writer became a figure in which the agents of literary culture explored the perceived absence and loss of tradition that attended the formation of an English literature in the late medieval and early modern periods. But when literary historians of the seventeenth and eighteenth centuries began to give form to an English literary history, they embodied it in a line of male authors of undisputed authority, from which the woman writer was excluded.[21] If women writers had been central to defining English literary history for an early literary historian like Bale, for a later figure like Cowley, the same terms by which Bale had earlier valorized women writers—their separation from tradition—made it possible to imagine that they never existed.

While the Middle Ages and Renaissance gave meaning and substance to the figure of "the lost woman writer," their representations never cohered into what might be called a lasting canon or tradition of women writers. Rather, the terms through which figures like the Henrician Bale or the Elizabethan Thomas Bentley defined women writers, as outside tradition and obscured from the official written record, posit their need to be continually rescued, a need that in turned requires that they be continually produced as objects of loss. Thus the "recovery" of individual women writers like Anne Askew or the women in Bentley's *Monument of Matrons* strangely hypostatizes, without repairing, the categorical "lostness" of "the woman writer." When, in the next century, Richard Brathwait identifies women writers with literary-historical oblivion, he is recalling the terms in which they were conceived in earlier models like Bale's or Bentley's. But where for Bale their loss made women writers emblematic of a new, Protestant English literary history that escaped the taint of tradition, later literary historians read that loss as nonexistence, thus identifying the woman writer with a history that never was.

Notes

INTRODUCTION

1. Richard Brathwait, *A Ladies Love-Lecture* (London, 1641), 449–50.

2. "Impale" is a heraldic term, meaning to divide a crest; see OED, s.v. "Impale." On the history of the frontispiece as a technology of authorship, see Margery Corbett and Ronald Lightblown, *The Comely Frontispiece: The Emblematic Title Page in England, 1550–1660* (London: Routledge and Kegan Paul, 1979), and Wendy Wall, *The Imprint of Gender: Authorship and Publication in the English Renaissance* (Ithaca: Cornell Univ. Press, 1993), 70–89. Brathwait's insistence that the printing press is the property of male authors alone confirms Wall's thesis that publication formed a key arena in which early modern ideas of masculine authorship were formed.

3. See Brathwait's other, better-known texts, *The English Gentleman, and the English Gentlewoman,* 3d ed., revised, corrected, and enlarged (London, 1641); and *A Comment upon the Two Tales of Our Ancient, Renowned, and Ever Living Poet Sr. Jeffray Chaucer, Knight . . . The Miller's Tale, and the Wife of Bath* (London, 1665).

4. See, for example, Susanne Woods and Elizabeth Hageman's "Foreword" to *The Examinations of Anne Askew,* ed. Elaine V. Beilin (Oxford: Oxford Univ. Press, 1996), ix, which introduces the series Women Writers in English 1350–1850 by asserting that "most of the writers represented in the series were well known and highly regarded until the professionalization of English studies in the later nineteenth century coincided with their excision from canonical status and from the majority of literary histories." As Jonathan Goldberg concludes from evidence to this effect, "the recovery of women authors from the early modern period in many instances means nothing more than the belated recognition in the academy of texts that once were more widely

known." *Desiring Women Writing: English Renaissance Examples* (Stanford: Stanford Univ. Press, 1997), 9.

5. From what follows, my debt to John Guillory's *Cultural Capital: The Problem of Literary Canon Formation* (Chicago: Univ. of Chicago Press, 1993), will be clear: as, for example, to his lapidary question, "If much feminist theory now problematizes the category of 'woman' itself, what theoretical inhibition disallows the problematization of the 'woman writer' in the canon debate?" (16). However, in its analysis of the reciprocal construction of "woman writer" and "English literature" in the medieval and early modern periods, this book approaches the question of women writers' relationship to the canons of early literature from a different angle from Guillory's (15).

6. The work in this field is surveyed in the notes to my second and third chapters in particular; representative works in the history of authorship and the idea of English literature in this period include Wall, *The Imprint of Gender*, and Jocelyn Wogan-Browne, Nicholas Watson, Andrew Taylor, and Ruth Evans, eds., *The Idea of the Vernacular: An Anthology of Middle English Literary Theory, 1280–1520*, (University Park: Pennsylvania State Univ. Press, 1999); I am grateful to Andrew Taylor for allowing me to see portions of this book in proof.

7. For this formulation I acknowledge my debt to Catherine Gallagher's *Nobody's Story: The Vanishing Acts of Women Writers in the Marketplace, 1670–1820* (Berkeley: Univ. of California Press, 1994), which argues that the terms "'woman,' 'author,' 'marketplace,' and 'fiction' . . . reciprocally defined one another" in the eighteenth century (xviii).

8. See, for example, Elaine Showalter, *A Literature of Their Own: British Women Novelists from Brontë to Lessing* (Princeton: Princeton Univ. Press, 1977); while she aims to define a "female tradition," Showalter also confronts the problems that such a project entails, noting that "we have never been sure what unites them as women, or, indeed, whether they share a common heritage connected to their womanhood at all" (3).

9. This observation calls on work in feminist theory that has sought to question the historical construction of "woman" and "women." For an analysis of "the ways in which women are positioned . . . as 'women,'" see Denise Riley, *"Am I That Name?" Feminism and the Category of "Women" in History* (Minneapolis: Univ. of Minnesota Press, 1988), 3; and Judith Butler, *Gender Trouble: Feminism and the Subversion of Identity* (New York: Routledge, 1990). For the related point that the historical activities of women writers were not "isomorphous with or even representative of the theoretical concept of 'the woman writer,'" see Margaret W. Ferguson, "Renaissance Concepts of the 'Woman Writer,'" in *Women and Literature in Britain, 1500–1700*, ed. Helen Wilcox (Cambridge: Cambridge Univ. Press, 1996), 151.

10. Virginia Woolf, *A Room of One's Own* (1929; reprint, New York: Harcourt Brace Jovanovich, 1981).

11. The argument that Woolf's definition of "women's writing" unproductively restricts the kinds of materials she considers—particularly when she omits manuscript circulation—has been cogently made by Margaret J. M. Ezell, *Writing Women's Literary History* (Baltimore: Johns Hopkins Univ.

Press, 1993); see especially Chapter 2: "The Myth of Judith Shakespeare: Creating the Canon of Women's Literature in the Twentieth Century."

12. On the contested early reception of the *Urania*, see Helen Hackett, "Courtly Writing by Women," in Wilcox, *Women and Literature in Britain*, 181.

13. Patricia Crawford, "Women's Published Writings, 1600–1700," in *Women in English Society, 1500–1800*, ed. Mary Prior (London: Methuen, 1985), 241, 235.

14. Hilary Hinds, *God's Englishwomen: Seventeenth-Century Radical Sectarian Writing and Feminist Criticism* (Manchester: Manchester Univ. Press, 1996).

15. A. J. Minnis, *Medieval Theory of Authorship: Scholastic Literary Attitudes in the Later Middle Ages*, 2d ed. (Philadelphia: Univ. of Pennsylvania Press, 1988); Ralph Hanna III, *Pursuing History: Middle English Manuscripts and Their Texts* (Stanford: Stanford Univ. Press, 1996).

16. Hanna, *Pursuing History*, 9.

17. Wogan-Browne et al., *The Idea of the Vernacular*; on the invention of tradition as part of the formation of national identity, see Eric Hobsbawm, "Introduction: Inventing Traditions," in *The Invention of Tradition*, ed. Hobsbawm and Terence Ranger (Cambridge: Cambridge Univ. Press, 1983).

18. I survey the rich body of work on the fifteenth- and sixteenth-century canonization of Chaucer in the notes to Chapters 1 and 2; for an exemplary analysis of the competing Henrician claims on Chaucer, see John Watkins, "'Wrastling for this World': Wyatt and Tudor Canonization of Chaucer," in *Refiguring Chaucer in the Renaissance*, ed. Theresa M. Krier (Gainesville: Univ. Press of Florida, 1998).

19. As John Guillory argues, "an ideology of tradition . . . collapses the history of canon formation into an autonomous history of literature, which is always a history of writers and not of writing" (*Cultural Capital*, 63).

20. On the secondariness of the vernacular, see M. L. McLaughlin, "Humanism and Italian Literature," in *The Cambridge Companion to Renaissance Humanism*, ed. Jill Kraye (Cambridge: Cambridge Univ. Press, 1996), 228–29, and on the cultural struggles between the vernacular and classical languages, see Rita Copeland, *Rhetoric, Hermeneutics, and Translation in the Middle Ages: Academic Traditions and Vernacular Texts* (Cambridge: Cambridge Univ. Press, 1991).

21. See Maureen Quilligan, *The Allegory of Female Authority: Christine de Pizan's "Cité des Dames"* (Ithaca: Cornell Univ. Press, 1991), 35.

22. On antifeminism as a component of the Latin education of boys, see Marjorie Curry Woods, "The Teaching of Writing in Medieval Europe," in *A Short History of Writing Instruction from Ancient Greece to Twentieth-Century America*, ed. James J. Murphy (Davis, CA: Hermajoras Press, 1990), and "Rape and the Pedagogical Rhetoric of Sexual Violence," in *Criticism and Dissent in the Middle Ages*, ed. Rita Copeland (Cambridge: Cambridge Univ. Press, 1996), as well as the essays collected in *The Tongue of the Fathers: Gender and Ideology in Twelfth-Century Latin*, ed. David Townsend and Andrew Taylor (Philadelphia: Univ. of Pennsylvania Press, 1998). The classic study of

early modern Latin pedagogy is Walter Ong, "Latin Language Study as a Renaissance Puberty Rite," *Studies in Philology* 56 (1959): 106–24.

23. "Few words are as resonant to contemporary feminists as 'voice,'" observes Susan Sniader Lanser in *Fictions of Authority: Women Writers and Narrative Voice* (Ithaca: Cornell Univ. Press, 1992), 3. Elizabeth D. Harvey offers a perceptive critique of the ways in which the idea of "voice" has become a "transhistorical" and "monolithic construction" that resists efforts to particularize it in different cultures; see her *Ventriloquized Voices: Feminist Theory and English Renaissance Texts* (London: Routledge, 1992), 5–6.

24. See, for an analysis of the theoretical and practical problems of editing women's writing, Ann M. Hutchison, ed., *Editing Women: Papers Given at the Thirty-First Annual Conference on Editorial Problems,* (Toronto: Univ. of Toronto Press, 1998); and Elizabeth H. Hageman, "Did Shakespeare Have Any Sisters? Editing Women Writers of the Renaissance," in *New Ways of Looking at Old Texts: Papers of the Renaissance English Text Society, 1985–1991,* ed. W. Speed Hill (Binghamton, NY: Medieval and Renaissance Texts and Studies, 1993). In a similar vein, Germaine Greer highlights the fact that the early texts by women that we now seek from the archives have been heavily mediated, critiquing the assumption that one can find "texts attributed to women that actually represent what women wrote and the way they wrote it. The further back we go from our own time, the more unlikely that is." *Slip-Shod Sibyls: Recognition, Rejection, and the Woman Poet* (New York: Viking, 1995), 172.

25. Julia Boffey, "Women Authors and Women's Literacy in Fourteenth- and Fifteenth-Century England," in *Women and Literature in Britain, 1150–1500,* ed. Carol M. Meale (Cambridge: Cambridge Univ. Press, 1993), 171.

26. In making this point I follow the lead of Katie King, "Bibliography and a Feminist Apparatus of Literary Production," *Text* 5 (1991): 91–103.

27. Gérard Genette, *Paratexts: Thresholds of Interpretation,* trans. Jane E. Lewin (Cambridge: Cambridge Univ. Press, 1987).

28. See, for example, Julia Boffey's chapter "Authorship and Composition" in her *Manuscripts of English Courtly Love Lyrics in the Later Middle Ages* (Woodbridge: D. S. Brewer, 1985); Cynthia Brown, *Poets, Patrons, and Printers: Crisis of Authority in Late Medieval France* (Ithaca: Cornell Univ. Press, 1995).

29. This point takes up Mary Jacobus's assertion that "women's writing occupies an unchallenged place in the politics of feminist criticism and in the classroom; yet the category itself remains problematic." *Reading Woman: Essays in Feminist Criticism* (London: Methuen, 1986), 5.

30. While I trace this topic more fully in my third chapter, see, as an exemplary discussion, Thomas Betteridge, "Anne Askewe, John Bale, and Protestant History," *Journal of Medieval and Early Modern Studies* 27 (1997): 265–84.

31. On this point, see D. C. Greetham, *Theories of the Text* (Oxford: Oxford Univ. Press, 1999), 461.

32. Ferguson, "Renaissance Concepts of the 'Woman Writer,'" 145.

33. Julian's assertion is cited and discussed by Nicholas Watson, "'Yf Wommen be Double Naturelly': Remaking 'Woman' in Julian of Norwich's *Revelation of Love,*" *Exemplaria* 8 (1996): 11.

34. Elizabeth Jocelin, Epistle Dedicatory, *The Mothers Legacy to her Unborn Child* (1624; reprint, Oxford, 1698), sig. C1ʳ; Elizabeth Hageman, "Women's Poetry in Early Modern Britain," in *Women and Literature in Britain, 1500–1700*, ed. Helen Wilcox (Cambridge: Cambridge Univ. Press, 1996), 201.

35. In relevant discussions, Clare Brant and Diane Purkiss exchange the notion of "women's 'private' or 'authentic' selves revealed in their writings" for "ways in which women's writings generate and negotiate speaking-positions in discourse" (Introduction, *Women, Texts, and Histories, 1575–1760*, ed. Brant and Purkiss [London: Routledge, 1992], 3); similarly, Martin Irvine finds that "the Abelard-Heloise correspondence . . . discloses that masculinity and femininity were not pure, absolute states but rather formed from ongoing negotiations among various kinds of (already) mixed subject positions." "Heloise and the Gendering of the Literate Subject," in *Criticism and Dissent in the Middle Ages*, ed. Rita Copeland (Cambridge: Cambridge Univ. Press, 1996), 107.

36. Watson, "'Yf Wommen be Double Naturelly,'" 11; Wall, *The Imprint of Gender*, 283–96. *Mothers Legacy*, sig. B2ʳ.

37. "Phyllyp Sparowe," in John Skelton, *The Complete English Poems*, ed. John Scattergood (New Haven: Yale Univ. Press, 1983); line numbers cited are to this text. My brief reading of the poem complements the views of Susan Schibanoff, for whom it is a poem "about reading," and Richard Halpern, for whom it is about writing; see Schibanoff, "Taking Jane's Cue: Phyllyp Sparowe as a Primer for Women Readers," *PMLA* 101 (1986): 832–47; Halpern, *The Poetics of Primitive Accumulation: English Renaissance Culture and the Genealogy of Capital* (Ithaca: Cornell Univ. Press, 1991).

38. For a survey of attitudes toward English, see Richard Foster Jones, *Triumph of the English Language* (Stanford: Stanford Univ. Press, 1953).

39. Thus see A. C. Spearing, *Medieval to Renaissance in English Poetry* (Cambridge: Cambridge Univ. Press, 1985), which finds that in *Troilus and Criseyde*, Chaucer "is introducing the conception of what we now call 'literature', and with it that of a history of literature in which a work in English may have a place, however modest, alongside the great writers of antiquity" (33); and René Wellek, *The Rise of English Literary History* (Chapel Hill: Univ. of North Carolina Press, 1941): "The sketch of English poetry from Chaucer to Sidney is conceived as a uniform advance, and the ethos behind Puttenham's consciousness of the difference of English poetry is purely patriotic and nationalistic. . . . But patriotism and nationalism were most important factors in the establishment of literary history, as they helped to create the concept of an independent national tradition and turned men's minds towards the search for an honorific past" (10).

40. *The Riverside Chaucer*, ed. Larry D. Benson et al. (Oxford: Oxford Univ. Press, 1987), *Troilus and Criseyde*, 5.1792; George Puttenham, *The Arte of English Poesie*, facsimile reprint, ed. Baxter Hathaway (Kent, OH: Kent State Univ. Press, 1970), 77.

41. See K. B. McFarlane, "William Worcester: A Preliminary Survey," in his *The Nobility of Later Medieval England* (Oxford: Clarendon Press, 1973), 202.

42. Paul de Man, "Literary History and Literary Modernity," in *Blindness and Insight: Essays in the Rhetoric of Contemporary Criticism*, 2d ed. (Minneapolis: Univ. of Minnesota Press, 1983), 148.

43. Brian Stock, *Listening for the Text: On the Uses of the Past* (Baltimore: Johns Hopkins Univ. Press, 1990), 167.

44. Alice A. Jardine, *Gynesis: Configurations of Woman and Modernity* (Ithaca: Cornell Univ. Press, 1985), 25.

45. Thus Simpson, in an argument with which my own shares similar goals from a different historical perspective, traces the development of "a kind of feminism [that emerges] . . . in counterpart to almost every shift in the dynamics of modernization since the Renaissance and perhaps earlier. As such, these feminisms have often attempted a resistance to *feminization*, to the gendering of certain undesirable or disavowed social and personal characteristics as the natural properties of women." See David Simpson, "Feminisms and Feminizations in the Postmodern," in *Feminism and Postmodernism*, ed. Jennifer Wicke and Margaret Ferguson (Durham: Duke Univ. Press, 1994), 55–56; reprinted in Simpson, *The Academic Postmodern and the Rule of Literature: A Report on Half-Knowledge* (Chicago: Univ. of Chicago Press, 1996).

46. For a thoughtful discussion of this point, see Juliet Fleming's review of Barbara K. Lewalski, *Writing Women in Jacobean England* (Cambridge: Harvard Univ. Press, 1993), in *Huntington Library Quarterly* 57 (1994): 199–204.

47. Stock, *Listening for the Text*, 38.

48. On the problem of "modernity" in the Middle Ages, see Brigitte Cazelles, Introduction, *Modernité au moyen âge: Le défi du passé*, ed. Cazelles and Charles Méla, Recherches et Rencontres 1 (Geneva: Librairie Droz, 1990), along with the other essays contained in this volume. See also Stephen G. Nichols, "The New Medievalism: Tradition and Discontinuity in Medieval Culture," in *The New Medievalism*, ed. Marina S. Brownlee, Kevin Brownlee, and Stephen G. Nichols (Baltimore: Johns Hopkins Univ. Press, 1991).

49. *The Norton Anthology of Literature by Women*, ed. Sandra M. Gilbert and Susan Gubar (New York: Norton, 1985), collapses the "Middle Ages" and "Renaissance" only out of perceived necessity, because its editors believe women's writing in this period to be so scarce as not to warrant separate sections: "That, in order to represent the earliest writings of English women, we have had to conflate three periods into one is simply the most dramatic sign of women's literary marginality in the years from 700 to 1600" (4). The historical premise behind this decision has been critiqued by Ezell, *Writing Women's Literary History*, and by the Brown Women Writer's Project; here, it bears remarking that existing categories of periodization are seen as appropriate for women's writing. Nicholas Watson cites the example of Margery Kempe's frequent, and mistaken, classification as a fourteenth-century writer, presumably to make her a contemporary of Chaucer's Wife of Bath: see Watson, "Censorship and Cultural Change in Late-Medieval England: Vernacular Theology, the Oxford Translation Debate, and Arundel's Constitutions of 1409," *Speculum* 70 (1995): 823.

50. See, for example, *Seeking the Woman in Late Medieval and Renaissance Writings: Essays in Feminist Contextual Criticism*, ed. Sheila Fisher and Janet E. Halley (Knoxville: Univ. of Tennessee Press, 1989); Carole

Levin and Jeanie Watson, *eds.*, *Ambiguous Realities: Women in the Middle Ages and Renaissance*, (Detroit: Wayne State Univ. Press, 1987).

51. Joan Kelly, "Did Women Have a Renaissance?" *Women, History, and Theory: The Essays of Joan Kelly* (Chicago: Univ. of Chicago Press, 1984), 19.

52. The epochal model of "medieval" and "Renaissance" has been the subject of productive critique by medievalists; see Lee Patterson, "On the Margin: Postmodernism, Ironic History, and Medieval Studies," *Speculum* 65 (1990): 92–95; David Wallace, "Carving Up Time and the World: Medieval-Renaissance Turf Wars; Historiography and Personal History," University of Wisconsin–Milwaukee Center for Twentieth-Century Studies, Working Papers No. 11 (1990–91). See also Judith M. Bennett, "Medieval Women, Modern Women: Across the Great Divide," in *Culture and History, 1350–1600*, ed. David Aers (Detroit: Wayne State Univ. Press, 1992).

53. David Hult, *Self-Fulfilling Prophecies: Readership and Authority in the First "Roman de la Rose"* (New York: Cambridge Univ. Press, 1986); A. J. Minnis, *Medieval Theories of Authorship: Scholastic Literary Attitudes in the Later Middle Ages*, 2d ed. (Philadelphia: Univ. of Pennsylvania Press, 1988); Jeffrey Masten, *Textual Intercourse: Collaboration, Authorship, and Sexualities in Renaissance Drama* (Cambridge: Cambridge Univ. Press, 1997); Joseph Loewenstein, "Idem: Italics and the Genesis of Authorship," *JMRS* 20 (1990): 205–24.

54. Michel Foucault, "What Is an Author?" trans. Josué V. Harari, in *The Foucault Reader*, ed. Paul Rabinow (New York: Pantheon Books, 1984), 111.

55. Quilligan, *Allegory of Female Authority*; see also my discussion in Chapter 2.

56. Wellek, *Rise of English Literary History*, 1.

57. Fredric Jameson, "Overview," in *Rewriting Literary History*, ed. Tak-Wai Wong and M. A. Abbas (Hong Kong: Hong Kong Univ. Press, 1984), 344. For an important development of this point's significance for the history of the book, see D. F. McKenzie, *Bibliography and the Sociology of Texts*, The Panizzi Lectures, 1985 (London: British Library, 1986).

58. It should be noted that the term "tradition" has always had a problematic history in feminist literary criticism; even Elaine Showalter, who influentially coined the term "the female tradition," stresses its limitations: see *A Literature of Their Own*, 3. For a broader discussion of "tradition" in relation to feminist literary history, see Florence Howe, ed., *Tradition and the Talents of Women* (Chicago: Univ. of Illinois Press, 1991), especially Howe's introduction, "T. S. Eliot, Virginia Woolf, and the Future of 'Tradition.'" Margaret J. M. Ezell discusses the limitations of evolutionary models of tradition for women's writing in *Writing Women's Literary History*, 19–20, 28.

59. For Terry Eagleton, Freud's *fort-da* game "is perhaps the shortest story we can imagine: an object is lost, and then recovered." See Eagleton, *Literary Theory: An Introduction* (Minneapolis: Univ. of Minnesota Press, 1983), 185–86.

CHAPTER ONE

1. Gavin Douglas, *Eneados*, in *The Poetical Works of Gavin Douglas*, ed. John Small (Edinburgh, 1874), 2:17.

2. Jill Mann, "Chaucer and the 'Woman Question,'" in *This Noble Craft: Proceedings of the 10th Research Symposium of the Dutch and Belgian University Teachers of Old and Middle English and Historical Linguistics*, ed. Erik Kooper (Amsterdam: Rodolpi, 1991); the topics raised in this essay are developed further in Mann's *Geoffrey Chaucer* (Hemel Hempstead: Harvester Wheatsheaf, 1991).

3. See Arlyn Diamond's pioneering essay, "Chaucer's Women and Women's Chaucer," in *The Authority of Experience: Essays in Feminist Criticism*, ed. Diamond and Lee R. Edwards (Amherst: Univ. of Massachusetts Press, 1977), 60–61. For a review of the outlines of this debate, and a critique of its premises, see Elaine Tuttle Hansen, *Chaucer and the Fictions of Gender* (Berkeley: Univ. of California Press, 1992), 11–12, 39–57, as well as Monica Brzezinski Potkay and Regula Meyer Evitt, *Minding the Body: Women and Literature in the Middle Ages, 800–1500* (New York: Twayne Publishers, 1997), 140–42, for a reconsideration of Douglas's famous remark.

4. R. James Goldstein, "Writing in Scotland, 1058–1560," in *The Cambridge History of Medieval English Literature*, ed. David Wallace (Cambridge: Cambridge Univ. Press, 1999), 245. On Douglas's "self-styled status as a vernacular *auctor*," see Daniel J. Pinti, "The Vernacular Gloss(ed) in Gavin Douglas's *Eneados*," *Exemplaria* 7 (1995): 443–64; Jerome E. Singerman, *Under Clouds of Poesy: Poetry and Truth in French and English Reworkings of the Aeneid, 1160–1513* (New York: Garland, 1986), 217–85; and Priscilla J. Bawcutt, *Gavin Douglas: A Critical Study* (Edinburgh: Univ. of Edinburgh Press, 1976). On Douglas's self-placement in relation to Chaucer, see Gregory Kratzman, *Anglo-Scottish Literary Relations, 1430–1550* (Cambridge: Cambridge Univ. Press, 1980), 22–23, 104–28, 169ff.

5. On the difficulties that Spenser encountered in transporting an idea of Virgilian "manhoode" to Chaucer, see Kevin Pask, *The Emergence of the English Author: Scripting the Life of the Poet in Early Modern England* (Cambridge: Cambridge Univ. Press, 1996), 32–34. Unless otherwise noted, all references to Chaucer are to *The Riverside Chaucer*, ed. Larry D. Benson et al. (Oxford: Oxford Univ. Press, 1987), with line numbers noted parenthetically.

6. Douglas, *Eneados*, 2:17.

7. Marilynn Desmond, *Reading Dido: Gender, Textuality, and the Medieval "Aeneid"* (Minneapolis: Univ. of Minnesota Press, 1994).

8. For analyses of Chaucer's identification with Ovid against Virgil, see John M. Fyler, *Chaucer and Ovid* (New Haven: Yale Univ. Press, 1979), and Jesse M. Gellrich, *The Idea of the Book in the Middle Ages: Language Theory, Mythology, and Fiction* (Ithaca: Cornell Univ. Press, 1985), 170–75. On Ovid's disruptive poetics, see Florence Verducci, *Ovid's Toyshop of the Heart* (Princeton: Princeton Univ. Press, 1985).

9. A. C. Spearing, *Medieval to Renaissance in English Poetry* (Cambridge: Cambridge Univ. Press, 1985), 59, 34.

10. A. J. Minnis, *Medieval Theory of Authorship: Scholastic Literary Attitudes in the Later Middle Ages*, 2d ed. (Philadelphia: Univ. of Pennsylvania Press, 1988); M. B. Parkes, "The Influence of *Ordinatio* and *Compilatio* on the Development of the Book," in J. J. G. Alexander and M. T. Gibson, eds.,

Medieval Learning and Literature: Essays Presented to Richard Hunt (Oxford: Clarendon Press, 1976); Ralph Hanna III, *Pursuing History: Middle English Manuscripts and Their Texts* (Stanford: Stanford Univ. Press, 1996), 13.

11. On the relationship between the terms "canonical" and "noncanonical," see John Guillory, *Cultural Capital: The Problem of Literary Canon Formation* (Chicago: Univ. of Chicago Press, 1993), especially Chapter 1, "Canonical and Noncanonical: The Current Debate." The importance of this work for my own thinking about these terms will become clear in the following discussion. On Chaucer's relation to his Middle English predecessors and contemporaries, see Nicholas Watson, "The Politics of Middle English Writing," in *The Idea of the Vernacular: An Anthology of Middle English Literary Theory, 1280–1520,* ed. Jocelyn Wogan-Browne, Nicholas Watson, Andrew Taylor, and Ruth Evans (University Park: Pennsylvania Univ. Press, 1999), especially "Chaucer and the Idea of English as a Literary Language." For a reconsideration of Chaucer's originality in relation to Middle English, see Christopher Cannon, *The Making of Chaucer's English* (Cambridge: Cambridge Univ. Press, 1998).

12. Thomas Usk is excerpted in *Chaucer: The Critical Heritage. Volume 1: 1385–1837,* ed. Derek Brewer (London: Routledge and Kegan Paul, 1978), 43; John Dryden, "Preface to Fables Ancient and Modern," in *Of Dramatic Poesy and Other Critical Essays,* ed. George Watson (London: J. M. Dent, 1962), 2. Jonathan Brody Kramnick argues that eighteenth-century literary historians located the origins of the nascent vernacular canon in the early English past as a way of guaranteeing that canon's masculinity; see Kramnick, *Making the English Canon: Print-Capitalism and the Cultural Past* (Cambridge: Cambridge Univ. Press, 1998); of course, such a vision of an exclusively masculine literary past overlooks evidence of the women who wrote literary texts in the English medieval and early modern periods, evidence that was available during this period, as Margaret Ezell establishes in *Writing Women's Literary History* (Baltimore: Johns Hopkins Univ. Press, 1993).

13. Carolyn Dinshaw, *Chaucer's Sexual Poetics* (Madison: Univ. of Wisconsin Press, 1989).

14. Thomas Greene, *The Light in Troy: Imitation and Discovery in Renaissance Poetry* (New Haven: Yale Univ. Press, 1982), 12.

15. The Chaucerian woman writer might thus be considered in light of what Judith Butler calls "the excluded and illegible domain that haunts the former domain as the spectre of its own impossibility, the very limit to intelligibility, its constitutive outside." *Bodies That Matter: On the Discursive Limits of "Sex"* (New York: Routledge, 1993), xi. On the reciprocally shaping relationship between "tradition" and "modernity," see Brian Stock, *Listening for the Text: On the Uses of the Past* (Baltimore: Johns Hopkins Univ. Press, 1990), 166.

16. Maureen Quilligan makes a related point about this passage: "The most important thing that the Wife of Bath can teach us is that the discursive slot in the literary system which allows for greatest resistance to authority has already been labeled 'female writer' by Chaucer." *The Allegory of Female Experience: Christine de Pizan's "Cité des Dames"* (Ithaca: Cornell Univ. Press, 1991), 35. While the women writers Chaucer represents in the works I

will examine here cannot be called "resistant," Quilligan's point dovetails with the argument I develop about Protestant women writers in Chapter 3.

17. Compare, for example, my reading of the passage with the one that prefaces the section on "Literature of the Middle Ages and the Renaissance" in *The Norton Anthology of Literature by Women: The Tradition in English*, ed. Sandra M. Gilbert and Susan Gubar (New York: W. W. Norton, 1985), 4.

18. On Trotula, see Monica H. Green, "'Traittié tout de mençonges': The *Secrés des dames*, 'Trotula,' and Attitudes toward Women's Medicine in Fourteenth- and Early Fifteenth-Century France," in *Christine de Pizan and the Categories of Difference*, ed. Marilynn Desmond (Minneapolis: Univ. of Minnesota Press, 1998), and *Women and Literate Medicine in Medieval Europe: Trota and the "Trotula"* (Cambridge: Cambridge Univ. Press, forthcoming); I am grateful to Monica Green for sharing her work on Trotula with me. On Heloise and modern debates over her authorship, see Barbara Newman, "Authority, Authenticity, and the Repression of Heloise," *Journal of Medieval and Renaissance Studies* 22 (1992): 121–57, reprinted in *From Virile Woman to WomanChrist: Studies in Medieval Religion and Literature* (Philadelphia: Univ. of Pennsylvania Press, 1995), and especially 65–66, where this passage is discussed.

19. This line has generated a rich vein of feminist Chaucer criticism: see Mary Carruthers's classic essay, "The Wife of Bath and the Painting of Lions," reprinted in *Feminist Readings in Middle English Literature: The Wife of Bath and All Her Sect*, ed. Ruth Evans and Lesley Johnson (London: Routledge, 1994); Sheila Delany, "Strategies of Silence in the Wife of Bath's Recital," *Exemplaria* 2 (1990): 49–69, especially 51–56; Elaine Tuttle Hansen, *Chaucer and the Fictions of Gender* (Berkeley: Univ. of California Press, 1992), 35; Renate Haas, "Lionesses Painting Lionesses? Chaucer's Women as Seen by Early Women Scholars and Academic Critics," in *A Wyf Ther Was: Essays in Honour of Paule Mertens-Fonck*, ed. Juliette Dor (Liege: Univ. of Liege Press, 1992).

20. *Riverside Chaucer*, 871.

21. The most persuasive case in favor of Marie's *Del Leun e del Vilein* as Chaucer's source is put forward by Marjorie M. Malvern, "'Who Peyntede the Leon, Tel Me Who?': Rhetorical and Didactic Roles Played by an Aesopic Fable in the *Wife of Bath's Prologue*," *Studies in Philology* 80 (1983): 238–52; Delany is among those who accept that "besides scriptural and classical texts, the Wife refers to a relatively modern source, Marie de France's version of the Aesopian fable of the lion" (51).

22. On the diversity of medieval women's writing practices, see Julia Boffey, "Women Authors and Women's Literacy in Fourteenth- and Fifteenth-Century England," in *Women and Literature in Britain, 1150–1500*, ed. Carol M. Meale (Cambridge: Cambridge Univ. Press, 1993).

23. Margaret Ferguson makes the relevant point that the totality of historical women writers and their written activities is not "isomorphous with or even representative of the theoretical concept of 'the woman writer'" such as it became meaningful in early modern literary culture; see Ferguson, "Renaissance Concepts of the 'Woman Writer," *Women and Literature in Britain, 1500–1700*, ed. Helen Wilcox (Cambridge: Cambridge Univ. Press, 1996), 151.

24. Terry Eagleton, "History, Narrative, and Marxism," in James Phelan, ed., *Reading Narrative: Form, Ethics, Ideology* (Columbus: Ohio State Univ. Press, 1989), 276.

25. On the intersections between Chaucer's vernacular ambitions and those of Dante, see David Wallace, "Chaucer's Continental Inheritance: The Early Poems and *Troilus and Criseyde*," in *The Cambridge Chaucer Companion*, ed. Piero Boitani and Jill Mann (Cambridge: Cambridge Univ. Press, 1986).

26. Dante, *De Vulgari Eloquentia*, edited in a parallel-text version and translated by Steven Botterill (Cambridge: Cambridge Univ. Press, 1996); see Dante's discussion of the different forms of the Italian vernacular in Book 1, I–XVI.

27. Hanna, *Pursuing History*; see especially the argument as formulated on pages 3–5. On the instability of texts and authorship in a manuscript culture, see Stephen G. Nichols, "Introduction: Philology in a Manuscript Culture," *Speculum* 65 (1990): 8. For a discussion of the specific attributes of texts and their circulation in one sector of late-medieval manuscript culture, see Julia Boffey, *Manuscripts of English Courtly Love Lyrics in the Later Middle Ages* (Woodbridge, Suffolk: D. S. Brewer, Ltd., 1985).

28. Consider, in this light, John Guillory's assertion that "canonicity is not a property of the work itself but of its transmission, its relation to other works in a collocation of works—the syllabus in its institutional locus, the school." Guillory, *Cultural Capital: The Problem of Literary Canon Formation* (Chicago: Univ. of Chicago Press, 1993), 55. Thus, as David Wallace argues, "medieval literature cannot be understood (does not survive) except as part of transmissive processes—moving through the hands of copyists, owners, readers and institutional authorities—that form part of other and greater histories (social, political, religious and economic)." General Preface, *Cambridge History of Medieval English Literature*, ed. Wallace (Cambridge: Cambridge Univ. Press, 1999), xxi.

29. Hanna, *Pursuing History*, 12.

30. See Lee Patterson, *Chaucer and the Subject of History* (Madison: Univ. of Wisconsin Press, 1991), for a reading of how, in mid-career works like *Troilus and Criseyde* and *Anelida and Arcite*, "Chaucer invoked the world of antiquity in order to distance himself from the immediate past" (21).

31. On the problems of literary authority in *The House of Fame*, see, among others, Jacqueline T. Miller, *Poetic License: Authority and Authorship in Medieval and Renaissance Contexts* (Oxford: Oxford Univ. Press, 1986), and Jesse M. Gellrich, *The Idea of the Book in the Middle Ages* (Ithaca: Cornell Univ. Press, 1985). I will discuss these and related issues in the poem in a later section in this chapter.

32. *Riverside Chaucer*, 363 n.1229.

33. Alfred David, "How Marcia Lost Her Skin: A Note on Chaucer's Mythology," in *The Learned and the Lewed: Studies in Chaucer and Medieval Literature*, ed. Larry D. Benson (Cambridge: Harvard Univ. Press, 1974), 19–29; A. C. Spearing, *Medieval to Renaissance in English Poetry* (Cambridge: Cambridge Univ. Press, 1985), 29, 336 n.30; on Marsyas's re-gendering, see also David Wallace, *Chaucerian Polity: Absolutist Lineages and Associational Forms in England and Italy* (Stanford: Stanford Univ. Press, 1997), 250.

34. Dante Alighieri, *Paradiso*, trans. Allen Mandelbaum (New York: Bantam Books, 1984), 2–3.

35. Dinshaw, *Chaucer's Sexual Poetics*, 4; in the context of Marcia's skin, see Dinshaw's discussion of the fleshliness of "Adam Scriveyn," 3–14.

36. On this conflict between philology and the materiality of texts, see Stephanie H. Jed, *Chaste Thinking: The Rape of Lucretia and the Birth of Humanism* (Bloomington: Indiana Univ. Press, 1989), 69–70.

37. Janet Gurkin Altman, *Epistolarity: Approaches to a Form* (Columbus: Ohio Univ. Press, 1982), 135.

38. Piero Boitani reads this opening moment as both a comic tribute to and a critique of a humanist-inspired antiquarian culture devoted to old books; "Old Books Brought to Life in Dreams: The *Book of the Duchess*, the *House of Fame*, the *Parliament of Fowls*," in *The Cambridge Chaucer Companion*, 40.

39. Gellrich, *The Idea of the Book in the Middle Ages*, 170.

40. See Desmond, *Reading Dido*, 34.

41. Hansen, *Chaucer and the Fictions of Gender*, 91.

42. On this point, see Lawrence Lipking, *Abandoned Women and Poetic Tradition* (Chicago: Univ. of Chicago Press, 1988), who argues that "the epic hero . . . tends to define himself by leaving a woman behind" (xvi).

43. Ovid, *Heroides and Amores*, ed. and trans. Grant Showerman, 2d ed. (Cambridge: Harvard Univ. Press, 1977), 82–83.

44. Ovid, *Heroides*, 96–97.

45. Ovid, *Heroides*, 98–99.

46. Ovid, *Heroides*, 132–33.

47. I am grateful to David Wallace for this point.

48. Gellrich, *The Idea of the Book in the Middle Ages*, 170–74.

49. Dinshaw, *Chaucer's Sexual Poetics*, 30; Fyler, *Chaucer and Ovid*, 34.

50. In this, Dido's writing embodies something similar to what Barthes describes as "that neutral, composite, oblique space where our subject slips away, the negative where all identity is lost, starting with the very identity of the body writing." Roland Barthes, "The Death of the Author," in *Image/Text/Music*, trans. Stephen Heath (New York: Hill and Wang, 1971), 142.

51. Louise O. Fradenburg, " 'Voice Memorial': Loss and Reparation in Chaucer's Poetry," *Exemplaria* 2 (1990): 169–202, 172.

52. Francesco Petrarca, *Letters on Familiar Matters: Rerum Familiarum Libri XVII–XXIV*, trans. Aldo S. Bernardo (Baltimore: Johns Hopkins Univ. Press, 1985), 344.

53. Vincent J. DiMarco, *Riverside Chaucer*, 991–92; see also Russell A. Peck, *Chaucer's Lyrics and "Anelida and Arcite": An Annotated Bibliography 1900 to 1980* (Toronto: Univ. of Toronto Press, 1983), 104–19.

54. A. S. G. Edwards, "The Unity and Authenticity of *Anelida and Arcite*: The Evidence of the Manuscripts," *Studies in Bibliography* 41 (1988): 177–88.

55. The rubric is cited from Bodleian MS Tanner 346, fol. 62ᵛ.

56. The three that reverse the order of the Complaint and Prologue are Bodleian MS Fairfax 16 and Bodley 638, and British Library MS Add. 16165.

57. Interestingly, and I think significantly, the text in which *The Legend of Good Women* precedes *Anelida and Arcite*, Bodleian MS Tanner 346, follows the canonical order (beginning on fol. 118ᵛ), suggesting, perhaps, that the Invocation's prayer to "continue" the poem indicates that the Complaint is

a continuation of the *Legend;* the two MSS in which *The Legend of Good Women* follows *Anelida and Arcite* present the Invocation and Complaint in reverse order, suggesting that *The Legend of Good Women* "continues" Anelida's complaint; see Bodleian MS Fairfax 16, in which "the complaint of fayre Anelida on fals Arcyte" (fol. 30ʳ) precedes the Invocation (fol. 32ᵛ), and Bodleian MS Bodley 638, in which "the complaint of fayre Anelida on fals Arcyte" (fol. 5ʳ) precedes "the boke of feyre Anelida and false Arcyte," which begins with the Invocation (fol. 7ᵛ).

58. On this extraordinary text, see Alexandra A. T. Barratt, "'The Flower and the Leaf' and 'The Assembly of Ladies': Is There a (Sexual) Difference?" *Philological Quarterly* 66 (1987): 1–24; Jane Chance, "Christine de Pizan as Literary Mother: Women's Authority and Subjectivity in 'The Floure and the Leafe' and 'The Assembly of Ladies,'" in *The City of Scholars: New Approaches to Christine de Pizan,* ed. Margarete Zimmermann and Dina de Rentiis (Berlin: Walter de Gruyter, 1994).

59. On Corinna's poetry, the only full-length study is D. L. Page, *Corinna* (London: Society for the Promotion of Hellenic Studies, 1953).

60. John Skelton, "Phyllyp Sparowe," in Skelton, *The Complete English Poems,* ed. John Scattergood (New Haven: Yale Univ. Press, 1983), 842; Juan Luis Vives, *Instruction of a Christian Woman* (1529), cited by Janis Butler Holm, "Struggling with the Letter: Vives's Preface to the *Instruction of a Christian Woman,*" in *Contending Kingdoms: Historical, Psychological, and Feminist Approaches to the Literature of Sixteenth-Century England and France,* ed. Marie-Rose Logan and Peter L. Rudnytsky (Detroit: Wayne State Univ. Press, 1991), 273.

61. Edgar F. Shannon, *Chaucer and the Roman Poets* (Cambridge: Harvard Univ. Press, 1929), 17.

62. Statius, *Thebaid,* trans. A. D. Melville (Oxford: Clarendon Press, 1992), 330; Dante Alighieri, *Purgatorio,* trans. Allen Mandelbaum (New York: Bantam Books, 1984), 206–7.

63. Greene, *The Light in Troy,* 12.

64. Patterson, *Chaucer and the Subject of History,* 64.

65. The five MSS in which Anelida's Complaint follows the Invocation and Story are British Library MS Harley 7333, Harley 372, Bodleian MS Tanner 346, Bodleian MS Digby 181, and Longleat 254; of the remaining seven, three produce them in reverse order and four contain the Complaint alone.

66. Fradenburg, "Voice Memorial," 173.

67. Lee Patterson, "Writing Amorous Wrongs: Chaucer and the Order of Complaint," in *The Idea of Medieval Literature: New Essays on Chaucer and Medieval Culture in Honor of Donald R. Howard,* ed. James M. Dean and Christian K. Zacher (London: Associated University Presses, 1992), 56–57. On Chaucer's relation to Ovid, see Fyler, *Chaucer and Ovid;* two studies of other medieval uses of the *Heroides* are Judith Miller Ortiz, "The Two Faces of Dido," *Romance Quarterly* 33 (1986): 421–30, and Gerald A. Bond, "Composing Yourself: Ovid's *Heroides,* Baudri of Bourgueil, and the Problem of Persona," *Medievalia* 13 (1989): 83–117. See also Marina Scordilis Brownlee, *The Severed Word: Ovid's Heroides and the Novela Sentimental* (Princeton: Princeton Univ. Press, 1990), esp. 28–30.

68. See Nancy Dean, "Chaucer's *Complaint:* A Genre Descended from the

Heroides," Comparative Literature 19 (1967): 1–27; John Kerrigan, *Motives of Woe: Shakespeare and "Female Complaint"* (Oxford: Oxford Univ. Press, 1991).

69. Linda Kauffman, *Discourses of Desire: Gender, Genre, and Epistolary Fictions* (Ithaca: Cornell Univ. Press, 1986), 33.

70. Spearing, *Medieval to Renaissance*, 32.

71. Spearing, *Medieval to Renaissance*, 33.

72. Spearing, *Medieval to Renaissance*, 33.

73. On this point, see Winthrop Wetherbee, *Chaucer and the Poets: An Essay on "Troilus and Criseyde"* (Ithaca: Cornell Univ. Press, 1984), 227.

74. On the circulation of the *litera Troili*, see W. A. Davenport, *Chaucer: Complaint and Narrative* (Cambridge: D. S. Brewer, 1988), 171; studies of Troilus's use of epistolary conventions include Norman Davis, "The Litera Troilu and English Letters," *RES* new series 16 (1965): 16–24, and John McKinnell, "Letters as a Type of Formal Level in *Troilus and Criseyde,*" in *Essays on Troilus and Criseyde,* ed. Mary Salu (Cambridge: D. S. Brewer, 1979), as well as Seth Lerer, *Courtly Letters in the Age of Henry VIII: Literary Culture and the Arts of Deceit* (Cambridge: Cambridge Univ. Press, 1997), esp. 7–10.

75. McKinnell, "Letters as a Type of Formal Level," 76, 82.

76. As Marcelle Thiébaux argues, "Of all the forms available to women writers, none has been so necessary and so congenial over the centuries as the letter. A literate woman would always find the need and opportunity to write letters without having to apologize for presuming to authorship." Introduction, *The Writings of Medieval Women* (New York: Garland, 1987), xiii; a similar argument is further developed by Karen Cherewatuk and Ulrike Wiethaus, "Introduction: Women Writing Letters in the Middle Ages," in *Dear Sister: Medieval Women and the Epistolary Genre,* ed. Cherewatuk and Wiethaus (Philadelphia: Univ. of Pennsylvania Press, 1993). On medieval women's letters and their significance for literary history, see Josephine Koster Tarvers, "In a Woman's Hand? The Question of Medieval Women's Holograph Letters," *Postscript* 13 (1986): 89–100; Sarah Stanbury, "Women's Letters and Private Space in Chaucer," *Exemplaria* 6 (1994): 271–85; Joan Ferrante, *To the Glory of Her Sex: Women's Roles in the Composition of Medieval Texts* (Bloomington: Indiana Univ. Press, 1997), esp. Chapter 1, "Women in Correspondence."

77. Virginia Woolf, *A Room of One's Own* (1929; New York: Harcourt, Brace, 1981), 62; in a similar vein, Michel Foucault asserts that "a private letter may well have a signer—it does not have an author." "What Is an Author?" trans. Josué V. Harari, in *The Foucault Reader,* trans. Paul Rabinow (New York: Pantheon Books, 1984), 107–8.

78. Janet Gurkin Altman, *Epistolarity: Approaches to a Form* (Columbus: Ohio Univ. Press, 1982), 135.

79. On the contrast between the lovers' letters, see also Jennifer Campbell, "Figuring Criseyde's 'Entente': Authority, Narrative, and Chaucer's Use of History," *Chaucer Review* 27 (1993): 347. See also Stanbury, "Women's Letters and Private Space," who examines the nexus of private space and female letter writing across Chaucer's works.

80. See Stephen G. Nichols, "An Intellectual Anthropology of Marriage in

the Middle Ages," in *The New Medievalism*, ed. Marina S. Brownlee, Kevin Brownlee, and Stephen G. Nichols (Baltimore: Johns Hopkins Univ. Press, 1991), 83–84; Peter Dronke provides an illuminating survey of these conventions in *Women Writers of the Middle Ages* (Cambridge: Cambridge Univ. Press, 1984), 88–97; see also Sylvia Huot, *From Song to Book: The Poetics of Writing in Old French Lyric and Lyrical Narrative Poetry* (Ithaca: Cornell Univ. Press, 1987), 131–51.

81. John of Salisbury, quoted by M. T. Clanchy, *From Memory to Written Record: England 1066–1307*, 2d ed. (Oxford: Blackwell, 1993), 202.

82. Eugene Vance similarly notes this connection, pointing out that Criseyde's letter shows how "in *written* speech too is change." See *Mervelous Signals: Poetics and Sign Theory in the Middle Ages* (Lincoln: Univ. of Nebraska Press, 1986), 304.

83. Anne Middleton, "Chaucer's 'New Men' and the Good of Literature in the *Canterbury Tales*," in *Literature and Society*, ed. Edward W. Said (Baltimore: Johns Hopkins Univ. Press, 1980), 24–26.

84. On the *Canticus Troili*, see Robert O. Payne, *The Key of Remembrance: A Study of Chaucer's Poetics* (New Haven: Yale Univ. Press, 1963); James I. Wimsatt, "The French Lyric Element in *Troilus and Criseyde*," *Yearbook of English Studies* 15 (1985): 18–32, and *Chaucer and His French Contemporaries* (Toronto: Univ. of Toronto Press, 1991), esp. xi; Vance, *Mervelous Signals*; Thomas C. Stillinger, *The Song of Troilus: Lyric Authority and the Medieval Book* (Philadelphia: Univ. of Pennsylvania Press, 1992). For a consideration of the gendering of lyric in *Troilus and Criseyde* that forms an interesting counterpart to the poem's gendering of writing, see Clare Regan Kinney, "'Who Made This Song?' The Engendering of Lyric Counterplots in *Troilus and Criseyde*," *Studies in Philology* 89 (1992): 272–92.

85. On "Adam Scriveyn"'s dangerous textuality, see Dinshaw, *Chaucer's Sexual Poetics*, 3–10; Seth Lerer, *Chaucer and His Readers: Imagining the Author in Late Medieval England* (Princeton: Princeton Univ. Press, 1993), 121–22, 132–37.

86. Huot, *From Song to Book*, 150–51; Stillinger makes a similar observation about "the 'writtenness' of the voice" in the *canticus Troili* (*The Song of Troilus*, 183).

87. Derek Pearsall, "The *Troilus* Frontispiece and Chaucer's Audience," *YES* 7 (1977): 70. On the other hand, it also recalls contemporary practices of orality that Joyce Coleman establishes to have been far more prevalent in late medieval literary culture than previously appreciated; see Coleman, *Public Reading and the Reading Public in Late Medieval England and France* (Cambridge: Cambridge University Press, 1996).

88. This contrast between Troilus's "disembodied" letters and Criseyde's "bodily" ones bears comparison to Geraldine Heng's reading of gender difference in *Sir Gawain and the Green Knight*, where Gawain functions as "a disembodied voice" while "the Lady *incarnates* a language of desire: produces, in other words, a bodily script that represents desire as momentarily visible and legible." "A Woman Wants: The Lady, *Gawain*, and the Forms of Seduction," *The Yale Journal of Criticism* 5 (1992): 109. Gayle Margherita makes a related point when she asserts: "To the extent that she becomes associated with an

irreducible and intractable materiality, woman embodies the losses and divisions wherein a poetic subjectivity originates." *The Romance of Origins: Language and Sexual Difference in Middle English Literature* (Philadelphia: Univ. of Pennsylvania Press, 1994), 100.

89. I quote Boccaccio's *Filostrato* from the parallel-text edition of *Troilus and Criseyde*, ed. B. A. Windeatt (London: Longman, 1984), 470–71.

90. On this point, see C. David Benson, "The Opaque Text of Chaucer's Criseyde," in *Chaucer's Troilus and Criseyde: "Subgit to alle Poesye,"* ed. R. A. Shoaf with Catherine S. Cox (Binghamton, NY: MRTS, 1992).

91. Middleton, "Chaucer's 'New Men,'" 39.

92. Gerald L. Bruns, "The Originality of Texts in a Manuscript Culture," in *Inventions: Writing, Textuality, and Understanding in Literary History* (New Haven: Yale Univ. Press, 1982), 44–59; Jed, *Chaste Thinking*, 26; on the changing relationship between medieval textuality and ideas of authorship, see also Robert S. Sturges, "Textual Scholarship: Ideologies of Literary Production," *Exemplaria* 3 (1991): 109–31.

93. Susan Schibanoff, "The New Reader and Female Textuality in Two Early Commentaries on Chaucer," *Studies in the Age of Chaucer* 10 (1988): 100; on the substitution of the "immediate, aural audience from the opening books" for "a more remote 'redere'" over the course of *Troilus and Criseyde*, see Paul Strohm, *Social Chaucer* (Cambridge: Harvard Univ. Press, 1989), 56.

CHAPTER TWO

1. Christine de Pizan has been the subject of burgeoning scholarly interest that has produced a dynamic body of work that is too large, and too quickly growing, to be cited in full here. Much was initially stimulated by Earl Jeffrey Richards's translation of *The Book of the City of Ladies* (New York: Persea, 1982), and it has been sustained by the work of Charity Cannon Willard for many years; see her biography and survey of Christine's works, *Christine de Pizan: Her Life and Works* (New York: Persea, 1984). For a good bibliography of scholarship on Christine, see the collection of essays from the 1995 Binghamton University conference "Christine de Pizan: Texts/Intertexts/Contexts," *Christine de Pizan and the Categories of Difference*, ed. Marilynn Desmond (Minneapolis: Univ. of Minnesota Press, 1998), 257–77.

2. The sumptuously illuminated collection of her complete works, British Library MS Harley 4431, was a gift from Christine herself to Isabel of Bavaria, queen of Charles VI, in 1407, and it later passed into the libraries of the Duke of Bedford and Anthony Woodville, the Earl Rivers, who used it as a source for his fifteenth-century English translations of her work; see Sandra Hindman, "The Composition of the Manuscript of Christine de Pizan's Collected Works in the British Library: A Reassessment," *British Library Journal* 9 (1983): 93–123. Other important manuscripts of Christine's works, including British Library MSS Harley 219, Royal 19 B XVIII, and Royal E VI, show signs of having been copied in England or directly for English owners; see P. G. C. Campbell, "Christine de Pisan en Angleterre," *Revue de Littérature Comparée* 5 (1925): 659–70, and Carol M. Meale, "Patrons, Buyers, and Owners: Book Production and Social Status," in Jeremy Griffiths and Derek Pearsall, eds. *Book Production and Publishing in Britain, 1375–1475* (Cambridge: Cambridge Univ.

Press, 1989), esp. 208. For an overview of Christine's works' circulation in England, see Jane Chance, "Christine de Pizan as Literary Mother: Women's Authority and Subjectivity in 'The Floure and the Leafe' and 'The Assembly of Ladies,'" in *The City of Scholars: New Approaches to Christine de Pizan*, ed. Margarete Zimmermann and Dina de Rentiis (Berlin: Walter de Gruyter, 1994).

3. The following discussion will elaborate this development in greater detail, with more particular references. On the rise of literature as a gentlemanly pursuit from the mid-fifteenth through the early sixteenth century, see Ruth Kelso, *The Doctrine of the English Gentleman in the Sixteenth Century*, University of Illinois Studies in Language and Literature 14 (1929), 15 and passim; J. H. Hexter, "The Education of the Aristocracy in the Renaissance," *Journal of Modern History* 22 (1950): 1–20. While Kelso and Hexter trace the rise of the literary-minded gentleman to the beginning of the sixteenth century, K. B. McFarlane convincingly pushes its origins back to the mid-fifteenth century in "The Education of the Nobility in Later Medieval England," in *The Nobility of Later Medieval England* (Oxford: Clarendon Press, 1973).

4. "A cette époque, il faut l'avouer, on s'intéressait surtout à l'oeuvre écrite, fort peu à l'écrivain" (Campbell, "Christine de Pisan en Angleterre," 669). Since Campbell's article, there has been a recent rekindling of interest in the English publication of Christine de Pizan. To my knowledge, the first work to explore the relevance of this topic to contemporary concerns about female authorship is a still-important article by Susan Schibanoff, "Early Woman Writers: In-Scribing, or, Reading the Fine Print," *Women's Studies International Forum* 6 (1983): 475–89. The most recent work on this topic reached my attention too late to be considered in this chapter: see Laurie A. Finke's chapter, "Christine de Pizan in England," in her *Women's Writing in English: Medieval England* (London: Longman, 1999). See also Dhira Mahoney, "Middle English Regenderings of Christine de Pizan," *The Medieval Opus: Imitation, Rewriting, and Transmission in the French Tradition*, ed. Douglas Kelly (Amsterdam: Editions Rodolpi, 1996), and Jane Chance, "Gender Subversion and Linguistic Castration in Fifteenth-Century English Translations of Christine de Pizan," in *Violence against Women in Medieval Texts*, ed. Anna Roberts (Gainesville: Univ. Press of Florida, 1998).

5. On "the extraordinary uncertainty and elusive fluidity of authors' names" in early printed texts, see E. Ph. Goldschmidt, *Medieval Texts and Their First Appearance in Print*, Bibliographical Society Transactions, Suppl. 16 (London, 1943), 86; on the textual construction of authors' names in early print culture in France, see Cynthia J. Brown, *Poets, Patrons, and Printers: Crisis of Authority in Late Medieval France* (Ithaca: Cornell Univ. Press, 1995).

6. See, for example, Mahoney, "Middle English Regenderings of Christine de Pizan," and Chance, "Gender Subversion and Linguistic Castration."

7. These two arguments also reflect, in different form, another recent, similar split between what might be termed a postmodern archaeology of humanist authorship and feminist efforts to resuscitate the humanist author figure for women writers; see W. Speed Hill, "Editing Nondramatic Texts of the English Renaissance: A Field Guide with Illustrations," in *New Ways of Look-*

ing at Old Texts: Papers of the Renaissance English Text Society, 1985–1991, ed. Hill (Binghamton: Medieval and Renaissance Texts and Studies, 1993), 23–24, as well as the other essays collected in the volume.

8. On Chaucer's construction as an author during the fifteenth and sixteenth centuries, see Seth Lerer, Chaucer and His Readers: Imagining the Author in Late-Medieval England (Princeton: Princeton Univ. Press, 1993); David R. Carlson, "Chaucer, Humanism, and Printing," University of Toronto Quarterly 64 (1995): 274–88; Theresa M. Krier, ed., Refiguring Chaucer in the Renaissance (Gainesville: Univ. Press of Florida, 1998); Joseph A. Dane, Who Is Buried in Chaucer's Tomb? Studies in the Reception of Chaucer's Book (East Lansing: Michigan State Univ. Press, 1998); Christopher Cannon, The Making of Chaucer's English (Cambridge: Cambridge Univ. Press, 1998).

9. Gérard Genette, Paratexts: Thresholds of Interpretation, trans. Jane E. Lewin (Cambridge: Cambridge Univ. Press, 1997), 2. New work bringing together traditional bibliographical practices with literary-critical concerns has made fruitful use of paratexts in early books: see, for example, Kevin Dunn, Pretexts of Authority: The Rhetoric of Authorship in the Renaissance Preface (Stanford: Stanford Univ. Press, 1994); Evelyn B. Tribble, Margins and Marginality: The Printed Page in Early Modern England (Charlottesville: Univ. Press of Virginia, 1993).

10. On the early French editions, see Cynthia J. Brown, "The Reconstruction of an Author in Print: Christine de Pizan in the Fifteenth and Sixteenth Centuries," in Christine de Pizan and the Categories of Difference, ed. Marilynn Desmond (Minneapolis: Univ. of Minnesota Press, 1998); see also Michal-André Bossy, "Arms and the Bride: Christine de Pizan's Military Treatise as a Wedding Gift for Margaret of Anjou," in the same volume.

11. Kevin Brownlee, "Discourses of the Self: Christine de Pizan and the Rose," Romanic Review 79 (1988): 199–221; Brownlee, "Ovide et le moi poétique 'moderne' à la fin du moyen âge: Jean Froissart et Christine de Pizan," in Modernité au moyen âge: Le défi du passé, ed. Brigitte Cazelles and Charles Méla (Geneva: Droz, 1990); Maureen Quilligan, The Allegory of Female Authority: Christine de Pizan's "Cité des Dames" (Ithaca: Cornell Univ. Press, 1991). As Quilligan cogently argues, "Christine de Pizan very early anticipated the position of 'author' and inhabited it—however briefly—becoming an accidental occupier of a theoretically possible social slot in part because, as a female, no other cultural model was available to her" (5). See also Lori Walters, "The Woman Writer and Literary History: Christine de Pizan's Redefinition of the Poetic Translatio in the Epistre au dieu d'amours," French Literature Series 16 (1989): 1–16.

12. Christine de Pizan, Le livre du chemin de long estude, ed. Robert Püschel (1887; repr., Geneva: Slatkine, 1974), lines 119–21; these lines are cited by Jacqueline Cerquiglini, "L'étrangère," Revue des Langues Romanes 92 (1988): 242; the English version is from Renate Blumenfeld-Kosinski in her translation of the article as "The Stranger," in The Selected Writings of Christine de Pizan, ed. Blumenfeld-Kosinski (New York: Norton, 1997), 268.

13. The French text of Christine's work is cited from the only current edition of the original, Maureen Cheney Curnow's dissertation, The "Livre de la Cité des Dames" of Christine de Pisan: A Critical Edition (Ph.D. dissertation,

Vanderbilt Univ., 1975), 628. The English text is from Christine de Pizan, *The Book of the City of Ladies*, trans. Earl Jeffrey Richards (New York: Persea, 1982), 10. Hereafter, references to the *Cité de Dames* will be to these editions—unless otherwise noted—with page numbers noted in parentheses.

14. Cerquiglini, "L'étrangère." See also Earl Jeffrey Richards, "'Seulette a part'—The 'Little Woman on the Sidelines' Takes Up Her Pen: The Letters of Christine de Pizan," in *Dear Sister: Medieval Women and the Epistolary Genre*, ed. Karen Cherewatuk and Ulrike Wiethaus (Philadelphia: Univ. of Pennsylvania Press, 1993), which examines how Christine manipulates a "constructed female authorial persona [as the *seulette a part*, literally, 'little lonely woman on the sidelines'], with its explicit emphasis on the stereotypical diminutive and marginalized position of women," into a position of authority (140).

15. A. J. Minnis, *Medieval Theory of Authorship: Scholastic Literary Attitudes in the Later Middle Ages*, 2d ed. (Philadelphia: Univ. of Pennsylvania Press, 1988); M. B. Parkes, "The Influence of the Concepts of Ordinatio and Compilatio on the Development of the Book," *Scribes, Scripts, and Readers: Studies in the Communication, Presentation, and Dissemination of Medieval Texts* (London: Hambledon Press, 1991); Roger Dragonetti, *Le mirage des sources: L'art du faux dans le roman médiéval* (Paris: Seuil, 1987): "écrire, pour un auteur médiéval, n'est-ce-pas avant tout se référer aux réserves d'une tradition dont les textes s'écrivent les uns dans les autres, copies de copies faisant palimpseste et compilation . . . ?" (41).

16. On the medieval divisions between "chevalerie" and "clergie" as competing models of masculinity, see Simon Gaunt, *Gender and Genre in Medieval French Literature* (Cambridge: Cambridge Univ. Press, 1995), 12.

17. On Christine's separation of chivalry and courtly love, see Charity Cannon Willard, "Christine de Pizan on Chivalry," in *The Study of Chivalry: Resources and Approaches* (Kalamazoo, Mich.: Medieval Institute Publications, 1988). On Christine's challenge to the misogyny of the medieval court of love, see particularly Helen Solterer, *The Master and Minerva: Disputing Women in French Medieval Culture* (Berkeley: Univ. of California Press, 1995), 151–75.

18. Christine de Pizan, *L'épistre au dieu d'amours*, in *Poems of Cupid, God of Love*, ed. and trans. Thelma S. Fenster and Mary Carpenter Erler (New York: E. J. Brill, 1990); I have slightly modified the translation of these lines, 163–64.

19. See Charity Cannon Willard, "Christine de Pizan on the Art of Warfare," in *Christine de Pizan and the Categories of Difference*, ed. Desmond; and Jane Chance, "Afterword: Chivalry and the Other," in *The Rusted Hauberk: Feudal Ideals of Order and Their Decline*, ed. Liam Purdon and Cindy Vitto (Gainesville: Univ. Press of Florida, 1994), 309–20; see also Nadia Margolis, "Christine de Pizan: The Poetess as Historian," *Journal of the History of Ideas* 47 (1986): 361–75.

20. Stephen Scrope, trans., *The Epistle of Othea*, ed. Curt F. Bühler, EETS 264 (Oxford: Oxford Univ. Press, 1970), 40; for Scrope's translation of "dompter," see Bühler's note on 144. I cite Christine's original from British Library MS Harley 4431, fol. 109ʳ.

21. Scrope, 7; B.L. MS Harley 4431, fol. 96ʳ.

22. *L'épistre au dieu d'amours*, lines 260–63.

23. On the division between women and clerks, see Susan Crane, "The Writing Lesson of 1381," in *Chaucer's England: Literature in Historical Context*, ed. Barbara A. Hanawalt (Minneapolis: Univ. of Minnesota Press, 1992).

24. Lori Walters, "Chivalry and the (En)Gendered Poetic Self: Petrarchan Models in the 'Cent Balades,'" in *The City of Scholars: New Approaches to Christine de Pizan*, ed. Margarete Zimmerman and Dina de Rentiis (New York: Walter de Gruyter, 1994), 46; see also Brownlee, "Discourses of the Self."

25. Diane Bornstein, *Mirrors of Courtesy* (Hamden, CT: Archon Books, 1975), 51.

26. See David Starkey, "The Age of the Household: Politics, Society, and the Arts, c. 1350–c. 1550," in *The Later Middle Ages*, ed. Stephen Medcalf (London: Methuen, 1981). The growth of the aristocratic household appears to be linked to the end of the war, which settled significant sums of money in the hands of aristocratic soldiers, enabling minor aristocrats to buy land and landed aristocrats to expand their holdings and augment their private living standards; see K. B. McFarlane, "War, the Economy, and Social Change: England and the Hundred Years War," in *England in the Fifteenth Century: Collected Essays* (London: Hambledon Press, 1981). On the aristocratic household see Kate Mertes, *The English Noble Household: Good Governance and Politic Rule* (Oxford: Basil Blackwell, 1988), 52–74, 121–38; Christopher Dyer, *Standards of Living in the Later Middle Ages: Social Change in England, c. 1200–1520* (Cambridge: Cambridge Univ. Press, 1989), esp. 50 and 108.

27. On the rise of "laymen employed in administrative work" for royal government, see R. L. Storey, "Gentlemen-Bureaucrats," in *Profession, Vocation, and Culture in Later Medieval England*, ed. Cecil H. Clough (Liverpool: Liverpool Univ. Press, 1982). According to McFarlane, the "rise of the gentleman bureaucrat was one of the most significant results of the growth of lay literacy." See K. B. McFarlane, "William Worcester: A Preliminary Survey," *England in the Fifteenth Century*, 202. Ethan Knapp's work on Hoccleve establishes the importance of this development for English literary culture in the fifteenth century; see "Bureaucratic Identity and the Construction of the Self in Hoccleve's Formulary and La Male Regle," *Speculum* 74 (1999): 357–76, in which Knapp argues that the new bureaucrats "might well be considered the first class one could point to whose identity was based solely on a relationship to the written word" (366).

28. See Storey, "Gentlemen-Bureaucrats," on the secularization of literacy in administrative positions.

29. See Roberto Weiss, *Humanism in England during the Fifteenth Century*, 3d ed. (Oxford: Oxford Univ. Press, 1967).

30. Susan Crane, "Anglo-Norman Cultures in England, 1066–1460," in *The Cambridge History of Medieval English Literature*, ed. David Wallace (Cambridge: Cambridge Univ. Press, 1999), 52.

31. On the provenance of Christine's manuscripts, see Sandra L. Hindman, "The Composition of the Manuscript of Christine de Pizan's Collected Works in the British Library: A Reassessent," *British Library Journal* 9 (1983): 96; Carol Meale, "Patrons, Buyers, and Owners," 207–8.

32. George Warner, Introduction, *The Epistle of Othea to Hector or the Boke of Knyghthode* (London: J. B. Nichols and Sons, 1904), xxxiv.

33. *Henry V*, 5.2.166–67; *The Norton Shakespeare*, ed. Stephen Greenblatt et al. (New York: W. W. Norton, 1997).

34. Malcolm Richardson, "Henry V, the English Chancery, and Chancery English," *Speculum* 55 (1980): 741; John H. Fisher, "Chancery and the Emergence of Standard Written English in the Fifteenth Century," *Speculum* 52 (1977): 879. On the continued French influence in England, see Elizabeth Salter, *English and International: Studies in the Literature, Art, and Patronage of Medieval England*, ed. Derek Pearsall and Nicolette Zeeman (Cambridge: Cambridge Univ. Press, 1988), especially the chapters in the section entitled "An Obsession with the Continent." See also John Burrow, "Hoccleve and the Middle French Poets," in *The Long Fifteenth Century: Essays for Douglas Gray*, ed. Helen Cooper and Sally Mapstone (Oxford: Clarendon Press, 1997), 44–45.

35. Lee Patterson, "Making Identities in Fifteenth-Century England: Henry V and John Lydgate," in *New Historical Literary Study: Essays on Reproducing Texts, Representing History*, ed. Jeffrey N. Cox and Larry J. Reynolds (Princeton: Princeton Univ. Press, 1993).

36. David A. Lawton, "Dullness and the Fifteenth Century," *ELH* 54 (1987): 793; on Lancastrian criticisms of Richard's Francophile court, see Patricia J. Eberle, "The Politics of Courtly Style," in *The Spirit of the Court: Selected Proceedings of the Fourth Congress of the International Courtly Literature Society*, ed. Glyn S. Burgess and Robert A. Taylor (Woodbridge: D. S. Brewer, 1985); Ardis Butterfield, "French Culture and the Ricardian Court," in *Essays on Ricardian Literature in Honour of J. A. Burrow*, ed. A. J. Minnis, Charlotte C. Morse, and Thorlac Turville-Petre (Oxford: Clarendon Press, 1997), 94; See also the essays of J. W. Sherborne, "Aspects of English Court Culture in the Later Fourteenth Century," and V. J. Scattergood, "Literary Culture at the Court of Richard II," in *English Court Culture in the Later Middle Ages*, ed. V. J. Scattergood and J. W. Sherborne (London: Gerald Duckworth, 1983), 20. On Richard's French marriage and anti-French prejudice, see May McKisack, *The Fourteenth Century, 1307–1399* (Oxford: Clarendon Press, 1959), 151. The link between Richard II and French love poetry may be grounded in more than popular prejudice: in one of the only contemporary accounts of Richard II's literary tastes and practices as a patron, Jean Froissart describes presenting the English king a book of poems: "Then the king asked me what it [the book] dealt with. I said to him, 'Of love.' He was pleased with this reply and looked into the book. . . . Then he gave it to one of his knights who was called Sir Richard Credon to take to his [i.e., the king's] private chamber, and he welcomed me even more pleasantly and entertained me marvellously well." Cited by V. J. Scattergood, "Literary Culture at the Court of Richard II," in *English Court Culture in the Later Middle Ages*, 33.

37. While the literary community of the Fastolf household is especially masculine, women did participate in other literary households of this period; see Susan Groag Bell's classic article, "Medieval Women Book Owners: Arbiters of Lay Piety and Ambassadors of Culture," reprinted in *Women and Power in the Middle Ages*, ed. Mary Erler and Maryanne Kowaleski (Athens: Univ. of Georgia Press, 1988). But the formal lines of patronage that developed in these households mimicked the ties of an earlier form of lordship that were pre-

dominantly between men; see J. M. W. Bean, *From Lord to Patron: Lordship in Late Medieval England* (Manchester: Manchester Univ. Press, 1989). Dyer, *Standards of Living in the Later Middle Ages*, points out that "households were predominantly masculine societies, because with the exception of a few female companions for the lady, and washerwomen, the officers and servants were always male" (50); Mertes, *The English Noble Household, 1250–1600*, cites a number of contemporary courtesy books that warn against the dangers of employing unmarried women in the household (57–58).

38. On Fastolf, see K. B. McFarlane, "The Investment of Sir John Fastolf's Profits of War," in McFarlane, *England in the Fifteenth Century.*

39. On the Fastolf household, and the place of Scrope and Worcester within it, see Jonathan Hughes, "Stephen Scrope and the Circle of Sir John Fastolf: Moral and Intellectual Outlooks," *Medieval Knighthood IV: Papers from the Fifth Strawberry Hill Conference*, ed. Christopher Harper-Bill and Ruth Harvey (Woodbridge: Boydell Press, 1992). Ethan Knapp offers an incisive reading of how translation mediated the troubled relationship between Scrope and his stepfather Fastolf in his paper "Bought and Sold Like a Beast: Stephen Scrope's Translation of *The Letter of Othea to Hector*," delivered at the 1996 Sixteenth Century Studies Conference; I am grateful to him for sharing this work with me.

40. *The Paston Letters*, ed. James Gairdner, 6 vols. (London: Chatto and Windus, 1904), 3:302; see also William Worcester, *The Boke of Noblesse*, ed. John Gough Nichols (London: Roxburgh Club, 1860), lix.

41. M. G. A. Vale, "New Techniques and Old Ideas: The Impact of Artillery on War and Chivalry at the End of the Hundred Years War," and N. A. R. Wright, "*The Tree of Battles* of Honoré Bouvet and the Laws of War," both in *War, Literature, and Politics in the Later Middle Ages*, ed. C. T. Allmand (Liverpool: Univ. of Liverpool Press, 1976); Arthur B. Ferguson, *The Chivalric Tradition in Renaissance England* (Washington: Folger Books, 1986), 39–40; Philippe Contamine, *La guerre au moyen âge* (Paris: Presses Universitaires de France, 1980), 272–76.

42. Scrope's translation survives as Longleat MS 253 and is edited by Curt Bühler, as *The Epistle of Othea*, EETS 264 (London: Oxford Univ. Press, 1970), 121; see also *The Epistle of Othea to Hector, or The Book of Knighthood*, ed. Sir George Warner (London: Roxburghe Club, 1894), which contains an account of the relationship between Fastolf and Scrope, xxxiii–xxxix. On Fastolf and Scrope, see also Curt Bühler, "The Revisions and Dedications of *The Epistle of Othea*," *Anglia* 76 (1958): 266–70. Bühler puts the date of the translation "between 1440 and 1459" (xxi).

43. Christine de Pizan, *Epistle of Othea*, 122.

44. Christine de Pizan, *Epistle of Othea*, 122.

45. Christine de Pizan, *Epistle of Othea*, 122–23.

46. On the source of Scrope's translation, see George Warner's introduction to his edition of *The Epistle of Othea to Hector, or the Boke of Knyghthode*, xxxiv; see also Gianni Mombello, "Per una edizione critica dell' "Epistre Othea," *Studi Francesi* 25 (1965): 1–12; Campbell, "Christine de Pisan en Angleterre," 665–66. Kathleen Chesney argues that Scrope's source is Bodleian MS. Laud 570, a copy of the original manuscript that Christine pre-

sented to the Duke de Berry: see "Two Manuscripts of Christine de Pisan," *Medium Aevum* 1 (1932): 35–41. Curt F. Bühler believes this to be a "sister-manuscript" to Scrope's original source because of irregularities in the translation: see Bühler, "Sir John Fastolf's Manuscripts of the Epître d'Othea and Stephen Scrope's Translation of This Text," *Scriptorium* 3 (1949): 123–28. Whatever the case, Scrope clearly worked from a source that identified Christine in a preface to the Duke de Berry.

47. Christine de Pizan, *Epistle of Othea*, 8.

48. Fastolf, who suffered defeat in France under the leadership of Joan of Arc, whom Christine de Pizan would eulogize in her *Ditie de Jehanne d'Arc*, would not have objected to the proposition that chivalry in all its forms belonged to men. (See *Dictionary of National Biography*, s.n. "John Fastolf," 236.)

49. William Worcester, *The Boke of Noblesse* (1475), ed. John Gough Nichols (London: Roxburgh Club, 1860); I have also consulted the manuscript (British Library MS Royal 18 BXXII), as well as Nichols's own manuscript notes and emendations to the edition he edited, which are also housed at the British Library. On Worcester, see K. B. McFarlane, "William of Worcester: A Preliminary Survey," who holds that Worcester began the book in 1451 and then revised it twice, in 1461 and the 1470s, when it might have been rededicated by his son (214–15). See also McFarlane, "William Worcester and a Present of Lampreys," *Medium Aevum* 30 (1961): 176–80; Norman Davis, "The Epistolary Usages of William Worcester," in *Medieval Literature and Civilization: Studies in Memory of G. N. Garmonsway*, ed. D. A. Pearsall and R. A. Waldron (London: Athlone Press, 1969); and William Worcestre [sic], *Itineraries*, ed. J. H. Harvey (Oxford: Clarendon Press, 1969).

50. Worcester, *Boke of Noblesse*, ed. Nichols, 64–65.

51. Worcester, *Boke of Noblesse*, ed. Nichols, 54; British Library MS Royal 18 BXXII, fol. 28ʳ.

52. Brown, " Reconstruction of an Author in Print."

53. Campbell, "Christine de Pisan en Angleterre."

54. "In general, the mention of an author's name in a heading or colophon must denote some attempt on the part of a manuscript-compiler to 'place' the piece with which it is associated, and to supply background or context." Julia Boffey, *Manuscripts of English Courtly Love Lyrics in the Later Middle Ages* (Woodbridge, Suffolk: D. S. Brewer, 1985), 65.

55. Michel Foucault, "What Is an Author?" in *The Foucault Reader*, ed. Paul Rabinow (New York: Pantheon, 1984), 107.

56. Thus we could see these translations overturning what Deborah McGrady sees as the construction of Christine's authorship in Harley 4431, in which, as she argues, "the benefactor's authority over the text is subverted in the name of the author's." See McGrady, "What Is a Patron? Benefactors and Authorship in Harley 4431, Christine de Pizan's Collected Works," in *Christine de Pizan and the Categories of Difference*, ed. Marilyn Desmond (Minneapolis: Univ. of Minnesota Press, 1998), 196.

57. Teresa de Lauretis, *Technologies of Gender: Essays on Theory, Film, and Fiction* (Bloomington: Indiana Univ. Press, 1987), 4–5.

58. Peter Stallybrass and Margreta de Grazia, "The Materiality of the Shakespearean Text," *Shakespeare Quarterly* 44 (1993): 276.

59. William Blades, *The Life and Typography of William Caxton, England's First Printer*, 2 vols. (London, 1861), 2:207. At a time when other nineteenth-century editors and antiquarians were inclined to doubt Christine's authorship, Blades's efforts to establish it are noteworthy; his description of Caxton's *Morale Prouerbes* offers a laudatory biographical note about her (in which he claims that "Cristyne de Pise was, with the single exception of Joan of Arc, the most famous woman of her age" [2:47]), and in a letter bound with John Gough Nichols's notes in the British Library, Blades responds to Nichols's assertion that "Christina de Pisan was a poetess: and it is not likely that she had much . . . to do with [Caxton's *Fayttes of Armes and of Chyvalrye*]" by upbraiding him for "denying [Xtine of Pise] her authorship of 'Les fais d'Armes'" (letter of 28 March 1862; see Worcester, *Boke of Noblesse*, ed. Nichols, vi).

60. The manuscript note is in the British Library MS Royal 20 C VIII, *L'arbre des battailles composé par Honoré Bonet Prieur de Sallon en Prouuence*; this book formerly belonged to John, Lord Lumley (1534–1609), as did the manuscript *Book of Noblesse*, and for this reason John Gough Nichols concludes that the reader's note is Lumley's own. (See Nichols, Introduction, *Boke of Noblesse*, iv.)

61. See Charity Cannon Willard, "Pilfering Vegetius? Christine de Pizan's *Faits d'Armes et de Chevalerie*," in *Women, the Book, and the Worldly: Selected Proceedings of the St. Hilda's Conference, 1993*, vol. 2, ed. Lesley Smith and Jane H. M. Taylor (Cambridge: D. S. Brewer, 1995).

62. *The Lumley Library: The Catalogue of 1609*, ed. Sears Jayne and Francis R. Johnson (London: Cambridge Univ. Press, 1956), 135, 149, 156; Carol Meale establishes that in the Middle Ages MSS of Boccaccio's *De claris mulieribus* often circulated with MSS of Christine's *Cité des dames*; this might have contributed to Lumley's confusion over whether Christine herself was included as a character in Boccaccio's collection of famous women. See Meale, "Legends of Good Women in the European Middle Ages," *Archiv* 229 (1992): 55–70.

63. See Christine de Pizan, *The Book of Fayttes of Armes and of Chyualrye*, trans. William Caxton, ed. A. T. P. Byles, EETS 189 (Oxford: Oxford Univ. Press, 1937), 291.

64. On Fastolf, see K. B. McFarlane, "The Investment of Sir John Fastolf's Profits of War," in McFarlane, *England in the Fifteenth Century*. Scrope was disfigured as the result of an illness, which prevented him from pursuing a military career of his own; see Hughes, "Stephen Scrope and the Circle of Sir John Fastolf," 111.

65. *The Paston Letters*, ed. Gairdner, 3:334.

66. On the historical significance of the rise of this group of literate laymen replacing ordained clergy in administrative positions, see Storey, "Gentlemen-Bureaucrats."

67. McFarlane, *Nobility of Later Medieval England*, 44; Colin Richmond, *The Paston Family in the Fifteenth Century: Fastolf's Will* (Cambridge: Cambridge Univ. Press, 1996), 55; see also McFarlane, "William Worcester: A Preliminary Survey," 201. These assessments of Worcester's "modernity" revise the earlier opinion of R. Weiss, in *Humanism in England during the Fifteenth*

Century (Oxford: Oxford Univ. Press, 1941), that Worcester was "unaffected by modern values. He was only a dilettante without qualifications for scholarship whose accomplishments lay rather in the direction of antiquarianism, as his voluminous compilations testify" (178).

68. McFarlane, "William Worcester: A Preliminary Survey," 212. William Worcestre [sic], *Itineraries*, ed. John H. Harvey (Oxford: Clarendon Press, 1969).

69. Worcester himself was born "on the fringes of the gentry" (McFarlane, "William Worcester: A Preliminary Survey," 201).

70. *Paston Letters*, ed. Gairdner, 1:431.

71. Gordon Kipling, *The Triumph of Honour: Burgundian Origins of the Elizabethan Renaissance* (The Hague: Leiden Univ. Press, 1977).

72. Thomas Walsingham, *Historia Anglicana* (1387), cited by Eberle, "The Politics of Courtly Style," 169.

73. See Joel Blanchard, "'Vox Poetica, vox politica:' L'entree du poete dans le champ politique au XVe siecle," in *Actes du Colloque International sur le Moyen Francais, Milan, 6–8 mai 1985* (Milan: Vita e Pensiero, 1986).

74. See Jacqueline Cerquiglini, "L'étrangère," 239–51.

75. Ann Rosalind Jones, "Surprising Fame: Renaissance Gender Ideologies and Women's Lyric," in *The Poetics of Gender*, ed. Nancy K. Miller (New York: Columbia Univ. Press, 1986), 75; on the thesis "that the ideal setup for the [Renaissance] lady is essentially Christian in its character, and the ideal for the gentleman is essentially pagan," see Ruth Kelso, *Doctrine for the Lady of the Renaissance* (1956; reprint, Urbana: Univ. of Illinois Press, 1978), 25.

76. On Caxton's uses of patronage, see my "William Caxton, Margaret Beaufort, and the Romance of Textual Production," in *Women, the Book, and the Worldly: Selected Proceedings of the St. Hilda's Conference, 1993*, ed. Lesley Smith and Jane Taylor (Suffolk: D. S. Brewer, 1995).

77. Curt F. Bühler, *The Fifteenth-Century Book: The Scribes, the Printers, the Decorators* (Philadelphia: Univ. of Pennsylvania Press, 1960), 44; Karl Schottenloher, *Books and the Western World: A Cultural History*, trans. William D. Boyd and Irmgard H. Wolfe (London: McFarland, 1989), 86.

78. Natalie Zemon Davis, "Printing and the People," in *Society and Culture in Early Modern France* (Stanford: Stanford Univ. Press, 1975), 192.

79. Christine de Pizan, *The Morale Prouerbes of Cristyne*, trans. Anthony Woodville (Westminster: William Caxton, 1478), sig. 1ʳ. See William Blades, *The Life and Typography of William Caxton, England's First Printer*, 2 vols. (London, 1861), 2:47–48.

80. Christine's French and Anthony Woodville's English are presented together as an appendix to the facsimile reprint of Caxton's *Morale Prouerbes (1478)*, intro. William Blades (London, 1859), n.p.

81. W. J. B. Crotch, ed., *The Prologues and Epilogues of William Caxton* (1928; reprint, New York: Burt Franklin, 1971), 32. The short verse has occasioned controversy between scholars who claim it as Caxton's work and those who see it as the work of the text's translator, Anthony Woodville, the Earl Rivers; see N. F. Blake, *William Caxton and English Literary Culture* (London: Hambledon Press, 1991), 143.

82. For a discussion of the trope of "rehearsal" as an indication of second-

ariness, see A. J. Minnis, *Medieval Theory of Authorship*, 2d ed. (Philadelphia: Univ. of Pennsylvania Press, 1988), 194.

83. Richard Firth Green, "The *Familia Regis* and the *Familia Cupidinis*," in *English Court Culture in the Later Middle Ages*, ed. V. J. Scattergood and J. W. Sherborne (London: Gerald Duckworth, 1983), 98–105; see also Green, *Poets and Princepleasers: Literature and the English Court in the Late Middle Ages* (Toronto: Univ. of Toronto Press, 1980), 129.

84. N. F. Blake, *Caxton's Own Prose* (London: Andre Deutsch, 1973), 74; this passage is discussed by Susan Schibanoff in "'Taking the Gold Out of Egypt': The Art of Reading as a Woman," in *Feminist Readings in Middle English Literature*, ed. Ruth Evans and Lesley Johnson (London: Routledge, 1994).

85. Caxton's emphasis on the patron's authorizing role is consistent with the larger critical project that he develops in his prologues and epilogues, which locate the cultural authority of books not in their authors but in the figures responsible for their reproduction. As Seth Lerer has observed, one of the chief critical effects of Caxton's prologues and epilogues is "the controlled displacement of authority from writer onto reader, from the originator of a text to those who transmit and interpret it." *Chaucer and His Readers*, 163.

86. Crotch, *Prologues and Epilogues of William Caxton*, 32.

87. A compelling discussion of the secretary in Renaissance English literary culture is Richard Rambuss, *Spenser's Secret Career* (Cambridge: Cambridge Univ. Press, 1993).

88. Blake, *Caxton's Own Prose*, 70.

89. Blake, *Caxton's Own Prose*, 71.

90. Geoffrey Chaucer, *The Canterbury Tales* (London: Richard Pynson, c. 1495), sig. Ai[v].

91. Alice S. Miskimin, *The Renaissance Chaucer* (New Haven: Yale Univ. Press, 1975), 244. See also, as relevant to this context, Joseph A. Dane's discussion of Pynson's self-described relation to Caxton; *Who Is Buried in Chaucer's Tomb? Studies in the Reception of Chaucer's Book* (East Lansing: Michigan State Univ. Press, 1998), 44.

92. Miskimin, *The Renaissance Chaucer*, 244.

93. *Here Begynneth the boke of fame, made by Geffray Chaucer: with Dyuers other of his Workes* (London: Richard Pynson, 1526), sigs. Ciii[v]–Cv[r]; on this edition, see Julia Boffey, "Richard Pynson's Book of Fame and the Letter of Dido," *Viator* 19 (1988): 339–53; and A. S. G. Edwards, "Pynson's and Thynne's Editions of Chaucer's *House of Fame*," *Studies in Bibliography* 42 (1989): 185–86.

94. On "Truth," see *The Riverside Chaucer*, ed. Larry D. Benson (Oxford: Oxford Univ. Press, 1987), 653, 1084–85.

95. Alice Miskimin affirms that Caxton was Pynson's source for the *Morall Proverbes*, but she mistakenly holds that Caxton attributed the proverbs to Woodville; see *The Renaissance Chaucer* (New Haven: Yale Univ. Press, 1975), 244.

96. On women's "ventriloquization" by male authors, see Elizabeth D. Harvey, *Ventriloquized Voices: Feminist Theory and English Renaissance Texts* (London: Routledge, 1992).

97. See especially Lerer, *Chaucer and His Readers,* and Boffey, "Richard Pynson's Book of Fame," which advances this argument about Pynson's selection of apocrypha in his edition of Chaucer.

98. On the popularity of "Truth" in the Henrician period, see Ralph Hanna III, "Authorial Versions, Rolling Revision, Scribal Error? Or, the Truth about *Truth,*" *Studies in the Age of Chaucer* 10 (1988): 27; the essay is reprinted in Hanna's *Pursuing History: Middle English Manuscripts and Their Texts (Stanford: Stanford University Press, 1996).* On the demand for moral and edifying literature, see David Lawton, "Dullness and the Fifteenth Century," *ELH* 54 (1987): 761–99. On Chaucer's reputation as a love poet among the early printers, see Francis Bonner, "Genesis of the Chaucer Apocrypha," *Studies in Philology* 48 (1951): 465; on the shifting valences of the term "truth," see Richard Firth Green, *A Crisis of Truth: Literature and Law in Ricardian England* (Philadelphia: Univ. of Pennsylvania Press, 1999).

99. On Pynson's status as a humanist printer, see David Carlson, *English Humanist Books: Writers and Patrons, Manuscript and Print, 1475–1525* (Toronto: Univ. of Toronto Press, 1993), 133–41.

100. See Paul Strohm, "Chaucer's Fifteenth-Century Audience and the Narrowing of the 'Chaucer Tradition,'" *Studies in the Age of Chaucer* 4 (1982): 3–32. That fifteenth-century poets saw Chaucer "as preeminently a court poet and a poet of love" is discussed by Lois A. Ebin, *Illuminator, Maker, Vates: Visions of Poetry in the Fifteenth Century* (Lincoln: Univ. of Nebraska Press, 1988), 9ff; for a discussion of the "strong, and non-Chaucerian, moral undertow" of fifteenth-century public literature, see Lawton, "Dullness and the Fifteenth Century," 768.

101. Boffey, "Richard Pynson's Book of Fame," 340.

102. See Green, "The *Familia Regis* and the *Familia Cupidinis.*"

103. James E. Blodgett discusses Pynson's version of "La Belle Dame Sans Mercy" in *Editing Chaucer: The Great Tradition,* ed. Paul G. Ruggiers (Norman: Pilgrim Books, 1984), 42.

104. See Hanna, "Authorial Versions, Rolling Revision, Scribal Error?" 27.

105. George Pace and Alfred David, *Variorum Edition of the Works of Geoffrey Chaucer. Volume 5: The Minor Poems* (Norman: University of Oklahoma Press, 1982), 49.

106. Pynson's reading of Chaucer thus brings to the fore Chaucer's own administrative career, which, according to Lee Patterson, anticipated that of the "gentleman-bureaucrat" of the fifteenth century: see Patterson, *Chaucer and the Subject of History* (Madison: Univ. of Wisconsin Press, 1991), 37–38.

107. Blodgett, "William Thynne," in Ruggiers, *Editing Chaucer,* 38. On the uses of Chaucer in the Henrician court, see Lerer, *Courtly Letters in the Age of Henry VIII: Literary Culture and the Arts of Deceit* (Cambridge: Cambridge Univ. Press, 1997).

108. These policies reverse earlier uncertainty about Chaucer's orthodoxy, since in 1464 a defendant's ownership of *The Canterbury Tales* was considered potentially damning evidence in a heresy trial; see Nicholas Watson, "Censorship and Cultural Change in Late-Medieval England: Vernacular Theology, the Oxford Translation Debate, and Arundel's Constitutions of 1409," *Speculum* 70 (1995): 831. On Tudor restrictions on vernacular material, see

Frederick S. Siebert, *Freedom of the Press in England, 1476–1776: The Rise and Decline of Government Controls* (Urbana: Univ. of Illinois Press, 1952), 41–63. On Chaucer's status in such bans, see *Chaucer: The Critical Heritage, Volume 1: 1385–1837*, ed. Derek Brewer (London: Routledge and Kegan Paul, 1978), which reproduces the text of "An Act for Thaduancement of True Religion and For Thabolisshment of the Contrarie" (1542–43), exempting "Chaucers bokes" from a general ban on vernacular printed books (98); from the same volume, see also William Tyndale's objection to Chaucer's protection from pre-Reformation restrictions on vernacular material, on the grounds that Chaucer promoted "fables of love & wantones & of rybaudry as fylthy as herte can thinke," at the same time that vernacular scripture was banned (87). Brian Cummings makes the point that Chaucer's exemption from such bans also brings his works "within the legitimate remit of the king's scrutiny"; see Cummings, "Reformed Literature and Literature Reformed," *Cambridge History of Medieval English Literature*, 843. On the production of Chaucer as a canonical poet in the Henrician court, see John Watkins, "'Wrastling for this World': Wyatt and the Tudor Canonization of Chaucer," in *Refiguring Chaucer in the Renaissance*, ed. Theresa M. Krier (Gainesville: Univ. Press of Florida, 1998).

109. On Chaucer's paternal identifications in connection with the Henrician court, see Jonathan Goldberg, *Sodometries: Renaissance Texts, Modern Sexualities* (Stanford: Stanford Univ. Press, 1992), 53.

110. *The Boke of the Cyte of Ladyes* (London: Henry Pepwell, 1521), reproduced in facsimile in *Distaves and Dames: Renaissance Treatises for and about Women*, ed. Diane Bornstein (Delmar, NY: Scholars' Facsimiles and Reprints, 1978). On Pepwell, see E. G. Duff, "The Stationers at the Sign of the Trinity," *Bibliographica* 1 (1895): 175–93, and *Westminster and London Printers, 1476–1535* (Cambridge: Cambridge Univ. Press, 1926), 147–50. Peter Blayney discusses Pepwell's bookshop on Paternoster Row in *The Bookshops in Paul's Cross Churchyard*, Occasional Papers of the Bibliographical Society 5 (London: Bibliographical Society, 1990), 19. On Pepwell's edition of Christine, see also Maureen Cheney Curnow, "*The Boke of the Cyte of Ladyes*, an English Translation of Christine de Pizan's *Le Livre de la Cité des Dames*," *Les Bonnes Feuilles* 3 (1974); Constance Jordan, *Renaissance Feminism: Literary Texts and Political Models* (Ithaca: Cornell Univ. Press, 1990), 105–16, and John Rooks, "*The Boke of the Cyte of Ladyes* and Its Sixteenth-Century Readership," in *The Reception of Christine de Pizan from the Fifteenth through the Nineteenth Century: Visitors to the City*, ed. Glenda K. McLeod (Lewiston, NY: Edwin Mellen Press, 1991).

111. Curnow, "*The Boke of the Cyte of Ladyes*," 619; Richards, trans., *The Book of the City of Ladies*, 4.

112. Susan Groag Bell, "A New Approach to the Influence of Christine de Pizan: The Lost Tapestries of 'The City of Ladies,'" in *Sur le Chemin de Longue Etude: Actes du Colloque d'Orléans, Juillet 1995*, ed. Bernard Ribémont (Paris: Honoré Champion Editeur, 1998). I am grateful to Susan Bell for sharing her work on Christine de Pizan with me.

113. *The Boke of the Cyte of Ladyes* (London: Henry Pepwell, 1521), sig. Aaiv^r. A facsimile of Pepwell's edition appears in Bornstein, *Distaves and*

Dames; Bornstein's introduction to this volume discusses the figures in Pepwell's prologue, xii–xiv.

114. In his survey of early English printers and patrons, H. B. Lathrop points out that Pepwell's address to the Earl of Kent "is the last reference which I have found to an aristocratic secular patron" by a printer, suggesting that "the special form of patronage which was so real a fact in the business of Caxton, and which continued to influence printers perceptibly, though with dwindling power, down to about 1510, now died out." Lathrop, "The First English Printers and Their Patrons," *The Library,* 4th ser. 3 (1922–23): 95–96.

115. *D.N.B.,* s.v. Richard Grey, Earl of Kent. See also Bornstein, *Distaves and Dames.*

116. See Starkey, "Age of the Household," 276–77; Storey, "Gentlemen-Bureaucrat," 108; on the centralization of the Tudor court and its effect on the aristocracy, see G. R. Elton, "Tudor Government: The Points of Contact. III. The Court," *Transactions of the Royal Historical Society,* 5th ser. 26 (1976): 211–28.

117. This manuscript note appears in the British Library's copy of *The Boke of the Cyte of Ladyes* (London: Henry Pepwell, 1521), sig. ²Biiᵛ.

118. The French text of Christine's work is from the only current edition of the original, Maureen Cheney Curnow's dissertation, *The "Livre de la Cité des Dames" of Christine de Pisan: A Critical Edition* (Ph.D. dissertation, Vanderbilt University, 1975), 617. The English text is from Christine de Pizan, *The Book of the City of Ladies,* trans. Earl Jeffrey Richards (New York: Persea, 1982), 3.

119. On the early sixteenth-century market for misogynistic satire, see H. S. Bennett, *English Books and Readers, 1475–1557,* 2d ed. (Cambridge: Cambridge Univ. Press, 1989), 148.

120. Roger Chartier cautions against the assumption "that it is possible to establish exclusive relationships between specific cultural forms and particular social groups," *The Cultural Uses of Print in Early Modern France,* trans. Lydia C. Cochrane (Princeton: Princeton Univ. Press, 1987), 3; see also Davis's point that "popular books are not necessarily written by *petite gens.* . . . Nor are popular books bought and read only by *petite gens*" ("Printing and the People," 192).

121. J. W. Saunders, "The Stigma of Print: A Note on the Social Bases of Tudor Poetry," *Essays in Criticism* 1 (1951): 139–64.

122. On the emergence of courtesy literature as a late development of books of chivalry, see Bornstein, *Mirrors of Courtesy,* 112–13.

123. In this discussion of "gentillece," Christine may share with the Wife of Bath a common source in Dante's *Convivio* Book IV, a reference for which I am grateful to David Wallace.

124. On the poetry of Henry VIII, see Peter C. Herman and Ray Siemens, "Henry VIII and the Poetry of Politics," in *Reading Monarchs Writing: The Poetry of Henry VIII, Mary Stuart, Elizabeth I, and James I,* ed. Herman (New York: MRTS, forthcoming).

125. Bornstein, "Chivalric Games at the Field of the Cloth of Gold," in *Mirrors of Courtesy.*

126. Helen Miller, *Henry VIII and the English Nobility,* (Oxford: Blackwell, 1986), 38–39.

127. On the reproductive and patrilinear crises of the Henrician court, see Seth Lerer, *Courtly Letters in the Age of Henry VIII,* 44–48.

128. Miller, "Creations and Promotions," *Henry VIII and the English Nobility.*

129. On this genre, see Roger Chartier, "From Texts to Manners, a Concept and Its Books: *Civilité* between Aristocratic Distinction and Popular Appropriation," in *The Culture of Print: Power and the Uses of Print in Early Modern Europe,* trans. Lydia G. Cochrane (Princeton: Princeton Univ. Press, 1989); and in later periods, Ruth Kelso, *The Institution of the Gentleman in English Literature of the Sixteenth Century: A Study in Renaissance Ideals* (Urbana: Univ. of Illinois Press, 1923); Frank Whigham, *Ambition and Privilege: The Social Tropes of Elizabethan Courtesy Theory* (Berkeley: Univ. of California Press, 1984); Anna Bryson, *From Courtesy to Civility: Changing Codes of Conduct in Early Modern England* (Oxford: Clarendon Press, 1998).

130. See Driver, "Christine de Pisan and Robert Wyer: The .C. Hystoryes of Troye, or L'Epistre d'Othea Englished," *Sonderdruk aus Gutenberg-Jahrbuch* (1997): 137, and Edward Hodnett, *English Woodcuts, 1480–1535* (1935; reprint, Oxford: Oxford Univ. Press, 1973), 59. On Christine's clothing in illustrations, see Laura Rinaldi Dufresne, "A Woman of Excellent Character: A Case Study of Dress, Reputation, and the Changing Costume of Christine de Pizan in the Fifteenth Century," *Dress* 17 (1990): 104–17. I am grateful to Amy Tigner for helping me to understand these conventions of female costume.

131. Curnow, *The "Livre de la Cité des Dames" of Christine de Pisan,* 788, 790; Richards, trans., *The Book of the City of Ladies,* 100, 101–2.

132. Curnow, *The "Livre de la Cité des Dames" of Christine de Pisan,* 794; Richards, trans., *Book of the City of Ladies,* 103–4.

133. Helen Solterer, *The Master and Minerva: Disputing Women in French Medieval Culture* (Berkeley: Univ. of California Press, 1995), 171.

134. Caxton, *Morale Prouerbes,* n.p.

135. Quilligan, *The Allegory of Female Authority,* 105; on the Sybils, see 104–17.

136. See Miller, *Henry VIII and the English Nobility,* chapters 3–5.

137. As Daniel Kempton finds of *Le trésor de la cité des dames,* the virtue of *Prudence Mondaine* "teaches princesses, and other estates of women in turn, how to look to their own advantage while living under the power of someone else, under 'la poissance de [lor] seigneur[s].'" "Christine de Pizan's *Cité des Dames* and *Trésor de la Cité:* Toward a Feminist Scriptural Practice," in *Political Rhetoric, Power, and Renaissance Women,* ed. Carole Levin and Patricia A. Sullivan (Albany: SUNY Press, 1995), 32.

138. Stephen Greenblatt's *Renaissance Self-Fashioning* (Chicago: Univ. of Chicago Press, 1980), provides an interesting point of reference here, not only because it offers a convenient term for understanding the literate work of Pepwell's gentlemen, but also because it illuminates the later developments of a masculine courtiership that I would like to imagine to have been on some level founded by Christine de Pizan.

139. See Quilligan, *The Allegory of Female Authority,* especially Chapter 1: "The Name of the Author."

140. Martha Driver, "Chaucer, Christine, and Melibee: Morgan M 39," paper delivered at the New Chaucer Society Congress, Los Angeles, 28 July 1996. I am grateful to Martha Driver for sharing this provocative work with me.

141. Curt Bühler revisits and debunks this attribution in "The Morgan Manuscript (M 39) of 'Le Livre de Melibee et de Prudence,'" *Studies in Language and Literature in Honour of Margaret Schlauch,* ed. Mieczyslaw Brahmer, Stanislaw Helsztynski, and Julian Krzyzanowski (Warsaw: Polish Scientific Publishers, 1966).

CHAPTER THREE

1. Recent efforts to rethink such epochal models of the Reformation include the essays collected in *England's Long Reformation, 1500–1800,* ed. Nicholas Tyake (London: UCL Press, 1998), as well as those collected in the special issue "From Medieval Christianities to the Reformation," *Journal of Medieval and Early Modern Studies* 27 (1997); see especially David Aers's preface, 139–44.

2. Patrick Collinson, *The Birthpangs of Protestant England: Religious and Cultural Change in the Sixteenth and Seventeenth Centuries* (London: Macmillan, 1988), 94.

3. Brian Cummings, "Reformed Literature and Literature Reformed," *The Cambridge History of Medieval English Literature,* ed. David Wallace (Cambridge: Cambridge Univ. Press, 1999), 824.

4. See Tyake, ed., *England's Long Reformation.* On political contests over medieval women's religious writing, see Susan Dickman, "Margery Kempe and the Continental Tradition of the Pious Woman," in *The Medieval Mystical Tradition in England,* ed. Marion Glasscoe (Cambridge: D. S. Brewer, 1984).

5. Claire Cross, "'Great Reasoners in Scripture': The Activities of Women Lollards, 1380–1530," in *Medieval Women,* ed. Derek Baker (Oxford: Blackwell, 1978).

6. This observation about female prayer—that it offers a form of authority through its very appearance of disclaiming authority—is consistent with other scholars' observations about the nature of mystical female authorship in the Middle Ages. See, for related discussions, Sarah Beckwith, "Problems of Authority in Late Medieval English Mysticism: Language, Agency, and Authority in the Book of Margery Kempe," *Exemplaria* 4 (1992): 171–89; Lynn Staley, *Margery Kempe's Dissenting Fictions* (University Park: Pennsylvania State Univ. Press, 1994), especially chapter 1, "Authorship and Authority"; and Sara S. Poor, "Cloaking the Body in Text: Mechthild von Magdeburg and the Question of Female Authorship," *Exemplaria* (forthcoming, 2000). I am grateful to Sara S. Poor for sharing this and her other work on Mechthild von Magdeburg with me.

7. *The Feitis and the Passion of Our Lord Jhesu Christ* is reprinted in part from its unique manuscript, Bodleian MS Bodley Holkham Misc. 41, in Alexandra Barratt's anthology, *Women's Writing in Middle English* (New York: London, 1992), 205–18. On Parr's *Prayers,* see John N. King, "Patronage and Piety: The Influence of Catherine Parr," in *Silent but for the Word: Tudor*

Women as Patrons, Translators, and Writers of Religious Works, ed. Margaret Patterson Hannay (Kent, OH: Kent State Univ. Press, 1985). Elizabeth's *Miroir* is discussed in the following chapter.

8. On the place of books during the Reformation, see Cummings, "Reformed Literature and Literature Reformed," as well as the references that follow.

9. John Foxe, *Acts and Monuments,* ed. George Townsend, 8 vols. (New York: AMS Press, 1965), 3 : 720.

10. For this view, see Elizabeth L. Eisenstein, *The Printing Press as an Agent of Change* (Cambridge: Cambridge Univ. Press, 1979), 33, and John N. Wall, Jr., "The Reformation in England and the Typographical Revolution: 'By this Printing . . . the Doctrine of the Gospel Soundeth to all Nations,'" in *Print and Culture in the Renaissance: Essays on the Advent of Printing in Europe,* ed. Gerald P. Tyson and Sylvia S. Wagonheim (Newark: Univ. of Delaware Press, 1986). For an important critique of this view, see Tessa Watt, *Cheap Print and Popular Piety, 1550–1640* (Cambridge: Cambridge Univ. Press, 1991).

11. Until recently it was possible for Reformation historians like A. G. Dickens to downplay the work of pre-Reformation English printers as culturally insignificant; see Dickens's classic *The English Reformation* (London: B. T. Batsford Ltd., 1964), which depicts a pre-Reformation literary culture in which "ideas were still chiefly communicated by speech, memories still unimpaired by oceans of print" (13). However, recent work by Martha Driver, David Carlson, and Mary Erler suggests to the contrary that the press played an important cultural role in England before the Reformation. Historians of the Reformation are divided in their use of the terms "Protestant" and "Catholic" to describe the forces of opposition in England from 1520 to 1560; here I use them for convenience and specificity, rather than the terms "Pre-Reformation" and "Post-Reformation," because I am focusing on the decades of Reformation themselves, when England's religious identity was both divided and shifting.

12. These editions are listed in the Appendix, "Handlist of Publications by Wynkyn de Worde, 1492–1535," H. S. Bennett, *English Books and Readers, 1475–1557,* 2d ed. (Cambridge: Cambridge Univ. Press, 1969); see also F. A. Gasquet, "The Bibliography of some Devotional Books Printed by the Earliest English Printers," *Transactions of the Bibliographical Society* 7 (1904): 163–89; on the first generations of print, see M. T. Clancy, "Looking Back from the Invention of Printing," in *Literacy in Historical Perspective,* ed. Daniel P. Resnick (Washington, D.C.: Library of Congress, 1983).

13. Bennett, *English Books and Readers,* 75.

14. On the *Legenda Aurea's* popularity in print, see Bennett, *English Books and Readers,* 74. For examples of iconography from Foxe's *Acts and Monuments* that adapts and reshapes that of the *Legenda,* see Margaret Aston and Elizabeth Ingram, "The Iconography of the *Acts and Monuments,*" in *John Foxe and the English Reformation,* ed. David Loades (Aldershot, Hants.: Scolar Press, 1997), esp. 113–14.

15. On the link between women religious and the development of Middle English prose, see N. F. Blake, "Middle English Prose and Its Audience," *An-*

glia 90 (1972): 437–55; Bennett, *English Books and Readers*, 8–9. Two works that draw out the cultural implications of this link in relation to the history of women are Elizabeth Robertson, *Early English Devotional Prose and the Female Audience* (Knoxville: Univ. of Tennessee Press, 1990), and Bella Millett, "Women in No Man's Land: English Recluses and the Development of Vernacular Literature in the Twelfth and Thirteenth Centuries," in *Women and Literature in Britain, 1150–1500*, ed. Carol Meale (Cambridge: Cambridge Univ. Press, 1993).

16. In addition to the studies cited in the preceding and following notes, see Anne Clark Bartlett, *Male Authors, Female Readers: Representation and Subjectivity in Middle English Devotional Literature* (Ithaca: Cornell Univ. Press, 1995). Andrew Taylor suggests that these works' preoccupation with the imagined female reader arose more from the cultural anxieties that she produced, which triggered in turn "a greater effort to monitor or shape women's reading practice," than from the actual demographics of female readership: Taylor, "Authors, Scribes, Patrons, and Books," in *The Idea of the Vernacular: An Anthology of Middle English Literary Theory, 1280–1520*, ed. Jocelyn Wogan-Browne, Nicholas Watson, Andrew Taylor, and Ruth Evans (University Park: Pennsylvania State Univ. Press, 1999), 363.

17. Riddy asserts, "It seems clear that the literary culture of nuns in the late fourteenth and fifteenth centuries and that of devout gentlewomen not only overlapped but were more or less indistinguishable." Felicity Riddy, "'Women Talking about the Things of God': A Late Medieval Sub-Culture," in *Women and Literature in Britain, 1150–1500*, ed. Carol Meale (Cambridge: Cambridge Univ. Press, 1993), 110. On Syon Abbey as a center of female literacy, see Martha Driver, "Pictures in Print: Late Fifteenth- and Early Sixteenth-Century English Religious Books for Lay Readers," in *De Cella in Seculum: Religious and Secular Life and Devotion in Late Medieval England*, ed. Michael Sargent (Cambridge: D. S. Brewer, 1989).

18. See my "William Caxton, Margaret Beaufort, and the Romance of Textual Production," in *Women, the Book, and the Worldly: Selected Proceedings of the St. Hilda's Conference, 1993*, ed. Lesley Smith and Jane Taylor (Suffolk: D. S. Brewer, 1995).

19. See George K. Keiser, "The Mystics and the Early English Printers: The Economics of Devotionalism," in *The Medieval Mystical Tradition: Papers Read at Dartington Hall, July 1987*, ed. Marion Glasscoe (London: D. S. Brewer, 1987), 11; on "the influence of the women of the nobility" on early English printers, see further 23–24.

20. See, for example Bodleian MS Bodley 939, which records the name of "Elina" and "Aleanora," or British Library Additional MS 37787, which records its ownership by "uxor Ihohanni Rudalli" in the early sixteenth century.

21. On this point, see Millet, "Women in No Man's Land," 87–91.

22. Cited by Vincent Gillespie, "Vernacular Books of Religion," in *Book Production and Publishing in Britain, 1375–1475*, ed. Jeremy Griffiths and Derek Pearsall (Cambridge: Cambridge Univ. Press, 1989), 321.

23. *The Ancren Riwle*, ed. James Morton, Camden Society 57 (London, 1853), 287; *The Myroure of Oure Ladye*, EETS e.s. 19 (London, 1873), chapter 2; see also Ann M. Hutchison, "Devotional Reading in the Monastery

and in the Late Medieval Household," in *De Cella in Seculum: Religion and Secular Life and Devotion in Late Medieval England*, ed. Michael G. Sargent (Cambridge: Brewer, 1989), who cites a rubric in one Middle English devotional compendium that encourages readers to "rede and use bokes in to þis entente: for formys of preysyng and preynge to god, to oure lady, saynte marye, and to all þe seyntes" (British Library MS Harley 1706, fol. 212ᵛ, cited p. 224).

24. Cited in L. M. J. Delaissé, "The Importance of Books of Hours for the History of the Medieval Book," in *Gatherings in Honor of Dorothy E. Miner*, ed. Ursula E. McCracken et al. (Baltimore: Walters Art Gallery, 1974), 203. See also Virginia Reinburg, "Prayer and the Book of Hours," in *Time Sanctified: The Book of Hours in Medieval Art and Life*, ed. Roger S. Wieck (Baltimore: Walters Art Gallery, 1988); Paul Saenger, "Books of Hours and the Reading Habits of the Later Middle Ages," in *The Culture of Print: Power and the Uses of Print in Early Modern Europe*, ed. Roger Chartier (Oxford: Polity Press, 1989); and Sandra Penketh, "Women and Books of Hours," in *Women and the Book: Assessing the Visual Evidence*, ed. Lesley Smith and Jane H. M. Taylor (London: British Library, 1996).

25. See *The Goodman of Paris*, trans. Eileen Power (London: George Routledge and Sons, 1928), 47–51.

26. I cite *The Fifteen Oes* from William Caxton's edition (1491), sig. aiiiᵛ. On *The Fifteen Oes*, see Martha Driver, "Nuns as Patrons, Artists, Readers: Bridgettine Woodcuts in Printed Books Produced for the English Market, " in *Art into Life: Collected Papers from the Kresge Art Museum Medieval Symposia*, ed. Carol Garrett Fisher and Kathleen L. Scott (East Lansing: Michigan State Univ. Press, 1995), 252–60; Rossell Hope Robbins, "Popular Prayers in Middle English Verse," *Modern Philology* 36 (1939): 337–50; Charity Meier-Ewert, "A Middle English Version of the *Fifteen Oes*," *Modern Philology* 68 (1971): 355–61; Eamon Duffy, *The Stripping of the Altars: Traditional Religion in England, 1400–1580* (New Haven: Yale Univ. Press, 1992), 249–56.

27. The legend is recounted, but without *The Fifteen Oes*, in a late fifteenth-century devotional commonplace book, Bodleian MS Tanner 407, edited and published as *The Commonplace Book of Robert Reynes of Acle*, ed. Cameron Louis (New York: Garland Publishing, 1980), 264–68; it accompanies the prayers in other manuscripts, for example, in a Northern English collection of prayers and devotional materials from the thirteenth and fifteenth centuries, British Library Additional MS 3381, 152ʳ. Likewise, the fifteenth-century *Treatise concerning St. Bridgit's Vision of the Number of Christ's Wounds* (British Library MS Harley 172, fol. 36) begins, "Here beginnythe a treatyse of a solytarye and a recluse woman" and ends "Hit ys seyde and tolde that the womans Name was Seynt Bryde that fule many reuelacyons and grete graces she hadde of oure lorde Jhesu cryste" (indexed in *Fifteenth-Century English Prayers and Meditations: A Descriptive List of Manuscripts in the British Library*, ed. Peter Revell [London: Garland, 1975], 33).

28. In *The Prymer of Salysbury Use* (1534), the prayers are called simply "orationes sancte brigide," sig. 91ʳ. On the apocryphal attribution of *The Fifteen Oes* to St. Bridget, see F. R. Johnson, "The English Cult of St. Bridget of Sweden," *Anelecta Bollandiana* 103 (1985): 75–93.

29. *The Minor Poems of John Lydgate*, ed. Henry Noble MacCracken, EETS o.s. 107 (London: Oxford Univ. Press, 1911), 1:238–50.

30. RSTC 5949, 15884; see Driver, "Nuns as Patrons, Artists, Readers," 254–56.

31. The prayer, "Ave Rose Sine Spinis," appears in many texts, including *The Prymer of Salysburye Use* (1532), sig. 228ʳ, which also includes *The Fifteen Oes* with an indulgence, sig. 108ʳ. For the cultural context of this form of Marian devotion, see Thomas J. Heffernan, "The Virgin as Aid to Salvation in Some Fifteenth-Century English and Latin Verses," *Medium Aevum* 52 (1983): 229–31; Carol M. Meale, "The Miracles of Our Lady: Context and Interpretation," in *Studies in the Vernon Manuscript*, ed. Derek Pearsall (Cambridge: D. S. Brewer, 1990). On pre-Reformation prayer as an invocation of "supernatural assistance," the effect of which was "to encourage the idea that there was virtue in the mere repetition of holy words," see Keith Thomas, *Religion and the Decline of Magic* (New York: Charles Scribner and Sons, 1971), 40–42.

32. Bodleian MS Bodley 850, fol. 93ᵛ.

33. For example, a woodcut preserved as Bodleian Arch G. e. 35; see Henry Bradshaw, "On the Earliest English Engravings of the Indulgence Known as the 'Image of Pity,'" in *Collected Papers of Henry Bradshaw* (Cambridge: Cambridge Univ. Press, 1889).

34. Claire Sponsler, *Drama and Resistance: Bodies, Goods, and Theatricality in Late Medieval England* (Minneapolis: Univ. of Minnesota Press, 1997), 111.

35. Jocelyn Wogan-Browne and Glyn S. Burgess make the point that "the text of a saint's life was often understood in the Middle Ages as the form of a relic"; see their introduction, *Virgin Lives and Holy Deaths: Two Exemplary Biographies of Anglo-Norman Women* (London: Everyman, 1996), xi. See also Alain Boureau, "Franciscan Piety and Voracity: Uses and Strategems in the Hagiographic Pamphlet," in *The Culture of Print: Power and the Uses of Print in Early Modern Europe*, ed. Roger Chartier, trans. Lydia G. Cochrane (Oxford: Polity Press, 1989).

36. John N. King cites Caxton's woodcuts in the *Legenda Aurea* as an example of how "reading or hearing such a text was considered a pietistic deed," and likewise, "woodcut images of the saints, the crucifixion, and the Corpus Christi procession served as objects of lay devotion." *English Reformation Literature: The Tudor Origins of the Protestant Tradition* (Princeton: Princeton Univ. Press, 1982), 39–40.

37. For example, A. G. Dickens finds that during the Reformation, "emphasis in religion shifted steadily from the image to the printed word, from pictures to literary ideas." *The English Reformation*, 11. Similarly, Imogen Luxton asserts of late medieval devotion that "popular beliefs and superstitions flourished within a religious culture in which the emphasis . . . was on visual representation rather than on the written word." "The Reformation and Popular Culture," in *Church and Society in England: Henry VIII to James I*, ed. Felicity Heal and Rosemary O'Day (London: Macmillan, 1977), 63; for a reading that critiques the dichotomy between books and images that such a

reading produces, see Kathleen Kamerick, "Art and Moral Vision in Angela of Foligno and Margery Kempe," *Mystics Quarterly* 21 (1995): 148–58.

38. See Gregory the Great, "Epistola XIII ad Serenum Massiliensem Episcopum," *Patrologia Latina* vol. 77, column 1128.

39. On woodcuts associated with Syon Abbey, including those of Sts. Catherine and Bridget, see Driver, "Pictures in Print."

40. Edward Dering, Preface to the Reader, *A Briefe & Necessary Instruction, Very Needeful to bee Knowen of all Householders* (London, 1572), sig. Aii v, Aiii r.

41. Michael Camille, *The Gothic Idol* (Chicago: Univ. of Chicago Press, 1989), xxvi.

42. William Marshall, *Certen Prayers and Godly Meditacyons Very Nedefull for Every Christian* (London, 1538), sig. Bi r–Bii r.

43. *Certeyne Sermons or Homilies, appointed by the Kinges Majestie* (London, 1547), sig. K1.

44. Dering, Preface to the Reader, *A Briefe & Necessary Instruction*, sig. Aiii r.

45. William Tyndale, *The Obedience of a Christian Man*, in *The Works of the English Reformers: William Tyndale and John Frith*, ed. Thomas Russell, 3 vols. (London, 1831), 1:313.

46. Tyndale, *The Obedience of a Christian Man*, 1:335.

47. Marshall, *Certen Prayers and Godly Meditacyons*, sig. Ai r.

48. Edgar Hoskins, *Horae Beatae Mariae Virginis, or Sarum and York Primers with Kindred Books and Primers of the Reformed Roman Use* (London: Longmans, Green, 1901), 201.

49. Bodleian MS Bodley 850, fols. 90 v–100 r.

50. Bodleian MS Bodley 850.

51. British Library Additional MS 37787; the defaced rubric preceding *The Fifteen Oes* is on fol. 71 v.

52. *Goodly Prymer in English Newly Corrected and Printed* (London, 1535), sig. Aiii v.

53. *The Manuall of Prayers, or the Prymer in Englyshe, set out at lengthe* (London, 1539), sig. Xiv r. See Helen C. White, *The Tudor Books of Private Devotion* (Madison: Univ. of Wisconsin Press, 1951), 217.

54. On the post-Reformation afterlife of *The Fifteen Oes*, see White, *Tudor Books of Private Devotion*, 176–77; 216–29.

55. White, *Tudor Books of Private Devotion*, 229.

56. Duffy, *The Stripping of the Altars*, 4; G. R. Elton, *Policy and Police: The Enforcement of the Reformation in the Age of Thomas Cromwell* (Cambridge: Cambridge Univ. Press, 1972). Duffy's book has attracted controversy: see David Aers, "Altars of Power: Reflections on Eamon Duffy's *The Stripping of the Altars*," *Literature and History* 3 (1994): 90–105, and Anne Hudson, Review, Eamon Duffy, *The Stripping of the Altars*, *Notes and Queries* 238 (1993): 523–25.

57. Christopher Haigh, *English Reformations: Reform, Politics, and Society under the Tudors* (Oxford: Clarendon Press, 1993).

58. Watt, *Cheap Print and Popular Piety*, 325.

59. For an analysis of the English Reformation that substitutes terms like

"negotiation" for "imposition" or "enforcement," see Patrick Collinson, "England," in *The Reformation in National Context*, ed.Bob Scribner, Roy Porter, and Mikulás Teich (Cambridge: Cambridge Univ. Press, 1994).

60. On the Reformation institutions of textual control, see Fredrick Seaton Siebert, *Freedom of the Press in England, 1476–1776* (Urbana: Univ. of Illinois Press, 1952); Cyprian Blagden, *The Stationers' Company: A History, 1403–1959* (Cambridge: Harvard Univ. Press, 1960); D. M. Loades, "The Press under the Early Tudors," *Transactions of the Cambridge Bibliographical Society* 4 (1964): 32–45; D. M. Loades, *Politics, Censorship, and the English Reformation (London: Pinter Publishers, 1991)* On these institutions' contribution to new models of authorship, see Joseph F. Loewenstein, "*Idem:* Italics and the Genetics of Authorship," *Journal of Medieval and Renaissance Studies* 20 (1990): 205–24, and "Legal Proofs and Corrected Readings: Press Agency and the New Bibliography," in *The Production of English Renaissance Culture,* ed. David Lee Miller, Sharon O'Dair, and Harold Weber (Ithaca: Cornell Univ. Press, 1994); and Roger Chartier, *The Order of Books* (Stanford: Stanford Univ. Press, 1992), especially his argument on page 32.

61. *The Seconde Tome of Homelyes* (London, 1563), sigs. Yy1ʳ–2ᵛ.

62. *The Seconde Tome of Homelyes,* sigs. Yy1ʳ–2ᵛ.

63. See Penketh, "Women and Books of Hours," 269; Deschamps is cited by Erwin Panofsky, *Early Netherlandish Painting,* 2 vols. (Cambridge: Harvard Univ. Press, 1953), 1:68, 387–88.

64. White, *Tudor Books of Private Devotion,* 33. On popular Marian devotion, see Meale, "The Miracles of Our Lady," and Heffernan, "The Virgin as Aid to Salvation."

65. Roger S. Wieck, *Time Sanctified: The Book of Hours in Medieval Art and Life* (Baltimore: Walters Art Gallery, 1988), 161.

66. *The Prymer off Salysburye Use . . . With Many Prayers/ and Goodly Pyctures yn the Kalender* (London, 1532), sig. 32ᵛ.

67. *The Manual of Prayers, or the Prymer in Englyshe, set out at Lengthe* (London, 1539), sig. Ciᵛ, Ciiʳ.

68. Susan Schibanoff, "Botticelli's *Madonna del Magnificat:* Constructing the Woman Writer in Early Humanist Italy," *PMLA* 109 (1994): 190–206.

69. *A Goodly Prymer in Englyshe, Newly Corrected and Printed* (London, 1535), sig. Aiiʳ.

70. Martin Luther, "The Magnificat Translated and Explained" (1520–21), trans. A. T. M. Steinhaeuser, in *The Works of Martin Luther* (Philadelphia: Muhlenberg Press, 1930)

71. Luther, "The Magnificat Translated and Explained," 127.

72. *A Goodly Prymer in Englyshe, Newly Corrected and Printed* (London, 1535), sigs. Ciiiiᵛ, Diʳ.

73. Joan W. Scott, "The Evidence of Experience," *Critical Inquiry* 17 (1991): 773–97.

74. That text is now housed at University Library, Cambridge. On de Worde's edition, see Sue Ellen Holbrook, "Margery Kempe and Wynkyn de Worde," in *The Medieval Mystical Tradition in England: Papers Read at Dartington Hall, July 1987,* ed. Marion Glasscoe (London: D.S. Brewer, 1987), and Marion Glasscoe, *English Medieval Mystics: Games of Faith* (London: Long-

man, 1993), 269. For a discussion of both printed editions, see Karma Lochrie, *Margery Kempe and Translations of the Flesh* (Philadelphia: Univ. of Pennsylvania Press, 1991), 220–25.

75. It is instructive to compare the sixteenth-century selections with those that appear in twentieth-century anthologies. *The Norton Anthology of Literature by Women*, ed. Sandra M. Gilbert and Susan Gubar (New York: W. W. Norton, 1985), emphasizes Margery's troubled sexual relations with men, selecting excerpts from chapter 3 in which Margery expresses the desire "to live apart from her husband," from chapter 4 on "her temptation to adultery with a man," and from chapter 11, when "she and her husband argue as to their carnal relationship to each other" (22–27). The excerpts in *The Norton Anthology of English Literature*, 6th ed., ed. M. H. Abrams et al. (New York: W. W. Norton, 1993), emphasize the worldly details of Margery's life as "a medieval housewife," focusing on "The Birth of her First Child," "Her Pride and Attempts to Start a Business," and her "Pilgrimage to Jerusalem," among other events (298–308).

76. Edmund G. Gardner, Introduction, *The Cell of Self-Knowledge* (London: Chatto and Windus, 1925), xx.

77. Holbrook, "Margery Kempe and Wynkyn de Worde," 35.

78. Anthony Goodman, "The Piety of John Brunham's Daughter, of Lynn," in *Medieval Women*, ed. Derek Baker (Oxford: Blackwell, 1978), 357–58.

79. Nicholas Watson, "The Composition of Julian of Norwich's *Revelation of Love*," *Speculum* 68 (1993): 637–83; Sarah Beckwith offers an apposite point when she observes that "the anchoress's cell provides an interesting spatial symbolism for the liminal position of women mystics in medieval society, both structurally supporting the church in their position under the eves and a potential pocket of subsidence." See "A Very Material Mysticism: The Medieval Mysticism of Margery Kempe," in *Medieval Literature: Criticism, Ideology, and History*, ed. David Aers (New York: St. Martin's Press, 1986), 55 n. 4.

80. Cross, "'Great Reasoners in Scripture.'"

81. Pepwell's book has appeared in full or part in two modern editions, Gardner's *Cell of Self-Knowledge* and *Richard of St. Victor's Treatise of the Study of Wisdom that Men Call Benjamin*, trans. and ed. Dick Barnes (Lewiston: Edwin Mellen Press, 1990). My discussion is based on the copy of the text now housed in the British Library: *Here foloweth a very devoute treatyse (named Benyamyn)* . . . (London: Henry Pepwell, 1521), with signatures noted in parentheses.

82. The fact that some manuscripts group these short texts with the Middle English *Benjamin Minor* led their modern editor, Phyllis Hodgson, to suggest that the *Benjamin* was also produced by the *Cloud* author; however, this ascription has been more recently contested by Roger Ellis. On the manuscript sources, see Hodgson, ed., *Deonise Hid Divinite and Other Treatises on Contemplative Prayer*, Analecta Cartusiana 3 (Salzburg, 1982), xiv, and *The Cloud of Unknowing and Related Treatises on Contemplative Prayer*, EETS OS 231 (London: Oxford Univ. Press, 1955), xxi–xxii; and Ellis, "Author(s), Compilers, Scribes, and Bible Texts: Did the *Cloud*-Author Translate *The Twelve Patriarchs?*" in *The Medieval Mystical Tradition in England, Exeter Symposium V*, ed. Marion Glasscoe (Cambridge: D. S. Brewer, 1992), and "Sec-

ond Thoughts on the Authorship of *The Treatyse of þe Stodye of Wysdome*," *Neuphilologische Mitteilungen* 95 (1995): 307–17.

83. On the differences between their implied audiences, see Ellis, "Author(s), Compilers, Scribes, and Bible Texts," 194, 196. Alistair Minnis, "*The Cloud of Unknowing* and Walter Hilton's *Scale of Perfection*," *Middle English Prose: A Critical Guide to Major Authors and Genres*, ed. A. S. G. Edwards (New Brunswick: Rutgers Univ. Press, 1984), 65–67, draws a similar comparison between the *Cloud* and the *Benjamin Minor* that is relevant here.

84. *Here foloweth a very devoute treatyse (named Benyamyn)*, sigs. Hii^r, Gi^r.

85. Mary Bateson, ed., *Catalogue of the Library of Syon Monastery, Isleworth* (Cambridge: Cambridge Univ. Press, 1898), 105, 113, 115, 121. Although no catalogue exists of their library, the nuns were famously literate and we can assume some continuity with the monks' reading. On the reading of the Syon nuns, see Driver, "Nuns as Patrons, Artists, Readers"; Ann M. Hutchison, "Devotional Reading in the Monastery and in the Late Medieval Household"; and Mary Carpenter Erler, "Syon Abbey's Care for Books: Its Sacristan's Account Rolls 1506/7–1535/6," *Scriptorium* 2 (1985): 293–307.

86. Compare these verses with the "Querela Divina" of British Library MS Addit. 37049, reprinted in *Religious Lyrics of the Fifteenth Century*, ed. Carleton Brown (Oxford: Oxford Univ. Press, 1939), 168:

> O man unkynde / hafe in mynde
> My paynes smerte!
> Beholde & see / þat is for þe
> Percyd, my hert.

87. See Henry Bradshaw, "On the Earliest English Engravings of the Indulgence Known as the 'Image of Pity,'" in *Collected Papers of Henry Bradshaw* (Cambridge: Cambridge Univ. Press, 1889); Campbell Dodgson, "English Devotional Woodcuts of the Late Fifteenth Century, with Special Reference to Those in the Bodleian Library," *Walpole Society* 17 (1928–29): 95–108; Flora Lewis, "Rewarding Devotion: Indulgences and the Promotion of Images," in "The Church and the Arts," special issue, *Studies in Church History* 28 (1992): 179–94, together with Lewis's other remarkable work on devotional images and objects; Mary Erler, "Pasted-In Embellishments in English Manuscripts and Printed Books c. 1480–1533," *The Library* 14 (1992): 185–206; Driver, "Nuns as Patrons, Artists, Readers," 239.

88. Emile Mâle, *Religious Art in France: The Late Middle Ages*, trans. M. Mathews (Princeton: Princeton Univ. Press, 1986), 96; see also Duffy, *The Stripping of the Altars*, 243.

89. *The Book of Margery Kempe*, ed. Sanford Brown Meech with Hope Emily Allen, EETS 212 (Oxford: Oxford Univ. Press, 1940), 148. Subsequent citations, except when otherwise noted, will be from this text, with page numbers indicated in parentheses.

90. The meanings and uses of imagistic piety in the Middle Ages are the subject of a rich body of work. Relevant to Margery Kempe are Kathleen Kamerick, "Art and Moral Vision in Angela of Foligno and Margery Kempe," *Mystics Quarterly* 21 (1995): 148–58; and Sarah Stanbury, "Regimes of the

Visual in Premodern England: Gaze, Body, and Chaucer's *Clerk's Tale*," *New Literary History* 28 (1997): 261–89.

91. *Here foloweth a very devoute treatyse (named Benyamyn)*, sigs. Dvi^v, Eii^r, Eiii^r. These selections are reprinted in *The Book of Margery Kempe*, ed. Meech and Allen, 356–57.

92. See Susan Dickman, "Margery Kempe and the Continental Tradition of the Pious Woman," in *The Medieval Mystical Tradition in England*, ed. Marion Glasscoe (Cambridge: D. S. Brewer, 1984).

93. S. S. Hussey, "The Audience for the Middle English Mystics," in *De Cella in Seculum: Religion and Secular Life and Devotion in Late Medieval England*, ed. Michael G. Sargent (Cambridge: Brewer, 1989), 121. On aristocratic female readerships for such texts, see Hutchison, "Devotional Reading in the Monastery and in the Late Medieval Household."

94. On the increased popular acceptance of "pilgrimage without travel" by the fifteenth and sixteenth centuries, see Jonathan Sumption, *Pilgrimage: An Image of Mediaeval Religion* (London: Faber and Faber, 1975), 295–302.

95. On Wycliffite objections to the doctrine of indulgence, see Anne Hudson, ed., *English Wycliffite Writings* (Cambridge: Cambridge Univ. Press, 1978), 19.

96. On this controversy, see Richard Rex, "The English Campaign against Luther in the 1520s," *Transactions of the Royal Historical Society*, 5th series, 39 (1989): 85–106; William A. Clebsch, *England's Earliest Protestants: 1520–1535* (New Haven: Yale Univ. Press, 1964), 11–20.

97. D. M. Loades, *Politics, Censorship, and the English Reformation*; Loades, "The Press under the Early Tudors," *Transactions of the Cambridge Bibliographical Society* 4 (1964): 32.

98. Roger Ellis, "'Flores ad Fabricandam . . . Coronam': An Investigation into the Uses of Revelations of St. Bridget of Sweden in Fifteenth-Century England," *Medium Aevum* 51 (1982): 163–86. On Henry V's uses of indulgences and Syon Abbey to support his political interests, see Peter Heath, *Church and Realm: 1272–1461* (London: Fortuna, 1988), 251, and Jeremy Catto, "Religious Change under Henry V," in *Henry V: The Practice of Kingship*, ed. G. L. Harris (Oxford: Oxford Univ. Press, 1985).

99. Joseph Ames and William Herbert, *Typographical Antiquities*, ed. Thomas Frognall Dibdin, 3 vols. (London, 1816), 3:15–16.

100. On Pepwell's career, see E. G. Duff, "The Stationers at the Sign of the Trinity," *Bibliographica* 1 (1895): 175–93; Duff, *Westminster and London Printers, 1476–1535* (Cambridge: Cambridge Univ. Press, 1926), 147–50; Duff, *Hand-Lists of English Printers, 1501–1556* (London: Blades, 1895); Henry R. Plomer, *Wynkyn de Worde and His Contemporaries, from the Death of Caxton to 1535* (London: Grafton and Co., 1925), 211–12; Cyprian Blagden, *The Stationers' Company: A History, 1403–1959* (Cambridge: Harvard Univ. Press, 1960), 21–23.

101. Carolyn Walker Bynum, *Fragmentation and Redemption: Essays on Gender and the Human Body in Medieval Religion* (New York: Zone Books, 1992), 195. See also Jo Ann McNamara, "The Rhetoric of Orthodoxy: Clerical Authority and Female Innovation in the Struggle with Heresy," in *Maps of*

Flesh and Light: The Religious Experience of Medieval Women Mystics, ed. Ulrike Wiethaus (Syracuse: Syracuse Univ. Press, 1993).

102. For the rejection of indulgences, see *Tudor Royal Proclamations,* ed. Paul L. Hughes and James F. Larkin, 3 vols. (New Haven: Yale Univ. Press, 1964–69), 1: 237 (1 January 1536).

103. *Act against Superstitious Books and Images* (3 and 4 Edward VI c10), 1550; cited in C. E. Wright, "The Dispersal of the Libraries in the Sixteenth Century," *The English Library before 1700,* ed. Francis Wormald and C. E. Wright (London: Athlone Press, 1958), 165–66.

104. Watt, *Cheap Print and Popular Piety,* 131.

105. Duffy, *The Stripping of the Altars,* 418.

106. Collinson, *Birthpangs of Protestant England,* 94.

107. John Harryson [pseud], *Yet a Course at the Romysche Foxe: A Dysclosynge or Openynge of the Manne of Synne* (1543).

108. René Wellek, *The Rise of English Literary History* (Chapel Hill: Univ. of North Carolina Press, 1941), 4–6. For more recent assessments of Bale's contribution to English literary history, see Trevor Ross, "Dissolution and the Making of the English Literary Canon: The Catalogues of Leland and Bale," *Renaissance and Reformation* 15 (1991): 57–80; James Simpson, "Ageism: Leland, Bale, and the Laborious Start of English Literary History, 1350–1550," *New Medieval Literatures* 1 (1997): 213–35; Anne Hudson, "*Visio Baleii:* An Early Literary Historian," in *The Long Fifteenth Century,* ed. Helen Cooper and Sally Mapstone (Oxford: Clarendon, 1997). The recent recuperation of Bale's historical reputation began with Margaret Aston, "English Ruins and English History: The Dissolution and the Sense of the Past," *Journal of the Warburg and Courtauld Institutes* 36 (1973): 231–55.

109. Ross, "Dissolution and the Making of the English Literary Canon," 57; similarly, Roger Chartier credits Bale for creating in his catalogues a "library without walls," *The Order of Books* (Stanford: Stanford Univ. Press, 1992), 71.

110. On Bale's unwillingness "to confront the politics of Dissolution," see Ross, "Dissolution and the Making of the English Literary Canon," 59.

111. John Bale, ed., *The Laboryouse Journey and Serche of Johan Leylande, for Englandes Antiquitees, geven of hym as a New Yeares Gyfte to Kyng Henry the viii* (London, 1549), sigs. Bviii ᵛ, Ci ʳ.

112. On the emergence of textual scholarship as a humanist methodology, see Stephanie H. Jed, *Chaste Thinking: The Rape of Lucretia and the Birth of Humanism* (Bloomington: Indiana Univ. Press, 1989).

113. Bale, ed., *Laboryouse Journey,* sig. Cv ʳ⁻ᵛ.

114. Bale, "To the Reader," *Laboryouse Journey,* sig. Aviii ʳ. See St. Paul, Ephesians 5; Chaucer, *Parson's Tale,* lines 745–50.

115. Bale, *Laboryouse Journey,* sig. Giii ʳ.

116. Peter Stallybrass, "Worn Worlds: Clothes and Identity on the Renaissance Stage," in *Subject and Object in Renaissance Culture,* ed. Margreta de Grazia, Maureen Quilligan, and Peter Stallybrass (Cambridge: Cambridge Univ. Press, 1996), 290–91.

117. Bale, "Conclusion," *Laboryouse Journey,* sig. Evii ᵛ.

118. Bale, "Conclusion," *Laboryouse Journey*, sig. Gi[v].

119. Bale, *Laboryouse Journey*, sig. Eii[r].

120. John Bale, letter to Matthew Parker, Archbishop of Canterbury, 30 July 1560; cited in Wright, "The Dispersal of the Libraries," 154.

121. N. R. Ker, *Medieval Libraries of Great Britain: A List of Surviving Books*, 2d ed. (London: Royal Historical Society, 1964), reports that the Royal Collection in the British Library comprises 250 books from monasteries, of which "the main interest is in works by or supposedly by English authors," and calls the period between 1560 and 1640 "the golden age of the English private collector" (xii).

122. Amy Boesky describes how, with the rise of antiquarianism, "sacerdotal objects were being devalued—rosaries, saints' teeth or hair, crucifixes, holy relics" in their transfer from the reliquary to the collector's cabinet. See Boesky, "'Outlandish-Fruits': Commissioning Nature for the Museum of Man," *ELH* 58 (1991): 7.

123. Aston, "English Ruins and English History," 335 n. 93; D. R. Woolf, "The Dawn of the Artifact: The Antiquarian Impulse in England, 1500–1730," *Studies in Medievalism* 4 (1992): 11.

124. John Earle, *Microcosmographie* (1628), cited by C. E. Wright, "The Elizabethan Society of Antiquaries and the Formation of the Cottonian Library," in *The English Library before 1700*, ed. Wormald and Wright, 176.

125. Letter of John Butler, Nicholas Eliot, Nicholas Patridge, and Bartholomew Traheron to Henry Bullinger, 8 March 1539, cited in Gilbert Burnet, *The History of the Reformation of the Church of England*, ed. Nicholas Pocock (1865; reprint, Oxford: Clarendon Press, 1969), 252; I am grateful to Michael Jones for this reference.

126. Miri Rubin, *Corpus Christi: The Eucharist in Late Medieval Culture* (Cambridge: Cambridge Univ. Press, 1991), 325; Sarah Beckwith, *Christ's Body: Identity, Culture, and Society in Late Medieval Writings* (New York: Routledge, 1993), 3.

127. Hughes and Larkin, *Tudor Royal Proclamations* 1: 279 (26 Feb. 1539).

128. Cited in Duffy, *The Stripping of the Altars*, 428.

129. On the sign theory of the Eucharist, see John S. Pendergast, "Pierre Du Moulin on the Eucharist: Protestant Sign Theory and the Grammar of Embodiment," *ELH* 65 (1998): 47–68.

130. See Aston, "English Ruins and English History," 239–42.

131. On the use of the monumental epitaph to construct Chaucer's simultaneous authority within and absence from early humanist literary culture, see Seth Lerer, *Chaucer and His Readers: Imagining the Author in Late-Medieval England* (Princeton: Princeton Univ. Press, 1993), 158–60.

132. *Proclamation Against Breakinge or Defacing of Monumentes of Antiquitie, beyng set up in churches or other Publique Places for Memory, and not for Supersticion* (London: Richarde Jugge and John Cawood, 1560); cited in Helen White, *Tudor Books of Saints and Martyrs* (Madison: Univ. of Wisconsin Press, 1963), 90–91.

133. Bale, *Laboryouse Journey*, sig. Evi[v].

134. Bale, *Laboryouse Journey*, sig. Hv[v].

135. Bale, *Laboryouse Journey*, sig. Diii[r].

136. The term is Walter Benjamin's, from *Origin of German Tragic Drama;* cited by Camille, *The Gothic Idol,* 349.

137. John Bale, *Index Britanniae Scriptorum,* ed. Reginald Lane Poole and Mary Bateson, intro. Caroline Brett and James Carley (Cambridge: D. S. Brewer, 1990), 105–6, 348–49, 430, 572–73.

138. Considering the Middle English texts that were preserved in print recalls the fact that a sanctioned view of England's literary past began to be shaped in the early fifteenth century, when Arundel's Constitutions placed draconian restrictions on the circulation of Middle English writings in order to ensure their orthodoxy; see Nicholas Watson, "Censorship and Cultural Change in Late-Medieval England: Vernacular Theology, the Oxford Translation Debate, and Arundel's Constitutions of 1409," *Speculum* 70 (1995): 822–64. Bale's policy of cataloguing only texts by named authors makes him a forerunner of modern, author-centered literary history; nonetheless, it leads him to omit anonymous works, thus paradoxically leaving him with a much more orthodox topography of Middle English literature than he might have found had he expanded his criteria for inclusion; see Hudson, "*Visio Baleii,*" 318–19.

139. *The Examinations of Anne Askew,* ed. Elaine V. Beilin (Oxford: Oxford Univ. Press, 1996), 19. Recent work on Anne Askew has focused productively on her status in Bale's edition and that edition's broader historical aims; see Thomas Betteridge, "Anne Askew, John Bale, and Protestant History," *Journal of Medieval and Early Modern Studies* 27 (1997): 265–84; Diane Watt, *Secretaries of God: Women Prophets in Late Medieval and Early Modern* England (Cambridge: D. S. Brewer, 1997), 81–109; Megan Matchinske, *Writing, Gender, and State in Early Modern England* (Cambridge: Cambridge Univ. Press, 1998), 28–52.

140. Elizabeth Tudor, *A Godly Medytacyon of the Christen Sowle,* ed. John Bale (Basel, 1548); I will be citing this text and noting signatures in parentheses. A facsimile of Elizabeth's original manuscript and transcription of Bale's "Epistle Dedicatory" and "Conclusion" to the printed version appear in Marc Shell, *Elizabeth's Glass* (Lincoln: Univ. of Nebraska Press, 1993).

141. On Foxe's treatment of Lollards, see Rosemary O'Day, *The Debate on the English Reformation* (London: Methuen, 1986), 22; Betteridge, "Anne Askewe, John Bale, and Protestant History," 269.

142. On the thaumaturgic saint's life, see Alain Boreau, "Adoration et Devoration: Uses and Strategems in the Hagiographic Pamphlet," in *The Culture of Print: Power and the Uses of Print in Early Modern Europe,* ed. Roger Chartier, trans. Lydia G. Cochrane (Oxford: Polity Press, 1989).

143. On the iconography of this woodcut, see John N. King, *English Reformation Literature: The Tudor Origins of the Protestant Religion* (Princeton: Princeton Univ. Press, 1982), 73, and *Tudor Royal Iconography: Literature and Art in an Age of Religious Crisis* (Princeton: Princeton Univ. Press, 207–9.

144. John King even suggests that Askew is holding "a quill pen" in her hand. King, *English Reformation Literature,* 73.

145. Foxe, *Acts and Monuments,* 1:xxvi–xxvii. As Knott suggests, Foxe's work "reflects unresolved tensions between his own sense of martyrdom and that found in Eusebius and other early sources. . . . The most obvious [source

of tension . . .] is the sense of supernatural manifestations associated with the death of the martyr and, subsequently, with his [or, in this case, her] relics or shrine." John R. Knott, *Discourses of Martyrdom in English Literature, 1563–1694* (Cambridge: Cambridge Univ. Press, 1993), 42.

146. Cited by O'Day, *The Debate on the English Reformation,* 26–27.

147. *Examinations of Anne Askew,* ed. Beilin, 48n.

148. Donald Weinstein and Rudolph M. Bell, *Saints and Society: The Two Worlds of Western Christendom, 1000–1700* (Chicago: Univ. of Chicago Press, 1982), 179.

149. On the uses of hagiography to support orthodoxy, see Kathleen Biddick, "Genders, Bodies, Borders: Technologies of the Visible," *Speculum* 68 (1993): 389–418; reprinted in Biddick, *The Shock of Medievalism* (Durham: Duke Univ. Press, 1998).

150. John Foxe, *Acts and Monuments,* 1:xxv.

151. Suzanne W. Hull, *Chaste, Silent, and Obedient: English Books for Women, 1475–1640* (San Marino: Huntington Library, 1982), 92. Thomas Bentley, *The Monument of Matrones: Conteining Seven Severall Lamps of Virginitie, or distinct treatises* (London, 1582); subsequent citations of the text will be noted in parentheses by "Lamp" (volume) and page number.

152. See Helen Hackett's argument that Bentley's book "surreptitiously exploit[s] Marian resonances" in its representation of Elizabeth, thus producing "the Virgin herself as a source of typological comparison" to the Queen. Hackett, *Virgin Mother, Maiden Queen* (Basingstoke: Macmillan, 1995), 124, 199.

CHAPTER FOUR

1. George Puttenham, *The Arte of English Poesie,* facsimile reproduction ed. Baxter Hathaway (Kent, OH: Kent State Univ. Press, 1970); all subsequent references to the *Arte,* unless otherwise noted, are to this edition, with page numbers cited in the text parenthetically.

2. René Wellek, *The Rise of English Literary History* (Chapel Hill: Univ. of North Carolina Press, 1941), 9.

3. Francis Meres, *A Comparative Discourse of Our English Poets, with the Greek, Latine, and Italian Poets* (1598), reprinted in *Ancient Critical Essays upon English Poets and Poesy,* ed. Joseph Haslewood (London, 1811), 2:155.

4. Edmund Spenser, "The Teares of the Muses," in *Poetical Works,* ed. J. C. Smith and E. de Selincourt (Oxford: Oxford Univ. Press, 1985), 486.

5. Thomas Heywood, ΤUΝΑΙΚΕΙΟΝ, or Nine Bookes of Various History Concernynge Women (London: Adam Islip, 1624), 398; Edmund Bolton, *Hypercritica* (1610–17), reprinted in *Ancient Critical Essays upon English Poets and Poesy,* ed. Joseph Haslewood (London, 1811), 2:246–48.

6. Leah S. Marcus, "Queen Elizabeth I as Public and Private Poet: Notes toward a New Edition," in *Reading Monarchs Writing: The Poetry of Henry VIII, Mary Stuart, Elizabeth I, and James I,* ed. Peter C. Herman (New York: MRTS, forthcoming). The forthcoming *Speeches, Letters, Prayers, and Poems of Queen Elizabeth I,* ed. Leah S. Marcus, Janel Mueller, and Mary Beth Rose (Chicago: Univ. of Chicago Press, 2000), will establish Elizabeth's *oeuvre* to be much more substantial than previous editions have allowed. Horace Walpole

cites Camden in his own voluminous record of Elizabeth's writings, contained in his *Catalogue of the Royal and Noble Authors of England, Scotland, and Ireland, with Lists of Their Works*, rev. ed. by Thomas Park (London, 1806), 1:84–112.

7. This translation is reprinted in *The Poems of Elizabeth I*, ed. Leicester Bradner (Providence: Brown Univ. Press, 1964); see also *Queen Elizabeth's Englishings of Boethius, "De Consolatione Philosophiae," A.D. 1598; Plutarch, "De Curiositate," A.D. 1598; Horace, "De Arte Poetica" (partial), A.D. 1598*, ed. Caroline Pemberton (London, 1899).

8. Cited from Henry Savile's preface to his translation of Tacitus, *The Ende of Nero* (Oxford, 1591).

9. Bolton, *Hypercritica*, 2:248.

10. See Kevin Sharpe, "The King's Writ: Royal Authors and Royal Authority in Early Modern England," in *Culture and Politics in Early Stuart England*, ed. Sharpe and Peter Lake (London: Macmillan, 1994); Peter C. Herman and Ray Siemens, "Henry VIII and the Poetry of Politics," in *Reading Monarchs Writing*, ed. Herman.

11. On these various personifications of the Queen's authority (but notably excluding Sappho), see Winfried Schleiner, "*Divina Virago*: Queen Elizabeth as Amazon," *Studies in Philology* 75 (1978): 163–80; and Frances A. Yates, *Astraea: The Imperial Theme in the Sixteenth Century* (London: Pimlico, 1975).

12. Jan van der Noodt, *A Theatre Wherein be Represented as wel the Miseries & Calamities that Follow the Voluptuous Worldlings, as also the Greate Ioyes and Pleasures which the Faithfull do Enioy* (1569; reprint, New York: Scholar's Facsimiles and Reprints, 1936), sig. Aiiii ʳ–Aiiii ᵛ; see also J. W. Saunders, "From Manuscript to Print: A Note on the Circulation of Poetic MSS in the Sixteenth Century," *Proceedings of the Leeds Philosophical and Literary Society* 6 (1951): 508, and on Spenser's translation see Jonathan Crewe, *Hidden Designs: The Critical Profession and Renaissance Literature* (New York: Methuen, 1986), 93–118.

13. British Museum Cotton Vesp. E. VIII, folio 169ʳ; the *Partheniades* are also reprinted by Haslewood, *Ancient Critical Essays upon English Poets and Poesy*, 1:xix–xxxviii.

14. Joan DeJean, *Fictions of Sappho, 1546–1937* (Univ. of Chicago Press, 1989); on other early modern representations of Sappho, see Elizabeth D. Harvey, *Ventriloquized Voices: Feminist Theory and English Renaissance Texts* (London: Routledge, 1992), chapter 4: "Ventriloquizing Sappho, or the Lesbian Muse," and Paula Blank, "Comparing Sappho to Philaenis: John Donne's 'Homopoetics,'" *PMLA* 110 (1995): 358–68.

15. Susan Dwyer Amussen, "Elizabeth I and Alice Balstone: Gender, Class, and the Exceptional Woman in Early Modern England," in *Attending to Women in Early Modern England*, ed. Betty S. Travitsky and Adele F. Seeff (Newark: Univ. of Delaware Press, 1994).

16. On Elizabeth's iconic self-fashioning and performances of femininity, see S. P. Cerasano and Marion Wynne-Davies, "'From Myself, My Other Self I Turned': An Introduction," in *Gloriana's Face: Women, Public and Private in the English Renaissance*, ed. Cerasano and Wynne-Davies (Detroit: Wayne

State Univ. Press, 1992), and Susan Frye, *Elizabeth I: The Competition for Representation* (Oxford: Oxford Univ. Press, 1993), who explores Elizabeth as "a woman who ruled through the simultaneous invocation and disruption of accustomed gender roles" (16).

17. This topic has been widely covered; for representative studies and good bibliographies on English women and humanism, see Valerie Wayne, "Some Sad Sentence: Vives' *Instruction of a Christian Woman*," in *Silent but for the Word: Tudor Women as Patrons, Translators, and Writers of Religious Works,* ed. Margaret Patterson Hannay (Kent, OH: Kent State Univ. Press, 1985), and Hilda L. Smith, "Humanist Education and the Renaissance Concept of Women," in *Women and Literature in Britain, 1500–1700,* ed. Helen Wilcox (Cambridge: Cambridge Univ. Press, 1996).

18. Leonardo Bruni, "On the Study of Literature: To Lady Battista Malatesta of Montrefeltro," *The Humanism of Leonardo Bruni: Selected Texts,* trans. Gordon Griffiths, James Hankins, and David Thompson (Binghamton, NY: Medieval and Renaissance Texts and Studies, 1987), 240–51; page numbers from this edition are cited parenthetically in the text. The letter is cited and discussed at length in Anthony Grafton and Lisa Jardine, *From Humanism to the Humanities: Education and the Liberal Arts in Fifteenth- and Sixteenth-Century Europe* (Cambridge: Harvard Univ. Press, 1986), 32–33.

19. Elizabeth Cary, *The Tragedy of Mariam, The Fair Queen of Jewry,* ed. Barry Weller and Margaret W. Ferguson (Berkeley: Univ. of California Press, 1994), 114.

20. Cary, *Mariam,* 131. On the link between women's public speech and sexual licentiousness, see especially Patricia Parker, *Literary Fat Ladies: Rhetoric, Gender, Property* (London: Methuen, 1987), 104–7.

21. See Grafton and Jardine, *From Humanism to the Humanities,* 38.

22. "A Most Excellent and Remarkable SPEECH Delivered by that Mirrour and Miracle of Princes, Queen *Elizabeth,* of famous memory, in the Honourable the High Court of Parliament, in the seventeenth yeere of her reigne." The speech exists in a 1643 copy at the Folger, the text of which is now available through the Brown University Women Writers Project and was recently reprinted in *The Brown University Women Writers Project Newsletter* 3 (1997): 3.

23. "Latin Oration at Cambridge University, 1564," in *The Public Speaking of Queen Elizabeth,* ed. George P. Rice (New York: Columbia Univ. Press, 1951), 71.

24. Rice, *The Public Speaking of Queen Elizabeth,* 75.

25. "The Queenes Most Excellent Majesties Oration in the Parliament House, Martii 15, 1575," in John Harington, *Nugae Antiquae,* ed. Thomas Park, 2 vols. (London, 1804), 1:121.

26. Frances Teague, "Queen Elizabeth in Her Speeches," in *Gloriana's Face: Women, Public and Private in the English Renaissance,* ed. A. P. Cerasano and Marion Wynne-Davies (Detroit: Wayne State Univ. Press, 1992).

27. Bruni, "On the Study of Literature," 242: "I would not have her ignorant of writing."

28. Margaret Ferguson opens a productive line of inquiry in this direction

when she pointedly asks, "Could not writing be construed in opposition to public speech rather than in conjunction with it? . . . Did authoritative classical and early Christian injunctions against women's public speech . . . clearly define a woman's act of writing (especially to a 'private' audience) as sinful?" "A Room Not Their Own: Renaissance Women as Readers and Writers," in *The Comparative Perspective on Literature: Approaches to Theory and Practice,* ed. Clayton Koelb and Susan Noakes (Ithaca: Cornell Univ. Press, 1988), 101–2.

29. See Margaret J. M. Ezell, *The Patriarch's Wife: Literary Evidence and the History of the Family* (Chapel Hill: Univ. of North Carolina Press, 1987), and "Elizabeth Delaval's Spiritual Heroine: Thoughts on Redefining Manuscript Texts by Early Modern Women Writers," *English Manuscript Studies, 1100–1700* 3 (1992): 216–37.

30. Printed editions include *A Godly Medytacyon of the Christen Sowle* (Wesel, 1548); *A Godly Meditation of the Inward Loue of the Soule* (London, 1568); and *A Godly Meditation of the Soule* (London, 1580); extracts of the text also appeared in the first volume of Thomas Bentley's *The Monument of Matrones* (London, 1582); a recent combined critical study and edition of the text is Marc Shell, *Elizabeth's Glass* (Omaha: Univ. of Nebraska Press, 1993). See also Ruth Hughey, "A Note on Queen Elizabeth's 'Godly Meditation,'" *The Library* 15 (1934): 237–40; David Scott Kastan, "An Early Metrical Psalm: Elizabeth's or John Bale's?" *Notes and Queries* 219 (1974): 404–5; Ann Lake Prescott, "The Pearl of Valois and Elizabeth I: Marguerite de Navarre's *Miroir* and Tudor England," in *Silent but for the Word: Tudor Women as Patrons, Translators, and Writers of Religious Works,* ed. Margaret P. Hannay (Kent, OH: Kent State Univ. Press, 1985).

31. Cited by Louis Wright, *Middle-Class Culture in Elizabethan England* (Chapel Hill: Univ. of North Carolina Press, 1935), 109.

32. Jonathan Goldberg, *Writing Matter: From the Hands of the English Renaissance* (Stanford: Stanford Univ. Press, 1990), 140–41; for an argument about embroidery as a model of feminine writing that stands apart from masculine literary authority, see Marjorie Garber, "'Greatness': Philology and the Politics of Mimesis," in *Feminism and Postmodernism,* ed. Margaret Ferguson and Jennifer Wicke (Durham: Duke Univ. Press, 1994), 270.

33. John N. King, "Patronage and Piety: The Influence of Catherine Parr," in *Silent but for the Word: Tudor Women as Patrons, Translators, and Writers of Religious Works,* ed. Margaret Patterson Hannay (Kent, OH: Kent State Univ. Press, 1985), 43.

34. See Prescott, "The Pearl of Valois and Elizabeth I."

35. John Soowthern, *Pandora, the Musyque of the Beautie, of his Mistresse Diana* (London, 1584), which includes the verse:

> Even so dooth Cupid, that infaunt, God, of amore,
> Flie about the tombe, where she lyes all in dolore,
> Weeping for her eies, wherin he made soiourne. (sig. Di^r)

The poem's attribution to Elizabeth is listed as doubtful by Elaine V. Beilin in her valuable "Current Bibliography of English Women Writers, 1500–1640," in *The Renaissance Englishwoman in Print: Counterbalancing the Canon*, ed. Anne M. Haselkorn and Betty S. Travitsky (Amherst: Univ. of Massachusetts Press, 1990), 356.

36. See Philippa Berry, *Of Chastity and Power: Elizabethan Literature and the Unmarried Queen* (London: Routledge, 1989), particularly the introduction, which asserts the importance of "Elizabeth's forgotten ties to other women" (5).

37. Richard Halpern, *The Poetics of Primitive Accumulation: English Renaissance Culture and the Genealogy of Capital* (Ithaca: Cornell Univ. Press, 1991); in my discussion of the relationship between oratory and poetry, I am indebted to Halpern's consideration of the topic in his chapter 1, "A Mint of Phrases: Ideology and Style Production in Tudor England," as well as to Daniel Javitch's central argument in *Poetry and Courtliness in Renaissance England* (Princeton: Princeton Univ. Press, 1978).

38. William Webbe, *A Discourse of English Poetrie* (1586), reprinted in *Elizabethan Critical Essays*, ed. G. Gregory Smith, 2 vols. (London: Oxford Univ. Press, 1904), 1:228.

39. Webbe, *A Discourse of English Poetrie*, 1:267.

40. Quintillian, *Institutio Oratoria*, trans. H. E. Butler, 4 vols. (Cambridge: Harvard Univ. Press, 1969), x.i.27–28.

41. Webbe, *A Discourse of English Poetrie*, 1:231. Compare Puttenham's tactic to Sir Philip Sidney's *Defense of Poetry*, which stresses the affinity between poetry and oratory; see Margaret W. Ferguson, *Trials of Desire: Renaissance Defenses of Poetry* (New Haven: Yale Univ. Press, 1983), 139–42.

42. Louis Adrian Montrose, "Of Gentlemen and Shepherds: The Politics of Elizabethan Pastoral Form," *ELH* 50 (1983): 438.

43. See, in this light, Javitch's comparison between Cicero's *De Oratore* and Castiglione's *Cortegiano*, in *Poetry and Courtliness in Renaissance England*, 46–49.

44. Relevant to this discussion is Jonathan Goldberg's argument that the lines of gender and identification in Puttenham's text multiply the possible configurations of desire far beyond the heterosexual binary of male and female; *Sodometries: Renaissance Texts, Modern Sexualities* (Stanford: Stanford Univ. Press, 1992), 29–61.

45. Javitch, *Poetry and Courtliness in Renaissance England*, 28–29.

46. Webbe, *A Discourse of English Poetrie*, 1:231.

47. With the point that follows I depart from the specific conclusions of Dolan's reading of Puttenham, although I find her larger analysis of cosmetics and rhetoric apt and convincing; see Frances Dolan, "Taking the Pencil out of God's Hand: Art, Nature, and the Face-Painting Debate in Early Modern England," *PMLA* 108 (1993): 229–39.

48. Relevant to this discussion of the feminization of poetic ornament is John Guillory's observation that "the development in the early modern period of new discourses of truth (the scientific) occasioned . . . the epistemological bracketing of the poetic genres as 'fiction,' and the identification of ornament as defining the linguistic difference of those genres." See Guillory, *Cultural Capital: The Problem of Literary Canon Formation* (Chicago: Univ. of Chicago Press, 1993), 213.

49. As discussed in the section that follows below.

50. On the Mary Queen of Scots affair, see J. E. Neale, *Queen Elizabeth I* (London: Jonathan Cape, 1934), and *Elizabeth and Her Parliaments, 1559–1581* (London: Jonathan Cape, 1953), 226–34, 241–90; see also Alison Plowden, *Two Queens in One Isle: The Deadly Relationship of Queen Elizabeth I and Mary Queen of Scots* (Sussex: Harvester Press, 1984).

51. Spenser, *Poetical Works*, 407.

52. Montrose, "Of Gentlemen and Shepherds," 443.

53. Sir John Harington refers to Puttenham when he charges, "For though the poore gentleman laboreth greatly to proue, or rather to make Poetrie an art, and reciteth as you may see, in the plurall number, some pluralities of patters and parcels of his owne Poetrie, with diuerse pieces of Partheniads and hymnes in praise of the most praisworthy, yet whatsoeuer he would proue by all these, sure in my poore opinion he doth proue nothing more plainly then that which M. Sidney and all the learneder sort that haue written of it do pronounce, namely that it is a gift and not an art. I say he proueth it, because making himselfe and manie others so cunning in the art, yet he sheweth himselfe so slender a gift in it." Preface, *Orlando Furioso (1591)*, in *Elizabethan Critical Essays*, ed. G. Gregory Smith, 2 vols. (Oxford: Oxford Univ. Press, 1904), 2:196–97.

54. On the significance of this motto, see Mary Thomas Crane, "'Video et Taceo': Elizabeth I and the Rhetoric of Counsel," *SEL* 28 (1988): 1–15.

55. On this and other portraits of Elizabeth, see Roy C. Strong, *Portraits of Queen Elizabeth I* (Oxford: Clarendon Press, 1963); Andrew and Catherine Belsey, "Icons of Divinity: Portraits of Elizabeth I," in *Renaissance Bodies*, ed. Lucy Gent and Nigel Llewellyn (London: Reaktion Books, 1990); Cerasano and Wynne-Davies, "'From Myself, My Other Self I Turned.'"

56. As Montrose notes, "Of Gentlemen and Shepherds," 443.

57. See the notes of Gladys Doidge Willcock and Alice Walker in their edition of *The Arte of English Poesie* (Cambridge: Cambridge Univ. Press, 1936), civ–cv.

58. The text has been printed as "A Justificacion of Queene Elizabeth in Relacion to the Affaire of Mary Queene of Scottes" (1587–88) in *Accounts and Papers Relating to Mary Queen of Scots*, ed. Allan J. Crosby and John Bruce (London, 1867); in the discussion that follows, citations are to this edition, with page numbers noted parenthetically. The manuscripts are: British Library MS Add. 48027, fol. 451–76; and British Library MS Harley 831; the Additional MS contains this marginal gloss at the title: "It is thought that this book was made by George Puttenham" (fol. 451ʳ); the complete title of the Harleian MS is as follows: "An apologie or true defence of her Ma[jesties] hono[r] and good renowne against all such as haue unduelie sought or shall seek to blemish the same with any injustice, crueltie, or other unprincely behaviour in any parte of her Ma[jesties] proceedings against the late Scotisch Queene. Be it for her first surprice, imprisonment, process, attaynder, or death. By uery firme reasons, authorities warrantable by the law of God and of man. Writen by GEORGE PUTTENHAM to the servece of her Ma[jestie] and for large satisfaction of all such persons both princely and private who by ignorance of the case, or partiallitie of mind shall happen to be irresolute and not well satisfied in the said cause."

59. Patricia Fumerton, *Cultural Aesthetics: Renaissance Literature and the Practice of Social Ornament* (Chicago: Univ. of Chicago Press, 1991); Richard Rambuss, *Spenser's Secret Career* (Cambridge: Cambridge Univ. Press, 1993).

60. Horace, "The Art of Poetry," trans. Elizabeth I, in Bradner, ed., *Poems of Elizabeth I*, 50.

61. Such a strategy is similar to what Jonathan Goldberg calls "the trope of state secrets," by which James I effected "the transformation of privacy into public discourse," *James I and the Politics of Poetry: Jonson, Shakespeare, Donne, and Their Contemporaries* (Baltimore: Johns Hopkins Univ. Press, 1983), preface, xii.

62. Rosalie L. Colie, *The Resources of Kind: Genre-Theory in the Renaissance*, ed. Barbara K. Lewalski (Berkeley: Univ. of California Press, 1973), 37; see Colie's larger discussion on emblems, 36–75. Javitch, *Poetry and Courtliness in Renaissance England*, 65.

63. Thus Colie stresses "the psychological appeal of the emblem to its readers, inducing a set for solving problems" (*The Resources of Kind*, 62).

64. On the manuscripts of "The Doubt of Future Foes," see Steven W. May, *The Elizabethan Courtier Poets: The Poems and Their Contexts* (Columbia: Univ. of Missouri Press, 1991), 317–18; and Herman, *Reading Monarchs Writing*.

65. Ruth Hughey, ed., *The Arundel Harington Manuscript of Tudor Poetry*, 2 vols. (Columbus: Ohio State Univ. Press, 1960), 1:276–77; 2:386–87.

66. Harington dedicated his translation of Cicero's *De Amicitia* (London, 1550) to Katherine Willoughby, Duchess of Suffolk, who might be the "Lady Wiloughby" here.

67. Arthur Marotti, *Manuscript, Print, and the English Renaissance Lyric* (Ithaca: Cornell Univ. Press, 1995), 49, 61; see his larger discussion titled "Women and the Manuscript System," 48–61. On women and manuscript circulation, see also Ezell, *The Patriarch's Wife*, especially chapter 3: "Women Writers: Patterns of Manuscript Circulation and Publication"; see also Ezell's "Elizabeth Delaval's Spritual Heroine: Thoughts on Redefining Manuscript Texts by Early Women Writers," *English Manuscript Studies 1100–1700* 3 (1992): 216–37. On the culturally defined "femininity" of manuscript, see Ann Baynes Coiro, "Writing in Service: Sexual Politics and Class Position in the Poetry of Aemilia Lanyer and Ben Jonson," *Criticism* 35 (1993): 359.

68. Jeffrey Masten, " 'Shall I Turne Blabb?': Circulation, Gender and Subjectivity in Mary Wroth's Sonnets," in *Reading Mary Wroth: Representing Alternatives in Early Modern England*, ed. Naomi J. Miller and Gary Waller (Knoxville: Univ. of Tennessee Press, 1991), 79.

69. Roger Ascham, *The Schoolmaster (1570)*, ed. Lawrence V. Ryan (Ithaca: Cornell Univ. Press, 1967), 56.

70. On the social production of handwriting in the Renaissance, see Jonathan Goldberg, *Writing Matter: From the Hands of the English Renaissance* (Stanford: Stanford Univ. Press, 1990), and on the female hand, see especially 137–56.

71. Coiro, "Writing in Service," 359.

72. The dialectic of privacy and "publication" is particularly charged in the

case of the *Urania*, given its own problematic history in print: for a consideration of this dialectic, see Helen Hackett, "Courtly Writing by Women," in *Women and Literature in Britain, 1500–1700*, ed. Helen Wilcox (Cambridge: Cambridge Univ. Press, 1996), 180–85.

73. Margaret Ferguson stresses "how complex and permeable the boundaries between manuscript and print publication were" in the early modern period, a point that is illustrated by Puttenham's *Arte of English Poesie* itself, which in many ways approximates the form of a manuscript commonplace book in print; see Ferguson, "Renaissance Concepts of the 'Woman Writer,'" in *Women and Literature in Britain, 1500–1700*, ed. Helen Wilcox (Cambridge: Cambridge Univ. Press, 1996), 162.

74. J. W. Saunders, "The Stigma of Print: A Note on the Social Bases of Tudor Poetry," *Essays in Criticism* 1 (1951): 139–64. Wendy Wall has developed the implications of Saunders's argument to rethink the combined influences of gender, print, and authorship in the Renaissance; *The Imprint of Gender: Authorship and Publication in the English Renaissance* (Ithaca: Cornell Univ. Press, 1993).

75. Samuel Daniel, *Poems and A Defence of Rhyme*, ed. Arthur Colby Sprague (Chicago: Univ. of Chicago Press, 1930), 9.

76. Arthur F. Marotti, "The Transmission of Lyric Poetry and the Institutionalizing of Literature in the English Renaissance," in *Contending Kingdoms: Historical, Psychological, and Feminist Approaches to the Literature of Sixteenth-Century England and France*, ed. Marie-Rose Logan and Peter L. Rudnytsky (Detroit: Wayne State Univ. Press, 1991); see also Harold Love, "Scribal Publication in Seventeenth-Century England," *Transactions of the Cambridge Bibliographical Society* 9 (1987): 130–54; and Richard B. Wollman, "The 'Press and the Fire': Print and Manuscript Culture in Donne's Circle," *Studies in English Literature* 33 (1993): 85–97.

77. Crewe, *Hidden Designs*, 78.

78. See Betty S. Travitsky, "Reconstructing the Still, Small Voice: The Occasional Journal of Elizabeth Egerton," *Women's Studies* 19 (1991): 194, and "His Wife's Prayers and Meditations: MS Egerton 607," in *The Renaissance Englishwoman in Print: Counterbalancing the Canon*, ed. Anne M. Haselkorn and Travitsky (Amherst: Univ. of Massachusetts Press, 1990).

79. Cited by Travitsky, "Reconstructing the Still, Small Voice," 245.

80. Or, as Elizabeth Hageman characterizes it, "a female variant of the humility topos" by which a woman writer "generally 'acknowledg[es]' in a comic or defiant way that she is 'only a woman.'" Hageman, "Women's Poetry in Early Modern Britain," in *Women and Literature in Britain, 1500–1700*, ed. Helen Wilcox (Cambridge: Cambridge Univ. Press, 1996), 201.

81. My model of "restricted circulation" draws from Pierre Bourdieu's essay "The Market of Symbolic Goods," reprinted in *The Field of Cultural Production: Essays on Art and Literature*, ed. Randal Johnson (London: Polity Press, 1993).

82. Consider, in this light, Alan Stewart's discussion of Lady Margaret Hoby's practice of withdrawing into her "closet": "The closet is thus constructed as a place of utter privacy, of total withdrawal from the public sphere

of the household—but it simultaneously functions as a very *public* gesture of withdrawal, a very public sign of privacy." "The Early Modern Closet Discovered," *Representations* 50 (1995): 76–100.

83. On the imaginary nexus of women's private places and state secrets, see Patricia Parker, "*Othello* and *Hamlet:* Spying, Discovery, Secret Faults," in *Shakespeare from the Margins: Language, Culture, Context* (Chicago: Univ. of Chicago Press, 1996).

84. Alan Haynes, *Invisible Power: The Elizabethan Secret Services, 1570–1603* (Wolfeboro Falls, NH: Alan Sutton Publishing, 1992); see also Alison Plowden, *The Elizabethan Secret Service* (New York: St. Martin's Press, 1991), and John M. Archer, *Sovereignty and Intelligence: Spying and Court Culture in the English Renaissance* (Stanford: Stanford Univ. Press, 1993).

85. William Camden, *The History of the Most Renowned and Victorious Princess Elizabeth, Late Queen of England,* ed. Wallace T. MacCaffrey (Chicago: Univ. of Chicago Press, 1970), 263–64.

86. William Warner, *Albion's England* (London, 1597), 249.

87. Camden, *The History of the Most Renowned and Victorious Princess Elizabeth,* 267.

88. "A speech made by her ma[jes]tie tochinge the treasons of the Quene of Scotte," Inner Temple Library, Petyt MS 538 vol. 10, folio 6ᵛ.

89. On this example see Masten, " 'Shall I Turne Blabb?' " On "blabbing" as a sign of women's shameful garrulity, see Parker, *Literary Fat Ladies,* 106.

90. Allison Heisch, "Queen Elizabeth I: Parliamentary Rhetoric and the Exercise of Power," *Signs* 1 (1975): 50. Related interpretations of Elizabeth's speeches are offered in two other studies. Nona Fienberg notes that in her speeches, Elizabeth "seems to brood to herself, and to allow Parliament access to a personal meditation. She grants that liberty, however, in a most calculated, controlled manner, just as the sonneteer permits the public to enter a private world, but shaped carefully into public, conventional form." See Fienberg, *Elizabeth, Her Poets, and the Creation of the Courtly Manner: A Study of Sir John Harington, Sir Philip Sidney, and John Lyly* (New York: Garland, 1988), 22–23. Similarly, Frances Teague points to "Elizabeth I's own manipulation of her image, her politically knowing alteration of her own texts," in "Queen Elizabeth in Her Speeches," 75.

91. *The Letters of Mary, Queen of Scots,* ed. Agnes Strickland, 2 vols. (London, 1848), 1:104–5.

92. My spelling and punctuation follow the manuscript of Mary's poem in British Library MS Cotton Calig. B.V., fol. 316. The English translation of the first stanza is Constance Jordan's; it appears in her essay "States of Blindness: Doubt, Justice, and Constancy in Elizabeth I's 'Avec L'Aveugler si Estrange,' " in *Reading Monarchs Writing: The Poetry of Henry VIII, Mary Stuart, Elizabeth I, and James I,* ed. Peter C. Herman (New York: MRTS, forthcoming). Another English translation appears in *The Paradise of Women: Writings by Englishwomen of the Renaissance,* ed. Betty Travitsky (New York: Columbia Univ. Press, 1989), which also reprints a slightly modified French text of the poem, 198 and 262.

93. Translation in Jordan, "States of Blindness."

94. Petrarch's lyrics are published in Italian and English in *Petrarch's Lyric*

Poems, trans. and ed. Robert M. Durling (Cambridge: Harvard Univ. Press, 1976), 270, 334. On the English influence of Petrarch's ship poems, see Thomas C. Stillinger, *The Song of Troilus: Lyric Authority in the Medieval Book* (Philadelphia: Univ. of Pennsylvania Press, 1992).

95. Translation in Jordan, "States of Blindness." Another early modern woman poet in French, Catherine des Roches, makes use of the Petrarchan image in her "Son[n]ets de Sincero a Charite" (1578, 1579) to describe a man's lovesickness:

> *Ma nef au gré des vens dedans l'onde pousee,*
> *Erroit de toutes parts quand vostre heureuse main,*
> *Piteuse de mon mal me retira soudain,*
> *En me sauvant des flotz de la mer courroucee.*

> (My ship, tossed at random among the waves, /
> Veered every way until your blessed hand / Pitying
> my suffering, suddenly released me, / Saving me
> from the waters of the wrathful sea)

This text is cited and discussed by Ann Rosalind Jones in *The Currency of Eros: Women's Love Lyric in Europe, 1540–1620* (Bloomington: Indiana Univ. Press, 1990), 66–67.

96. *Letters of Mary, Queen of Scots,* 1:177.

97. Horace, *Odes and Epodes,* trans. C. E. Bennett (Cambridge: Harvard Univ. Press, 1988), 42–43; For a valuable discussion considering the relations between Petrarch and Horace in these poems, see Stillinger, *The Song of Troilus,* 196.

98. For a reading of Mary's position in "The Doubt of Future Foes" and contemporary literary works, see James Emerson Phillips, *Images of a Queen: Mary Stuart in Sixteenth-Century Literature* (Berkeley: Univ. of California Press, 1964), esp. 81.

99. *English Women Writers before 1800,* ed. Mary Mahl and Helene Koon (Bloomington: Indiana Univ. Press, 1977), 48–49.

100. Frances Teague, "Elizabeth I," in *Women Writers of the Renaissance and Reformation,* ed. Katharina M. Wilson (Athens: Univ. of Georgia Press, 1987), 529.

101. Livy, *History* (1.54), cited in H. J. Leon, "Classical Sources for the Garden Scene in *Richard II,*" *Philological Quarterly* 29 (1950): 65.

102. See Leon, "Classical Sources for the Garden Scene in *Richard II,*" 67–68.

103. Letter from Nicholas White to Sir William Cecil, 1569, cited in Roy Strong and Julia Trevelyan Oman, *Mary Queen of Scots* (London: Secker and Warburg, 1972), 45.

104. Neale, *Queen Elizabeth I,* 258; see Margaret Swain, *The Needlework of Mary, Queen of Scots* (New York: Van Nostrand Reinhold Co., 1973).

105. William Camden, *Annales, or the History of the Most Renowned and Victorious Princesse Elizabeth, Late Queen of England,* 3d ed. (London, 1635), 269.

106. The tapestry, on display at Oxburgh Hall in Norfolk and now owned

by the Victoria and Albert Museum in London, is pictured and described by Francis de Zuleta in *Embroideries by Mary Stuart and Elizabeth Talbot at Oxburgh Hall, Norfolk* (Oxford: Oxford Univ. Press, 1923), 8, and by Rozsika Parker in *The Subversive Stitch: Embroidery and the Making of the Feminine* (New York: Routledge, 1989), 11. On the Petrarchan resonance of the motto "virescit vulnere virtus," see Thomas Greene, *The Light in Troy: Imitation and Discovery in Renaissance Poetry* (New Haven: Yale Univ. Press, 1982), 103.

107. *The Tryal of Thomas Duke of Norfolk by His Peers* (London: 1709), 68; on the embroidery's significance in Norfolk's trial see also Neville Williams, *A Tudor Tragedy: Thomas Howard Fourth Duke of Norfolk* (London: Barrie Books, 1964), 236.

108. Geoffrey Whitney, *A Choice of Emblemes* (1586), facsimile ed. Henry Green (1866, repr. New York: G. Olms, 1971), 98; a similar emblem adorns the title page of Elizabeth Cary's *Mariam*, which features an image of a naked woman being scourged from above: the motto reads "Verita Verescit Vulnerae." While this appears to be the mark of the printer Thomas Creede (whose initials are inscribed between the woman's feet), it is not inappropriate to the gendered concerns of the drama.

109. Swain, *The Needlework of Mary, Queen of Scots*, 60.

110. On Mary's manipulation of martyrdom, see Goldberg, *James I and the Politics of Literature*, 17.

111. *Mary Queen of Scots: Facsimiles*, ed. Jennifer S. Baker, Public Record Office Museum Pamphlets 12 (London: H. M. Stationery Office, 1981), 3.

112. The famous phrase is from Suzanne W. Hull, *Chaste, Silent, and Obedient: English Books for Women, 1475–1640* (San Marino: Huntington Library, 1982).

AFTERWORD

1. Richard Flecknoe's gendering of Elizabethan writing is cited and discussed by Patricia Parker, who affirms that "the shift of [writing] style between sixteenth- and early seventeenth-century England was also associated with the shifting of the monarch's gender." See Parker, "Virile Style," in *Premodern Sexualities*, ed. Carla Freccero and Louise Fradenburg (New York: Routledge, 1996), 206.

2. Samuel Daniel, *A History of England*, cited by Ruth Kelso, *Doctrine of the English Gentleman in the Sixteenth Century* (Urbana: Univ. of Illinois Press, 1929), 16; Daniel, *A Defense of Rhyme* (1607), in *Critical Essays of the Seventeenth Century*, ed. J. E. Springarn (Bloomington: Indiana Univ. Press, 1957), 2:372.

3. George Chapman, *A Defense of Homer*, in *Elizabethan Critical Essays*, ed. G. Gregory Smith (Oxford: Clarendon Press, 1904), 2:302.

4. Laura Runge, *Gender and Language in British Literary Criticism, 1660–1790* (Cambridge: Cambridge Univ. Press, 1997), 49; see especially chapter 2, "Dryden's Gendered Balance and the Augustan Ideal."

5. Jonathan Brody Kramnick persuasively makes the case for the invention of an all-male literary tradition, beginning in the seventeenth century but taking hold in the eighteenth century, in part as a guard against the perceived

femininity of English literary culture with increasing levels of popular literacy; see Kramnick, *Making the English Canon: Print Capitalism and the Cultural Past, 1700–1770* (Cambridge: Cambridge Univ. Press, 1998). Timothy J. Reiss pushes the origins of this masculinization of literature to the seventeenth century, when, he argues, "literature had adopted the 'masculine' job of founding rational public society" and therefore denigrated women writers; see Reiss, *The Meaning of Literature* (Ithaca: Cornell Univ. Press, 1992), 196.

6. Consider, for example, Michael Drayton's "Epistle to Reynolds" (1627), which imagines a continuous line of succession from Virgil to the English poets, beginning with Chaucer and Gower and extending through Sidney, Marlowe, Shakespeare, and Chapman. That this poetic tradition is masculine by definition is confirmed by the homoerotic scene between child and tutor in which Drayton frames it, which equates "poet" and "man":

> Clasping my slender armes about his thigh,
> O my deare master! cannot you, quoth I,
> Make me a Poet? doe it if you can,
> And you shall see Ile quickly be a man.

Michael Drayton, "Epistle to Henry Reynolds, Esquire, Of Poets and Poesie," in *Critical Essays of the Seventeenth Century*, ed. J. E. Spingarn (Bloomington: Indiana Univ. Press, 1959), 1:135.

7. For the increasing numbers of women writers in print through the seventeenth century, see Richard Bell and Patricia Crawford, "Appendix 2: Statistical Analysis of Women's Printed Writings, 1600–1700," in *Women in English Society, 1500–1800*, ed. Mary Prior (London: Methuen, 1985).

8. Abraham Cowley, "On the Death of Mrs Katherine Philips," *Poems by the Most Deservedly Admired Mrs Katherine Philips, the Matchless ORINDA* (London, 1667), n.p. On Cowley and Philips, see also Margaret J. M. Ezell, *Writing Women's Literary History* (Baltimore: Johns Hopkins Univ. Press, 1993), 77; Stella P. Revard, "Katherine Philips, Aphra Behn, and the Female Pindaric," in *Representing Women in Renaissance England*, ed. Claude J. Summers and Ted-Larry Pebworth (Columbia: Univ. of Missouri Press, 1997).

9. Cowley, "On the Death of Mrs Katherine Philips," n.p.

10. On Margaret Cavendish's promotion of her own uniqueness, see Catherine Gallagher, "Embracing the Absolute: The Politics of the Female Subject in Seventeenth-Century England," *Genders* 1 (1988): 24–39.

11. *Playes Written by the Thrice Noble, Illustrious, and Excellent Princess, the Lady Marchioness of Newcastle* (London, 1662), sig. A7ᵛ.

12. On the significance of Jonson's 1616 *Workes* for establishing masculine authorship in print, see Stephen Orgel, "What Is a Text?" *Research Opportunities in Renaissance Drama* 2(1981):3–6; Wendy Wall, *The Imprint of Gender: Authorship and Publication in the English Renaissance* (Ithaca: Cornell Univ. Press, 1993), 18–19.

13. See Jeffrey Masten's discussion of this passage in his *Textual Intercourse: Collaboration, Authorship, and Sexualities in Renaissance Drama* (Cambridge: Cambridge Univ. Press, 1997), 159–60.

14. *Playes Written by . . . the Lady Marchioness of Newcastle*, sig. A7ᵛ.

15. E. Top, "To Her Excellence, the Lady Marchioness of Newcastle,"

Poems and Fancies (London, 1664), n.p. On Elizabeth Top, see Douglas Grant, *Margaret the First: A Biography of Margaret Cavendish, Duchess of Newcastle, 1623–1673* (London: Rupert Hart-Davis, 1957), 229–30.

16. Margaret Cavendish, "Epistle to My Readers," *Nature's Pictures, Drawn by Fancies Pencil* (London: A. Maxwell, 1971), n.p.

17. On this title, see Gallagher, "Embracing the Absolute," 27.

18. "The She-Anchoret" appears in *Nature's Pictures* (London, 1966); Cavendish, "A True Relation of My Birth, Breeding, and Life," in *Her Own Life: Autobiographical Writings by Seventeenth-Century Englishwomen*, ed. Elsbeth Graham et al. (New York: Routledge, 1989), 98. Robin Valenza's work in progress on Cavendish and the cultural memory of anchoresses offers a promising direction for understanding this figure's significance in Cavendish's work.

19. Virginia Woolf, *A Room of One's Own* (1929; reprint, New York: Harcourt Brace Jovanovich, 1981), 62.

20. Woolf, *A Room of One's Own*, 113.

21. For the development of the male author in the seventeenth century, see Kevin Pask, *The Emergence of the English Author: Scripting the Life of the Poet in Early Modern England* (Cambridge: Cambridge Univ. Press, 1996).

Index

manuscripts, 2, 9, 69, 76; coterie, 98, 185–
90, 192–93, 202; humanist study of,
141, 154; transmission of, 13, 133,
170. *See also* textual exchange
Marcia/Marsyas, 30–32, 43
Marcus, Leah, 165
Margaret, Saint, 113
Margherita, Gayle, 225–26n.88
margins/marginality, 8, 28, 71, 77, 81, 96,
103, 105–6, 160, 202, 209. *See also*
paratext
Marguerite de Navarre, 147, 168–69; *Le
miroir de l'ame pécheresse,* 147, 168
Marie de France, 27, 50
Marotti, Arthur, 186, 188
Marshall, William, 119, 124
Marshall Primer, 120
Martial, 139, 148
martyrdom, 131, 135, 149, 151–55, 199.
See also hagiography
Marx, Karl, 142
Mary of Oignies, 135
Mary, Queen of Scots, 7, 164, 171–72,
175–76, 178, 181–82, 190–95, 197–
202
Masten, Jeffrey, 18, 187, 206
Matchinske, Megan, 148
Mathéolus, 93
Maxentia, 155
McFarlane, K. B., 79, 227n.3, 230n.27
McGrady, Deborah, 233n.56
McKinnell, John, 51
Meres, Francis, 164
Middleton, Anne, 53, 57
Milton, John, 6; *Areopagitica,* 4
Minnis, A. J., 6, 18, 25, 66, 235–36n.82
Miskimin, Alice, 88, 236n.95
"modesty trope," 189, 192. *See also* apol-
ogy, genre of
Montrose, Louis, 172, 177
monuments, 144–46, 156–58, 160–61
mourning, 148, 150, 205
Myracles of Oure Blessyd Lady, 113
Myroure of Oure Ladye, The, 114

Neale, J. E., 198
Nichols, John Gough, 234nn.59–60

oratory, 15–16, 166–68, 170–74, 183,
187, 202–3
Orcherd of Syon, The, 128–29
Orgel, Stephen, 265n.12

originality, 66, 206–7, 09
ornamentality, 15, 70, 99; and emblems,
184–85; of poetic language, 172–77,
202–3, 258n.48. *See also* covertness
Osritha, Saint, 155–56
Ovid, 11–12, 24–25, 29, 43–44, 46–47,
49, 57–58, 85, 197; *Heroides,* 24, 35–
38; *Metamorphoses,* 31; *Tristia,* 47
Oxburgh Hanging, 199–201

Pace, George, 91
paratext, 8, 10, 14, 19–20, 64–65, 70–71,
82, 93, 95; dedicatory epistles, 62, 64–
65; epilogues, 82, 84–85, 236n.85;
frontispieces, 2; prefaces and prologues, 64, 82, 120, 157, 236n.85;
titles, 64. *See also* illuminations;
margins/marginality; woodcuts
Parker, Patricia, 262nn.83 and 89, 264n.1
Parkes, M. B., 25, 66
Parr, Catherine, 147, 151, 168–70, 190;
*Prayers Stirryng the Mynd unto Heav-
enlye Medytacions,* 111
Paston, Sir John, 70
patronage, 19, 62, 68, 71, 76–88, 92, 95–
98, 103–5, 107, 239n.114; of devotional works, 113, 115. *See also* aristocratic households
Patterson, Lee, 44, 47, 221n.30, 237n.106
Paul, Saint, 141
Pearsall, Derek, 54
pen: and martyr's palm, 152; and needle,
168; and sword, 36, 152
Pepwell, Henry, 93, 95–96, 98–100, 126–
40, 152, 156, 161, 238n.110, 239n.114;
The Boke of the Cyte of Ladyes, 93,
95–101, 103–5, 107; *Here foloweth a
very devoute treatyse (named Benyamyn),* 128–29, 133–35
periodization, 17–18
Petrarch, 175, 183–84; *Canticus Troili,*
54; Canzone 132, 195; Canzone 189,
195; *Familiares,* 40, 52
Petrarchanism, 165, 175, 183–84, 195
Philips, Katherine, 205–7, 209
pilgrimage, 129–33. *See also* indulgences
Pindar, 43
Plutarch, 43, 148
poetics of queenship, 179, 182, 190, 193–
94, 201
poetry, 7, 12–16, 31–37, 41, 91–92, 163–
66, 170–85, 190–93, 197, 201–2